Propaganda and
Censorship
During Canada's
Great War

Propaganda
and Censorship
During Canada's Great War

Jeffrey A. Keshen

 The University of Alberta Press

Published by
The University of Alberta Press
Athabasca Hall
Edmonton, Alberta
Canada T6G 2E8

Copyright © The University of Alberta Press 1996

ISBN 0–88864–279-2

Canadian Cataloguing in Publication Data

Keshen, Jeff, 1962–
Propaganda and Censorship during Canada's Great War

ISBN 0–88864–279–2

1. World War, 1914–1918—Propaganda. 2. World War, 1914–1918—Censorship—
Canada. 3. Propaganda, Anti-German—Canada—History. 4. Propaganda, Canadian—
History. I. Title.
D639.P7C2 1996   940.4'889711   C96-910093-0

Printed on acid-free paper. ∞
Printed and bound in Canada by D.W. Friesen & Sons Ltd., Altona, Manitoba.

Frontispiece: "Your Chums Are Fighting—Why Aren't You?" C.J. Patterson,
offset lithograph, 96.5 x 63. C–029484, National Archives of Canada.

COMMITTED TO THE DEVELOPMENT OF CULTURE AND THE ARTS

Contents

Acknowledgements

For giving generously of their time, I would like to thank my thesis board—Professors Jack Saywell, Christopher Armstrong, Reginald Whitaker and Fred Fletcher of York University, along with the Hon. John English, formally of the University of Waterloo. As so many other first books, this manuscript represents a revised version of my doctoral dissertation. At the University of Alberta, valuable suggestions were offered by Professors Rod Macleod, Doug Owram, Paul Voisey and David Mills. Also appreciated were the incisive comments of Professor Reginald Roy of the University of Victoria, Dr. Leila Mitchell-Mckee of the University of Toronto, and two anonymous readers for the Social Science Federation of Canada.

The Social Science and Humanities Research Council of Canada and the Ontario Graduate Scholarship programmes provided funds in the form of doctoral fellowships to make much of this research possible. The University of Alberta awarded me a Killam Postdoctoral Fellowship that permitted the time for the revisions necessary for publication.

Antonio Lechasseur and Glenn Wright of the National Archives of Canada helped me locate several records, as did Leon Warmsky at the Archives of Ontario. The staff at the Canadian War Museum, the Metropolitan Toronto Public Library, the Multicultural History Society of Ontario, as well as the Public Records and the House of Lords Record Offices in London were most helpful in my research. I would also like to express my gratitude to archivists at the Document Delivery Unit at the University of New South Wales in Sydney, Australia.

Thanks are also due to Norma Gutteridge, former director of the University of Alberta Press, for her encouragement and patience, and as well to Mary Mahoney-Robson for her superlative editorial work. This book has been published with the help of a grant from the Social Science Federation of Canada, using funds provided by the Social Sciences and Humanities Research Council of Canada.

As it is customary, my greatest debts are saved until last. Without the guidance of my Ph.D. supervisor, J.L. Granatstein, this manuscript would have taken far longer to complete and perhaps have turned out half as good. But I remain responsible for any mistakes in the text. I would also like to thank my parents, James and Rosaline Keshen, and my family for their encouragement. For years of patience, support, and many valuable suggestions that appear in these pages, my deepest felt acknowledgement goes to my wife, Deborah Moynes-Keshen.

Introduction

Never easily balanced in wartime is the public's eagerness for information with the need to safeguard security and bolster morale. Admittedly, initiatives such as censorship possess the potential to make proclaimed crusades against tyranny appear rather ludicrous; but countering this is the official perception that it is necessary to repress news providing the enemy with strategic and/or psychological advantages. In the case of the Great War, a free flow of information might well have proven disastrous. This was, after all, a contest calling upon countries to amass unprecedented numbers of men and amounts of materiel, and engendered a level of battlefield slaughter still unsurpassed. Few, if any, anticipated its magnitude. In August 1914, Britain's Foreign Secretary said that Lord Kitchener's prediction of a three-year struggle requiring a million-man British army (the actual number ended up being five times higher) was "unlikely if not incredible."[1] Once realizing that victory was not "coming by Christmas," governments began introducing multitudinous measures to fully mobilize national strength, an endeavour that for the first time included formalized attempts at moulding the mass psyche.

In Canada, the federal government, in order to generate a supreme effort, armed itself not only with a host of new regulatory and taxing powers, but also entered the field of official news management. The same occurred elsewhere. In Britain, public agencies such as Wellington House and its successor, the Ministry of Information, distributed propagandistic pamphlets, posters, films and press releases at home and abroad; France's *Maison de la Presse* laboured to keep spirits buoyant despite a casualty toll eventually reaching 1.4 million dead; and starting on 9 April 1917, the United States launched its Committee on Public Information that, among other things, disseminated a profusion of cheery communiques, educational booklets, moving and still pictures, along with war trophies for state fair exhibitions.

Commencing with Walter Lippmann's 1922 pathbreaking study on *Public Opinion*, several European and American scholars have investigated this facet of the Great War experience.[2] By contrast, however, both academic and popular studies on the Canadian homefront usually stop at references to the unsuspecting elation accompanying the declaration of hostilities, the activities of assorted patriotic citizen associations, along with the suffering endured by enemy aliens. There still exists no systematic examination of the naivete, jingoism and nativism articulated through various means of mass communication, or how this affected society both during and after the conflagration.

Setting the stage for this analysis, the first chapter presents a nation in August 1914 both anxious for combat and nervous about internal subversion. It then proceeds to illustrate how such traits—based in pre-war imperialist, romantic and racialist philosophy—were stimulated throughout the conflict by privately-controlled propaganda like newspaper editorials, books, advertisements, movies, songs, church sermons and classroom lessons.[3] These sources sold most people on battle as adventurous, the foe and his worldwide minions as depraved, and continually emphasized that the Dominion's valiant and manly northern warriors were laying the seeds for ever-lasting national glory. Indeed, so prevalent did jingoism remain, at least outside of Quebec, that Ottawa was not compelled to fund a large-scale domestic-based propaganda network until early 1917 when the flow of recruits slowed, and food and fuel shortages along with a monetary crisis necessitated conscription, conservation, and Victory Bond drives— campaigns that a majority of Canadians responded to with idealistic enthusiasm.

Although drawing initial strength from pre-war philosophies, the enduring influence enjoyed by clichéd notions, despite nearly five years of bloodshed, points to the significant and successful management of information-dispensing systems. This issue is first addressed in chapter two.

Besides analyzing the appearance and effects of Canadian-based propaganda, different forms of officially-sanctioned news despatched to the Dominion from overseas will be examined.[4] Chapters three and four expand upon this theme by shifting the emphasis from information infusion to the kindred subject of censorship, initially of newspapers, and then of books, telegraphs, telephones, photographs, movies, theatrical productions and gramophone recordings.[5]

By and large, those in the Dominion read, saw or experienced relatively little to discredit chimerical notions about conflict. Logistics ensured that they were spared the Zeppelin or Gotha raids that reached London, the bombs of Big Bertha that rained down upon Parisians, or the physical displacement and severe food shortages afflicting millions across Europe. While long casualty lists were capable of providing a disturbing jolt, Canada's remoteness from the war also helped to ensure that its civilians remained sheltered from the grisly details responsible for sapping the spirits of many a frontliner. Whereas Tommy Atkins or the French *poilu* could reach home on leave time and divulge some horrendous aspects of combat—either verbally or through exhibiting disturbing personality alterations—for up to nearly half a decade Canadians remained separated from their khaki-clad kin. Never did they see troops fresh from the fray trudging down Yonge Street or Portage Avenue still bearing on their uniforms the mud and perhaps blood of the Western Front. Indeed, with the Dominion taking approximately 75 per cent of its casualties after August 1916, even the wounded did not became a common sight until the latter stages of the war.

Therefore, it was left to Canada's fourth estate to fill the void, a task for which it never seemed better prepared. Between Confederation and the Great War, newspaper circulation had, as a result of rising literacy and urbanization rates, more than tripled to exceed a million copies daily. When complimented by photography and the emerging film industry, the new mass media possessed the capacity to create some common comprehension between disparate societies—in this case the firing line and civvy street.[6] But obviously accompanying such force was the ability to manipulate popular opinion, a danger stressed by scholars including Harold Innis who, in the immediate post-World War Two period, expressed fear over what he perceived as the news industry's "bias" toward over-simplification and misrepresentation.[7] More recently, academics aligned to the Social Constructionist school have postulated that the news business, by virtue of its power to choose what stories to carry, has become a fundamental force in moulding public perception. Adding to this argument, Marxists, along with Social Control theorists, have pointed to elite press ownership as being responsible for a pattern of near-homogeneous copy legitimizing unequal power relations within a bourgeois capitalist system. In attempting to refute conspiratorial contentions, others emphasize the media's need as a profit-motivated concern to reflect—rather than manipulate—existing social values lest its message fall on deaf ears, as well as the belief that most journalists possess a professional code of conduct preventing capitulation to any type of agenda or authorized view.[8]

Without intending to offer sweeping conclusions upon the issue of media prejudice, it appears that at least in the context of the Great War, such safety valves against the emergence of an authorized view did not apply. The Dominion's jingoistic press did not encourage diversity of opinion, but rather fed off an imperialist dogma that many historians have asserted held considerable sway in pre-war Canada.[9] The same applied with respect to unrealistically blithe images about trench warfare. Before August 1914, most Canadians, like those in other nations, regarded armed combat as a rather majestic affair. History books, when not dwelling upon legendary battles and noble heroes that made Britain the world's envy, waxed eloquent about hearty Canadian Loyalists and their devoted descendants who vanquished Yankee invaders in 1812, the Fenians in 1866, traitorous half-breeds in 1885, and performed brilliantly against the Boers at places such as Paardeberg. Casualties from these encounters never reached proportions to challenge romanticized assumptions. Commenting upon the fact that only 224 countrymen died during the 1899-1902 Boer War (more than half from disease), the *Canadian Military Gazette* concluded that armed conflict was "becoming more humane, more restrained, more Christian."[10]

Besides tapping into public opinion, the ardent and continuing patriotism of the press also illustrated the prevailing state of journalism. The rise of profitable mass distribution newspapers had, by the time of the Great War, practically ended the tendency of Canadian publishers to solicit funds from political parties; still, strong echoes of this overtly partisan system remained in polemicized editorial pages, blatantly biased headlines, and news stories carrying a heavy dose of advocacy. The convention of objective reporting was a post-World War Two phenomenon resulting in part from the appearance of journalism schools. In 1914, the news profession, if one could call it that, was still largely perceived as a literary endeavour where correspondents, with encouragement from publishers and editors, produced purple prose not only to advance certain positions, but also to build readership. Thus, it was not a huge ethical leap for reporters to provide, and their newspapers to accept, ridiculously upbeat versions of battle. In fact, some in the business may have regarded the pattern as a natural and agreeable evolution from narrow partisan concerns to the far nobler purpose of defeating German authoritarianism.

But even had correspondents proven ideologically or professionally adverse towards producing jingoistic and sanitized descriptions of combat, technological considerations along with the limited clout of Canada's fourth estate ensured that they had little choice in this matter. At the front, military escorts guided the movement of journalists, photographers, and filmmakers, while specially-assigned officers checked everything they produced. If a reporter was cunning enough to avoid submitting copy to military authorities, his ability to promptly transmit the account still depended upon one rigorously monitored undersea cable linking Canada and Britain. This situation, along with the confiscation of wireless facilities on both sides of the Atlantic for military purposes, meant that there existed no instantaneous means of communication capable of circumventing censors. Meanwhile, for the Canadian-based correspondent submitting a disheartening story, not only did there exist the potential obstacle of a patriotic editor, but more important, the presence of Lieutenant-Colonel Ernest J. Chambers, the country's Chief Censor.

Normally, Canadian papers, like their British counterparts, were permitted to publish anything as long as it was not libelous; but in wartime, and without a constitutional guarantee for free expression, it seemed that their ability to promote this principle came down to power. With greater London containing more than a million inhabitants, and Britain as a whole being rather densely populated, several Fleet Street sources obtained massive circulation numbers and provided their proprietors with considerable influence. For instance, Lord Northcliffe, whose newspaper chain distributed each day twice that of all Canadian newspapers combined, was viewed by many at Westminster as literally possessing the means to make or break governments.[11] Therefore, the English press, though usually responding favourably to regulations outlined in the Defence of the Realm

Act, was still known to defy authorities by criticizing military strategy and reporting upon Allied losses that, they hoped, would improve performance on the battlefield and rally people to the tough task ahead. Probably Ottawa would have balked at sanctioning the prohibition of major Canadian dailies, and it is telling that Chambers phrased some of his admonitions to principal sources in tactful tones. Nonetheless, it is clear that when compared to their colleagues in the mother country, those running Canadian newspapers were not so self-assured. Rather than confronting Chambers when informed of a transgression, quite often an editor's humble apology flowed into the censor's office along with a pledge to never repeat the mistake.

Utilizing such legislative and *de facto* authority, Chambers forged a demanding standard, one more rigid in its attempt to coddle citizens and repress dissent than censorship systems established in the United Kingdom or the United States. Frequently, he banned material circulating in Britain, reasoning that the mother country's proximity to the war zone had partially accustomed its citizens to the grittiness of war—at least moreso than geographically-sheltered Canadians who, he suggested, were tied to combat more by idealistic sentiment than any imminent concern about national survival. Indeed, he postulated that those in the Dominion, if presented with similar information as the British, might well have developed something akin to a civilian version of neurasthenia. As far as U.S. sources were concerned, Chambers claimed, with considerable exaggeration, that even after Washington declared war, its First Amendment constitutional rights made it too difficult for officials there to stifle dissent, a perception for which he more than amply compensated when it came to the ability of questionable American tracts and films to circulate north of the international border. Finally, most prohibited publications were written in languages other than English or French, thus demonstrating Chambers's capacity to vigorously apply the imperialist-connected faith of "Anglo conformity" that cast so-called outsiders as inferior, deceitful and disloyal.[12] All told, throughout his term, that ended with the lapse of the War Measures Act on 1 January 1920, Canada's Chief Censor suppressed 253 publications, approximately 90 per cent of which were American-based and two-thirds written in a foreign language.

In Chambers's defence, there is no doubt that numerous sources from the neutral United States were hostile to the Allied cause. As well, in over-emphasizing the surveillance of certain ethnic groups as presumably pro-German, or, after the war, as plotting a Canadian-based Bolshevik revolution, the Chief Censor mirrored a repressive social consensus shown, for instance, by the overwhelming support extended to the internment of enemy aliens. One might argue that it was reasonable for him to apply rough justice and err on the side of caution. While not wishing to overstate circumstances, it is only with the benefit of hindsight that it becomes easy to dismiss the smattering of German fifth columnists and potential invaders in a neutral America, as well as factions within other ethnic groups openly hostile to Britain. Certainly, the presence of such parties was stressed by a fledgling Canadian secret service network that, though sometimes prone to embellish matters, still represented the most plausible source of gauging potential threats. In addition, by 1918, wartime inflation, conscription and the inspirational events in Russia, provided Canada's radical left with unprecedented strength. But even if partly absolved by community-wide mores, or the need to win the war and maintain social stability following the armistice, it is clear that Chambers exuded too little dispassion and too much zeal. Often his decisions were based far more upon racism than anything approaching bona fide evidence and at times he even exceeded what other cautious officials considered as appropriate safeguards. Still, by ceaselessly pursuing and identifying so-called subversive elements, censorship in Canada helped set the foundation for oppressive post-war legislation focusing upon ethnic and political minorities as well as the emergence of a permanent peacetime internal security network.

Both censorship and propaganda also played key roles in creating some painful legacies for society-at-large. Undeniably, Great War veterans from all countries had difficulty readapting to civilian life, but in Canada there is good reason to suspect that their sense of displacement was more profound and long-lasting. Those fortunate enough to survive the carnage returned to a place where press copy, books, and other post-war ideological indicators suggested that despite 60,000 dead, idealistic conceptions about war still dominated. This is not to say that Canadians were unaffected by years of unprecedented sacrifice; the need to escalate censorship and eventually introduce large-scale domestic propaganda pointed to some weariness. Yet, having been inundated with cheery accounts and spared by geographic remoteness from first-hand evidence that challenged pristine perspectives, civilians, in November 1918, from the vantage point of their cocoon-like environment, stood far more ready to welcome home the brave and Christian conquering heroes manufactured by opinion-makers instead of men frequently marred in some manner by their combat experience.

In order to illuminate the extent to which Canada's homefront became disconnected from reality, Part III turns to the views of those who left for adventure and glory overseas. Quickly and sorely testing Johnny Canuck's quixotic expectations was the monotony of training, followed by a two-week voyage in a crowded and stinking vessel, along with the myriad privations and terrors of front-line life. Ardent young men who had once worried about hostilities finishing before they had a chance to participate soon expressed concern over a never-ending battle; those who had anticipated that the *elan* of combatants would decide this contest found a place where technology and firepower seemed far more decisive; and volunteers who had envisaged military life as providing physical and spiritual enhancement, discovered themselves in a setting where profanity, drunkenness and sexual promiscuity became release mechanisms. As significant as their proverbial sense of disillusionment, however, was the fact that censorship provisions imposed by the military, along with the desire of recruits to bear the brunt like real men, confined the preponderance of embittered commentary to sources meant only for those in uniform.

One such source was the somewhat restrained but still revealing pages of censored battalion newspapers that are analyzed in chapter five. Here, military authorities, besides including patriotic and inspirational copy, endeavoured to maintain morale by allowing satirical accounts that reflected the depressing incongruity of this *Great War*—hoping that soldiers would laugh at their predicament and thus vent frustrations. This schism between a secluded homefront and those whose pre-war naivete was shattered by bombs, bullets and blood is made yet more evident in chapter six that compares letters written home by troops with diary entries as well as some images lodged in their long-term memories.[13]

In abiding by censorship rules and the so-called code of manly conduct, Johnny Canuck unwittingly contributed to the agonizing experiences associated with this bloodbath. Namely, he widened the intellectual chasm and ultimately intensified a peacetime clash with a civilian society manipulated by an information control system whose capacity to project an appealing picture of combat and its participants was bolstered by logistical, ideological, technical and social factors. How long this schism persisted after repatriation depended upon individual wartime experiences and the dynamics within each family. On a community-wide basis, however, it was not until perhaps the early 1930s that the divide between soldiers and the rest of society narrowed substantively. By that time many veterans were prepared to reveal their ordeals in a series of harrowing memoirs—works that took a decade or more to write not only as a result of the time required to adequately comprehend the psychological effects of combat, but also because only then could veterans address a civilian audience that finally dismissed the Great War as an agent of social progress and appeared prepared to accept its more tragic consequences.

From such narratives, argued Paul Fussell in his brilliant cultural analysis of the conflagration, a "modern memory" of war was created, one that forever displaced romanticised "high diction" with an "ironic mode" to reflect a front-line verity that emerged in contrast to the once-high hopes of idealistic recruits.[14] But in Canada, the fixation upon rats, mud, trenches and death represents only one part of the prevailing perception. There also persists the picture of soldiers who, through their extraordinary bravery, won the hardest and most important battles—particularly Second Ypres and Vimy Ridge—and thus emerged as a singular and heroic force in transforming Canada from colony to nation. Admittedly, it is "modern memory" for which information control is not solely responsible. Also relevant was that Canadians, unlike the British or Americans, carried into this contest the aspiration of winning greater status, either within the Empire or as an independent country. Still, it is not stretching credulity to suggest that it became easier to affix a rather quixotic interpretation upon the post-war growth in autonomy when for nearly five years the stupendous qualities of and critical role played by Johnny Canuck in garnering worldwide esteem went unchallenged. With the help of pre-war jingoism and naivete, geographic isolation, along with press corps' patriotism and relative tractability, Canadian propagandists and censors were able to exert a level of influence that not only made it possible for romantic notions about combat to survive the butchery, but also, where post-armistice events provided some rationality, to practically predestine that they surface as core explanations. Such a pattern also suggests that to their dying day, some distance remained between the heroes of popular consciousness and Canada's real Great War veterans who frequently proved psychologically incapable of leaving the battlefield behind.

PROPAGANDA

1

A Nation Rallies to the Cause

Quickly escalating Serb-Austrian tensions, precipitated by the June 1914 assassination of Archduke Franz Ferdinand, appeared to many Canadians as just another episode in the seemingly endless turmoil of Central European politics. Indeed, Prime Minister Borden, as most Members of Parliament, was vacationing when the Kaiser's army, as directed by the Schlieffen Plan, by-passed French defences and invaded Belgium, thus prompting, on August 4th, Britain's declaration of war against the Central Powers.

In Canada, initial shock was promptly replaced by a sense of exhilaration. Clarion calls were issued. "Gallant, little" Belgium lay imperiled. In this fight, imperialists claimed, Canadians would finally demonstrate the loyalty, grit and fortitude qualifying the Dominion for a major share in deciding Empire affairs. Citizens would not just be performing God's work in helping to destroy a barbaric foe proclaimed many religious leaders, but would also project their nation to a higher plane of conduct since the Great War had clearly infused the multitudes with that Christian spirit of sacrificing on behalf of others.[1] For countless men, the conflict was perceived as a one-time opportunity to exchange the sedate routines of civilian life for a ticket to new lands and manly adventures then celebrated in popular adventure stories, especially those written by Rudyard Kipling or Edgar Rice Burroughs.

The heady days of August 1914 promised much. Even the festivities commemorating Canada's entry into the war seemed symbolic. Almost everyone lent their voices to support this noble venture, prompting some to conclude that the apparent unity heralded a fresh start within a society recently plagued by increasingly bitter socio-economic and racial divisions.[2] For not only had Canadian industrialisation produced some major strikes and radical unions, but a series of political events, perhaps starting with the 1885 Riel execution, exacerbated the Dominion's French-English division. However, within those August throngs cheering the fiery speeches of politicians and other community leaders, workers and capitalists stood shoulder-to-shoulder, and newspaper reports noted that crowds in Montreal exceeded those in Toronto. To oppose participation in such a hallowed campaign appeared akin to lunacy. So discovered Judson Davidson of Guelph who, that month, was sentenced by local authorities to an asylum for writing an anti-war pamphlet.[3]

At the outset of hostilities, J. Castell Hopkins wrote in his *Canadian Annual Review*, "the Conservative press…supported immediate aid to the Empire," while Liberal tracts "clearly enunciated the doctrine that when Britain was at war so was Canada."[4] At one level this reflected the country's legal status as a colony. Yet, if the Dominion had decided not to despatch troops, England was incapable of forcing compliance. Quickly making large-scale participation a foregone conclusion, however, was an imperialist ethos born of Canada's British heritage, cultivated in Victorian and Edwardian times by the belief in Anglo-Protestant superiority, and strengthened by the hope that once the Dominion proved itself on the battlefield, an equal partnership between Ottawa and London would result. Moreover, with little collective knowledge about warfare, bold and idealized rhetoric seemed pervasive, even emanating from sources serving French-Canada such as *La Presse* that called upon young Quebecois to form a regiment and "join France's heroic army."[5] Also typical in its reaction to hostilities was the Toronto-based *Industrial Banner*, arguably Canada's most important labour newspaper, from whose pages came a rallying cry to crush "Prussian authoritarianism," under which, it asserted, the "common man suffered most."[6]

Politicians did not disappoint when it came to supplying patriotic gestures and hyperbole. Toronto's city council, similar to several other municipal governments, offered free insurance policies to volunteers. In Ottawa, an imperialist-minded Prime Minister Borden proclaimed that "we stand shoulder to shoulder with Britain," while Opposition leader Sir Wilfrid Laurier, though concerned about the potential of war to exacerbate Canada's French-English cleavage, nevertheless pledged his patriotic support.[7] And after consulting some prominent Quebec priests, even nationaliste leader, Henri Bourassa, who had opposed involvement in the Boer War, initially conceded that "it is Canada's national duty to contribute according to her resources."[8]

A spirit of voluntarism consumed much of the public. After a week's hostilities, the Montreal financier, Herbert Ames, told Borden that citizens were enquiring "how…[to] help in the common endeavour." Many soon channelled their energies into assisting the Canadian Patriotic Fund, started that August by an Act of Parliament, with Ames as Honourary Secretary, to raise money for those left financially destitute by the absence or death of a family member in uniform. In three months, it raised a remarkable $6 million and by 1916 supported some 25,000 families. Others devoted their time to many different causes including the Red Cross and Tobacco Fund (which sent soldiers cigarettes), along with Belgian, Serbian and Armenian relief.[9]

Hand-in-hand with jingoism and imperialism came the desire to ferret out and crush the unpatriotic, a tendency also drawing upon the related and well-established creed of nativism. For generations, newcomers to Canada harbouring customs, beliefs or racial backgrounds preventing easy assimilation into white Anglo-Protestant society were denounced as inferior, and resented for threatening to draw the Dominion from its British roots. The war, with its emphasis upon total loyalty and conformity, intensified such intolerance. Prior to August 1914, Germans, since they were caucasian and predominantly Protestant, actually constituted a favoured group. Some noted the Kaiser's blood ties with Britain's royal family. But with hostilities, xenophobia was expanded to recast Teutons as a dark and mongrel race that, according to some scientific experts, were shown by "flattish heads" to possess Turkish roots.[10] This portrait also emphasized their savage and devious nature. Soon characterizing the sentiments of countless citizens was the Toronto *Star*'s conclusion that though the 170,000 Canadians of Teutonic background and 8,000,000 German-Americans were "under no legal obligation to serve…the fatherland," most still likely stood "ready to do criminal work for their masters."[11]

Reflecting such fears, Ottawa introduced measures to combat spies, saboteurs and the possibility of invasion. Not since pre-Confederation battles against the Fenians had Canada engaged in significant secret service work. That changed quickly. In August 1914, the Department of Justice was provided with an extra $100,000 to increase the Royal North-West Mounted Police [R.N.W.M.P.] roster from 763 to 1,268. Many ended up in France as soldiers, but a portion were assigned to internal security work in Alberta and Saskatchewan. Heading up efforts in British Columbia was the Immigration Branch, particularly its inspectors, Malcolm J. Reid and Colonel J. Hopkinson, who, before the war, directed some surveillance of Canadian Sikhs and Hindus for signs of support towards anti-colonial insurgents in their homeland. Throughout the rest of the country, security was organized by the Dominion Police, a unit initially created to guard politicians and public buildings following the 1868 assassination of D'Arcy McGee. During the first year of the Great War, its budget was almost doubled to $154,225 to better coordinate activities with the R.N.W.M.P. and various local constabularies in the fight against supposed internal subversives.[12] Its commander, Colonel Percy Sherwood, was among those counselling Borden on the need to carefully monitor Germans, especially in areas close to the international border. Enemy success overseas, he warned, could give confidence to "bodies of armed men drawn from certain [Teutonic] societies, united with members of the [anti-British Irish-Catholic group] Clan-na-gael," reproducing on "a larger scale" the Fenian raid of 1866.[13] Therefore, investigators were also hired from the Pinkerton and Theil Detective Agencies to frequent, both in Canada and the United States, saloons and social clubs in German neighbourhoods, a service for which the latter collected $117,000 during the first two years of the war.[14]

With no central body to filter and assess the quality of various despatches, for months jittery politicians gave considerable credence to alarmist reports from operatives who may have exaggerated threats to demonstrate the importance of their job, held personal biases regarding German treachery, or simply could not distinguish reality from the boasts of men in bar rooms. In one of many such reports, Borden was advised that Michigan-based Germans, in coordination with their Canadian brethren, were preparing a massive raid. Consequently, up to 16,000 militia personnel maintained patrols along the international border, as well as at arsenals, railway stations, docks, canal locks, grain elevators and other facilities considered militarily or economically essential.[15] From this charged atmosphere there sometimes flowed unfortunate results. One of the more extreme cases occurred in December 1914 when two American hunters were killed near Niagara Falls by anxious soldiers who assumed that they were advance scouts for a hostile force.[16]

Only after literally hundreds of baseless tips did Canadian authorities, though still alert to the possibility of sabotage, develop a more sober assessment of the invasion scenario. In mid 1915, Major-General Sir Willoughby Gwatkin, the Chief of the General Staff, assured Borden that the likelihood of an armed foray was at best remote. Furthermore, by stressing the ability of recruits in each military district to repel any would-be invader, he convinced the government to curtail the use of special border patrols. From various detectives ominous warnings persisted, but by November 1915 even Percy Sherwood conceded that he was no longer "disposed to treat such information seriously."[17] The following year, the Dominion Police roster was cut from 355 to 245, and, in September 1916, the services of the Theil agency were temporarily discontinued.[18]

Still, the public remained tense. It took only a few incidents, all of which were given front page newspaper coverage, to retain the atmosphere of a witch hunt. In 1915, the international railway bridge at Vanceboro, Maine was dynamited by a German reservist (though traffic was halted for only six hours),[19] and eight New York-based Teutons were convicted of planting time bombs on board the Marseilles-bound cargo ship *Kirke Oswald*. Such episodes, headlines blared, represented the handiwork of Captains Carl Boy-Ed and Franz von Papen, two enemy military attaches who, though expelled by Washington soon after the British passenger liner *Lusitania* was sunk, had, it was reasoned, left behind a network of operatives working across North America. For example, there was no shortage of ominous speculation about the February 1916 fire that demolished the House of Commons. Said the Ottawa *Evening Journal*: "The Justice Department was warned from Providence, Rhode Island, that a German plot was being hatched...to blow up or otherwise destroy the buildings."[20]

In this milieu, accusations of disloyalty against German-Canadians became the norm, accusations that, in fact, had little, if any, corroborating evidence. For instance, remaining Ontario jail registers from the era, which indicate ethnic background and cover areas of heavy Teutonic settlement, do not reveal a single German serving time for war-related subversive activities.[21] Nevertheless, typical of public attitudes was the story of Berlin, Ontario. Despite having raised $96,000 for the Patriotic Fund and just over $49,000 for the Red Cross in 1914 (the latter figure exceeding money obtained in Prince Edward Island, New Brunswick, and Manitoba), the community was cast as a hotbed of disloyalty because of its large German population. Determined to erase the stigma, those of Anglo-Protestant background took action three weeks after Canada declared war by tossing a statue of Kaiser Wilhelm I, which had stood in the town park for sixteen years, into Victoria Lake.[22] Residents such as J.H. Baetz recalled as a child being beaten for speaking German in public.[23] Moreover, the business elite of this thriving industrial community, fearing a loss of commerce from surrounding districts, led a campaign in 1916 to have the town's name changed to Kitchener to commemorate the British War Minister who drowned that spring in the Irish Sea. Typifying the temper of the debate, which soon resulted in Berlin's disappearance from the map, were soldiers from the nearby 118th Battalion who ransacked the German-dominated Concordia and Acadian Clubs, both of which suspended meetings a year earlier following the sinking of the *Lusitania*.[24]

However, because most German-Canadians had family roots stretching back in the Dominion for several generations, they at least were spared the indignity of internment. Experiencing such misery and humiliation were thousands of unnaturalized enemy aliens, most of whom were of Ukrainian descent—a scenario that, it is unfortunate to say, epitomised much of their treatment since arriving in Canada. For instance, large-scale migration from Eastern Europe during the late nineteenth century elicited comments from numerous Canadians about "dirty, poor, sickly, rebellious, and immoral" people. Moreover, their propensity for block settlement was not interpreted as a reaction to bigotry, but rather as a sign of antipathy to the dominant culture, a conclusion that in wartime added to questions about their loyalty.[25]

In the opening days of the war, the federal government promised enemy aliens fair treatment as long as they obeyed the laws of the land.[26] But intense public pressure and cynical economic considerations rapidly altered the situation. Regulations prevented these people from owning firearms or handling explosives, restrictions that proved especially onerous to farmers facing wild animals, or those working in mines. As well, to stop such disloyal people from stealing employment from "real" Canadians, enemy aliens were required to disclose their ethnic background when applying for a job.[27] These measures, however, only constituted the thin edge of the wedge. Commencing in October 1914, 5,954 Ukrainians, most of whom were born in the Austro-Hungarian controlled province of Galicia, joined 2,009 Germans reservists as internees. Each month, thousands more Ukrainians were compelled to report upon their whereabouts to a designated officer, who could prevent those naturalized after 1911 from residing or being in any place believed "prejudicial to public safety."[28]

In initiating these measures, federal officials disregarded the fact that Galicia's status as a belligerent was a result of a pre-war Austro-Hungarian military incursion into the province. What caught the attention of authorities instead were inflammatory remarks made by a few individuals belonging to the ethnic group, such as the Western Canadian Ukrainian spiritual leader, Bishop Nicholas Budka, who, in August 1914, issued a pastoral decree advising his followers "to support the peace-loving Emperor Franz-Joseph...." A week later Budka recanted, insisting that all Ukrainians were "faithful citizens of...the British Empire...."[29] Understandably, most Canadians looked upon the second comment as a ruse, but unfairly they also assumed that a majority of Galicians would blindly obey Budka's subversive advice.[30] Therefore, in further rationalizing its harsh approach towards this ethnic group, Ottawa cited its responsibility to protect them from the possibility of mob justice.

The new homes and duties provided by the government, however, hardly suggested that benevolence was a guiding concern. Galician males were transported to remote northern communities such as Petawawa,

Kapuskasing and Spirit Lake, leaving behind families who often fell into abject poverty. At these camps, internees were compelled to perform tasks such as clearing roads, planting trees and constructing rifle ranges. Ottawa spent only 25 cents a day to pay, feed and provide shelter for each man, a policy that in large part accounted for abnormally high rates of frostbite, tuberculosis and pneumonia. To maintain discipline, some prisoners were hanged by their wrists for hours, a control mechanism that, along with other outrages, produced some attempted escapes and uprisings during which a total of six Ukrainians were killed by guards.[31]

More than a few officials in Ottawa knew full well that assumptions about Galician disloyalty were by and large unfounded, thus making the internment programme even more deplorable. For example, Solicitor-General Arthur Meighen, a strong advocate of internment, confessed to the Prime Minister in late 1914 that he "would be very much surprised" if these people caused any trouble.[32] Indeed, it is likely that in establishing the camps, not only was the federal government gratifying wartime nativistic rage, but also demonstrating a need to reduce an employment surplus. Throughout 1914, Canada was in the midst of an economic downturn and the prevailing presumption about a quick triumph over Germany promised little job creation. In fact, four days after hostilities commenced, Labour Minister Thomas Crothers advised municipal governments to prepare for "much unemployment and destitution next winter." Local authorities in Port Arthur and Fort William, for example, responded by arresting all unnaturalized and jobless Austro-Hungarians. Nationwide, the number of indigent enemy aliens soon swelled as patriotic employers added thousands of Galicians to the ranks of the unemployed.[33] Clearly, from both economic and political angles, it proved expedient for Ottawa to remove a number of these people, via internment, from a tight job market. Meanwhile, two years later, when the labour surplus transformed into a shortage, more than half of the internment camps ceased operations and paroled a majority of Galicians.[34] But as a condition of their release, many Galicians were contracted out as cheap farm labour, while others found themselves assigned to railway work sites where long hours, paltry pay and confinement to the immediate locale were rigidly enforced. And for those who talked about unionization or strikes, more often than not their payoff was in the form of a free trip back to one of the remaining prison camps.[35]

Not even the cessation of hostilities softened public attitudes towards groups who, because of their ethnic background, were presumed as unpatriotic. On 12 November 1918, in Smooth Rock Falls, Ontario, George Miller, the German superintendent of the Mattagami Pulp and Paper Company, was forced by a crowd of 300 to kiss the Union Jack after failing to blow the factory whistle at 11 a.m. the previous day to commemorate the armistice. The following March, in Monkton, Ontario, several Lutherans were beaten and their church ransacked because a Reverend Wohlert neglected to meet a wounded local boy arriving at the nearby Stratford train station.[36] Finally, in mirroring such a mood, the 1919 Immigration Act barred from Canada any prospective citizen coming from a former enemy country.[37]

From the first shot to the final artillery salvo, Canadian communication networks reflected and augmented imperialist and romantic notions of duty, honour and warfare, and buttressed virulent sentiment against Germany and its suspected worldwide web of spies, saboteurs and other servile agents. Having firmly established its roots by the early twentieth century, the print- and pictorial-based mass media held extraordinary and unprecedented power to produce and retain such opinions. In the case of newspapers, nineteenth century technological advances with papermaking, typesetting machines and photoengraving, along with, most important, the appearance of high speed steam-powered cylinder-presses, allowed pioneers such as Lord Northcliffe in England and Jacob Pulitzer in the United States to provide inexpensive daily publications to increasingly urbanized and literate societies. This was a process duplicated in Canada where, between 1891 and 1911, the nonrural population more than doubled to 3.3 million, and public school attendance displayed almost identical growth.[38] During the 30 years prior to the Great War, the number of newspapers in the Dominion jumped from 46 to 138, and their size and appeal magnified with the introduction of international news service reports, as well as sports, entertainment and society pages, thus resulting in total daily circulation tripling to just over one million.[39]

Besides carrying official front-line despatches, it was through their editorial pages and stories by in-house reporters and columnists that the Canadian press emerged as propaganda source. The apparent lack of concern with so-called objective standards said much about early twentieth century journalism. Although new mass circulation publications earned enough revenue to end the longstanding practice of editors and publishers seeking financial support from political parties, both were still known to serve as informal advisors to the country's leaders and were sometimes offered senatorial appointments as a reward for favourable coverage.[40] Widespread acceptance of explicit partisanship—a situation then largely unchallenged partly due to the absence of professional journalism schools preaching the principle of balanced coverage—no doubt made it easier for the fourth estate to quickly hone a wartime pattern. Of this trend, the Toronto *Globe*'s editor, Dr. J.A. Macdonald, claimed that those who "wield[ed] the pen" were determined to make "every citizen know what Canada is fighting for and what success or failure means."[41]

With the exception of socialist and pacifist tracts, along with some anti-imperialist rural and French-Canadian publications (which, if wishing to continue circulating, muted their rancour considerably), the press, throughout the conflict, propounded loyalty to the mother country, pride in the accomplishments of Johnny Canuck, the adventure and relative bloodlessness of battle, the saintliness of those who made the supreme sacrifice, and incredulity over German fiendishness. From a mere glance readers could glean these themes: from bold headlines heralding yet another Allied triumph; via political cartoons showing, for example, the archetypal spike-helmeted Hun clutching a sword dripping with blood; or through newspaper spots placed by citizen organizations like Red Cross depicting images such as the proverbial female angel of mercy treating a soldier with minor wounds on a pastoral-like battlefield.[42]

Especially acclaimed in newspaper columns was the grit displayed by Canadian lads. "They seem…to have something heroic and almost divine about them," declared the Toronto *News* after the Second Battle of Ypres, a clash whose 6,000 Canadian casualties actually shocked Prime Minister Borden to the point of leading him to demand greater consultation with the British when it came to the future use of Dominion troops.[43] In its reaction to the losses, however, the Manitoba *Free Press* insisted that "above the tears…there rose steady and clear the voice of thankfulness to God…that they were permitted in their death to make so splendid a sacrifice."[44] Through several bloody encounters this romanticized pattern persisted, and perhaps was most prominent following the April 1917 clash at Vimy Ridge since it represented the first bona fide test and triumph for the newly-formed Canadian Corps. There, Commander Julian Byng, in coordination with General Arthur Currie, replaced conventional, costly and all-too-often failed linear attack strategy with platoon formations and rolling artillery barrages. The result saw the capture of 54 large guns, 104 trench mortars, 4,000 soldiers and an objective that some military men, following failed French and British assaults, began considering as impenetrable. Newspapers such as the Winnipeg *Tribune* were certainly accurate in describing "citizens [who] thrill[ed]" over the conquest, but were far less forthright when depicting "German troops…who were scattered like chaff before the vigour of the…attack." In fact, by glossing over grisliness and playing up the superhuman conduct of Johnny Canuck, it seemed that such accounts helped produce a populace proud and euphoric enough to barely pause over an unprecedented single battle casualty toll reaching approximately 10,000 Canadians.[45]

Besides attracting men into service by sanitizing combat, countless publications also championed recruitment drives. The Toronto *Star* not only printed the names of local inductees, but also endorsed a technique where military officers went into cinemas and other public places to demand that all able-bodied single men in civvies stand up and explain why they were not in uniform. National Service questionnaires distributed in December 1916, and interpreted by many as a prelude to conscription, enjoyed spirited media support throughout English-Canada. The Manitoba *Free Press* condemned those trade unions demanding that wealth first be drafted for "hiding behind bleeding France, martyred Belgium, valorous Britain, and their Allies…."[46] Also from a majority of English-Canadian sources came unconditional support for compulsory service. Besides stressing that such a measure would compel Quebec to sacrifice as much as the rest of the country, these tracts also touted conscription to opponents within the labour movement as the most class-free system because, as one editorial contended, it "takes no account of wealth or social pretensions, but regards all citizens as equal and exacts from all the same compliance."[47] Indeed, based upon such convictions, long-time Laurier advisor and Manitoba *Free Press* editor, J.W. Dafoe, once accepting his inability to convince the party leader to join Borden in a pro-draft coalition Union government, played a key role in arranging the defection of several high-profile Anglo-Canadian Liberals.[48]

Helping to explain the fervent endorsement of such measures was the connection made in many publications between war and the advancement of civilization. *Saturday Night*, one of Canada's few national magazines, insisted that only the total destruction of Germany would "better humanity and extend the bounds of freedom."[49] To ensure that Canadians understood what defeat meant, several sources supplied lurid tales of enemy conduct. In May 1915, extensive coverage was given to Britain's "Report on Alleged German Outrages in Belgium" that, as revealed after the war, was based upon falsified testimony from refugees. "In Sempst," read a standard account paraphrased by the Halifax *Herald*, "a girl of seventeen, dressed only in a chemise...[was] dragged into a field, stripped naked and violated...."[50] The same month, the *Lusitania* was sunk, with a loss of 1,198 lives, including 170 Canadians. Berlin's assertion that the vessel carried ammunition (a fact recently confirmed by an underwater investigation team)[51] was denounced as a vicious lie spread by a satanically-inspired race accused of striking a medal to honour those who committed the monstrous deed. That October, attention shifted to the British nurse, Edith Cavell, who was shot for espionage. The press depicted her as a glowing example of Christian British womanhood who selflessly risked her life to care for enemy wounded, and, despite her innocence, bravely confronted death at the hands of cowards devoid of manly chivalry. Exclaimed the Winnipeg *Tribune*: "This deed of hell will dog their steps for another century."[52]

It was the Hun, citizens were reminded, who introduced poison gas against their sons at Second Ypres, and later utilized flame throwers summoning up Dantesque-type visions of hell. Playing upon the religious theme of the Great War as symbolizing a struggle between the forces of darkness and light, several sources reported as fact the rumour that the enemy crucified a Canadian soldier on a barn door with bayonets. It was not surprising, wrote *Saturday Night*, that such pagans possessed no guilt about deliberately aiming artillery at places of worship. In 1917, it told readers that the enemy destroyed 173 French and Belgian churches, but conveniently failed to mention that the Allies used their steeples as observation posts.[53] And while Canadians were informed about the exceptional care provided to German P.O.W.'s, it was maintained that their sadistic adversary displayed contempt for international law. For instance, based upon testimony from a lance-corporal released in a Swiss-arranged prisoner exchange, the Hamilton *Spectator* described Allied inmates forced to subsist on "grass soup…cheese (inedible), raw fish, coffee made from roasted acorns and tea made from barkwood shavings."[54]

Even in parts of their newspapers not intended to convey any news, Canadians still encountered messages and images shaping and obscuring their perception of trench warfare. This was apparent with commercial advertising whose presence in major publications directly paralleled the growth of cities and the concomitant rise of mass manufacturing and retailing. By World War One, ad agencies had appeared across Britain and North America and began applying new public relations theories hypothesizing that successful campaigns invariably tapped into positive social desires or symbols.[55] Thus, to generate a response from consumers, advertisers often attempted to affiliate their goods with this celebrated conflict, or, if at all possible, to present their products as the buyer's patriotic choice. For example, in giving Doctor Cassell's Dyspepsia Tablets his endorsement, the fictional Sergeant MacNeil managed to convey the impression that among the biggest problems faced by servicemen overseas was rather severe indigestion caused by having to eat on the run more frequently. Also representative were solicitations from the Gillette Razor Corporation. While careful not to denigrate army life in any way, still it informed families that its merchandise could make the soldiers' life yet more comfortable. "It's a luxury the lucky ones share with their pals, so send along plenty of extra blades," proclaimed one pitch depicting a group of smiling, snappily-clad front-line troops at an inspection.[56]

The other principal source of printed war-related information came from books, a medium that also witnessed trends of expanding volume, falling prices and spiralling popularity throughout the nineteenth century, culminating with the famed dime-store novel. Between 1914 and 1918, approximately 1,000 works, ranging in sales from 100 to 40,000, deluged the Canadian market to satisfy the insatiable curiosity of citizens to know more about the electrifying events from which they were physically isolated. However, the majority of entries did little more than confirm propagandistic news copy. Censorship provisions, patriotism, possibly an author's concern about sales, along with the fact that some writers possessed scant knowledge about the butchery overseas, saw publications continue to cater to an audience that demonstrated in the immediate pre-war years a prefer-ence for adventure stories whose male protagonist embodied the highest physical and spiritual standards, or imperialistically-inclined historical accounts commemorating heroes such as General Gordon of the Sudan whose battlefield bravery exemplified the qualities of Anglo-Saxondom and built a glorious Empire. Not surprising, in 1919, after having surveyed a multitude of material juxtaposing German guilt, greed and cruelty, against Allied fair play, honour and courage, Hugh Eayrs of the newly-started *Canadian Bookman* concluded that publishers and authors "treated their calling in these war years as a serious and a high one, and without their efforts the light of propaganda could not have shone with half the effect."[57]

The first bona fide Canadian war novel, appearing in early 1915, was Harry Woodson's *Private Warwick: Musings of a Canuck in Khaki*. To strengthen homefront determination, its main character warned readers that "German rule means serfdom." Meanwhile, Warwick's mother resolved that if her "own should fall in battle...Christ's words will comfort: `Greater love hath no man than this, that a man may lay down his life for his friends'."[58] With Canadians tasting action later that year, stirring dis-plays of manly courage began filling works such as S.W. Dawson's *The Faith of a Belgian: A Romance of the Great War*. The protagonist, Joseph, "was twice struck by flying pieces of shrapnel, but he pressed on."[59] For the acclaimed Canadian author, Reverend Charles Gordon, alias Ralph Connor, military service was not just a matter of duty, but provided each participant with an opportunity to display his mettle and even attain redemption. In *The Major*, Connor celebrated the conversion of Larry Gwynne, once a Quaker and pacifist, who in war discovered a reservoir of masculine resolve after coming to understand that there was "no possibility of peace or sanity for the world" until everyone realized the necessity of destroying "that race of mad militarists."[60]

Bolstering the legitimacy of such novels were factual narratives supplied by combatants. In addition to delineating German insanity, they stressed the high ideals and high adventure of war, and, in terms of style, were com-posed in the high diction typical of the romantic genre. Such accounts, which were especially coveted by citizens who sought the real scoop on front-line life, were affected not only by censorship, patriotism, and per-haps the pecuniary considerations of the author and/or publisher, but also the desire of troops to fulfil manly stereotypes by embellishing their exploits and hiding any emotional weakness. In *The Glory of the Trenches*, Lieutenant Corningsby Dawson of the Canadian Expeditionary Force insisted that soldiers did not fear death but instead derived serenity from the knowledge that those who fell in such a righteous cause earned the right to "hang beside Christ." Military life, he asserted, did not retard individualism but rather called forth the best in men. Until he "became a part of the war," Dawson doubted the "nobility" in others; but after witnessing the courage of his comrades in combat, he was convinced that such a quality was "latent in everybody, and only awaits the opportunity to call it out."[61]

Displays of extraordinary valour and a life of daring-do were also prominent themes in those works focusing upon men who soared above the battlefield. The aviator's life furnished a sense of individuality, escape from the muddy trenches, and, in Canada's case, produced a number of esteemed aces.[62] But early aviation also often translated into tedium. For days on end, pilots and their mechanically-undependable machines waited for decent flying weather. Moreover, the majority of flights were not combat missions but involved taking pictures of enemy trenches. Nevertheless, given their understanding of events, civilians responded eagerly and uncritically to heroic narratives, especially that written by the country's Victoria Cross winner, Major William A. Bishop, whose death-defying feats and 72 victories were recorded in *Winged Warfare*. Air combat, he wrote, was great sport, akin to a "hunting trip," and provided one with "glory...both in victory and...in death." And while Billy Bishop exuded fearlessness, the dastardly Hun was cast as cowardly, always loath to *play the game* "unless...outnumber[ing] us by at least three to one,"[63] even though it was not until early 1918 that the Se5(a) and Sopwith Camel provided the Allies with air superiority over the Fokker, Albatross and Halberstadt.[64]

Contrasting with stories of action were several accounts from Medical Corps personnel that, in attempting to allay homefront consternation, frequently provided a rather inflated portrayal of the skills made available to the maimed. Although the war years witnessed many startling advances in surgical technique, F. McKelvey Bell's *First Canadians in France* definitely embellished matters by claiming that "a large percentage of men shot through the brain...recover[ed]." Because current masculine stereotypes called for strength and stoicism under adversity, Bell highlighted the fact that even though some soldiers had "bandages about their head or hands or feet," from none came cries of pain or complaints.[65] However, on occasion, a few less than uplifting images were utilized to invoke hatred against the enemy. Following the gas attack at Ypres, Colonel George G. Nasmith's *On the Fringe of the Great Fight* described men at a casualty clearing station lying on a floor with blue faces, choking and gasping for air. "As I stood and watched them," he wrote, "I felt that the nation who had planned in cold blood, the use of such a foul method of warfare, should...be taken and choked until it, too, cried for mercy."[66]

But for sheer focus upon German savagery, nothing exceeded narratives from escaped or released P.O.W.s. "I can quite easily see," wrote Lieutenant J. Harvey Douglas in *Captured*, "how men who have been in German hospitals or camps for two or three years become despondent, nervous wrecks and often go stark staring mad." Enemy doctors, he charged, used Allied prisoners as teaching specimens. In one account, a German head specialist, after inadequately applying an anaesthetic, removed an eye from a Canadian soldier. Medical students sat around impassively while the surgeon snipped each nerve and muscle, calling out their names and slowly explaining their function, while the victim, still refusing to break before his adversary, "drew blood from his lower lip with his teeth in trying to keep from screaming out with pain."[67] Worse yet were accusations in *Escape of a Princess Pat*. Here George Pearson told of a Winnipeg lad forced "to put his hands above his head...[while] his captor placed the muzzle of his rifle squarely against the palm [of one] and blew it off," leaving a "bloody and broken mass dangling from the wrist."[68]

Employed as well to rally and incense Canadians were more modern, and perhaps also more popular, means of communication. In 1895, the first nickelodeons opened in New York, and, by 1907, some 1.5 million Americans had witnessed a motion picture. Contrary to the then popular belief, audiences were drawn from all walks of life, not just the so-called ignorant masses.[69] Two years later, in Montreal, Canada's first movie house was constructed. By the time the Great War erupted, Canadian newspapers were carrying full-page advertisements for film spectaculars such as

Carmen, Cleopatra and *Tarzan*, and ran daily profiles of matinee idols. In 1916, *Maclean's* estimated that 1,500 places in Canada were registered for showing films, a number that in Toronto, translated into ten times as many movie houses as stage theatres.[70]

Canadians, as multitudes elsewhere, flocked to war films in order to see the unvarnished truth. However, many filmmakers, cognizant of public preconceptions as well as censorship decrees, and harbouring a determination to pitch in for victory, portrayed an event characterized by thrilling escapades, dashing heroes and beautiful heroines. Absent from Canada's celluloid war were mud, rats, lice, gory death and other such grisliness; presented instead were Allied triumphs and an archetypal romantic conflict in which every young man dreamt of participating.

While Canada obtained most official newsreels from Britain, it acquired a majority of full-length fictionalized war movies from America, a trend no doubt attributable to the emergence of the Hollywood film industry. In 1916, some 230 million feet of motion pictures were imported into the Dominion from the United States.[71] Those involved with Canadian-based cinematography were simply incapable of funding the multi-reel battlefield epics soon demanded by audiences. From small outfits such as James & Sons of Toronto came only short clips such as of the 204th Battalion conducting a "sham battle" in High Park.[72] Indeed, between 1914 and 1918, only nine movies longer than two reels were produced in Canada.[73]

Not all U.S. motion pictures made during America's neutrality years were acceptable from a Canadian perspective. To attract viewers, directors staged mock battles sometimes containing rather intense death scenes that censorship authorities feared could thwart recruiting. Caution also was shown because a few individuals sympathetic to the Central Powers held important positions within the U.S. movie-making industry. Among those entries prohibited in Canada was *The Battle and Fall of Przemsyl*. Released in late 1914 by Albert Dawson's American Correspondent Film Company, whose cameramen were permitted access to enemy lines, this film highlighted a successful eastern front offensive against the Allies, and, in the words of the United States trade magazine, *Motion Picture World*, "glorified the prowess of Germany...."[74] Still, Canadian film distributors were able to find ample material mirroring an ideological atmosphere where five times as many major American newspapers in 1915 sympathized with the Entente nations as compared to their foe. One of the more extreme, but also immensely popular entries, was J. Stuart Blackston's *Battle Cry of Peace* that argued for military preparedness by showing the marauding Hun coming across the Atlantic to pillage, rape and ultimately destroy the Capitol Building and the White House.[75]

After America declared war in April 1917, Canadians were literally besieged with U.S. film propaganda. That month, William Brady, President of the National Association of the Motion Picture Industry, organized Hollywood directors such as King Vidor, Cecil B. de Mille, Jesse Lasky and D.W. Griffith into a group that coordinated with Washington's new Committee on Public Information.[76] A prominent theme continued to be the abominable conduct of German soldiers. In *Johanna Enlists*, audiences were moved to hysterics and then cheers by America's Canadian-born sweetheart, Mary Pickford, who fought off a lecherous German and then declared as a spokesperson for her adopted nation: "I was neutral till I saw your soldiers destroying women and shooting old men!" Meanwhile, Universal Studios promised Canadian film distributors that *The Kaiser: The Beast of Berlin* would make "audiences boil" by presenting "the rape of Belgium, and the decorating of the man who torpedoed the *Lusitania*." For their lobbies, the studio supplied theatre owners with a 15 by 18 foot frame cutout of the German leader, his sword pointing downward at a woman cringing with fear. Public response was indeed overwhelming. At Montreal's Holman theatre *The Beast* took in twice as much money in eight days as any previous billing, while in Toronto, it became necessary to accommodate the overflow crowd at Loew's at the nearby Winter Garden Theatre.[77]

If not motivated by the need to crush this cruelty, young men may have aspired to emulate *The Warrior* who single-handedly attacked an Austrian mountain hideout where two officers fought over his sweetheart. Others perhaps obtained inspiration from *The Unbeliever* that told "how the war made a man and a hero out of an able bodied young idler."[78] Fostered by several comedies was not only the notion of the Great War as rather amusing, but also as demonstrating, at least in *Kicking the Germ out of Germany*, that in this splendid fight even the inept could prove valiant. Here, Harold Lloyd volunteered after learning that the girl of his dreams was captured while performing Red Cross work and sent to the Kaiser as a trophy.

Through a series of comic adventures, Lloyd infiltrated Berlin, disposed of the general staff, rescued his love, and acted "real rough with the Kaiser."[79]

Finally, linking events overseas with intrigue, excitement and just a hint of romance (out of deference to moral and, in some cases, racial codes), as well as fuelling the nativistic crusade against internal subversion, were several tales of espionage. Stirring exploits and rendezvous with mysterious women in far-off lands characterized entries such as *For the Freedom of the East*, where an American diplomat teamed up with a beautiful Oriental princess to foil German attempts at undermining China's recent decision to join the Allies.[80] Meanwhile, in focusing upon matters closer to home, one advertisement carried in numerous Canadian newspapers for *The Spy* read: "Do you know that the Prussians have 10,000…secret police lurking and scheming in the United States?" No doubt to the eventual consternation of many non-Anglos, it was predicted that those attending this movie would soon be asking: "Do I know my neighbour?"[81]

When it came to home-based entertainment, one of the more popular forms was the singalong, an activity that, by 1914, was reaching a crest with the democratization of the gramophone, which could be purchased for as little as $20. If anything, the war bolstered this pastime by inspiring approximately 300 primarily cheery, rousing and patriotic tunes copyrighted by Canadians. Many songs obtained considerable fame such as *When We Wind up the Watch on the Rhine* by Gordon V. Thompson, which sold 100,000 copies.[82] Through both their lyrics and uncomplicated rhyming structure, these songs revealed a child-like naivete about combat where intrepid men bravely went forth to battle for all that which was good and pure.

Through songs, young men still wearing civilian garb were made to feel cowardly. Inspired by the famous recruiting poster of a pointing Lord Kitchener, Muriel Bruce asked in a melody that became the anthem of local recruitment leagues: "Why aren't you in Khaki?/ This means you!/ Any old excuse won't do…." In Harry Taylor's *We'll Love You More When You Come Back Than When You Went Away*, a mother urged her reluctant son to his duty and the attainment of manly self-respect, both of which she knew were to be found on the battlefields of France.[83] Also exemplifying clichéd conceptions of masculinity was Keith Hardyside's tune assuring that those in uniform got "all the girls," because they were "simply mad" about those with the "toothbrush moustache, military dash/ Khaki to boot, snappy salute...."[84]

To soothe apprehension, several songs dwelt upon a triumphant homecoming.[85] When death was mentioned, lyrics consoled the grieving by assuring them that Heaven's grandeur along with the ever-lasting homage of their countrymen served as rewards for those whose altruistic acts brought the supreme sacrifice. Of the typical casualty, H. Rose wrote reverently: "All his comrades called him brave/ [And] he found a hero's grave."[86] Standard as well was an undying devotion to the Empire and pride in the Dominion's battlefield accomplishments. Certainly Canadian imperialists sang with gusto H. Keane's ballad about "Men who bravely dared and nobly died/ For rights that the [Union Jack] maintained."[87] And to commemorate those who repelled the Germans at Second Ypres, Marion Templeton told of "The pick of our gallant manhood/ [Whose] fame shall stand forever...," while a few years later, J.B. Spurr exalted Canadians who "Were first in the battles that ended in victory/ At Mons and around Cambrai...."[88]

Verses cheering the country's Christian soldiers onward to victory also rang through cathedrals and chapels across the land. Like citizens in all warring nations, Canadians were assured that theirs was a divinely inspired crusade. An "apocalyptic struggle" against those "serving the Kingdom of Evil" was how Dr. T.B. Kirkpatrick of the Presbyterian Church characterized the Great War. Reverend P.P. Pedley, a Congregationalist, explained that "in Germany, nationalism in its form of Pan-Germanism ha[d] divorced itself from Christ."[89] To establish Berlin's malevolence, clergymen often turned to rather detailed Biblical analysis; one prominent interpretation, based upon passages from the Old Testament, depicted Germany's "envy" of Anglo-Saxondom as paralleling Haman's jealousy for Mordecai, a sin that provoked an attempted massacre of the Hebrews.[90]

In the quest to extinguish German wickedness, clerics invited army recruiters to speak at church services. In London, Ontario, Catholic Bishop Michael Fallon went a step further, telling his parishioners that he had "no sympathy at all with the mothers who are hanging on to the coat tails of their sons nor with the wives who are clinging to their husbands."[91] Ministers and priests absolved those who questioned whether the Bible justified taking another's life. Canada's Methodist Superintendent S.D. Chown insisted that "even Christ...would not stand with limp hands if a ruthless soldier should attempt to outrage His holy mother as the women of Belgium were violated." In fact, Methodists, who constituted the second largest Protestant denomination in English-Canada,[92] assumed a leadership role in promoting national registration, Union Government and conscription, activities that caused the resignation of future Co-operative Commonwealth Federation leader, Reverend J.S. Woodsworth. In reconciling such bellicosity with the Social Gospel doctrine of which Methodists had long been leading advocates, many adherents stressed the war's role in encouraging selfless sacrifice, a greater role by government in economic affairs, and, during the final year of hostilities, the introduction of prohibition.[93] Envisaging such progressive trends at work, Reverend Doctor George Workman, Toronto's Methodist Superintendent, confidently predicted that once having defeated the devil's foot soldiers, there would emerge "a new era where love of peace will triumph over love of power."[94]

The scholarly community proved no more dispassionate. To certify the loyalty of his academy, University of Toronto President Robert Falconer, during the opening weeks of the war, arranged for the removal of three German professors. He also implored students to unite behind the Union Jack, contending that "to live by shirking one's duty is infinitely worse...than to die."[95] Other academics utilised their intellectual skills to certify the fierce nature of German aesthetics. *Kultur*, which the enemy presented as a spiritual leap toward nobler nonmaterial mores was, in Canadian academic writing, habitually rendered into a gross simplification of Nietzschean philosophy, principally the dictum, "that which hurts makes me strong."[96] George Wrong, then the University of Toronto's most esteemed history professor, argued that such depraved thoughts explained the emergence of a militaristic society obsessed with making "the world sit obediently at its feet."[97]

In numerous elementary and high schools there occurred an intensification of pre-war indoctrination achieved, for example, through turn-of-the-century texts like *Deeds that Won the Empire*, and in Ontario, the patriotic marches organized for youth on Empire Day since 1899. As part of the crusade against Germany, children were organized into clubs whose activities included fund-raising for myriad war charities, collecting scrap metal, and writing supportive letters to men overseas. In Ontario, Education Minister Robert Pyne even directed that first formers be taught "how to make a Union Jack" and the "Grand march with flags."[98] New books appeared on the high school curriculum such as *How Britain Strove for Peace* and *Germany's Swelled Head*. Another favourite for adolescents was the 31-volume *Children's History of the War*. To inspire young minds and build the stuff of future soldiers, its British author, Sir Edward Parrot, depicted scenes of "sweating gunners [who] worked like inspired giants, and flung a perfect hurricane upon German positions."[99] Also imported from England for Canadian secondary schools were copies of [Louis] *Raemaker's Cartoons on the War*. Intended by British propagandists for distribution in neutral nations, this well-known Dutch illustrator presented, among other images, the enemy burning a woman representing Belgium at the stake and Germany crucifying Christ. Finally, at the end of term, students were given examinations asking them to discuss topics such as "The value of the flag" or the importance of "The naval victory at Jutland."[100] To ensure that the correct answers were provided, *The School*, the official magazine of the Ontario Teachers' Federation, directed instructors to consistently emphasize the Allies' perspective, while in several communities across the land, local boards even required educators, under the threat of dismissal, to take an oath expressing their "pro-British… sympathies.…"[101]

While reading, worshipping, studying, singing or even shopping, Canadians were besieged with messages propounding patriotism, duty and honour, and learned about the monstrous nature of their foe. Words and images from privately-controlled means of communication both reflected and intensified a mass psyche largely disposed toward imperialist, romantic and nativist beliefs. From 1914 to 1918, citizens, primarily but not exclusively in English-Canada, were told that the war constituted an exhilarating competition played by the bold and chivalrous; that death in a just cause ensured eternal life; that through his noble sacrifice, Johnny Canuck was forging a record of renown; and that the Germans were not just extraordinarily fiendish, but had countless fifth columnists working on their behalf. Thus, thousands of newspaper editors, journalists, advertisers, theatre owners, church leaders, academics, authors and book publishers all helped convince Canadians that they had a legal and historical obligation to aid the mother country, a moral responsibility to uphold democracy, and a right if not obligation to suppress those *legitimately* assumed as unpatriotic.

These convictions, while not eliminating war weariness nor dissent, nevertheless continued to exert a profound impact despite more than four years of hostilities, 60,000 dead, and the strains wrought by conscription. Even in Quebec, opposition remained framed more in terms of pre-war anti-imperialism rather than a new-found understanding of and revulsion towards mass slaughter. But to fully explain the preponderance of such guilelessness and jingoism, especially when expressed through conduits not officially attached to the government, requires the exploration of elements beyond ideological predilection. For after all, a positive pre-war attitude did not prevent the once-ardent Johnny Canuck from abandoning many idealized notions about war. However, while the views of those in uniform derived from grisly experience, pivotal was the fact that the family and friends they left they behind were subject to a system of formal information control that, due to a series of determinants particularly relevant to Canada, managed to keep citizens largely ignorant about grim realities transpiring across the Atlantic.

2

Official Propaganda: Canada's Great War of Deception

Journalistic despatches, photographs and moving pictures destined for Canada from the front were first perused by military personnel in France attached to General Headquarters [G.H.Q.] and often again in London by Press Bureau officials or the British Board of Film Censors. Only then were they conveyed via steamship or the one underwater cable linking North America and England. To prevent the spread of German propaganda to a neutral United States, on 2 August 1914, the Royal Navy severed all other lines, while military authorities, both in Britain and in Canada, ordered that wireless facilities with trans-Atlantic capabilities be placed at their disposal.[1] To patriotic correspondents who by and large accepted the need for concocted copy, these controls had marginal effect. Nevertheless, with few, if any, means of evading designated channels, particularly when involving the quick despatch of news to Canadian publications demanding current battlefield accounts, these safeguards emerged as an extra and sometimes applied insurance policy.

Consequently, for more than four years, civilians in the Dominion read about and saw only a truly *Great* War, and, in the process, grew philosophically divorced from those whose front-line experiences led them to see the irony of such venerable nomenclature.

On 18 August 1914, Britain's Colonial Office informed the Canadian Press Association [C.P.A.] that it could send one correspondent to the front. But ten days later the offer was revoked after the London *Times*, in an effort to spur more men into service, reported upon Allied forces in a desperate retreat from Mons. To Britain's War Minister, Lord Kitchener, who already was disposed against the press for criticizing his leadership during the Boer War, such material demonstrated the necessity of keeping the fourth estate on a short leash.

Brief journalistic tours were started in December, but correspondents, operating under the threat of a six-month jail term, were prohibited from travelling within 20 miles of the front. Not until March 1915 did pressure from Fleet Street produce the accreditation of six British newsmen. Before that date, practically every front-line report carried throughout the Empire came from Colonel Ernest Swinton, formally of the London *Daily Chronicle*, who was given the title of official *eye-witness*. His despatches, aptly termed "eyewash" by several newsmen, described war in terms of "plucky cavalry charges."[2] In the opening weeks of the conflict, with the Allies reeling before Central Power forces and experiencing a 40 per cent casualty rate in some sectors, Swinton emphasized the "enormous losses sustained by the Germans...[and the] brilliant and victorious assaults by the Lancers and Scots Greys."[3]

The presence of bona fide journalists was accepted reluctantly by Kitchener after some War Office colleagues pointed out that despite prevailing controls, Britain's influential press had obtained considerable information through connections at other departments including the Foreign Office. As well, it was learned through ex-President Theodore Roosevelt that German reporters were successfully despatching copy to U.S. newspapers via a New York-based information office because

American editors considered them as a more legitimate source than official government news.[4]

In terms of substance, however, Kitchener's liberalization meant little. Accredited correspondents were billeted at a chateau well to the rear in St. Omer. Each was assigned a military chaperon who ensured that newsmen were kept from the most sensitive areas and did not talk to troops without advance permission. If they wished to have their story transmitted the next day, it was necessary that copy be submitted to a press officer by 10:30 p.m. to provide time for the *blue pencilling* of militarily sensitive or upsetting material, a definition that included troop locations, strength, actual or rumoured manoeuvres, flagging morale, and criticism of plans or leaders.[5]

Sometimes reporters muttered about "being employed" by the army "as...a department of propaganda," and on occasion were known to differ from military authorities on what constituted patriotic copy. Still, having come from a fourth estate well-immersed in partisan conduct, they were not professionally adverse towards *doing their bit*. Certainly, Brigadier General Manley-Sims, who was stationed at G.H.Q., was on safe ground when claiming that "even if totally absolved from the restraint of censorship...not one journalist would consciously damage Allied prospects."[6] With few exceptions, their accounts exaggerated Entente gains while deriding both the accomplishments and behaviour of the enemy. For example, though more than 60,000 British casualties were endured during the opening day (1 July 1916) of the Somme offensive, an event Field Marshal Sir Douglas Haig later characterized as "a costly failure," Canadians received news about a glorious conquest during which several thousand German soldiers mutinied and called for "death to the Kaiser."[7] Even if not completely ignoring disheartening details, journalists almost always showed the wherewithal to shroud them in euphemism—a "brisk" or "sharp" encounter, for instance, actually meant a casualty rate perhaps reaching 50 per cent.[8]

The drive for front-line Canadian press representation mounted after the country's troops saw action in March 1915 at Neuve Chapelle. As well, members of Canada's fourth estate noted that in the Middle East, Commander-in-Chief Sir Ian Hamilton had recently provided the Australian journalist, Charles Bean, with permission to cover the Anzacs. The timing of this pressure from Canada also proved fortuitous since the arrival of British correspondents in France had the Colonial Office again

» *William Maxwell Aiken in uniform. (National Archives of Canada. PA 22714)*

broaching to Ottawa the idea of an official press emissary. Yet, stiff competition among and uncompromising attitudes assumed by both Canada's morning and evening daily newspapers precipitated considerable bickering over who constituted the best delegate. Each suspected that a reporter with ties to a particular source would transmit stories back at an hour to provide their former employer and those papers published at the same time with the scoop. The federal government, therefore, took matters in hand and appointed William Maxwell Aitken, perhaps then Canada's most famous expatriate in Britain, to perform any future *eye-witness* duties.[9]

Having made his fortune in the Dominion by 1910, primarily through the sale of industrial bonds, Aitken had set off to conquer London. Within a year, he had obtained a controlling interest in the Rolls-Royce Company, a substantial piece of the London *Daily Express*, and ran successfully for Parliament in the Manchester suburb of Ashford-Under-Lyne. A man of keen intellect, boundless energy (despite his chronic asthma) and considerable charisma, Aitken soon acquired several powerful friends in Britain such as future Colonial Secretary Bonar Law to go along with a Canadian coterie including Militia Minister Sam Hughes.

Possessing important allies at home, the apparent capacity to exert influ-ence abroad, and a professed imperialist philosophy, Aitken was first appointed in late 1914 as Canada's unofficial delegate at the British War Office.[10] The immediate stepping stone to his emergence as the Dominion's official press representative, or *eye-witness*, was traced to a January 1915 appointment as director of the Canadian War Records Office [C.W.R.O.], a job involving the gathering of documents relating to the country's war effort. In addition to $25,000 provided by the federal govern-ment, Aitken also poured some of his own money into the project, claiming that the information accumulated would record for posterity how Canadian heroism won for the nation a new level of respect and status — enthusiasm that, along with his practical experience as publisher of a mass market daily newspaper, unquestionably confirmed to many in Ottawa that he was the right person to provide news for the homefront. Finally, and cer-tainly as important, was that the title of *eye-witness* was a post Aitken coveted. Besides furnishing an opportunity to elevate Canada's position within the Empire as well as the Dominion-based war effort, Aitken real-ized that since he was not an ally of Prime Minister Herbert Asquith, little possibility then existed of him landing an important role with the British government.[11]

On 27 March 1915 Aitken formally assumed the job of *eye-witness* and immediately began issuing from the C.W.R.O.'s Lombard Street office in London a stream of reports that appeared primarily in Canadian, but also in English and American newspapers. Some information for his despatches came from unit war diaries that he and a C.W.R.O. writing staff of approximately ten twisted into inspiring tales of triumph. Copy also came from some soldier-correspondents acquired by the agency, prin-cipally Major Theodore G. Roberts (the younger brother of the famed New Brunswick author, Charles G.D. Roberts) and Henri Bourassa's cousin Captain Talbot Papineau (who in 1916 resigned from this job over guilt about leaving his regiment for a soft assignment, a decision that, a year later at Passchendaele, cost him his life). Furthermore, the C.W.R.O. hired cameramen and artists to record Canada's magnificence in this titanic struggle. Aitken, despite his title as *eye-witness*, purposefully made few return trips across the English Channel after viewing the gut-wrenching results of Second Ypres, a battle that he cast as an uplifting and heroic struggle where Canada's superior fighting men sowed the seeds of a proud nationalism.[12]

Information Aitken received from the War Office, unit diaries, soldier correspondents and cameramen, or as a result of his infrequent forays to France, revealed that circumstances for the Allies were far from rosy. Rather primitive intelligence gathering methods, such as aerial photographs incapable of distinguishing between convex and concave formations, brought no shortages of miscalculations and some pretty costly disasters.[13] In 1916, records from the St. Eloi theatre disclosed that many of Canada's 1,500 casualties (approximately three times that suffered by the enemy) were in fact attributable to poor air reconnaissance that incorrectly claimed that the Allies controlled "craters 2, 3, 4, 5…." Therefore, supporting artillery was aimed in the wrong direction as soldiers attacked abandoned craters 6 and 7 and in the process were cut down by machine gun fire from unanticipated sources.[14] For public consumption, however, Aitken told Canadians only of the "endurance, courage, and cheerfulness" of their sons whose "attacks were delivered with an unabated fury."[15] Such manipulation he saw as a small price to help attain victory. "It may not be pleasant to issue false news," he said, but if those at home "could be taken into our confidence I feel quite certain they would endorse the scheme."[16]

Realizing from experience in the news business that "the publicity of the press" represented a "powerful weapon," Aitken provided material not only to raise spirits within Canada, but also with an eye also towards promoting the country's image in Britain.[17] Besides C.W.R.O. news reports that always received ample coverage in his Daily Express, he arranged for the agency to sponsor art and photographic exhibits throughout England consisting largely of Canadian troops in action. While his zeal to champion Johnny Canuck was appreciated in Ottawa, complaints soon emanated from some British officials about an impression being created of Canadians as constituting most capable soldiers without whose presence the Allies would flounder.[18] Such a theme was especially evident in the coverage Aitken provided, both in article and book form, to Second Ypres. To at least 40,000 Canadians as well as multitudes of Britons who bought volume one of Canada in Flanders, Aitken juxtaposed French colonial soldiers who "fled before the German gas attack," with the Dominion's stalwart warriors who stood firm, "saved the day," and in the process ensured that "the mere written word Canada glow[ed]...with a new meaning before all the civilised world."[19]

In fact, a gauntlet of sorts was thrown down by British military censors with the second instalment of *Canada in Flanders*, an action that ironically strengthened the unrealistic perspective of warfare dominant among civilians in the Dominion. This was because Aitken, in order to ensure similar sales as the first narrative, included some graphic references alongside attempts to build the reputation of Johnny Canuck. Besides deleting the book's mention of particular units and its mild criticism of the British Northumberlanders for supposedly leaving behind poorly repaired trenches for Canadian soldiers, English military censors changed sentences such as "The crowded presence of the wounded men in the trench passed the limits of horror," to "The presence of the wounded made it far worse."[20] One can only assume the root cause for such cuts represented retaliation against Aitken's rather extreme pro-Canadian slant, for British newspapers often carried the names of regiments and equally intense descriptions of battle. In counterattacking, Aitken turned to several influential connections including Robert Borden. He insisted that by citing specific regiments, local pride and recruitment efforts would be enhanced; besides, he added, such information was undoubtedly known by the enemy for months.[21] Moreover, Aitken asserted that to excise the few dramatic sentences would "emasculate the form and substance" of the book, "mak[ing] it...devoid of interest." Ultimately he prevailed, but this fight delayed the release of volume two of *Canada in Flanders* by six months, thus dating its subject-matter, and, to the satisfaction of British military authorities, lessened its appeal—but also limited its capacity to enlighten Canadians about some displeasing aspects of trench warfare.[22]

Meanwhile, by 1916, Canada's journalistic community noted that even the neutral United States had nongovernment press representation at St. Omer. John Bohn of the Toronto *Star*, no doubt reflecting the growing exasperation, if not professional embarrassment, of many of his colleagues, charged that Aitken possessed no actual journalistic qualifications but had likely acquired the *eye-witness* post through a friendship with Sam Hughes. Reading the writing on the wall, a principal assistant to Aitken, Henry Beckles Willson, assured the C.W.R.O. chief that his eventual replacement by a C.P.A. reporter would change little. Besides being subject to censorship laws, Willson noted that English and Australian correspondents had demonstrated "a keen sense of patriotism."[23] Such a conclusion, however, Aitken had also likely reached, not just from the conduct of other country's correspondents, but also as a result of his role, starting in September 1915, in bringing over small parties of Canadian newsmen for brief visits to France. To obtain front-line access, many publishers wrote Aitken to ensure that patriotism, and not desire for sensationalism and newspaper sales, would guide their reporters. Typical was John Ross Robertson, founder of the Toronto *Telegram*, who promised that his correspondent would emphasize "men who have become famous through their prowess and heroism."[24]

By March 1917, the C.P.A. finally stopped squabbling long enough to accept Stewart Lyon, managing editor of the Toronto *Globe*, as its first official press correspondent.[25] After seven months he was replaced by W.A. Willson, the son of the Toronto *News*' editor and proprietor, J.S. Willson, while the following August, J.F. Livesay, former president of the Western Canadian Press Association and an assistant to Ernest J. Chambers in the domestic censorship service took over, thus assuring representation from newspapers affiliated with more than one region and political party. Seeing as they were providing news to all Canadians, Ottawa offered to pay the salary of these journalists, but the C.P.A. declined to avoid charges of serving an official agenda.[26]

Administrative independence, however, exerted no perceptual impact upon content. Typical was the press coverage given to the bloody encounter at Passchendaele. In late 1917, several British generals and the Canadian Corps' leader, Arthur Currie, advised Field Marshal Haig to refrain from relieving pressure upon French forces by launching this offensive. He may have prevailed over his military subordinates, but Haig was not so effective when it came to the enemy. Well-entrenched German forces and bog-like terrain made the venture foolhardy. For ten days prior to the assault, four million shells were hurled towards enemy lines, an effort that primarily served to churn the muck into a more impassable state. Unit diaries from the sector focused upon "waist deep" mud in which some of Canada's 16,000 casualties drowned.[27] Obviously, the last thing needed by Ottawa, then in the midst of a conscription crisis, was a faithful recounting of this debacle. Willson did not disappoint. Mud was mentioned in his despatches, but only as a means of bolstering the conviction that nothing

» *A rehearsed action shot supplied by the Canadian War Records Office.*
(National Archives of Canada, PA 130112)

could deter the Canadians from victory. As well, despite casualty lists running on for several newspaper pages, he resolutely maintained that only
"enemy losses" were truly "frightful," describing as proof, for instance, "a
veteran machine gun officer...having had as a target for an hour and a
quarter [German] reinforcements coming up in columns of four for use in
counter-attacks."[28]

Pictorial evidence also assumed a significant role in bolstering romantic
shibboleths. During the first months of the war, newspaper photographers,
like correspondents, were kept miles from the front. Practically every image
of the conflict despatched to the press came from two specially-assigned
English army officers who naturally ignored its disagreeable features. But,
just as with reporters, by mid 1915, the British government forced the military to relent after learning that some U.S. dailies preferred German
photographic sources because their military permitted newspaper cameramen more access to the battle zone.[29] Taking advantage of such
liberalization, the C.W.R.O., under Aitken's direction, launched an extensive programme to document Canada's war experience on film. Images
captured by Captains M. Knoble (who retired in early 1917 because of ill
health), Ivor Castle, and Lieutenant William Rider-Rider appeared regu-

larly in Canadian and British newspapers and periodically in American and French publications. Aitken reasoned that the right sort of pictorial evidence would promote "enthusiasm and eager interest in our army in France."[30] To achieve this goal, he sometimes authorized that photographs be fabricated. There was, for instance, the popular C.W.R.O. snapshot of Canadian troops scurrying over parapets at the Somme that was actually posed at a French training facility.[31] As well, countless authentic photos endeavoured to verify sanitized press reports (less uplifting images were usually placed in storage with the idea, said Aitken, that one day "they will form a source of information...for historians.").[32] Standard fare for Canadian civilians included pictures such as "enemy guns seized," "Germans quite happy to be prisoners," as well as images of devastated churches to prove the "wanton destruction of the Hun" who "like pagans of old" ravaged the "sanctuaries of God."[33] Even when it came to corpses, Aitken displayed his flair for propaganda, instructing cameramen to "cover up the Canadians before you photograph them...but don't bother about the German dead."[34]

Several British authorities, soon after hostilities commenced, made much of the fact that films such as the *Surrender of Kroonstad to Lord Roberts* had buoyed morale during the Boer War, while the 1913 *British Army Film* boosted the government's preparedness campaign against Germany.[35] In late 1915, one of the strongest advocates for movie propaganda, Charles Masterman, the Chairman of Wellington House, a British propaganda agency, convinced the War and Admiralty Offices to allow filmmakers front-line access. With alarm he relayed correspondence from Britain's ambassador in Washington, Sir Cecil Spring Rice, who, though inclined towards overstatement (on several occasions he warned Ottawa about an impending German-American invasion), still managed to raise concern in England about Berlin having obtained a virtual monopoly over newsreel distribution to America. By the armistice, Britain responded with a dozen feature-length movies and 240 newsreels, each of which was previewed by G.H.Q. and/or the London-based Board of Film Censors.[36]

Although importing most fictionalized war movies from Hollywood, Canada obtained a majority of its factual material from the mother country. In part this was attributable to a neutral United States acquiring some film footage from Germany; but a more important explanation relates to the ubiquitous Max Aitken. By late 1915, he had C.W.R.O. movie cameramen in the field, and had arranged for the Canadian-bound export of news-reels produced by the Topical Trade Commission, a consortium of British and Allied film companies whose services were utilised by Wellington House.[37] As with newspapers, Aitken was acutely aware of the appeal and potential power exerted by this medium. "The [present] generation," he contended, "will [want] to see the battle[s] as though we saw the Egyptian wars of the Eighties." In fact, it was with motion pictures that Aitken, in mid 1916, began to make his presence known within Britain's propaganda network. Besides insatiable personal ambition, probably Aitken felt grow-ing pressure to branch out. After all, Canada's journalistic community had expanded its lobbying for permanent front-line press representation, while the creation by Ottawa that spring of an Overseas Military Ministry threat-ened to (and in fact would soon) eliminate Aitken's informal post at the British War Office.

Aitken's opportunity came because the War Office, in light of mounting casualties and Britain's need to introduce conscription in February 1916, launched a campaign to usurp some control from Wellington House over newsreel production, claiming, in light of the expanding military crisis, that it was most qualified to determine what images were prudent to release. Aitken employed whatever influence he possessed at Westminster to support the War Office where, over the past 18 months, he had made some important contacts, such as principal secretary Sir Reginald Brade as well as Lloyd George who took over as Minister after Kitchener drowned in the Irish Sea. As it turned out, Aitken chose well. Despite having previously ruffled military feathers in promoting the intrepid Johnny Canuck, when the departmental dispute settled, Aitken, as a result of his support, strategic political alliances and in, sometimes grudging, recognition of his C.W.R.O. propaganda work, emerged as Chairman of the new War Office Cinematograph Committee.[38]

Under his guidance, the revamped agency expanded links with film companies to produce a bi-weekly newsreel called the *Topical Budget*. A standard entry carried five subjects, each of which ran approximately two minutes. To guarantee the appeal of these pictures in his former home-land, Aitken arranged that C.W.R.O. clips be spliced into the package or that a cameraman working for the Cinematograph Committee record the activities of Dominion soldiers.[39] In these productions, potentially contro-versial matter rarely survived the official vetting process. Cameraman

Brooks Carrington recalled that 90 per cent of the footage he took of dead bodies hit the cutting room floor. Technical considerations also worked towards guaranteeing a sanitized perspective of warfare. Bulky equipment weighing in excess of 100 pounds proved relatively immobile while lenses were inadequate for long distance shots. The result made soldiers charging across No Man's Land appear as ants. Therefore, rather than battle scenes, moviegoers often had to be satisfied with marching regiments, artillery firing, and pictures of churches or graveyards destroyed by the Germans.[40] To raise spirits, other clips recorded the Allies liberating towns where "great surging crowds raised their voices in song," pictures of P.O.W.s, as well as groups of smiling wounded Canadians smoking cigarettes at sparkling clean casualty clearing stations.[41] Also received in the Dominion were a few longer and more heavily publicized entries, one of the most popular being *Canadians at Courcelette.* C.W.R.O. and Cinametograph Committee personnel recorded not only the territory and enemy troops captured by Johnny Canuck during this 1916 encounter, but also, most exciting of all for theatregoers, the first moving pictures of tanks in action, something that subtitles proclaimed as a technical marvel sure to mow the Germans under. As with most propaganda, however, reality was far less impressive. While later versions of the tank were moderately effective, the Mark I, the model shown in this movie, often ended up providing enemy artillery with target practice due to its tendency to break down, especially when attempting to traverse shell-pitted terrain.[42]

Finally, starting in 1917, Canadian civilians flocked to auditoria and fairs to see even more concrete proof of the country's battlefield achievements such as captured howitzers, trench mortars, cloth from a Zeppelin, along with other German instruments of war.[43] The War Trophy programme, as it was called, germinated in the mind of the Dominion Archivist, Sir Arthur Doughty, who envisaged the artifacts as eventually forming a component for memorials to Canada's fallen heroes, as well as a national war museum. In late 1916, he arrived in London to commence the collection but first found it necessary to settle a score with the everpresent Aitken who, it was rumoured, planned not to transfer unit diaries held at the C.W.R.O. to the Canadian archives after the war. The anticipated row, however, actually turned out as serendipitous because after being convinced that no such intention existed, Doughty warmed up to Aitken and, in the process, secured an exceptionally resourceful ally. Through his various high level contacts, the C.W.R.O. director convinced the British and French War Ministries to hand over trophies such as the first gun seized by Canadian soldiers at Ypres. In displays across the country, these items were presented to civilians as symbolic of extraordinary courage. "The captured trophies," Doughty told the Montreal *Gazette*, "are not merely curiosities, but have been brought over by the blood of heroes."[44]

Doughty found himself overwhelmed with requests for presentations from sources that ranged from Toronto's Canadian National to Moose Jaw's Industrial Exhibition. Some communities staked their claim to a display by professing that on a per capita basis they had supplied more than the average number of recruits.[45] At these shows an appropriate atmosphere was created by suspending Union Jacks from ceilings and plastering walls with C.R.W.O. photographs (mainly of Canadian generals and Victoria Cross winners), plus recruiting, Victory Bond and food conservation posters. Wounded veterans were on hand to stress the courageous and thrilling story that lay behind the capture of each item. One such display in Vancouver attracted 22,000 people over five days. "The returns," wrote the Halifax *Herald* of an October 1917 demonstration at the local armouries, "exceeded the expectations of the most sanguine members of the committee."[46] Although there were plenty of disappointed applicants, by the end of 1919, the war trophy collection, or parts thereof, had visited 60 communities across Canada.[47]

As the emotional and economic strains associated with the war mounted, federal authorities, starting in earnest by late 1916, also began initiating massive domestic-based efforts at information infusion. Yet, their ability to have delayed for such time also made clear that privately-controlled propaganda when combined with and shaped by various forms of official front-line news, went a long way towards maintaining jingoism, voluntarism and ingenuousness. Indeed, when finally forced to assume a proactive strategy to promote military enlistment, conservation and fundraising, federal politicians still discovered, even after years of conflict, a majority, divorced from morale-destroying realities, who remained most responsive to appeals framed in idealistic concepts about duty, honour and war—perceptions that a late-blooming domestic propaganda system undoubtedly fortified.

In August 1914, thousands were turned away from the First Contingent and there was no trouble meeting authorized troop increases to 150,000 in July and 250,000 in October 1915. Moreover, if one factors Quebec out of the picture (where even at the outset of hostilities many perceived the Great War as being Britain's struggle), Anglo-Canadian enlistment, despite pockets of opposition, surpassed rates in both New Zealand and Australia.[48] While it is true that the need for work motivated many of these people into military service, which in itself displayed naivete about the job awaiting in France, within months this factor became less relevant as the country began gearing up economically for a long fight. Based upon the ardour of young men to get overseas and prove their mettle, Sam Hughes, in early 1915, boasted to Parliament that he "could raise three more contingents inside of three weeks...."[49] To Borden, an imperial nationalist who equated more Canadian troops with increased input by the Dominion into Empire strategy, and who, later that year, faced intensified pressure from London to supply massive reinforcements following heavy Allied casualties at Ypres and Loos, such predictions were no doubt heartening. In January 1916, without consulting his caucus, the Prime Minister, demonstrating considerable faith in the population, publicly pledged Canada to supply a half-million man volunteer army.

Reacting, the Chief of the General Staff, Sir Willoughby Gwatkin, called the commitment unrealistic and predicted conscription. While the initial response—29,185 enlisting in January, 26,658 the next month, and 34,913 in March—appeared to bear out Borden's confidence, circumstances were indeed conspiring against success.[50] About two-thirds of the First Division were British-born. As the number of these expatriates dwindled, Ottawa discovered that other English-Canadians, though not usually antagonistic to the cause, still, in a greater proportion of cases, felt less compunction about rallying behind the mother country as compared to seizing growing economic opportunities at home. By 1916, approximately 300,000 Canadians had been drawn into relatively well-paid war industry jobs, and in the rural sector, unprecedented demand for produce provided for record profits.[51] As well, though few men fully understood its horrors, some must have comprehended that consistently longer casualty lists printed in newspapers meant warfare was probably a tad deadlier than the popular metaphor that talked about a glorified sporting match. In no month after June 1916, were more than 10,000 attracted to the colours, and in the thirteen months before the first call up of conscripts in January 1918, not one infantry battalion achieved full strength.[52]

Nonetheless, Borden might have achieved a 500,000 man volunteer army without conscription if recruitment had been handled differently. Despite the monumental task of building a military force from scratch (in July 1914, Canada's permanent active militia totalled 3,110 men and 684 horses),[53] enlistment procedures remained, until mid 1916, poorly directed and funded. As long as regiments filled their ranks, Ottawa remained uninterested in centralized management and a national publicity campaign.

In large part, the approach was traceable to Militia Minister Hughes, a man almost pathological in his opposition to bureaucratic red tape, and who possessed an unyielding faith in inexhaustible Canadian loyalty. To his high-ranking friends in charge of various regiments, Hughes gave almost complete responsibility for attracting legions of patriotic men, and provided no defined boundaries in which they were to concentrate their recruitment efforts.[54] Consequently, some locales were denuded of essential labour while others remained virtually untouched.[55] Moreover, in some sectors, competition between regiments (who sometimes hired civilian recruiters on a commission basis) brought charges of bribery, and played a part in permitting a number of men to slip into uniform as a means of obtaining free treatment for old ailments such as tuberculosis.[56]

Hughes's hands-off approach also meant that in most circumstances not more than $50 was issued annually by militia headquarters to each regiment in order to conduct propaganda (in total, around $27,000 during the first three years of the war).[57] Still, unemployment, slapdash standards about what constituted an acceptable recruit, and considerable naivete about the true temper of conflict, resulted in 69 of 71 infantry battalions authorized by Ottawa prior to September 1915 attaining full strength. Despite such numbers, the C.P.A., undoubtedly for financial self-interest but also perhaps in recognition of a few rural regiments taking longer than average to fill their ranks, advised Ottawa to re-evaluate its parsimonious approach. In August 1915, and especially in the weeks following Borden's announcement of a 500,000 man army, W.E. Springfield, the Press Association's president, said that a three-month nation-wide advertising blitz was possible for a cut-rate price of $50,000.[58] However, resistance by Hughes who interpreted such a campaign as an inherent insult to the patriotism of Canadian men, along with encouraging recruitment figures during the first quarter of 1916, convinced federal authorities to continue their penny-wise and pound-foolish behaviour.

In compensating for Ottawa's miserly conduct, commanding officers dipped into regimental funds and on occasion their own pockets. Yet, even with major daily newspapers charging pennies per line for advertising, most battalions could not indefinitely sustain a decent level of press publicity, especially when it came to providing large and attractive eye-catching displays. Therefore, to spread the word, voluntary community aid became indispensable. Women drummed up enlistees by distributing white feathers to suspected shirkers. In Montreal, the Citizens' Recruiting League obtained from employers the names of those not needed for homefront production and disseminated 20,000 booklets pleading with "mothers, wives and sweethearts...[to] think of your country by letting your sons go and fight."[59] Across the land, the Speakers' Patriotic League organized parades and meetings where both they and army recruiters harangued young men about their duty. Patriotic societies, fraternal associations, women's groups, the Boy Scouts, and myriad other volunteer organizations, also proved invaluable by plastering city streets, train stations, post offices and other public places with regimental posters enticing men into service on the basis of economic self-interest, duty, adventure, loyalty, nationalism and ethnic affiliation. For example, through broadsides, both the 21st and 86th Battalions told the jobless that for its members "pay begins at once." The 98th, exploiting popular notions about performing one's duty, declared that "to live in humiliation" would certainly surpass any despair encountered overseas. Reinforcing this were Sportsmen or Pals Battalions promoting combat as a comparatively safe and manly game. Imperialistic sentiments were utilised by Ottawa's 207th where an officer pointed to the Union Jack that he proclaimed "stands for liberty." To reflect the upsurge of Canadian nationalism following Second Ypres, another regiment displayed a Dominion flag bearing the names Langemark, St. Julien, Festubert and Givenchy; "More [battles] are coming—will you be there?" it asked. Meanwhile, the 236th Kilties depicted a soldier in tartan who desired to know "if you possess the fighting spirit of your forefathers?" And in Quebec, the 22e Regiment not only capitalized upon religious beliefs and common racial ties through illustrations of destroyed French and Belgian churches, but also challenged young men to emulate the proud traditions of ancestors such as folk hero Adam Dollard Des Ormeaux who, in the hallowed days of New France, also defended women and children from *savages*.[60]

Yet it was in Quebec that recruitment strategy was most dismally conceived. Hughes deluded himself into believing that a Huguenot ancestry and personal friendship with the well-known nationaliste, Armand Lavergne, was enough to rally Quebecois to his side. Instead, they focused upon Hughes's denunciations of separate French and Catholic schools, his opposition to Canadian Papal Zouaves, and his membership in the Orange Order.[61] Despite carrying such baggage, and notwithstanding his opposition to large-scale propaganda, in 1914, the Militia Minister was still presented with a chance to send a message to francophones that their perception of him, as well as their general view of the Canadian military as having long favoured Anglos, were unfair. Specifically, within the First Division were enough Quebecois to start a French-speaking regiment. But rather than seize this opportunity to build good feelings, Hughes, citing the need to forge a truly national military (and in the process ignoring the existence of some Scottish-Canadian regiments), decided to divide and then place these volunteers within two Anglo-dominated battalions. Furthermore, he helped convince Ottawa to reject an offer by Montreal doctor Arthur Mignault to fund a Quebec-based regiment. In fact, only considerable pressure from prominent French-Canadian politicians prompted the federal government to authorize the 22e Regiment within the Second Division, a group that, due to poor recruiting trends quickly established within Quebec, had to be comprised of francophones from across the nation.[62]

Naive presumptions by Hughes regarding the province also resulted in scant effort to ensure that French-speaking recruiters were utilized. When it finally dawned upon him that francophones, especially curés, were essential for success, few proved willing to help. Therefore, amazingly, during much of 1916, enlistment strategy in Montreal was directed by

Reverend C.A. Williams, a Methodist. Although sensitive to French-Canadian complaints, his presence produced little success. When the country's military reached 300,000, only 14,100 recruits were Quebecois.[63]

By mid 1916, the defects of Canada's recruitment programme were becoming blatantly apparent. For instance, by citing labour shortages in parts of the country that threatened to cripple war industry, the Fredericton legislature passed a resolution that spring urging the federal government to organize recruitment along "scientific means." Hughes resisted, casting such a suggestion as not only unnecessary and involving far too much bureaucracy, but also as a veiled attempt to usurp his control over the military. But while possessing some powerful allies in the Conservative Party and admirers across the land, by this time, Hughes was increasingly perceived by Borden as a political liability. Besides mounting recruitment problems, a recent Royal Commission investigation revealed that the Militia Minister's friend and appointee to the Shell Committee, J. Wesley Allison, had taken kickbacks for distributing munition contracts. Moreover, at the London-based army pay office, where Hughes's loyalists dominated, corruption was rife.[64] Finally, on a personal level, the behaviour of the Minister appeared rather erratic, if not verging on paranoia when it came to protecting his turf.

In April 1916, Hughes travelled to Britain to reassert his control over extra-territorial Canadian training and receive a peerage arranged for by Borden. Yet, rather than displaying gratitude for the honour, throughout the visit he denounced Ottawa for deciding to establish an Overseas Ministry to handle military matters outside Canada. In a last-ditch effort to retain his power, Hughes attempted, without Borden's permission, to organize a Sub-Militia Council in England directly answerable to him—an action that resulted in his dismissal from Cabinet soon after returning home that autumn.

Indeed, while Hughes was stirring up trouble abroad, Borden, probably already having decided to seek a replacement, began authorizing changes to Canadian enlistment practices. In August 1916, Thomas Tait, head of the Montreal branch of the Citizens' Recruiting League, was installed at militia headquarters in Ottawa as Director General of Recruiting. To relieve pressure on areas exhausted of labour and provide for a more effective sweep of the land, he appointed senior army officers to coordinate activities in nine military districts that were subdivided into precincts and then parcelled out among recruiters from various regiments.[65] The following month, in an effort to further improve the system and hopefully avoid conscription, Tait's position evolved into the Director of the National Service Board that, among other things, set priority classifications upon jobs so recruiters could focus upon occupational groups whose absence would not cripple the domestic economy.[66]

Some military authorities argued that on its own, such reorganization was incapable of reversing the dwindling trend of reinforcements. Exemplifying comments made by others, the Chief Recruiting Officer for Southeastern Ontario said that "there should be more money spent on judicious advertising."[67] Although a national publicity campaign failed to materialize, Ottawa did at least intensify efforts in Quebec where it obviously perceived the maximum number of available recruits. In November 1916, the federal government authorized a second regiment commanded by francophones, the 65e, and gave the job of Chief Enlistment Officer to the once-spurned Mignault.[68] He separated the province into 13 sectors for 82 recruiters and wrote practically every curé asking for the names of those in their parish not needed for farm or industrial work.[69] While not all priests were responsive, some, such as those from Rawdon, St. Marie and St. Honore proved cooperative.[70] Also, between 1 November 1916 and 14 March 1917, Mignault spent nearly $9,500 on newspaper advertising in a desperate attempt to make the prevailing conflict relevant to Quebecois. He emphasized that the fight overseas, far from just being a British imperial struggle or a campaign to save France (a country actually often denounced in Quebec as republican and atheistic), did in fact involve the defence of Canada against an enemy that no doubt had intentions of spreading its tentacles across the Atlantic.[71]

It was, however, a campaign launched too late. Hughes's insensitivity towards Quebec, when combined with the province's pre-war antipathy to British imperialism, as well as anger over discriminatory school language legislation in Ontario,[72] confirmed to a majority of francophones that Canada's contribution should not extend beyond one of strictly limited liability. Between 1 December 1916 and 1 February 1917, only 330 Quebecois joined the 65e. A last-ditch recruiting drive in May 1917 by P.E. Blondin, then Canada's Secretary of State, brought only 92 responses.[73] By the time Ottawa policy-makers accepted that administrative re-organization and extra efforts in Quebec were inadequate to address the task at hand, the government faced a crisis. In March 1917, three months before the introduction of the Military Service Act, A.R. Alloway, the C.P.A.'s assistant manager, wrote the new Minister of Militia, Sir Edward Kemp, to suggest a nationwide advertising campaign, this time for the Canadian Defence Force—a home-bound unit designed to free up more men for the front. The matter was discussed but authorities saw little point. Major-General Sydney Mewburn, who carried East Hamilton for the Unionists in the December 1917 election and succeeded Kemp, was one of many then advising against further expenditures to encourage voluntary enlistment, a position with which Borden apparently concurred.[74]

When the flow of reinforcements began ebbing in mid 1916, pressure mounted upon the Prime Minister to conscript men for overseas service. In April, Hamilton's Branch of the Citizens' Recruiting League formally inaugurated the process by producing a *memorial* stressing the need for *equality of sacrifice*. This principle promptly spawned groups such as the Canadian National Service League, which spotlighted Quebec's laggard performance. With 27.3 per cent of the population the province had, by 1917, provided only 14.2 per cent of recruits, and of that figure, the majority came from its 18 per cent Anglo contingent.[75]

Throughout the latter part of 1916, Ottawa also received entreaties from Britain to put a fifth Canadian division in the field to compensate for Allied losses sustained at the Somme. In situation perceived as approaching crisis proportions, that September, the National Service Board, now under the direction of Conservative M.P. Richard Bedford Bennett,[76] finally launched a new direction with propaganda. While producing a few booklets advocating thrift and conservation as part of the Board's drive to promote national service, the bulk of its publicity budget centred on a coast-to-coast advertising blitz during the last week of 1916 aimed at convincing all males of working age to mail back by 7 January answers to 24 questions dealing with matters such as age, health, marital status and occupation. Besides copious newspaper appeals, broadside production topped 60,000 and over 150,000 letters were mailed to union and business leaders, clergymen and the directors of various patriotic societies. While propaganda stressed the duty of citizens to fill out their National Service cards to secure the most efficient use of manpower, such appeals carefully avoided mentioning conscription. When pressed, Borden refused to state categorically that a draft would not flow from the survey, but such a pledge was made by Bennett, especially to prominent Quebec priests.[77] Suspicion persisted among those opposed to compulsion, but nevertheless, the campaign proved reasonably successful; over 80 per cent of the cards were returned, although of that number 15 per cent were blank or incomplete.[78]

Conscription did indeed follow and recriminations were heard not just about the government lying to Quebec, but worse yet, cynically using compulsion to salvage Conservative Party re-election prospects. Undoubtedly, at the time, the Tories were unpopular. Scandals over munition contracts and Quebec railway deals, rumours about wartime profiteering, as well as mounting inflation, accounted for seven straight provincial election defeats for the party between August 1915 and June 1917. So dubious were the Conservatives about their prospects that not one federal by-election was called between March 1915 and July 1917 despite 20 seats becoming vacant.[79] But conscription was not a sure-fire ticket to victory. Significant sources of opposition existed, not only in Quebec, but also among organized labour and in rural Canada. Furthermore, just the previous October, despite massive campaigning by Prime Minister William Hughes, Australian voters rejected a military draft.

The evidence strongly suggests that Borden acted out of a sincere belief in the absolute necessity of conscription. In early 1917, while in England, he was told about a gloomy situation. The Tsar's collapse was well underway thus permitting Germany to transfer more soldiers to the Western Front; Italy was faltering against Austria; and morale among French troops in the Champagne district had collapsed to the point where, after costly battles that May, a mutiny resulted. America's declaration of war offered hope, but its mobilization would take months. Most military experts predicted high casualties continuing well into 1919. One might also suspect that among his imperial colleagues then also in London to discuss strategy, it must have been especially difficult for Borden to resist demands for further reinforcements. In January 1917, it was learned that while Great Britain had 17 per cent of its male population in uniform, New Zealand

11.9 per cent and Australia 10.7 per cent, the Canadian total was just 9.6 per cent.[80] In addition, the National Service Board, in spite of sometimes sketchy information, soon reported that 286,796 civilians were eligible to fight.[81] It must have seemed all the more imperative to compel at least some of these men into uniform after Canadian wastage figures from the Vimy Ridge and Hill 70 campaigns in April and May, respectively, more than doubled the number of new inductees. Faced with these facts, Borden, who was also emotionally moved by visits to wounded Canadians while overseas, determined that coercion remained the only answer.

In May 1917, almost immediately after returning home, Borden instructed Solicitor-General Arthur Meighen to write a Military Service Act that he in turn promptly presented to Parliament as a measure that should transcend partisanship. To minimize the potential for cultural discord, Borden approached Laurier on the 25th with the idea of forming a coalition government whose cabinet would contain equal numbers of Liberals and Tories. The Opposition leader refused, citing philosophical antipathy towards compulsion, displeasure over Borden's introduction of the bill prior to offering the partnership, and, most important of all, his fear that such collaboration would hand Quebec over to the more extreme nationaliste forces and perhaps even precipitate civil war. Given this response, and since Parliament had already been extended once beyond the legal time limit, Borden was forced to face the electorate—a contest in which, despite his initial concerns about partisanship, he quickly determined had to be won over the "French, foreigners, and slackers."[82] Accordingly, based upon the old adage that the *end justifies the means*, legislation and extensive propaganda soon appeared that, as never before (or perhaps since) in post-Confederation Canada, displayed outright contempt for the democratic process.

Several pro-draft Liberals ultimately joined Borden's new Union party; but their's was a decision prompted not only by Laurier's ongoing refusal to compromise on conscription, but also by the passage that September, via closure, of the Wartime Elections and the Military Voters Acts. The first, most relevant to the political prospects of Prairie Liberals, denied the franchise to conscientious objectors and those of enemy background naturalized after 31 March 1902. The latter group, particularly Western Canada's large Ukrainian population, consistently voted Liberal. In their place, the wives, daughters and sisters of those in uniform, an agglomeration reasonably assumed as sympathetic to conscription, were extended the franchise. Since those denied the ballot were excused from the draft, Borden cast the Act as devoid of prejudice, and no doubt many of its victims were pleased with the swap. Yet such sophistry could not alter the fact that in order to enhance his chances for victory, the Prime Minister lent further credence to suspicions that the foreign-born, even those naturalized for nearly a generation, were untrustworthy. Meanwhile, the Military Voters Act, which undoubtedly constituted a threat to Liberals across English-Canada, permitted the governing party to determine the provincial distribution of overseas soldier ballots (also presumed as pro-conscription) where a specific riding was not indicated.

Government machinations did not stop with such odious legislation. Turning its attention to those in uniform, the Borden administration showed determination that Canadian soldiers not repeat Australian referendum results when 45 per cent of Anzacs cast ballots against compulsion either to avoid "polluting" their ranks with draftees, or, more commonly, to spare their kin from the carnage (particularly after having lost 23,000 at Pozieres just weeks before the October 1916 vote).[83] Therefore, arrangements were made with Aitken and the Ministry of Overseas Military Forces to provide Canadian troops with an abundance of pro-conscription material, avenues not meant for such partisan political activity. Propaganda assured servicemen that each family with an eligible son would be compelled to sacrifice before their siblings were drafted, and also suggested to members of the First Division that an extended furlough to Canada awaited once conscripts arrived at the front—a measure the government made only token gestures towards fulfilling.[84] If that was not enough, Liberal scrutineers complained about being kept physically away from polling stations where, they quite rightly alleged, election boxes were stuffed and officers watched as enlisted men marked their vote. It was therefore no wonder that approximately 90 per cent of soldiers supported the Unionists, a fact that, along with the gerrymandering of their ballots under the Military Voters Act, shifted perhaps 14 seats from Laurier.[85]

At home, Borden proclaimed that his party opposed "abusive language...towards those who may think differently."[86] Nevertheless, the Prime Minister refused to denounce scores of Anglo-Canadian tracts that argued, with various contemptuous modifications, that "a vote for Laurier...[will bring] tyranny, lawlessness and terror." Indeed, by

November, key Unionists such as Finance Minister Thomas White convinced Borden that with Quebec solidly backing Laurier, it was essential for the government to rally English-Canada by any means possible. Therefore, this contest saw the creation of the Union Government Publicity Bureau that flooded the country with recklessly inflammatory posters, pamphlets and press advertisements. For instance, through this agency, Laurier, and by implication Quebec, was charged with "deserting our men…and trailing Canada's honour in the mud," or caricaturized as Nero fiddling away as Europe was consumed by flames.[87]

When the votes were finally cast in December 1917, the Liberals took 62 of 65 seats in Quebec, 10 of 28 in the Maritimes, 8 of 82 in Ontario and 2 of 57 in Western Canada—a division that hardly seemed worthwhile considering that only 24,132 conscripts made it to France. Moreover, if forcing an equal sacrifice from Quebec constituted a major aim, then again the government came up short. Only 23 per cent of those drafted were French-speaking as most Quebecois, particularly those from agricultural families, successfully convinced conscription tribunals of their need at home.[88]

In defence of the Prime Minister, clearly it was impossible in 1917 to predict that Germany would collapse so quickly after its 1918 spring offensive fizzled. As well, so staunchly did Borden believe in the need for conscription that at one point he even offered to step down as Prime Minister in order to secure a coalition with Laurier. But in the final analysis, Borden's steadfast support for compulsion led him to support initiatives that, in the words of his most respected biographer, "did him no credit."[89] It was sadly ironic that in the cause of trying to arouse Canadians to what he perceived as a higher standard of service[90] that Borden capitalised upon bigotry, displayed gross disrespect for democracy, and implemented propaganda that tore deeply into Canada's delicate English-French duality.

The repercussions of paltry recruitment propaganda, while proving divisive if not somewhat calamitous, nevertheless, in becoming apparent by early 1917, perhaps helped convince Ottawa to develop a more dynamic approach towards information infusion when confronting other war-related predicaments. Moreover, the new energy placed upon mass manipulation during the last 18 months of the Great War reflected and received implicit encouragement from general political and economic trends. By 1916, with the conflict exerting rather severe material and monetary strains, Ottawa began introducing unprecedented regulatory controls over the economy. For example, an Imperial Munitions Board, which had supplanted the Shell Committee the previous year, moved beyond placing orders and setting profit guidelines to create several national armament factories. In 1917, new taxes were placed on incomes, and a trade board was established to market Canadian war products in the United States. Side-by-side with these and several other notable interventions came the expanded management of public opinion, not only to help urge the endorsement of conscription, but also to deal with the possibility of fuel and food shortages, and the difficulty of financing a war whose costs appeared to be growing exponentially.

In the winter of 1916-1917, periodic fuel deficiencies began affecting major munition production centres such as Toronto. Compounding the situation was that under Hughes's chaotic approach to recruitment, far too many miners were enlisted after it was discovered they performed well in France as sappers.[91] Furthermore, America's declaration of war threatened to drastically curtail exports of anthracite from Pennsylvania. Therefore, on 16 June 1917, C.A. Magrath, an Alberta Conservative and founder of the Northwestern Coal and Navigation Company, was appointed as Canada's Fuel Controller. He was given powers to regulate the delivery, sale and profit levels made from resources, enforce cuts in public consumption up to 30 per cent, and, if necessary, to nationalize mines where labour disputes threatened production.[92]

Considering that it remained possible to alleviate short-term fuel deficits through the periodic shut-down of nonessential train routes or places of entertainment, Magrath was spared the need to develop a major advertising strategy. Still, a steady flow of communiques were issued by the Fuel Controller to the C.P.A.'s Ottawa bureau beseeching citizens to keep house temperatures down, while newspaper advertisements advocated patriotic "gasless Sundays" and "heatless Mondays."[93] Some grumbling emanated that winter from the frigid Prairies over the delivery of lignite rather than superior Pennsylvania coal to generate heat, but generally speaking, Magrath garnered enough voluntary public compliance across the country to prevent the need for a formalized rationing scheme.[94]

Far more propaganda emanated from the Food Controller's Office, also created on 16 June 1917, and put under the direction of former Imperial Oil executive and Ontario Conservative William J. Hanna, whose task became to "ascertain the food requirements of Canada and to facilitate the export of the surplus." The situation overseas was critical. Between 1913 and 1917, France's wheat crop plunged by 57 per cent, while Germany's unrestricted U-Boat campaign scared off enough neutral shipping to necessitate the implementation of coupon rationing in Britain during the final year of hostilities. To try to relieve such conditions, Hanna was provided with powers over pricing, storage, distribution and consumption.[95] Ill-health forced his retirement in February 1918 but the duties were quickly assumed by the Canada Food Board, which was run by the Department of Agriculture.

On their own, farmers were incapable of solving the food supply crisis. By January 1918, military recruitment had caused agricultural labour shortages of 12,000 in Ontario, 7,000 in Manitoba, 10,000 in Saskatchewan, and 6,000 in Alberta. Laws appeared against hoarding and black marketeering, as well as to prevent restaurants from distributing large quantities of free bread, butter and sugar, or from serving beef and pork on designated days and never in quantities exceeding eight ounces per person. But since it was impossible to police every citizen, propaganda stressing public participation in conservation and production campaigns became a key ingredient in generating success. Between the inauguration of food control efforts and the end of the war, over $500,000 was spent on various promotional activities.[96] The response proved sufficient enough to negate the need for ration cards in Canada, for after only six months of largely voluntary food control, citizens were consuming 200,000 fewer barrels of flour per month and freeing up enough meat to feed 500,000 soldiers on an ongoing basis.[97]

Through Publicity and Educational Sections, the Food Controller and Food Board issued press releases, a departmental newspaper, posters, pledge cards, flyers, cookbooks and in 1918 produced a movie entitled *War Gardens* instructing urbanites on how to grow vegetables.[98] Daily communiques about half a newspaper column long entered, at its peak, 962 English- and 82 French-language publications. The *Canadian Food Bulletin*, started by Hanna in October 1917, targeted in its distribution approximately 45,000 opinion-makers such as clergymen, local politicians and business leaders. By reporting upon respective food control efforts, it created some friendly competition between communities. Compliance was also fostered through the threat of public shaming. Each issue of the *Bulletin* contained entries such as: "A fine of $100 and costs [was imposed] against a local restaurant man, _____, for serving veal at the mid-day meal."[99]

Furthermore, rather than relying upon existing volunteer groups to distribute propaganda in a possibly haphazard manner because such organizations were also busy with other war-related tasks, authorities went to the trouble of establishing provincial and local food control sub-committees under well-known community figures. As well, in each of 25 administrative districts, a major retailer was appointed to rally their business colleagues to the task of promoting conservation and food production, an initiative that ultimately reached consumers in over 700 locales. Many pamphlets circulated by these volunteers, as well as live demonstrations put on by women attached to a Domestic Economy Section, educated housewives on how to can food and in using more plentiful foodstuffs such as corn to prepare a variety of patriotic meals. Also distributed were more than a million cards for display in kitchens where people signed a pledge "to carry out conscientiously the advice and directions" of food control officials.[100] Meanwhile, broadsides, among other messages, reminded civilians that they were asked to make small sacrifices compared to the huge burdens borne by those overseas. "We are saving you, you save food," demanded a soldier pointing to an explosion off in the distance. Indeed, it was primarily through a massive dissemination of posters that a $25,000 Soldiers of the Soil campaign attracted over 20,000 adolescents to help out on farms. Here was an opportunity, said propagandists, for lads to emulate an older brother or father overseas, while at the same time serving King and Country. Declared one placard under a drawing of boys in the military-type uniform of this agricultural corps: "You couldn't look th[ose]…who are going straight in the eye if you proved a slacker in this emergency."[101]

For Ottawa there also the rapidly growing ordeal of financing the war whose daily costs between 1915 and 1917 doubled to $1 million. All traditional methods of raising funds—hikes to tariffs, cigarette and alcohol taxes, postage rates and railway tickets—were utilised by the end of 1914, but proved inadequate in alleviating the problem. By July 1915, the federal government was forced to go with *cap in hand* to New York's money markets, a source it preferred to avoid because of high interest rates. The following February, in an attempt to address its mounting fiscal burdens, as well as assuage escalating labour resentment over stories about wartime profiteering, Finance Minister Thomas White convinced the provinces not to push their shared constitutional power over levies upon individuals and corporations and allow without complaint passage of a new Business Profits Tax. Yet, this measure, which was capable of raising just $25 million annually, along with a temporary tax upon personal incomes the next year for which only 31,130 Canadians qualified, demonstrated that Ottawa, while willing to experiment in order to raise money, still remained cautious, both for ideological and jurisdictional reasons, about jettisoning what until the war had been a basically hands-off approach when it came to economic activity.[102]

The only remaining and clearly less controversial solution was to borrow on a massive scale from Canadians. Such a strategy called for voluntary sacrifice on the part of citizens, promised an ultimate and direct benefit for the money extended, and had not created big government when employed the previous century to build the nation's transportation infrastructure. Prior to the fourth Victory Loan in November 1917, war bond sales were conducted with little fanfare and secured funds mainly from financial institutions and the affluent. Advertising was sparse and unspectacular, only discussing the terms of the security. Consequently, while one in every 23 Britons owned a Victory Bond in mid 1917, the Canadian figure was one in 187.[103] White was reluctant to democratize the securities for fear of depleting and destabilizing what he perceived as a relatively small domestic financial market. However, degenerating economic circumstances along with a reluctance to institute massive taxation, forced the Minister to reconsider his cautious conduct.

A broader appeal for funds commenced in early 1917 with the War Savings Certificate programme. These securities, starting at $25 and issued for three years at five per cent interest, were made available at all banks and post offices. In three months, 79,509 subscribers, more than for previous Victory Bond issues, pledged in excess of $5 million.[104] Once fully appreciating the public's enthusiasm, as well as the fact that numerous citizens had saved substantial sums from wartime employment, White took the proverbial plunge. For the fourth Victory Loan, the propaganda floodgates were opened. In a drive employing every conceivable means of communication, citizens were told that duty, national pride and even self-interest demanded their patriotic response. Expectations were vastly exceeded. That November, 820,035 people subscribed to securities worth $413.6 million (double the third loan), while the following November, in 1918, 1.067 million citizens loaned Ottawa $660 million, an extraordinary tally in a country whose population barely topped eight million. Most important, the money allowed Canada to finance its various war-related commitments without meeting economic disaster.[105]

Promotional and organizational costs for the November 1917 campaign totalled just over $2.2 million; this, however, proved an excellent investment, amounting to only 0.5319 per cent of the revenue obtained.[106] Critical in securing such a response was the visible hand of professionalised management. A National Executive Committee based in the Finance Department arranged for banks, along with stock and bond houses, to receive a 0.5 per cent commission on each security sold. As well, to market bonds to the public-at-large, thousands of insurance salesmen (whose companies at this time handled most residential mortgages) were hired on a similar pay scale. White figured that with funds being solicited from people who had probably never before invested their money, it was crucial that the canvassers "project considerable knowledge of financial matters."[107]

Organizing propaganda efforts was a Dominion Publicity Committee. During the fourth loan it spent $163,000 on material besides newspaper advertising—broadsides, sandwich boards, pamphlets, buttons and inspirational letters. The following year, in a campaign that saw the appearance of an official Victory Loan *Honour Flag*, this figure leaped to $275,000.[108] Branches of the publicity division, supervised by prominent individuals, were established in each province, plus city and town of worthwhile size.[109] Also producing a profusion of propaganda were contracts signed between the Finance Department and the C.P.A., one result of which was a Dominion Feature News Service where the government paid members of the Press Association to provide publications with upbeat stories and facts about fund-raising efforts. Yet more pivotal was the agreement reached in the area of display advertising, for which Ottawa allotted over $350,000 to publicize the fourth and fifth loans. The C.P.A., acting as an agent for White's ministry, obtained the services of major advertising firms including Pearce and McKim of Toronto to furnish copy that ultimately appeared in over 1,000 sources.[110] Commencing six weeks prior to the Victory Bond issue date, and especially during the three-week purchasing period, it became virtually impossible for citizens to open a newspaper or magazine without confronting appeals to share their earnings. Not only was every conceivable romantic or idealistic theme effectively utilized,[111] but also points certain to have caught the attention of so-called practically-minded people. Particularly productive in Quebec was an appeal emphasizing that at five per cent interest, government securities constituted a better invest-ment than putting one's money in the bank.[112]

Even hermits or shut-ins could not escape government solicitations. White arranged for the Post Office to deliver nearly four million letters to households in which he implored that "money is urgently required…to support our gallant soldiers in the field…."[113] This tactic was especially use-ful during the November 1918 campaign when many citizens were quarantined because of the influenza epidemic. Also finding their way into every home were patriotic postage seals as well as jingoistic messages printed by stamp cancelling machines beseeching people to "buy Victory Bonds to the limit of your ability."[114]

Modern modes of mass communication were not neglected. For a fee of $15,000, the Finance Minister convinced American directors such as Adolph Zukor and Jesse Lasky to re-cast scenes in U.S. Liberty Loan pro-motions using Canadian uniforms and flags.[115] Audiences cheered when Hollywood matinee queen Mary Pickford bashed the Kaiser on the head with a baseball bat labelled "Victory Loan" in *100 per cent Canadian*.[116] Also presented at movie theatres and other public forums in 1918 was a gramophone recording in which White proclaimed that the money raised would support those "whose heroism and achievements…have inspired the admiration of all the Allies and indeed the whole world."[117]

Linkages between the mounting socio-economic strains exerted by the war and an expanding propaganda network were further demonstrated on 9 November 1917 when the federal government (also obviously trying to max-imize positive press coverage during the election campaign) created the Department of Public Information. As officially described by Ottawa, its was to funnel to the press via weekly news conferences factual data about events overseas and policies introduced at home. However, with its budget of approximately $75,000, its director, former Montreal *Mail* newspaperman, M.E. Nichols, made the agency into much more.[118] From its offices came the *Canadian Official Record*, a publication whose contents—such as the claim that nearly all bed-ridden wounded soldiers learned "a useful and interesting occupation" by the time of their discharge—consistently and sharply diverged from the connotation of its title.[119] Other material authorized by Nichols fortified well-worn themes and highlighted concerns not emphasized by other government offices disseminating propaganda. In an effort to reduce tensions in the wake of anti-conscription riots in Montreal and Quebec City during the 1918 Easter weekend, Nichols signed a contract that July with Montreal's Specialty Film Import Company to produce *The Call of Freedom* that depicted "the various phases of a draftee's life from the first call to the colours to the final turning out of a finished recruit," highlighting throughout "how the boys enjoy life in the military camps."[120] Meanwhile, growing anxiety over leftist strength towards the end of the war resulted in *Bolshevism in Russia*, a polemical pamphlet that, among other revelations, told of "thousands...[who were] left to rot in prisons under conditions to find parallel to which one must turn to the darkest annals of Indian or Chinese history."[121]

Most substantial, however, among the Department's activities was its War Lecture Bureau that, in January 1918, supplanted the citizen-run Speakers' Patriotic League so Ottawa could assume a more direct role in determining the issues emphasized at various times. For a monthly cost of $4,000, newsletters were mailed out every two weeks to approximately 10,000 volunteers in 150 communities drawn primarily from politics, journalism, the church, Boards of Trade, unions, women's groups and universities.[122] Within three months, their five-minute orations—the majority written by the Bureau's staff—reached approximately 400,000 Canadians in an effort to help boost the acceptance of conscription, as well the need to conserve scarce resources and purchase Victory Bonds.[123]

Finally, there remained the matter of peacetime reintegration for those who, the government stressed, had selflessly served the nation. Parents and wives were promised that all veterans, no matter their physical or psychological injuries, would, with generous public aid and a little gumption, soon be on the road to a full recovery and a productive life. To provide medical care and retraining, and to decide upon appropriate pensions, Ottawa created a Military Hospitals Commission [M.H.C.] in July 1915.

» *Propaganda promises a smooth transition for "real men" to civilian life.*
(National Archives of Canada, C 9528)

On 21 February 1918, the M.H.C. became part of the Department of Soldiers' Civil Re-Establishment [D.S.C.R.], which also devised strategy to aid veterans who were physically fit.

With the number of repatriated wounded soldiers growing dramatically by 1917, Ottawa began setting aside funds to manufacture information illustrating its remarkable work in helping such men re-adapt. Through press releases, the M.H.C. bragged that its pensions were more generous than annuities offered by other Allied nations and available to any serviceman in sliding scales no matter how slight their injury. Moreover, from its *Bulletin* came articles highlighting the more than 300 courses made available to the maimed, along with cases such as of legless and one-eyed veteran who became a silver polisher.[124] Those who failed to reintegrate and thrive, it was said, had only themselves to blame. This was the message in *Canada's Work for Wounded Soldiers*, a five-reel M.H.C. film depicting a variety of retraining programmes and "how these brave men set about cutting new niches for themselves in the industrial world." Only those veterans who "refus[ed] to try and achieve victory over [their] wounds," the film insisted, were destined for hardship.[125] The idea that anyone could, with a little effort, ultimately return to the mainstream was also conspicuous in live demonstrations set up by the D.S.C.R. at fall fairs across Canada in 1918 where blind veterans wove baskets and those with artificial limbs worked with lathes.[126] Recovery for the psychologically damaged was presented as a simple matter of getting the subject to face his fears. *Reconstruction* magazine, a D.S.C.R. publication, told of one former private continually forced back into a machine shop until he got used to the noise, thus suggesting that those not attempting the same were either cowards or just plain lazy.[127]

Information also assured citizens about an abundance of government support programmes practically guaranteeing success to those returning uninjured as long as they possessed a modicum of ambition. From the D.S.C.R.'s Repatriation Committee came pamphlets professing that veterans could easily re-establish themselves with the War Service Gratuity, a lump sum payment ranging up to 183 days' pay for three years of overseas service. As well, Ottawa boasted about employment offices established for soldiers across the land along with regulations providing veterans with easier access into the civil service. Expert training, superior land and excellent financial terms (no interest for the first two years and five per cent thereafter) were supposedly made available to any ex-soldier who desired to try his hand at farming. Indeed, a favourite flyer distributed by the government described the exploits of the fictional veteran, *Private Pat*. Proudly he shunned the dole, struggled under this programme to break the Prairie sod, and, soon enough felt that self-respect that came with re-establishing himself as a productive citizen and a man.[128]

Near the front and in Britain, controls imposed by military and civilian authorities clearly protected Canadians from upsetting portrayals of combat. For the most part, Aitken, C.P.A. journalists, and others involved with gathering information voluntarily composed copy with an eye towards raising morale. Still, the immediate transmission of their reports to Canadian newspapers demanding up-to-date data ensured that their accounts flowed through official channels and did not inadvertently leak something deemed sensitive or unsavoury. Beyond a well-monitored undersea cable, there was no other instantaneous means of trans-Atlantic communication available to European-based newsmen. Therefore, the patriotic disposition of and technical limitations relating to overseas correspondents and cameramen assured that practically all renderings of warfare remained romanticized and sanitized, and, as long as the British proved tolerant, moulded Johnny Canuck's exploits into something approaching fantasy.

When combined with propaganda from nongovernment sources, officially-sanctioned information helped retain an ideological environment partly explaining the surface-level success of Canada's poorly organized and niggardly recruitment programme. However, such a situation, though saving Ottawa money in the short-run, could very well have contributed to the eventual certainty of conscription. Having perhaps learned something from this pattern, and also drawing strength from general trends towards economic intervention, the federal government, throughout 1917, adopted a more hands-on approach towards managing the mass psyche not only to secure conscription, but also to deal with possible fuel, food and monetary shortages, as well as potential problems associated with returning soldiers. Significantly, propagandists, even after nearly three years of warfare, still encountered a majority who, at least in English-Canada, remained jingoistic and idealistic in their outlook. Therefore, though used divisively (albeit successfully) in the conscription campaign, propaganda was also able to generate enough of a patriotic response to avert the need for comprehensive compulsory rationing and produced sufficient funds to manage the war economy—problems that, if not solved, held out the potential of subverting the country's military effort.

In accounting for the perseverance of such enthusiasm, however, information infusion provides only half of the answer. Extensive efforts were also initiated within the Dominion to withdraw ideas from public discussion. And when it came to domestic censorship, Canada, in comparison to its allies, created a most thorough system. Taken together, these two sides of opinion formation, while serving valuable functions during the war, also played key roles in making the ailments suffered by and complaints of veterans almost incomprehensible to civilians who, during the struggle, confronted only anticeptized and quixotic accounts of conflict.

11

CENSORSHIP

» *Ernest J. Chambers as Gentleman Usher of the Black Rod.*
  (National Archives of Canada, C 1824)

3

A Loyal or Muzzled Press?

"**M**ake absolutely sure that you omit no power that the government may need."[1] So instructed Prime Minister Borden to Halifax lawyer, W.F. O'Connor, who helped draft Canada's War Measures Act. Passed on 22 August 1914 and made retroactive to 4 August, this statute, among other restrictions, provided for "censorship and control and suppression of publications, writings, maps, plans, photographs, communication and means of communication." Those contravening the Act were liable to receive a $5,000 fine, five years in jail, or both, and, contrary to traditional Common Law practice, once charged, the onus of proof lay with the accused to demonstrate innocence.[2]

In fretting about the potential of free expression to undermine morale and military security, Canadian authorities were not alone. Just prior to August 1914, the Committee on Imperial Defence noted with concern that during the 1899-1902 South African war, British generals complained about telegraphs being utilised by field correspondents to relay dangerously detailed accounts on troop positions that were subsequently published by English newspapers. In turn, these were transmitted by London-based enemy agents to Dutch embassies across Europe, and soon enough, ended up in the hands of Boer commanders on the Veldt.[3]

In fact, the leakage of some sensitive information by the press during the opening months of the Great War convinced Ottawa to move beyond the War Measures Act. On 10 June 1915, an Order in Council (PC 1330) established a Chief Press Censor's office. The man chosen for the job, Lieutenant-Colonel Ernest J. Chambers, received authority, subject to approval from the Secretary of State, to prohibit sources criticizing military policy, causing disaffection, "assisting or encouraging the enemy, or preventing, embarrassing or hindering the successful prosecution of the war." To enforce this and subsequent regulations, Chambers regularly sent detailed instruction sheets outlining permissable commentary on particular war-related events to approximately 1,500 publishers; other parties involved with printing, distributing, selling or displaying matter about the war; as well as federal, provincial and local constabulary services.[4]

As casualties mounted, recruitment ebbed, and dissidence became more prominent, Canadian censorship assumed wider proportions. In September 1915, PC 2073 provided Chambers with the authority to order telephone operators to monitor conversations, and directed telegraph companies to supply him or a designated agent with copies of messages carried over their landlines.[5] The following June, a Censorship Committee—comprised of the Secretary of State, Postmaster General, Solicitor General, Directors of Customs and Naval Service, along with the Ministers of Justice and Militia and Defence—was struck to consider yet more comprehensive legislation.[6] The result, PC 146, which became law in January 1917, supplemented endeavours by the National Service Board to balance maximum recruitment and homefront production, and appeared to anticipate conscription, by baring all material possibly "prejudic[ing] the operation or administration of any act or Order in Council concerning national service." As well, it furnished Chambers with the capacity to censor motion pictures arriving from America and London in ever-increasing numbers.[7] Further powers came in May 1918 as PC 1241 sought to contain growing internal dissent—especially in Quebec, where major anti-draft riots had occurred that Easter—by adding to the black list attempts to "persuade or induce any person...to resist or impede" the Military Service Act; false or unflattering statements regarding any branch of the armed service; derogatory comments about Great Britain or its harsh policies against Republican insurgents in Ireland; or anything "which tends to weaken or in any way detract from the united effort...in the prosecution of the war." Also classified as unacceptable was "any talking machine record which is calculated to arouse hostile national sentiment among the people of enemy country origin resident in Canada."[8]

Finally, just weeks before the conflict ended, the regulations applicable to newspapers serving certain less-favoured ethnic and political minorities became particularly ruthless. On September 25th, the Borden administration succumbed to nativist pressure, especially from the then politically powerful and potentially violent Great War Veterans' Association [G.W.V.A.], which threatened to destroy newspaper offices printing tracts in enemy languages. The response, PC 2381, outlawed German, Bulgarian, Hungarian, Turkish, Finnish, Ukrainian, Ruthenian, Estonian, Croatian and Livonian from print and at all public meetings.[9] Two months later, with the armistice signed, Ukrainian, Ruthenian, Estonian, Croatian and Livonian legally resurfaced in dual column format newspapers (an English translation appearing beside the foreign text). The following April, PC 703 allowed the parallel text system to lapse and granted legal status to most tongues, but Canada's so-called principal enemies—those of German, Austrian, Bulgarian, Hungarian and Turkish birth or descent—were only granted the right to read their language in sources solely dedicated to religious, literary, artistic or legal matters.[10] Meanwhile, to counteract an apparently growing Bolshevist threat, PC 2384 was passed on 28 September 1918. It was devised by the corporate lawyer and Tory advisor C.H. Cahan who, for the past six months, had, at Ottawa's behest, researched the danger posed by the country's radical left. In October, he was appointed as Director of Public Safety to oversee its implementation that banned 13 organizations and made it a crime, punishable by five years' incarceration, to advocate, teach, advise, defend, or in any way advertise "the use of force, violence or physical injury to person or property in order to accomplish governmental or economic change...."[11]

Perhaps exemplifying the parsimony that the federal government initially displayed towards propaganda, or simply Ottawa's inexperience in having to contend with extensive security concerns, censorship activities, for practically the first year of the war, possessed no centralized authority to direct the surveillance and, if necessary, translation of newspapers. The Post Office, operating under a 1906 statute permitting it to outlaw "obscene or immoral publications, prints, or photographs," along with a November 1914 Order in Council prohibiting the importation of material sympathetic to the enemy, suppressed a few tracts.[12] Also identifying the odd undesirable source were Militia and Defence, Immigration Branch and various local law enforcement authorities. But as a whole, this rather haphazard system, in which no one department focused its efforts exclusively upon censorship, proved capable of identifying and suppressing only the most obvious anti-British newspapers, such as the New York *Fatherland*, whose editor, George Sylvester Viereck, received a weekly payment of $250 from Austria's Ambassador to the United States.[13]

However, the most direct factor in precipitating the appointment of a Chief Press Censor related to the fact that some of those in charge of mass distribution newspapers envisaged the war as having created a new business opportunity. The public, eager for details about the great adventure, bought, for example, 30,000 extra copies of the Toronto *Globe* during the week of 4-11 August 1914. That month, a "Memorandum on the Duties of the Press in War" was drawn up by military authorities. Editors were requested to remove anything conceivably "useful to the enemy," or causing "alarm or despair."[14] Yet, so far as enforcement was concerned, federal authorities chose to rely upon press corps' patriotism rather than assume the cost and trouble of establishing a formal censorship department. To their disappointment, however, some publishers and editors who beat the jingoistic drums also tried to boost sales by "satisfy[ing] the insatiable demand of people for news," that, though not being of the nature to sap morale, was still viewed by numerous officials as best suppressed.[15]

Authorities were most perturbed when the Toronto *Globe*, in an effort to display the Empire's might, printed photographs of the H.M.S. *Centurion* and *Dartmouth* and included details such as their tonnage, quantity and calibre of weaponry, maximum speed, and the number of ships of similar class in the Royal Navy. Far more serious was the Montreal *Gazette*'s story telling curious families about the departure of the last ship carrying the First Canadian Contingent to England that even mentioned the amount of ammunition on board.[16] With a trans-Atlantic voyage taking approximately two weeks, some officials remarked that an American-based fifth columnist with access to a wireless facility could have employed such information to produce disastrous consequences. Bonar Law, Britain's Colonial Secretary, relayed the War Office's "concern" to Ottawa, especially in light of rumours about enemy U-Boats lurking near the mouth of the St. Lawrence.[17] As a result, in February 1915, Justice Minister Charles Doherty established a committee to produce an Order in Council giving "authorities power to exercise effective control over the press."[18]

Some journalists expressed concern over the prospect of a formalized censorship service. News, they argued, developed throughout the day and night, and, as a result, a reporter might have to wait several hours to get a story approved, thus missing their deadline and giving the edge to competitors printing a later edition.[19] Ottawa responded that no requirement would be placed upon newsmen to submit every story in advance, only those that, in the judgment of a reasonable person, transgressed the Orders in Council. A relatively low-profile network, the government hoped, would pacify editors, maintain the appearance of journalistic independence, and, perhaps most important, not arouse public suspicion over day-to-day official control extending well beyond extremists, disloyal minorities, and militarily-sensitive news. But to deal with those cases where the diplomatic approach seemed inadequate to secure newspaper quiescence over mass manipulation, regulations specified that editors expunge copy denouncing censorship or from indicating, either by direct commentary or the insertion of blank spaces, that stories were sometimes expurgated.

Despite some grumbling, most newsmen, in exemplifying pervasive jingoism, a resignation to new realities, and unencumbered by professional standards promoting dispassionate reporting, responded by promising greater efforts to help win the war. Many in the fourth estate, in fact, evidently welcomed Chambers's appearance based upon the premise that he would halt the practice of some publishers to print ill-advised stories that caused truly patriotic sources to suffer financially because they voluntarily complied with government requests to bury sensitive copy. F.A. Miller of the Toronto *Telegram* expressed the frustration of many colleagues by commenting that it was ludicrous for his paper to avoid mentioning the departure of troops from the city when such information appeared in both the *Star* and the *News*.[20]

Such a cooperative attitude was evident at a meeting held on 10 June 1915 between 25 Canadian Press Association [C.P.A.] representatives and Chambers. While those attending requested and obtained the creation of an advisory committee to voice from time to time concerns or grievances, they also pledged loyal conduct. John Ross Robertson, the proprietor of the Toronto *Telegram*, typifying comments from several others, said that while in principle he believed that "a muzzled...press spells doom for democracy," he also insisted that the prevailing crisis made controls necessary in order "to escape evils worse for the nation than the temporary infringements on personal liberty."[21]

The man selected to administer Canadian censorship, Ernest J. Chambers, was born on 16 April 1862 in Penkridge, England. Both his lineage and early life might be characterized as intertwined with the military and British pre-eminence in Canada. An edition of *Who's Who* noted: "An ancestor on the father's side [Rear Admiral Thomas Chambers] served in Saunders's fleet at Quebec, 1759, and, during the Revolutionary War, commanded the British squadron on Lakes Champlain and George."[22] In his formative years, Chambers displayed an affinity for army life, quickly progressing to commander of the Montreal School Cadet Rifles. His association with the militia was life-long, eventually earning him a citation for distinguished service and undoubtedly bringing him into close contact with the architects of Canada's military. One of these military associates, Major-General Sir Willoughby Gwatkin, appointed him as cable censor for the West Coast during the opening stages of the Great War.[23]

In the civilian world, Chambers, like his older brother Edward, became a journalist. As a cub reporter for the Montreal *Star*, he journeyed west in 1885 and relayed back accounts about patriotic Canadian forces who crushed the "arch-conspirator" Louis Riel. During this venture he volunteered for military service and fought at Fish Creek, Batoche, and against Big Bear and his tribe, efforts for which he received a medal and a clasp. When referring to the events in later years, he explained with pride that "it ha[d] always been my life's goal to take part on the field in defense of the Empire and of the Dominion."[24] During the late 1880s, Chambers took the job of managing editor for the newly-founded Calgary *Herald*. In 1898, he combined his work and interest in the militia with his talents as a newsman to write for the *Canadian Military Gazette*, that publication that led the charge for Dominion participation in the 1899-1902 Boer War.[25] Moreover, by that time he had moved back east and was also serving as Captain and Adjutant for Montreal's Sixth Fusiliers and soon after held the same ranks in the Canadian Grenadier Guards. Certainly his visibility in political circles soared when, in 1904, in recognition of his journalistic and military standing, Chambers was appointed as Gentleman Usher of the Black Rod, and, four years later, as editor of the *Canadian Parliamentary Guide*—posts he held until his death on 11 May 1921. Further connections to Canada's power-elite he also cultivated through his secretaryship of the Royal Academy and Royal College of Music; Montreal's Anglican Church Choral Society; Ottawa's branch of the Empire Parliamentary Association; and by membership in the Ottawa Golf and the Courlage Fish and Game Club.[26]

Continuing to move up the militia hierarchy, in 1911, Chambers was promoted to Major and as the new District Intelligence Officer for Southwest Quebec, a post that involved monitoring suspected threats to constituted authority and providing aid to the civil power, such as in the case of a violent labour dispute. By the time the Great War erupted, military commanders, in acknowledging this quasi-espionage role, had him elevated to Lieutenant-Colonel and relocated to the Corps of Guides, the forerunner of Canada's army intelligence corps.

As demonstrated by his government appointments, Chambers had been able to impress, as well as work effectively with Ottawa decision-makers. Military men must have considered him sympathetic to their interests, given his militia background and association with the *Gazette*. Experience as an intelligence officer most likely inspired confidence in his ability to ferret out undesirables. Thirty years in the news business provided substantive links with members of the fourth estate—something undoubtedly advantageous in helping him obtain compliance with censorship decrees. There is also evidence that Chambers possessed superior interpersonal skills. William Banks, a leading figure in the Orange Order and sometimes an adviser to Prime Minister Borden, described the Chief Censor as "genial," while Lieutenant-Colonel Charles Frederick Hamilton (the *Globe*'s Boer War correspondent who, starting in August 1914, directed the surveillance of international cable and wireless transmissions) asked Chambers on two occasions prior to the creation of the Chief Press Censor's post, to talk with C.P.A. representatives, noting that he was "particularly well suited" for such a task.[27]

As Chief Censor, Chambers had a small staff at his disposal: one filing clerk, two stenographers, one typist and by late 1916, a full-time German translator. His principal aides in Ottawa were Joseph Fortier (the monitor for French-Canadian publications), Ernest Boag and Ben Deacon, all journalists by training, each of whom were paid $8 per diem. In Winnipeg, J.F. Livesay, former president of the Western Canadian Press Association [W.C.P.A.], assisted by surveying Prairie and B.C. newspapers. When appointed as the C.P.A.'s overseas correspondent in August 1918, F.G. Aldham, also a W.C.P.A. board member, assumed this post.[28] Supplementing efforts in Winnipeg, Vancouver and Toronto were six C.P.A. employees each of whom received an honorarium of between $20 and $50 monthly to watch transmissions carried across news wires. Technically-speaking, Chambers worked for free since he remained on a daily salary of $10 that for years he had obtained as Gentleman Usher of the Black Rod. To the satisfaction of government officials who faced spiralling costs in so many other areas, censorship, under Chambers's self-sacrificing direction, remained a frugal operation, with total expenses running less than $25,000 per annum.[29]

Chambers's willingness to assume the Chief Censor's post with no extra remuneration was indicative of a man who looked upon this job as a calling—a chance to once again "take part on the field in defense of the Empire." To ensure a successful operation that would protect Canadians from inappropriate information while at the same time minimizing the alienation of patriotic newsmen, Chambers endorsed without complaint Ottawa's policy of keeping the censor's office open from 9 a.m. to midnight Monday through Saturday, and 8 p.m. to midnight on Sunday. In fact, he and his equally hard-working staff went even further. Regular hours," noted the Chief Censor, "were never considered." The department "was either open continuously day and night, week in and week out, or closed for a few hours after midnight when the opportunity to do so presented itself." Chambers personally answered almost all queries, with correspondence often exceeding one hundred letters per day. Twice during his term, which ran until 1 January 1920, he was forced to take time off for nervous exhaustion.[30]

As an ardent imperialist, Chambers proved untiring and unyielding in his fight to shelter citizens from anything that might compromise their loyalty for and conviction to aid Great Britain in whose hands, he asserted, lay the worldwide future of liberty. In pursuing this end, he concluded that the country's isolation from the front and dependence until late 1917 upon a volunteer army meant that extra efforts were necessary to keep enthusiasm strong. Among British civilians, Chambers maintained, combat was more real and immediate; in England's Southeast people heard artillery in France, while thousands in London experienced the terror of air raids or perhaps heard unpleasant tales about front-line life from soldiers on leave. To provide them with depressing information, he believed, possessed less potential to shock or produce catastrophic consequences compared to Canada where the Great War, both physically and intellectually, remained a far-off event to which people were tied more by idealistic sentiment than fears about national survival.

Given his small staff along with the intention of imposing a rigid agenda, Chambers often came to rely upon those whom he considered loyal. He looked to editors of mainstream newspapers as potential propagandists and watch dogs; cable and phone company owners and their employees as unofficial censors; while film distributors and booksellers were asked to contribute by refusing to circulate movies, printed matter and gramophone recordings considered undesirable.

As far as government departments were concerned, none was more helpful to the Chief Censor than the Post Office. At 27 principal exchanges through which all international mail passed, Deputy Postmaster General,

Dr. R.M. Coulter, partly as a result of requests made by Chambers, ulti-mately assigned approximately 120 employees to censorship duty, some of whom were fluent in enemy languages or trained in the use of chemicals to detect invisible ink. Following guidelines established a decade earlier by the Committee on Imperial Defence, they opened letters sent to or from enemy and neutral countries, or involving areas where substantial forces battled against the Allies.[31] However, this strategy, while perhaps appropri-ate for surveying the limited correspondence between Canada and places like the Philippines (where Germany had trade mission), was clearly not capable of effectively monitoring the approximately 400,000 items crossing the U.S.-Canada border weekly. In that context, Chambers directed Coulter to have postal workers concentrate upon mail involving someone whose surname indicated possible sympathy with the Central Powers, and, by late 1917, correspondence connected to known socialists and their orga-nizations. A frequently updated inventory of subsequently prohibited tracts delivered to or sent by such groups was distributed among postal employ-ees, along with names and addresses, and descriptions of the packages. One hit list circulated in February 1916 included over three hundred locations as well as instructions to examine all matter mailed in "buff envelopes about 10 1/2" x 7 1/2" prepaid…with a two cent stamp and posted from New York."[32]

Chambers also acquired his own small army of translators to control what he presumed was the negative influence exerted by certain foreign-language sources. Some personnel came *gratis* from other government departments, such as Miss E. Mercer who read German and worked for the Immigration Branch. He also recruited individuals believed competent for this work like McGill's Slavonic Studies' Professor, E. Tartak, who was paid on the basis of each paper deciphered. Finally, some people of foreign background heard or figured out that the government was looking at such publications and offered their services to obtain extra money. M. Sung of Vancouver made $36 for scanning nine day's worth of Chinese tracts, while a similar wage was provided to H. Eddelstein of Montreal for analyz-ing Yiddish and Hebrew sources.[33] Through these means, Chambers kept abreast of newspapers printed in 31 languages.[34]

Having forged a far-reaching apparatus through clever management and workaholic conduct, Chambers proceeded to exert a notable impact upon what Canadians read—influence he obtained not only through his ability to apply coercive legislation. He understood the importance of not needlessly alienating the mainstream press and risking, despite regulations, a negative view of censorship being presented to the public. It was here that his genial approach came to the fore. After being appointed as Chief Censor, Chambers attempted to solidify links with the principal members of Canada's fourth estate. In August 1915, he wrote C.W. Young of the Cornwall *Freeholder*, a C.P.A. director, to ask if at the next meeting he could "give a little spiel on censorship matters."[35] Attempting to promote good relations, he assured those assembled that "as an old newspaperman...I would refuse to act as an administrator of a Prussian system." Instead, Chambers presented himself as an advisor who could help editors determine the status of items over which they were uncertain. Also he pitched to their patriotism, relaying Major-General Gwatkin's flattering, but also sagacious, observation that press corps' compliance perhaps equated to a brigade raised for the front.[36]

When the censorship regulations were inadvertently transgressed by a source that Chambers regarded as essentially loyal, the admonishment delivered was usually courteous and diplomatic. For example, the Montreal *Mail* caused some concern by publishing one of Henri Bourassa's anti-war addresses; but rather than chastise the editor and possibly alienate a source of pro-war sentiment, Chambers wrote that "your staff have done so splendidly that I even hate to offer a hint, [yet]...I am following the policy of drawing...attention in a friendly way to everything that looks like a slight slip."[37]

Newsmen no doubt appreciated the velvet glove, desired to display loyalty, and possessed no sacrosanct principle of objectivity to uphold. However, many also realized their limited leverage in demanding total respect for the Common Law principle protecting their right to print all nonlibellous matter. Specifically, in lacking a constitutional guarantee for free expression, it became significant that C.P.A.'s advisory committee (which met only sporadically with Chambers) boasted no equivalent of say a Lord Northcliffe—a mogul whose newspaper empire stretched across England, and whom many British parliamentarians, in judging as possessing the power to topple governments, dared not attack.[38] Possessing such influence, his London *Times*, as well as other major British newspapers run by those dubbed as Fleet Street's "press barons," sometimes deliberately flouted censors such as by printing news of Allied defeats that, in their view, would rally the populace.

By contrast, Chambers did not hesitate to request that the Secretary of State prohibit sources that he thought acted with open defiance. On 27 June 1916, he secured a ban upon the Sault Ste. Marie *Express* for declaring in an editorial: "No More Canadian Soldiers for the Front."[39] By the end of the war, unacceptable copy carried in *Le Bulletin* of Montreal, Quebec City's *La Croix*, and the Victoria *Week* produced identical results.[40] Likely Ottawa would not have approved the repression of Canada's most prominent newspapers, but it appeared that their editors and publishers were unwilling to take that chance. Rather than vociferously challenge, let alone defy Chambers, most of those who were reprimanded promptly acquiesced, sometimes to the point of apologizing profusely and pledging extra care in future. Instructive was the case of *Maclean's* magazine. Despite its nearly 80,000 subscribers, talk of suppression circulated until publisher J.B. Maclean removed a proposed story copied from the British press outlining the Allied defeat at Cambrai. In vain, Maclean tried to explain to the censor that Canadians, particularly a working class increasingly inclined to strike for higher wages to maintain pace with inflation, needed a jolt to their complacency. He noted that in England "a large section of labour...kept in a fool's paradise by the suppression of bad news" were organizing walkouts at munition factories, but "when the realities of the situation were brought home to them," they promptly performed an about face and put their shoulder to the wheel. Ignoring Maclean's apparently loyal intent, and letting it be known that "action" would follow if the account ran, Chambers prevailed in enforcing (and thus augmenting the authenticity of) his presumption of British citizens, due to their propinquity to the war zone, as better equipped than Canadians to cope with unsettling truths.[41]

Ultimately, even the upstart nationaliste publication, *Le Devoir*, tempered its tone. As pressure mounted upon Quebec to supply a decent number of recruits, and in light of discriminatory school language legislation, Regulation XVII, remaining enforced in Ontario, *Le Devoir's* founder, Henri Bourassa, set aside any initial support for the Entente cause. Having been denied liberty for their children at home, Bourassa argued that Quebecois were right to refuse to die for democracy overseas, especially in a struggle that, in order to contain Canadian contributions, he increasingly cast as serving British commercial interests. On several occasions, Chambers counselled the federal government towards suppression but was rebuffed by politicians who feared a violent backlash should the newspaper be prohibited.[42] Borden, for example, reasoned that "Bourassa would like nothing better" than to become a martyr.[43]

During the final year of hostilities, things changed dramatically. *Le Devoir*, though never advocating violent resistance to the Military Service Act, was nevertheless seen by many as having helped precipitate the Easter 1918 anti-draft riots. Among other sources, the Vancouver *Sun* speculated that the passage of PC 1241 the next month was "probably aimed at *Le Devoir*."[44] It is impossible to know whether Ottawa would have ultimately sanctioned a warrant, but recognizing Chambers's determination to push the matter, Bourassa concluded that his only option was "to submit," leaving "it to the future to decide whether it [was] in conformity with the very best interests of the country." Although not completely terminating criticism of the Military Service Act, *Le Devoir's* acting editor, Georges Pelletier, submitted to the censor in advance all potentially contentious copy, none of which, significantly, proved sufficiently dangerous to require threats of suppression against the paper.[45]

Possessing the determination and legislative means to coddle Canadians, Chambers always gave wide latitude to his mandate. Even when dealing with stories focusing upon Canada, he strengthened that distinction between a fiendish foe and the civilized nature of Anglo-Saxon culture. While German mistreatment of Allied P.O.W.s was permitted unlimited coverage, the Chief Censor outlawed reports mentioning any abuse perpetrated against enemy soldiers held in Canada. Typical of the stories he endorsed was the Montreal *Star's* description of a Christmas feast organized for German reservists imprisoned at Kingston's Fort Henry complete with presents and a decorated tree.[46] Accordingly, Chambers became especially agitated over a piece in the Chicago *Tribune* relaying the tale of an Otto Miller who claimed to have escaped from an internment camp north of Montreal. "We had no heat," alleged the former prisoner, "very little clothing...[and] the food was poor and scanty." At the censor's behest, Canadian papers ignored this account, and to prevent the possibility of retaliatory action against Dominion soldiers held overseas, arrangements were made (via Herbert Vanderhoof, a Chicago-based publicist with connections to the U.S. Secret Service who years earlier was hired by Ottawa to attract American immigrants and investment) for Chambers to supply under an alias a "few contradictory paragraphs" for a subsequent issue. Yet, beside concerns over Canadian P.O.W.s held abroad was public opinion at home for the *Tribune* circulated in several Manitoba and Southwest Ontario communities. Consequently, Chambers's rebuttal—which claimed that "all prisoners...[were] comfortably housed, well clad and receive[d] exactly the same rations as [Dominion] soldiers in training"— was also supplied to, and, under his direction, reported by several Canadian newspapers as a retraction by the American source.[47]

When it came to the picture of Canadian trainees or military life in general, equal, if not greater sensitivity was displayed. Chambers expressed considerable consternation after several sources reported upon a July 1916 uproar involving 30,000 recruits at Barrie's Camp Borden made to wait on a parade square in blazing heat for several hours until the Prime Minister arrived. That month, he issued a circular instructing editors to disregard anything reflecting badly upon the training regimen, explaining that "as an officer of long experience, I know that soldiers...are natural grumblers...."[48] This decree, Chambers's conviction that Johnny Canuck be regarded as part of a divine crusade against evil and sin, along with a desire to retain the public's perception of army discipline as improving the morality of men, meant that the soon-to-be prohibitionist homefront also heard scant reference to excessive drinking among trainees. Editors for the Greenwood *Lodge* and Enderby *Press* were prevented from reporting upon a riot involving inebriated soldiers at the Vernon, British Columbia, camp during which a provost marshal was killed.[49]

Hardly surprising was that unpleasant tales about front-line life were forbidden. The Ottawa *Journal* was reprimanded for carrying a rather graphic report from the well-known author, Robert W. Service, then in France as an ambulance driver and part-time syndicated columnist for several American sources. In an account mailed to and carried in tracts across the United States, Service talked of one survivor whose skin was "a blueish colour and cracked open in ridges." Responding to the charge that the article could "seriously interfere with recruiting," a contrite editor, P.D. Ross, assured Chambers that in future any other material bearing the Service by-line would receive the strictest of scrutiny.[50] If choosing to reprint soldier correspondence, Chambers insisted that newspapers convey a far more unsullied image. While letters from the front were checked by military authorities, and most troops practised self-censorship in order to allay homefront worries and endure their lot *like men*, some material painting a less than glorious view still slipped through. Editors were reminded of their liability for carrying messages that revealed military secrets or damaged enlistment. Some, therefore, took the precaution of screening letters before Chambers, such as Fred Field of the *Monetary Times* who was helping the Sterling Bank start a magazine containing material written by employees serving in France. Heartily endorsed by the Chief Censor were selections stating things such as "the trenches were not so bad"; but when it came to Private Bloxham's claim that "the man who said war was hell did not know anything about it, for it [was] far worse," Chambers insisted that the scissors be applied.[51] Moreover, sometimes the censor asked newspapers to carry certain letters, such as that sent to him from the family of an injured Lieutenant C.G. Power who told of hospital facilities where troops were supplied with "comfortable beds...cigarettes, chocolates [and] lemonade."[52]

Although some respectful overtures were made to those running Canada's mainstream press, no such gestures were offered by Chambers when it came to tracts from a neutral America, written in languages other than English or French, or espousing leftist philosophy. Of the 253 sources banned in Canada, 222 came from south of the border, 164 were foreign-language, and 93 advocated some variant of Marxism.[53]

From the neutral United States Canada received its lion's share of paci-fist and anti-British publications. In banning these papers, Chambers faced little or no opposition from his elected superiors. They agreed such tracts were inappropriate for distribution, saw little point in issuing warnings to sources printed outside the country, and reasoned that any efforts to control the American press could create far more of a diplomatic flap than enforc-ing acceptable opinion within Canada. In refusing to cut such sources any slack, Chambers also obtained widespread societal endorsement. Among the many expressions of support for his suppression of Jehovah's Witness publications was *Saturday Night*'s accusation that the organization was unquestionably funded by Germany because there was no other way it could print and distribute so much material[54]—a belief that, along with the group's tendency to proselytize its pacifistic message rather forcefully, explained its eventual subjugation under PC 2384. In fact, it was Canada's religious community that often enlightened Chambers as to the existence of several U.S. evangelical papers like the subsequently-banned *Apostolic Faith* that quoted from Matthew 5:39 ("…but whosoever shall smite thee on my right cheek, turn to him the other also…") to claim that true Christians could not participate in the conflict.[55]

Probably the boldest initiative taken against an anti-British American source came on 11 November 1916 when Chambers secured an order ban-ning the 14 newspapers comprising the William Randolph Hearst press empire. It was a measure for which he again received sweeping support, not the least of which came from Canada's fourth estate. Besides ideologi-cal considerations, Canadian newspaper proprietors had long loathed the Hearst chain for taking away business in some centres by supplying, unlike themselves, a Sunday edition.[56] But even if the motivations of some were partly tainted, there is no denying that these newspapers were controversial. In several editorials, the Hearst dailies argued that the Great War traced to Britain's inability to compete economically against Germany. Some of the articles, in fact, were written by William Bayard Hale, a former employee of Berlin's New York-based Press Bureau.[57] Chambers's warrant was delayed only because England's Colonial Office advised that repressive action taken prior to the American Presidential election on 10 November could provide anti-Wilsonian forces such as Hearst with ammunition.[58] Despite having run on the slogan *he kept us out of war*, the Democratic

President was regarded as sympathetic to Britain and more likely than Republican nominee Charles Hughes to bring America into the melee.

Once Washington declared war on 6 April 1917, Hearst, though stressing the conscription of material rather than men, nevertheless radically transformed the position of his newspapers. A typical editorial now read: "Let us make reprisals upon German towns...[and] also upon the bodies of the German leaders." Both the British and French responded by ending their embargoes against the Hearst dailies and Hearst's news wire service, but Chambers refused to budge, successfully arguing to his superiors that what was appropriate elsewhere did not necessarily apply in Canada. In particular, he pointed out that while Britain and France already enjoyed the luxury of conscription, the issue was far from settled in the Dominion, thus providing Hearst with a chance to undermine the policy through what Chambers cast as the "insidious" anti-draft message still permeating his tracts.[59] In fact, once the Chief Censor banned a source, rarely did he reconsider the order. Rather than constantly recheck newspapers that had already proven untrustworthy, he maintained the logical use of limited resources dictated that efforts be focused upon catching others who spread discontent—an approach that kept the Hearst press, as well as several other American publications that shifted their allegiance towards the Allies, out of Canada until 1 January 1920.[60]

Comprising a majority of prohibited sources, both from the United States and Canada, were those written in a foreign-language. In approaching these tracts with extra suspicion, Chambers revealed his attachment to the precepts of *Anglo conformity*, an imperialist-connected philosophy that revolved around defending the Dominion's British heritage, and, as such, made the country into a most fertile ground for wartime repression through its long-established characterization of various immigrant groups as inferior, distrustful and/or prone towards political extremism. Over a four-and-a-half year term, Chambers, in applying this creed to full effect, obtained prohibition orders against 56 German, 27 Russian, 20 Ukrainian, 16 Finnish and 8 Yiddish newspapers, as well as tracts published in Polish, Hindustani, Chinese, Italian, Greek, Hungarian, Swedish, Norwegian, Serbian, Estonian, Romanian, Dutch, Arabic, Lettish and Syrian.[61]

German publications from a neutral America were closely monitored and banned at the first sign of antipathy to the Allies. In Chambers's defence, Berlin ran an information office in New York, and in a number of these newspapers translators found it easy to identify a multitude of provocative statements. Representative of many was the prohibited St. Louis *Mississippi Blatter* that proclaimed "we love German *Kultur*, German ways, German song and German speech, and our thoughts fly over the ocean to the old Fatherland and we hope it will continue to give good German blows."[62]

Equally evident, however, was that no shortage of injustices resulted from censorship policies formed in large part by prejudicial assumptions. This was especially apparent with the German-Canadian press that, with the declaration of war, usually advised its readers to suppress their feelings should they differ from the majority, or, as in the case of Winnipeg's *Der Nordwesten*, claimed that it was the "duty of all those who call Canada their home to pick up arms." Still, through myriad comments and actions, most Anglo-Canadians demonstrated their agreement with newspapers like the Calgary *Herald* that maintained that "a man born in Germany and natural-ized in Canada is in 99 cases out of a 100 just as strongly German in his views and sympathies as if he was not naturalized."[63] Chambers shared such misgivings. In 1916, he told J.F. Livesay that when the war com-menced, authorities should have "seized control of these publications …placed them under government editors," demanded that they print in English, or, at the very least, in a dual-language format.[64]

Convinced that German-language tracts surreptitiously stoked treaso-nous tendencies in an inherently disloyal audience, Chambers held them to a higher standard of conduct than so-called Canadian newspapers. There was, for example, the *Berliner Journal*, a small publication started in 1859 to serve the German-speaking residents of Southwestern Ontario. Admittedly, it celebrated Teutonic culture, but the paper also "castigated Prussia" for its "militaristic attitude."[65] No matter, easily was the censor convinced of its sinister nature. In August 1915, A.C. Laut of the London *Advertiser* told him that the *Journal* wrote the war began because of a British-German commercial rivalry. Responding immediately, Chambers asked then Secretary of State Louis Coderre for a warrant to suppress its fur-ther publication but soon discovered the request ill-advised. Probably because he was of German background, local M.P. William G. Weichel came to the paper's defence, informing Chambers that the *Journal's* pub-lisher and editor, Motz, served as county sheriff and was considered by all in the community as a man of impeccable character. Ultimately, Chambers admitted to Motz that he had been "somewhat misrepresented," but still he refused to admonish Laut. Instead, he proceeded to remind the sheriff that such mistakes were apt to occur because "being of German extraction…[this] imposes upon you certain standards of carefulness which might not be expected of others."[66]

In late 1917, Chambers obtained a most active ally in his quest to have federal authorities severely restrict the freedoms enjoyed by publications printed in enemy languages—the Great War Veterans' Association [G.W.V.A.]. After facing bombs and bullets overseas, ex-soldiers, most of whom were sent home early due to wounds, showed less hesitation than civilians about taking direct action in order to keep enemy aliens in their *rightful place*. The following April and again in August 1918, several hundred veterans, along with some trainees, rampaged through downtown Toronto destroying shops and beating those who, because of their ethnic background, were assumed as sympathetic to the enemy.[67]

Fear over such violence prompted the Regina *Der Courier* to voluntarily switch to a dual-language format on 4 September 1918, a gesture that, however, failed to dissuade veterans from sacking its presses the subsequent week. With nearly 100,000 members by this time, and the G.W.V.A. leadership predicting more such action if appropriate language legislation did not materialize,[68] Borden despatched the Hon. J.A. Calder, who hailed from Saskatchewan, to the Prairies to assess the threat. "Suppression should take place without delay," he telegraphed back, "otherwise look for serious trouble" at the offices of *Der Nordwesten*.[69] Publicly, the Prime Minister rationalized the resulting PC 2381 as a measure to protect Germans. Yet clearly, the decision was fundamentally political, for given the choice between supporting the rights of the already maligned and abused Teuton or complying with demands issued by an organization representing the nation's returned heroes, any other outcome was simply wishful thinking.

G.L. Maron, the editor of *Der Nordwesten* (a man Chambers once described as "possessing a mentality free from the peculiar distortion which distinguishes that of the average Teuton"), reacted bitterly, pointing out to the Chief Censor that "the German farmer is contributing…a very large production of food stuffs, while others, for instance the Jews, who scarcely produce one bushel of grain and who are hardly considered a desirable addition to the business life of any country, are permitted to retain their papers."[70] Chambers, in fact, shared some of Maron's misgivings, having ordered the translation and suppression of several U.S.-based Yiddish publications, but this in no way softened his opinion with respect to German-language sources. Therefore, even when liberalized the following April in PC 703, the censor consistently sought to fully enforce PC 2381. For example, that month, under the provisions of PC 703, *The Courier* (the paper's name under PC 2381) started a literary magazine called *Der Plauderer*. To ensure compliance with every particular of the amendment, Chambers insisted that this latest publication be mailed separately to avoid any association with a tract distributing hard news—a decree that added substantially to Maron's costs. In explaining the decision to the Secretary of State, Chambers insisted that it was crucial to "draw the line very firmly" because "the individual of German origin cannot get it out of his head that laws are to be evaded, particularly if the evasion suits his purpose."[71]

An equally uncompromising campaign was launched during the latter stages of the war against left-wing publications. Prior to the October 1917 Russian Revolution, only two socialist newspapers, *Russkoye Slova* and *Novy Mir* of New York, were prohibited in Canada, the result of a personal request made by the Tsar's Ottawa-based Consul-General who pointed out that both received funding from America's Russian Soviet Bureau (*Novy Mir* was once edited by Nicholai Bukharin and Leon Trotsky).[72] But once a Communist government was installed in Petrograd, the Chief Censor, reflecting what quickly became pervasive fear over the red menace, adopted a far more proactive stance.

For years government authorities had denounced and suppressed radical unions, but towards the end of the war this took on special intensity. If the apparently all-powerful Tsar could be overthrown, then, many figured, the same was possible in Canada. Quickly, the country's still rather disorganized and overlapping secret service network was mobilized into action. The Royal North-West Mounted Police and Dominion Police placed operatives in socialist organizations and coordinated their activities with military intelligence, provincial and local constabulary forces, the

Immigration Branch, the Canadian Pacific Railway's Department of Investigation, various private detective firms, as well as a few U.S. government agencies. Besides often-alarmist reports received from such investigators (who, as with German-Americans, possibly exaggerated threats due to their economic self-interest, inexperience, and/or personal prejudice), anxiety over a possible leftist upsurge was also being fed by domestic socio-economic conditions. Encouraging working class militancy was cumulative inflation reaching approximately 75 per cent between 1915 and 1918; the conscription of men and not wealth; profiteering scandals with armament production; the refusal by the Imperial Munitions Board to adopt a fair wage policy; and labour's exclusion from various government war committees. Between 1914 and 1917, the number of days lost to strikes soared from 491,000 to 1.124 million—a trend that, as publisher J.B. Maclean asserted, no doubt drew considerable encouragement from the feeling among complacent and sheltered Canadians that victory was a forgone conclusion, but that several nervous officials instead cast as the first stage in the revolutionary process.

Certainly this doomsday scenario was stressed by many after a large civic strike rocked Winnipeg in 1918, the concessions from which labour won further popularized among several factions of the working-class a militant approach towards collective bargaining. Indeed, that September, Western Canadian labour leaders, who had long supported industrial unionism rather than supposedly elitist and conservative craft organizations backed by the Central Canadian dominated Trades and Labor Congress [T.L.C.], and who still harboured resentment over the T.L.C.'s failed strategy of running candidates in the 1917 federal election to protest conscription instead of opting for a general strike, initiated efforts to form their own and clearly more radically-inclined association. Even those appointed to uphold constituted authority appeared susceptible to the revolutionary wave. In 1918, police forces in ten cities formed unions; in Toronto and Montreal constables went as far as to abandon their posts.[73]

To counteract such trends, in October 1918 Ottawa initiated efforts to better coordinate secret service work by appointing C.H. Cahan as its Director of Public Safety, one whose assessment of the situation exhibited the then popular nativist-inspired belief that to stamp out revolutionary philosophy, one had to concentrate upon the radical alien. "Since the outbreak of the present war," he wrote in a preliminary report for the government, in early 1918 "groups of Russians, Ukrainians and Finns" held meetings "to direct revolutionary propaganda." Their membership in Toronto alone he estimated at 1,000 to 1,200. His ensuing contribution was PC 2384, banning 13 groups, the majority representing newcomers to Canada, and made it clear to other advocates of Marxist theory that they were best advised to keep their views private.[74]

Prime Minster Borden shared such misgivings over the potential spread of this *political cancer*. Following the Treaty of Brest-Litovsk between Soviet and German forces on 7 May 1918, he authorized the despatch of 600 Canadians to Murmansk and Archangel to help prevent Allied supplies given to the Tsar's faltering army from falling into Bolshevik hands. After the armistice, 4,000 Canadians joined a larger force situated just outside of Vladivostok. Officially, their aim was to enforce an export embargo against Germany until a comprehensive peace treaty could be signed, but these troops also were made available to White forces supporting the Russian monarchy. On several occasions while overseas to help negotiate the Versailles agreement, Borden telegraphed acting Prime Minister Thomas White to advise that the Bolshevists, through what became known as the Comintern, were successfully building support throughout Europe and would soon likely undertake a major North American thrust.[75] In displaying his depths of loathing for and anxiety over this new enemy, Borden also endorsed an Allied plan allowing the German army to retain 50,000 machine guns so it could crush that country's increasingly potent socialist Sparticus movement.[76]

Newspapers also mirrored tensions over galloping socialism and the belief that behind the problem lay the radical alien, if not as leading the movement, then certainly as constituting the bulk of its shock troops. In its coverage of countless strikes, the press gave prominence to those with foreign-sounding names.[77] Strengthening the association between socialism and disloyalty was the accusation that the Reds and Huns worked in tandem. Lenin, it was noted, had lived in Germany and was allowed to leave Berlin for Petrograd, the hope being he would stir up enough trouble to get Russia out of the war. The Treaty of Brest-Litovsk that followed soon after provided circumstantial legitimacy to this theory. Headlines in the Winnipeg *Telegram* charged that the "Bolshevists [were] the Admitted Tools of Hun Intrigue."[78] Even after the armistice, *Maclean's* wrote that German financing lay behind recent labour troubles across North

America. "After all," it argued in an expose identifying an enemy spy ring based in New York led by a mysterious foreigner named Sateria Nuarteva, "we must recognize that it will pay Germany to spend millions to weaken Canada and the United States by seriously limiting the quantity and increasing the cost of production."[79]

In sharing this belief about a traitorous foreign-dominated movement, the Chief Censor fully capitalized upon his powers to defend constituted authority and the supposedly besieged Anglo-Canadian way of life. Beyond sympathetic public opinion, his ability to conduct such a crusade was made possible by time extensions to the War Measures Act, initially until the Versailles Treaty was ratified by Canada's Parliament, and then again until the end of 1919 in order to provide Ottawa with the necessary power to reorganize the national economy for peacetime production. Consequently, whereas all forms of military censorship (such as reports on troop movements) were revoked by December 1918, controls over political opinion remained very much in evidence during the post-armistice period. Of the 253 censorship warrants issued by Chambers, 70 were obtained after 11 November 1918.[80]

From his elected superiors the Chief Censor faced virtually no resistance when it came to banning scores of left-wing American publications. Typical of the tracts he prohibited was the *International Socialist Review* that Secretary of State Martin Burrell concurred was unacceptable in Canada because of its endorsement of solidarity strikes, as well as for leading a campaign to release fellow travellers Thomas Mooney and Warren Billings, who were incarcerated for allegedly plotting to plant bombs at a 1916 San Francisco preparedness parade.[81]

Equal success was enjoyed by Chambers when it came to prohibiting foreign-language socialist newspapers, definitely not an astounding trend when one notes that by 1917, numerous left-wing foreigners—especially Ukrainians and Finns—were being interned, even by County Court judges who, often without hard proof, removed from the community those they deemed as political threats.[82] Admittedly, within some ethnic groups there existed strong left-wing factions. In the case of the Ukrainians, perhaps starting with the migration of the outspoken Kyrilo Genyk in the early 1890s, the militancy bred within this largely peasant population by desperate economic circumstances and political repression under Russian monarchs was carried to Canada, and once there, fed off the juxtaposition between hopes for a better life and the reality of racism that condemned these people to the most menial jobs and urban slums. In 1907, the Ukrainian Social Democratic Party [U.S.D.P.] was founded in Canada and gained adherents by offering not just a forum for venting frustrations, but also a range of social activities and rudimentary welfare services.[83] Such success, however, also brought unwanted attention, especially during the war when the association's newspaper, the Winnipeg-based *Robotchyi Narod*, responded to hostilities in August 1914 by condemning militarism, accusing French authorities of murdering the well-known pacifist, Jean Jaures, and quoted freely from the German socialist, Karl Liebknecht, anti-war tendencies that resulted in some top U.S.D.P. officials being interned.[84]

Notwithstanding the arrests, the U.S.D.P. continued to gain strength. By 1918, the *Narod* went from being a monthly to a bi-weekly journal, while the same year, the U.S.D.P.'s membership peaked at around 2,500. Accounting for such fortunes was the collapse of Austrian rule in Eastern Galicia and the hope that the Russian Revolution would produce an independent Ukraine since Lenin had promised to respect its declared borders. Therefore, in 1917 the party leadership denounced a new Central Rada in their homeland as a product of bourgeois Kerenskyism and demanded recognition of the more militant workers' government formed in Kharkov. Despite many Ukrainian-Canadian socialists deviating from this extreme stance and backing the Rada, those like Chambers supported, and in fact helped lead, a campaign for *carte blanche* action against this ethnic group who, as internment policy showed, were already among the least trusted. In fact, his dogged pursuit, which resulted in the Secretary of State's office being supplied with reams of translator reports identifying practically any left-wing rhetoric, not only helped convince authorities to quash both the *Narod* along with its more moderate rival, the Toronto-based *Robitnyche Slovo*, but also played a role in paving the way for legislative bans against both the U.S.D.P. and the Ukrainian language, thus repressing as well, at least for a couple of months, a number of anti-communist and Catholic Ukrainian papers.[85]

Chambers was acutely aware of radical tendencies in Finland; its general strikes over the previous generation, its desire to rid itself of Tsarist domination, and its ill-fated Bolshevist rebellion in early 1918, revealed a pattern that he and several other officials stressed required the most prudent policing of Canadian Finns lest they try to achieve their revolutionary goals in the Dominion. It was true that within six years of its founding in 1911, the Finnish Socialist Organization of Canada [F.S.O.C.] encompassed perhaps 60 per cent of this immigrant group's population. Yet, like the U.S.D.P., its popularity was not attributable to some genetic propensity towards radicalism, but derived from economic and social discrimination in Canada combined with F.S.O.C. halls that functioned as social centres and dispensers of welfare—factors that failed to register with Chambers.[86]

While the Chief Censor prohibited a number of left-wing U.S. Finnish publications, for much of the war there was no Canadian-based newspaper to concern him because in 1915, *Tyokansa*, based in Sudbury, went bankrupt. Towards the end of hostilities, however, F.S.O.C. members in Sudbury and Port Arthur/Fort William began *Vapaus*. To increase his chances of discovering unacceptable material in its pages, Chambers assigned to monitor *Vapaus* a translator recommended by J.A. Mustonen, the editor of a rival right-wing Finnish newspaper called the *Canadan Uuitiset*. Despite these efforts, it proved impossible to make a case for repression under PC 1241 because *Vapaus* kept its criticisms of the war and conscription rather muted. Soon enough, however, both PC 2381 and PC 2384 solved the censor's dilemma. Taking further advantage of the situation, Chambers, in order to provide Finns with the proper ideological guide, reached an agreement in December 1918 with Mustonen allowing the *Uuitiset* to republish under a dual column format, while *Vapaus*, he insisted, remained banned until the following April.[87]

Relatively speaking, Chambers was satisfied with Ottawa's approach toward radical American and foreign-language tracts. Yet, sometimes he grew impatient over the federal government's hesitation to move as decisively against major Anglo-Canadian socialist sources for fear of further alienating a mainstream union movement disgruntled enough to run candidates in the December 1917 federal election. The *Western Clarion*, the Vancouver-based organ of the Socialist Party of Canada, was first brought to Chambers's attention in November 1917 by the Deputy Postmaster General. Throughout that month and the next, it minced no words over conscription, claiming that workers were "being scientifically slaughtered in a fight" having no relevance to their "class interests." Chambers sought a warrant but was rebuffed by Secretary of State Martin Burrell who told him of Ottawa's unwillingness to sanction such an extreme response during an election campaign.[88] Therefore, the following January, Chambers again sought a suppression order, submitting among other proof, a story accusing the United States of entering the war for economic gain. Continued reluctance from his elected superiors eventually prompted a different approach. During a trip west in September 1918, the Chief Censor visited the Pender Street office of the newspaper to make a direct appeal to its editor but, to his dismay, ended up meeting "several men...[who] professed an ignorance as to the *Western Clarion*...." Once more he beseeched Burrell, this time pointing out with dramatic flair about confronting "seven or eight men of a rough and most decidedly cut-throat type...[who were] accustomed to methods of avoiding giving information in the witness box." Finally, later that month, after nearly a year of lobbying to ban this source, the passage of PC 2384 provided Chambers with some satisfaction.[89]

His contentment was short-lived. In January 1919, a publication called *The Red Flag* surfaced in Vancouver. The location and timing of its appearance, along with the fact that its editor's name was concealed, led Chambers to surmise correctly that this was the *Clarion* in disguise. During the Winnipeg General Strike of May-June 1919, he told Burrell that Major-General Ketchen, commanding troops in the area, saw this source being distributed by those labelled as chief rabble rousers.[90] But before he could obtain another warrant, the Royal North-West Mounted Police [R.N.W.M.P.] reported that *The Red Flag* had most likely been replaced by the *Indicator*. The ensuing request for suppression was rejected because in this latest paper, explained the Secretary of State, one found "a complete absence of revolutionary buncombe and a marked disposition to stick to a discussion of labour and socialistic issues along more academic lines." While Chambers was pleased that "the efforts of authorities" eventually produced "a salutary political effect," he continued to assert to little avail that the best policy remained to ban, without exception, all leftist tracts whose mere presence encouraged subversive elements.[91]

In fact, federal officials, despite their fears over internal subversion, realized the necessity of sometimes restraining Chambers in his quest to control press copy. For example, the censor worried that years of disappointment under national economic policy such as high tariffs might make farmers susceptible to radical rhetoric. In 1916, the Canadian Council of Agriculture—reflecting such discontent as well as anger over Ottawa's wartime exhortations that farmers produce more with less agricultural labour—introduced a platform that included the nationalization of public utilities, elimination of monopolies, a progressive income tax, an end to all land speculation and lower tariffs. In April 1918, rural Canada was seething after PC 819 apparently cancelled draft exemptions for farmers' sons. The next month, 5,000 agriculturalists from Ontario and Quebec marched upon Parliament in protest.[92] To check such trends, Chambers attempted to utilise legislation at his disposal, but the Secretary of State determined that such an uncompromising approach would only aggravate bad feelings among too wide a cross-section of the population. For instance, the Chief Censor unsuccessfully lobbied for a warrant against the Alberta *Non-Partisan* because alongside its condemnations of federal policies was an article sympathizing with Russian peasants for challenging "autocracy."[93]

Since Canada lacked a Bill or Charter of Rights, in many cases the decision about whether or not to apply statutory restrictions against expression came down to political considerations. With regard to left-wing newspapers, those to whom Chambers answered proved far more willing to follow his advice when it came to American and foreign-language sources. Probably it was surmised that no way existed to influence the content of U.S. publications, and with both types of sources, politicians could anticipate little political fallout, especially after the Wartime Elections Act removed the franchise from numerous readers of non-Anglo tracts. Ottawa's readiness to act as arbitrarily with major English-Canadian socialist newspapers was sometimes lacking. When it came to such sources, Chambers confidentially complained to a friend in the Toronto police department that it seemed the government "feared that the implementation of repressive measures would give anarchistic and Bolshevistic agitators an excuse to claim that they [were] being subject to persecution."[94]

The goal of restricting leftist influence without needlessly creating martyrs also seemed to play a role in the federal government's prosecution of socialists arrested under the War Measures Act. Telling was the fact that though thousands of Canadians belonged to organizations banned under PC 2384, only 214 were formally charged between autumn 1918 and June 1919, 35 of whom were incarcerated.[95] This is not to trivialize state repression; several organizations experienced police raids, while those such as Michael Chartinoff, editor of *Robotchyi Narod*, was fined $1000 and given a three-year jail term.[96] Yet, if Ottawa had desired, the overall results could have been far worse. What the arrest pattern implies is that authorities concentrated upon making examples out of the socialist leadership, along with perhaps those considered as most vocal in their radicalism, while a stiff (and often physical) warning from the police or a moderate fine were used to intimidate a majority of rank and file membership into obeying the law.[97] Moreover, progressive-minded members of the Union government, namely former Liberals T.A. Crerar and N.W. Rowell, convinced most of their new political colleagues that not always was a strong-arm legislative approach most appropriate. The influential Rowell, who served as Clerk of the Privy Council, cautioned the government that it ran the risk of losing practically all support from (and perhaps even radicalizing) mainstream labour if it initiated or maintained bans under PC 2384 against comparatively moderate groups like the Social Democratic Party of Canada [S.D.P.C.], which addressed itself primarily to academic discussions of left-wing theory and endorsed change through peaceful means.[98]

In protesting against what he perceived as the government's generally soft treatment of subversives, its decision the previous December to legalize the S.D.P.C., and its refusal to transform the Public Safety Branch from a policy-advising and coordinating agency into Canada's premier spy organization with at least 100 detectives, C.H. Cahan, in January 1919, tendered his resignation.[99] Newspapers quoted his anger over "failed...support" for efforts to "eradicate pernicious propaganda,"[100] a protest that produced empathic noises from those such as Ontario Provincial Police Superintendent Joseph Rogers who charged that "when the labour movement cracks the whip the government falls in."[101] Chambers also desired a less flexible strategy, but ever the dutiful public servant, he kept his criticisms to private correspondence.

Soon enough, however, liberal nuances within the government waned and the unbending strategy advocated by Chambers and Cahan gained more strength. In May 1919, a most ominous threat to constituted authority was perceived in Winnipeg where 30,000 workers left their jobs in a general strike. Sympathetic walkouts followed in Vancouver, Edmonton, Calgary, Regina, Saskatoon, Brandon, Fort William, Port Arthur, Sault Ste. Marie, Hamilton, Montreal, Halifax and about 20 other smaller centres. Although the roots of the Winnipeg strike related to long-standing grievances over union recognition and wage scales, the scope of the event combined with the fiery oratory of the socialistically-inclined strike leadership, led many to panic about a Soviet-style government taking power in the city.

The legislative response rang sharp and clear. On 6 June 1919, Section 41 was added to the Immigration Act permitting the deportation of those, including unnaturalized British subjects, who destroyed property, advocated or defended "riot or public disorder," or, at any time after 4 May 1919, belonged to an organization mentioned in or conceivably falling under PC 2384 (thus establishing *ex post facto* guilt). Yet, despite most of the strike leadership in Winnipeg being British, Ottawa, in conforming to racist preconceptions, only applied this statute against "Russian" participants — meaning, in fact, a wide variety of Slavs. To expedite their removal, hearings were held *in camera*, a policy also adopted to avoid attracting attention from the liberally-inclined who, the government believed, would have loudly protested the denial of counsel or witnesses for the accused along with verdicts often resulting in their return, in the case of Slavs, to areas controlled by White forces areas where imprisonment or even execution loomed as possibilities.[102]

Those managing the strike in Winnipeg faced charges under Section 133 of the Criminal Code (which related to seditious conspiracies) and received jail terms ranging between one and two years. In order to dissuade others from copying their actions, in July 1919, Section 98 was added to the Criminal Code. It established a maximum penalty of 20 years' imprisonment against anyone printing, publishing, writing, editing, issuing, or offering for sale "any book, newspaper, periodical, pamphlet, picture, paper, circular, card, letter, writing, print, publication, or document of any kind in which it is taught, advocated, advised or defended...that the use of force, violence, terrorism or physical injury be used as a means of accomplishing any governmental, industrial or economic change."[103] Finally, in November, Ottawa further enhanced the country's secret service capabilities by amalgamating the Dominion and R.N.W.M. Police forces into a better funded, coordinated and manned Royal Canadian Mounted Police. This in turn set the stage for the emergence of a permanent peacetime "surveillance state"[104] that, along with repressive legislation, was used to crush dissent under far less justifiable circumstances than wartime or the post-armistice leftist surge.

Whether or not a Chief Censor existed, most mainstream Canadian publications would have cast the Great War in quixotic terms. However, Chambers ensured that the sanitized and idealized version of army life and combat also dominant in official despatches relayed from overseas, remained practically the sole interpretation presented to civilians. Ceaselessly he laboured in this post, viewing the job, like his venture against Riel, as an opportunity to perform sacred work on behalf of the Empire. To achieve maximum impact, he issued friendly advice to so-called Canadian newspapers deemed patriotic; threatened and thus managed to cleanse a number of others viewed as having strayed too far from the censorship regulations; banned scores of dubious American sources; and endlessly hounded both the ethnic and left-wing press, which to him, as well as a nativistic Canada, served and encouraged those bent upon replacing British democracy with a foreign dictatorship.

Reasonable grounds existed for many of his edicts. Lives could be lost if sensitive military information leaked, while the massive mobilization required of both men and materiel during the Great War certainly made the maintenance of high morale an important consideration. Given these concerns, many newspapers, both foreign- and English-language, and especially from a neutral America, carried copy genuinely inappropriate for distribution in wartime Canada. Moreover, by the armistice, the government, in light of mounting strike activity, was, as labour historian Gregory Kealey wrote, not being entirely "irrational" in regarding Bolshevism as a danger.[105]

Nonetheless, it is impossible to sweep aside the fact that in the name of supporting Anglo-Canadian mores as well as the Empire in its struggle, Chambers outlawed news acceptable in Great Britain, consistently assumed guilt by ethnic affiliation, and even managed at times to exceed the mandate placed at his disposal by repressive legislation. Internment policy and various Orders in Council demonstrate that his elected superiors were also stern, but at least in some circumstances—such as with *Le Devoir*, the *Non-Partisan*, and in the case of a few leftist tracts—they understood that a more subtle approach was required. Yet, despite any pragmatically-motivated respites from repression, on the whole, the effects as well as the legacies of what became a rather unyielding censorship programme were quite harsh. In the case of ethnic and political minorities, Chambers, by identifying *subversives*, helped lay the groundwork for ruthless legislation and a more elaborate secret service. And as far as society-at-large was concerned, the censor's nanny-like demeanour acted in concert with propagandists to widen a perceptual gulf between civilians and soldiers, the painful effects of which reverberated long after the guns fell silent.

4

The Censor's Extended Scope

"Why," the Honourable Charles Murphy asked Prime Minister Borden in early 1917, were "temperance books by Arthur Mees" (*The Fiddlers*, *Defeat* and *The Parasite*) able to circulate in England but banned in Canada? The action, Sir Robert replied, was requested by officials in London who believed Mees's description of British society as drunk-infested could convince Canadian farmers, especially in a land contemplating national prohibition, to reduce efforts at providing increased wheat and barley exports at a time when the German U-Boat campaign was moving the mother country towards coupon rationing. Reverend Benjamin Spence, leader of the country's main temperance organization, the Dominion Alliance, was incensed. "Canadians are no children," he complained, "and neither is their loyalty of such a quality that it cannot stand the strain of the knowledge these books give of old country conditions." Nowhere else "in the civilized world," he pointed out, were they prohibited.[1]

Having already acted on numerous occasions as a nanny for a population he viewed as particularly prone to shock, Ernest Chambers steadfastly supported the British. He reminded the Secretary of State that news received in 1914 about drunkenness among the First Division at Salisbury

Plain brought murmurings from temperance advocates about whether England was worth saving. Turning to Mees's work, he asserted that its "very extreme and gruesome view of the…drink situation in the mother country," was not only capable of undermining current food control efforts in Canada, but also its last-ditch recruiting initiatives. "No parent," he warned, "would willingly allow a son to proceed overseas" after reading accounts such as of "a Canadian soldier, helplessly drunk, at King's Cross station…tearing, crumpling up, and eating one pound notes."[2]

Thus the order stood and in mid 1918 resulted in Spence's arrest by the Ontario Provincial Police for possessing several copies of *The Fiddlers*. True to form, Chambers recommended a tough prosecution. However, a more politic Justice Minister Doherty decided it imprudent to incarcerate a clergyman who lauded Canadian soldiers as "the flower of our Anglo-Saxon manhood." As a result, Doherty advised Ontario's Attorney-General that Ottawa would not oppose dropping the matter (the eventual outcome) hoping that just the experience of having been arrested would convince Spence to act with more circumspection in future.[3]

Still, pragmatic intervention in this case did not undermine a general pattern where Chambers, just as with newspapers, exerted massive control over the contents of books encountered by Canadians. From the censor's office circulars were dispatched to leading book distributors and sellers across the country outlining regulations and soliciting help in identifying objectionable sources. The loyalty of such parties, combined with the knowledge that heavy fines and/or imprisonment could result from disseminating inappropriate matter, shortly brought dozens of books and pamphlets, mostly from America, to the Chief Censor's attention. Some material, such as all items released by the Open Court Publishing Company of Chicago, was banned for candidly expressing pro-German sympathies, books that included *What Could Germany Do for Ireland?* and *Germany Misjudged*.[4] With other books, the perceived danger related to a too realistic treatment of warfare. Before the L.W. Walter Company of Chicago was permitted to export Thomas Russell's *Europe's Greatest World War* to Canada, several less than uplifting photographs of Allied wounded were excised, as well as an illustration of a steel pencil that, when dropped from an airplane, would "penetrate a man from head to foot." Chambers was particularly enraged over Andreas Latzkoto's *Men in War*, published in New York by Boni and Livewright. Despite its distribution in wartime America where the New York *Post* expressed admiration for its "authenticity," he labelled the author an "abnormal neurotic" and outlawed the work for depictions such as of "two men taking turns at pulling a spurred boot out of another's head...."[5] Perhaps such material did cross the line of suitability, but hyper-sensitivity about conveying the right picture even had the Chief Censor insisting upon the removal of a couple of humorous passages about officers from F. McKelvey Bell's jingoistic *First Canadians in France* for fear of undermining discipline among fresh recruits.[6]

No means of communication escaped the scrutiny of Canadian censorship. On 2 August 1914, with the prospect of war imminent, Ottawa, acting upon plans drawn up six months earlier by the Committee on Imperial Defence, passed an Order in Council permitting the military to place personnel at international cable and wireless facilities, and, if necessary, to assume control of telephone lines.[7] These operations were directed by Lieutenant-Colonel Charles Frederick Hamilton. Initially he took orders from Militia as well as Naval Service headquarters in Ottawa along with the British War Office, and after June 1915, Hamilton also coordinated his efforts with Chambers. By examining cablegrams to and from points outside Canada, it was hoped to detect espionage activities, sabotage schemes, as well as companies trading with the enemy.[8] Only allowed for transmission therefore were messages indicating the sender's address; written in English, French or an approved code; not making reference to the position, movement or proper name of battalions, ships, or any other item of military importance; and over which cable operators possessed "no doubt."[9]

Although such safeguards failed to uncover spy rings or serious breaches of security, throughout the war, their necessity remained unquestioned. What did draw criticism, however, was the fact that on its own, the military-run system proved inadequate. Initially, no supervision was established over purely domestic transmissions, and during the first year of the war, this situation permitted information on troop transports, gold shipments and port schedules to reach newspapers whose editors often printed what they must have, or conveniently, presumed as permissable exceptions to the censorship guidelines. Thus, only months after creating a Chief Press Censor's post, the federal government provided Chambers, in PC 2073, with the authority to control Canadian-based landlines, and, at the same time, transferred to his office the administration of telephone surveillance.

The interpersonal skills the Chief Censor sometimes exhibited when dealing with newspaper editors also became evident in his conduct toward those managing inland telegraph and telephone companies. A lack of departmental funds and personnel, combined with the task of shattering the influence exerted by those of dubious allegiance, convinced Chambers to adopt a collegial disposition; rather than simply cite his legal powers, Chambers astutely drew upon the theme of loyalty and acquired the voluntary and even enthusiastic cooperation of those directing these sectors. At a considerable cost and without complaint, the presidents of the Grand Trunk, Canadian Pacific, Great North Western and Anglo American telegraph networks, instructed their employees, after the censor's request, to analyze countless cablegrams.[10]

Technically-speaking, the most critical aspect of inland cable surveillance involved controlling references to troop trains, ships, the location of arsenals or any other matter of military significance. Under Chambers's tutelage, sometimes this formal aspect of censorship was moulded to reinforce a particular understanding of events. For example, not only were the departure dates of merchant ships refused transmission, but also any wire service report saying that they shot at German U-boats.[11] Officially, the aim was to conceal Allied firepower, but such general information was well known to the enemy. Clearly, when describing sea battles and especially the sinking of a cargo vessel, Chambers wanted newspapers to arouse public furore by conveying the image of a heinous foe preying upon unarmed boats.

Not content to wait for cable employees to stumble across espionage rings, the Chief Censor instructed that operators meticulously inspect thousands of messages sent or received by potential traitors, the vast majority of whom were targeted because of their non-British background. Besides focusing upon Germans (and identifying a few individuals attempting to send money via the United States to family members overseas), Chambers directed that extensive efforts be centred in British Columbia. There, Hindus and Sikhs were suspected of conspiring to help anti-colonial factions in India, while the local Sino population was assumed as sympathetic to Germany because of friendly overtures by Berlin to Chinese Republican rebels who supported neutrality and renounced Peking's 1917 alliance with the Entente powers. During the war, Chambers prohibited four American newspapers representing the former and three espousing the latter position.[12]

As with his conduct towards other non-Anglo groups, the zeal with which the Chief Censor harassed Canada's East Indian population reflected and derived strength from long-established nativism. Condemned as dirty, diseased and unassimilable, the arrival in Vancouver of 4,700 Sikhs and Hindus during 1906 and 1907, played a fundamental role in precipitating major anti-Asiatic riots. Ottawa's response, drawn up by the then Deputy Minister of Labour, William Lyon Mackenzie King, assuaged public fury by demanding that all future East Indian migrants arrive via continuous voyage, a formidable request considering that no direct sea routes existed between these two members of the Empire. The most notable consequence of this measure occurred in July 1914 when, after a month-long stand-off, 376 Sikhs crowded on board the *Komagata Maru* were expelled from Canadian waters by the country's only active warship *H.M.S. Rainbow*.[13]

Such deep-rooted racism against people whose mere presence was perceived as a threat to Anglo-Canadian society was intensified by wartime pressures towards conformity. Still, it simplifies matters to cast bigotry as the sole reason for distrust. In 1907, Ottawa began receiving despatches from the Indian Home Office and London-based officials about Hindu and Sikh revolutionaries travelling abroad to garner support from expatriates for their crusade to oust the British Raj. In response, two years later, the Immigration Branch acquired the services of Colonel J. Hopkinson, formerly of the Calcutta Police, to monitor Canadian East Indians. He discovered a small network of anti-colonial militants extending up from San Francisco and Seattle into Victoria and Vancouver. Moreover, in 1913, some East Asian Canadians allied with the radical India-based Ghadar (Mutiny) party that openly advocated violence against the British. The next year, Tarkat Das of Vancouver was arrested for trying to smuggle arms to India, along with Bhag and Balwant Singh, respectively president and priest of a Sikh temple also in that city where, to a mixed response from parishioners, Indian nationalism became part of the dogma.[14] With the declaration of war, Sikh and Hindu radicals talked about a golden opportunity to launch an armed campaign for the liberation of their homeland since most British troops would relocate to Europe. That October, many Canadians undoubtedly concluded such heightened militancy had reached their shores when in broad daylight, outside a Victoria courthouse, Hopkinson was gunned down by a Sikh extremist.[15]

Through contacts with the Immigration Branch, Chambers kept close tabs on developments within Canada's 2,000 strong East Indian community (a number halved in less than a decade due to racism as well as the desire of these people to re-unite with family members who had emigrated to America, where, they also felt, better economic opportunities awaited). Soon after assuming the post of Chief Censor, Chambers was supplied with a report from British Intelligence identifying 58 worldwide addresses of key Sikh and Hindu conspirators. Although not a single location was in Canada, Chambers told cable companies to delay and examine all messages sent or received by those bearing Indian-sounding names. Given recent events, perhaps the action was initially justified, but quickly it became apparent that almost all messages were between points in British Columbia and related to job prospects. In fact, by August 1916, Dominion Police Commissioner, Colonel Percy Sherwood (who as shown earlier by the fears he expressed over a German-American invasion was not inclined to lightly dismiss potential hazards), told Chambers that he believed the surveillance was no longer necessary.[16] Nevertheless, the Chief Censor, motivated by an imperialist fervour to crush anti-colonials, and, due to the Hopkinson assassination, convinced of numerous traitors still lurking among these foreigners, sought from cable companies ongoing blanket coverage—not just until the armistice was signed, but for more than a year beyond that point, until the very day his job ended.

So far as the derisively dubbed *John Chinaman* was concerned, ever since arriving as cheap railway labour in the late nineteenth century, accusations abounded about his importation of disease, urban slums, organized crime, opium dens, and the "white slave trade." Therefore, to control the arrival of these people following the completion of the Canadian Pacific Railway, the government, in 1885, began applying head taxes (which, by

1903, increased ten fold to $500) and approved the practice of its medical inspectors to exclude numerous Asiatics on the specious and obviously racist grounds that they were particularly prone to eye disease.[17] Ironically, however, the catalyst connecting sinophobia to war-related concerns came courtesy of China's Canadian Consul-General who, in mid 1914, informed Ottawa that rebel forces intent upon destroying all vestiges of monarchy and establishing a republican form of government had travelled abroad to obtain money and weapons. Accordingly, he requested that federal authorities prohibit the sale of arms and ammunition to Canada's Chinese population who, as a result, promptly became a target of police surveillance.[18]

Chambers joined the picture three years later. When a provisional administration of Chinese warlords allied with the Entente nations, he quickly acted to suppress those opposing their right to govern — namely the Canadian followers of Republican leader, Dr. Sun Yat-Sen, who belonged to a group called the Chinese Nationalist League. In pursuing this policy, clearly Chambers's motivation derived in part from racist preconceptions about proverbial Chinese treachery and deceit. He told Admiral R.N. Stephens, the Director of Naval Service, that in the United States, thousands of Chinese, even if not active League members, were "more or less identified with German propagandists." Besides banning several publications received from America by Canadian-based Nationalist League members, thousands of telegrams involving any member of this racial group were intercepted, almost all of which, it soon became clear, were devoid of political commentary, or, at the very worst, concerned efforts by some republican adherents to establish new branches. Despite the innocuous pattern prevailing for months, Chambers assured cable companies that their efforts here were of great value, explaining that "many...travellers have stated the Chinese are pro-German...and at the bottom of the whole trouble is a desire by Berlin to keep the East in turmoil."[19]

The Chinese Consul-General in Vancouver was among those believed untrustworthy because he supposedly gave the editor of the New Republic — one of the Nationalist League's prohibited American-based magazines — a "clean bill of health." Yet the evidence uncovered actually pointed in the opposite direction, for correspondence between Vancouver and Peking showed that the consulate tried to prevent money from reaching places held by Republican rebels.[20] Only towards the very end of the war was Chambers able to show some justification for more than a year of intense scrutiny. In September 1918, the Nationalist League (along with its sister organization, the Chinese National Reform Association), was suppressed under PC 2384 following the assassination the previous month of Peking's Interior Minister during a visit to Victoria. Sun Yat-Sen's Canadian supporters vigorously denied sanctioning, let alone having any involvement with this incident, and no hard evidence existed to demonstrate otherwise. Ignoring such *trivialities*, Chambers, in responding to the murder, bombarded his superiors with provocative quotes about the Peking government clipped from the pages of the already-banned *New Republic*, an effort which, it is safe to assume, helped sway politicians also concerned about maintaining good inter-Allied relations to err on the side of caution.[21]

Telegraph surveillance was also employed by the Chief Censor to contain threats to constituted authority posed by socialists. Fearing that the Bolshevists were attempting to export their revolution, Chambers, after October 1917, instructed cable companies to stop all messages from the new Soviet government or its North American representatives—the only exception being those communiques urging some key Canadian socialists to emigrate and help establish a workers' government in Petrograd.[22] Furthermore, while relaxing the enforcement of military-related censorship over telegraph wires soon after the armistice, Chambers resolutely maintained his crusade to manage political ideology by utilizing a loophole that did not formally end controls over cable transmissions until every belligerent ratified the Treaty of Versailles. Throughout much of 1919, he had telegraph companies examine all incoming and outgoing messages involving Finns living in the Port Arthur-Fort William vicinity, some of which he forwarded to immigration officials who, if agreeing upon the existence of radical proclivities, often initiated deportation proceedings.[23]

Meanwhile, in attempting to scan over 1.5 million miles of telephone wire, Chambers directed that operators concentrate upon lines emanating from locations frequented by Germans, as well as long-distance calls made by those whose surname indicated possible sympathy for the enemy. In early 1917, such a classification also came to include Greeks, many of whom, Chambers hypothesized, were acting on behalf of Teutonic interests in response to Berlin's promise to support, if triumphant, pro-monarchical Athenian forces. Phone company directors, responding to legal obligations cleverly couched by Chambers within patriotic entreaties, pledged a supreme effort. Still, they also made clear that with a volume of calls requiring over 250 operators in Montreal alone, effective surveillance, at least over local conversations, without a specific and manageable number of individuals to focus upon, was nearly impossible.[24]

Accepting that the quantity and anonymous nature of telephone conversations made the phone company's plight far more problematic than that confronting telegraph firms, Chambers, once being assured that transnational communications were monitored, devoted less active attention to this facet of censorship. From time-to-time he provided general classifications of people upon whom he hoped operators could devote extra attention, but did not go to the trouble of supplying a comprehensive list of names that, since conceivably including entire ethnic groups, might well have run into the hundreds of thousands. As well, he realized that individuals desiring to evade scrutiny needed only to turn to a public phone. With this aspect of censorship, Chambers behaved in a more reactive manner, issuing relatively few directives and choosing to wait for operators (or others) to stumble across peculiarities. When reported, he responded swiftly, but to his disappointment, the results usually proved less than satisfactory, and, on a few occasions, even embarrassing. For example, in May 1917, W.H. Hobbs, Secretary to the Grand Trunk Railway president, told Chambers of an employee who, when calling his wife in Ottawa from Montreal, tapped into another discussion. "It seemed to be between a clerk and his employer," wrote Hobbs, "the latter instructing that someone meet the 9:20 train tomorrow as there would be some confidential mail on it. He then said to find out when the steamship *Baymaster* would sail, and whether direct to France." Understandably, Chambers contacted the Chief Commissioner of Police along with military intelligence and harbour authorities. However, soon he discovered that the dialogue involved a superior officer of the Imperial Munitions Board and a manager for the Montreal-based British Munitions Limited.[25]

Compared to policing what civilians uttered, it proved far easier for the censor to control the war-related matter that people viewed. With the enemy being able to use some visuals to advantage, the War Measures Act and the Order in Council establishing Chambers's office permitted the censorship of photographs and drawings. Fear over sabotage prevented A.C. Batten of the British and Colonial Press Service from taking pictures of Lindsay's arsenal, while the same response was given to Underwood and Underwood of New York with respect to the Vickers's shipyard in Montreal where submarines were being constructed.[26]

Beyond such technical considerations, Chambers was most anxious to control the spread of pictures contradicting an idealized version of war. Thus, while accepting Canadian War Record Office [C.W.R.O] photographs like "the unfailing cheerfulness of the British Tommy," he rejected for Canadian dissemination other agency snapshots displayed in England aimed at raising hatred against Germany by showing, for instance, "bodies of men and horses amid wreckage of a French city."[27] Equally revealing was a case where the Montreal *Standard* and Toronto *Star* were admonished for printing an advertisement depicting a few skeletons to publicize a British film called *War's Horrors*. "I will be much obliged," Chambers asked one of the editors, "if you will kindly let me know from what source you obtained these pictures."[28] When informed that they came from England's War Office Cinematograph Committee, the Chief Censor remained unfazed and simply explained that Canada's distance from and resulting unfamiliarity about front-line conditions could permit such images to exert far greater negative consequences.[29]

In Canada's movie war, the Chief Censor ensured that the trenches always remained dry, death clean and rare, and the enemy inhuman and regularly routed. Besides stressing the potential of this medium to petrify the country's sheltered multitudes, Chambers further rationalised the need for unstinting standards by pointing out to his superiors that as part of its U.S.-based information service, Berlin had given (and even after April 1917 he assumed was still providing) financial aid to firms such as the Messter and American Correspondent Film Companies.[30] Indeed, despite Washington's emergence as an ally, Chambers, in maintaining fine nativist form, stressed that much of the U.S. movie industry remained under the control "Germans, Poles and Jews" whose loyalties, he said, undoubtedly lay with the Central Powers.[31]

Given the lack of formal legislative authority to control film content until January 1917 (P.C. 146), Chambers turned to provincial movie censors who had been appointed before the war to safeguard morality, Canadian film distributors and over 1,500 theatre owners to enforce his wishes. He "noted with satisfaction" that each extended "the greatest co-operation" to guarantee that "nothing in the moving pictures be shown which might be calculated to produce an injurious effect on the minds of the public."[32] For example, to prevent revulsion towards combat, Chambers convinced such parties to quash screenings of the U.S. production, *Peace at any Price*, that, he professed, "served German interests" by emphasizing "the gruesome side of war through depictions of ghastly heaps of dead....graveyard scenes, etc."[33]

America's decision to enter the Great War provided Canada with a litany of easily passible propaganda films, but a wary Chambers, determined to protect civilians from what he perceived as the subtly subversive products from suspected pro-German movie makers, concluded that several post-April 1917 U.S. entries were unsuitable for Canadian audiences. For example, *The Last Zeppelin Raid*, released by Superfeatures of New York, was banned for "glorifying" the German character, not to mention the "Hun's might and prowess." As proof, Chambers pointed to scenes demonstrating the effectiveness of enemy air raids along the disturbing claim that some Teutons possessed a conscience, a characterization that, to say the least, twisted matters considerably. In its review, the American trade magazine, *Motion Picture World*, interpreted the film's overriding theme as anti-Kaiserism, for in this story, an airship commander, "converted by the brutality of his ruler's regime," secretly joined a "revolutionary society" whose aim was to establish democracy. While on a bombing raid, word came of the uprising, but when his crew refused to join him in the fight for liberty, the captain, rather than killing innocent civilians in the name of autocracy, destroyed the zeppelin.[34]

From England there came scores of rubber-stamped factual newsreels including the monumental *Britain Prepared*, a 1915 production from Wellington House that for three-and-one-half hours displayed a succession of English ships, regiments and armaments to demonstrate the mother country's fighting potential. Yet, given the Chief Censor's rigid demeanour, some British imports, even if not suspected of pro-Germanism, still proved problematic. In late 1916, Chambers requested provincial movie censors to delete parts from Wellington House's 77-minute epic, *Battle of the Somme*, a film that grossed over £30,000 at 2,000 British cinemas.[35] Admittedly, it was a departure from the typical propaganda entry as English authorities, in attempting to build support for conscription, decided to display some suffering inflicted by Germany upon Allied troops. Approximately 13 per cent of the movie was devoted to the dead and wounded, much of which was cut from the Canadian version.[36] After viewing the movie in its original form, Chambers concluded that though the *Somme* "could be shown without any results in England" where wounded men were a common sight, an unedited Canadian release, he predicted, would "cause women in motion picture theatres to become hysterical."[37]

Maybe the *Somme* was a tad extreme, but certainly far less justification existed for similar concerns voiced by Chambers nearly two years later over D.W. Griffith's less graphic *Hearts of the World*, an immensely popular propaganda effort financed by the British and French governments that portrayed the dreadful consequences of the German occupation upon a European village.[38] For months, it played before packed houses in London, Paris and New York. Once in Canada, however, the Chief Censor, probably to avoid intensifying prevailing tensions over conscription, ordered deletions of potentially disturbing images of combat, including a scene where men hit each other over the head with revolvers.[39]

The legislation providing Chambers with jurisdiction over film content also gave him the power to control stage productions. This prerogative he employed less frequently because with motion pictures being regarded as a more adaptable medium for depicting events overseas, the period witnessed the production of comparatively few war plays.[40] Still, there was enough to keep the censor interested. Even before the passage of PC 146, Chambers requested that theatre owners cancel some plays usually identified for him by William Banks who, in addition to his high-ranking status in the Orange Order, sometimes wrote theatrical reviews for the Toronto *Star*. Ironically, on one occasion at least, action here by the censor contributed to racial tolerance. To avoid a diplomatic spat with Japan, the Entente's most important Far Eastern ally, Chambers ordered the manager of Ottawa's Russell Theatre to discontinue performances of the U.S. production, *Daughter of the Sun*, that covered "the efforts of…[Tokyo's] agents…to gain possession of the island of Hawaii by intrigue."[41] However, most of his decrees proved far less progressive. For example, to retain a positive image of army life, Chambers even banned some vaudeville shows. "This may seem like a small matter," he told Banks, "but just imagine such songs being sung, jokes told or acts reflecting upon the honour of these men, at a time when we need to hearten everybody up."[42]

Finally, it was not until May 1918 (PC 1241) that the Chief Censor received authority to control gramophone recordings. Yet, as with movies and stage productions, Chambers's obsession with crushing supposed signs of subversion led him to overstep formal statutory limitations and acquire such a power in *de facto* terms. To control those he presumed as traitorous, Chambers, starting in mid 1915, wrote hundreds of record and book shops to halt the circulation of songs such as *The Watch on the Rhine* that he claimed were being "played in bar rooms frequented by those of Teutonic descent."[43] Besides drawing motivation from patriotism, few, if any, proprietors showed a willingness to place their commercial interests above the censors' request, realizing they would get little support in a country where, for example, couples were roundly denounced if playing Mendelssohn's *Wedding March* at their ceremony. With the introduction of PC 1241, Chambers carried the campaign a step further, demanding catalogues from Canadian distributors for U.S. companies like Columbia and Victor-Pathé and then asked a German translator to identify songs whose titles or lyrics seemed inappropriate. The result was a prohibition against the sale or playing of 34 tunes, most of which, like *Germany Above All*, probably could be classified as unsuitable—assuming, as Chambers obviously did, that such music possessed the potential to enrage rather than calm what he and countless others viewed as Canada's Teutonic beasts.[44]

Many factors can be posited as explanations for Canada's rigid World War One censorship programme—a programme that still ranks as among the most brazen affronts to democracy in the country's history. Of utmost concern was the necessity of stamping out information jeopardizing national security or morale. In the hands of spies, intelligence such as the date of a troopship departure represented the potential death of thousands, while to advertise enemy victories or the blood-curdling aspects of combat might well have enhanced despair and thwarted recruitment. Besides such basic concerns, Chambers believed extra vigilance was essential because for three-quarters of the conflict, Canada contended with a neutral giant on its doorstep containing a number of Germans who, as their newspapers indicated, were favourably disposed towards the Fatherland; Hindus, Sikhs and Irish-Catholics[45] who sought for their homelands independence from Britain; along with tracts, such as the yellow press put out by William Randolph Hearst, that were antagonistic to the mother country. In fighting such forces, the Chief Censor, ever the faithful imperialist, never deviated from a social consensus largely formed by well-entrenched pro-Empire sentiment and associated Anglo conformity, creeds that were bolstered by war-related euphoria, the aspiration that Canada acquit itself proudly in this first great national test, and, consequently, the desire of its citizens to stamp out all forms of dissidence. In Chambers's view, as well as that of countless countrymen, to permit enemy aliens or Bolshevists to challenge the precepts of British culture or the Dominion's connection to the Crown would not simply complicate the war effort, but subvert centuries of Canadian progress by imposing a foreign system that, as the history of continental Europe demonstrated, consistently begot turmoil, conflict and misery.

Factors relating to administration and geography also help to explain the harsh pattern of Canadian censorship. Given his small and overworked staff, Chambers believed it sensible to simply ban a tract rather than conduct on-going surveillance or attempt to persuade a newspaper to change its stance, that, if emanating from a neutral America, represented a remote possibility. Unlike the British or French, Canadians were physically isolated from the war. To an extent, this was a dichotomy whose ideological results Chambers overstated. While on leave in London, Robert Graves wrote contemptuously about citizens who spoke in "newspaper talk," while his comrade-in-arms, Siegfried Sassoon, poetically wished for "a tank to come down the stalls…of a music hall" to awaken multitudes who, he claimed, continually spewed jingoistic clichés.[46] Nonetheless, residents in Kent could hear artillery duels in France; Britain suffered more than 1,300 civilian deaths due to German air raids; and often Londoners saw troops on leave still wearing muddy, bloody and lice-ridden uniforms.[47] Convinced, with some reason, that English civilians were better equipped than Canadians to confront the macabre, Chambers imposed a higher level of censorship than that prevailing in the mother country, one that no doubt intensified the intellectual rifts that developed between Johnny Canuck and those whom he left behind to defend.

Aiding Chambers in fashioning such a rigid code was a legal condition flowing from the fact that Canada, with its conservative Loyalist and French-Catholic roots, did not, as its southern neighbour, whose society was born out of a revolution exalting individualism, enjoy a constitutionally-enshrined protection for free expression. Even after April 1917, Chambers, perhaps exuding some imperialist-based disdain for republicanism, argued that the Bill of Rights supposedly provided U.S. dissidents with enough leeway to made it "unwise to accept the licence issued to [American]…publishers as sufficient…for allowing them to circulate in Canada."[48] Although exaggerating liberal tendencies south of the border, still it appears that by operating under a constitution emphasizing "peace, order and good government," Canada's censor was provided with greater latitude to manage so-called troublemakers.

This is not to paint the U.S. wartime record on civil liberties as praiseworthy. Citizen groups such as the American Protective League rounded up suspected pro-Germans and Bolshevists, many of whom found themselves in local jails for months without formal charges being laid. As well, First Amendment rights failed to dissuade library boards from removing books written in enemy languages or works sympathetic to Teutonic historical figures.[49] At the national level, as soon as America declared war, a 1911 provision in the U.S. Criminal Code was utilized to outlaw the postage of "indecent material." Two months later, in June 1917, passage of the Espionage Act denied mailing rights and fixed a maximum $10,000 fine and/or 20-year jail term against those promoting the enemy's success, interfering with recruitment, or "causing or attempting to cause insubordination, disloyalty, mutiny, or refusal of duty in the military or naval forces of the United States." A rider in October 1917 to the Trading with the Enemy Act permitted local postmasters to demand translations from foreign-language sources of "any comment respecting the Government of the United States…[or] the state or conduct of the war."[50] Topping off this infamous legislative record was the April 1918 Sedition Act that established similar jail terms and fines as the Espionage Act for those printing, distributing, editing, selling, teaching, advocating or defending theories promoting the overthrow of the government by force. As a result, by the end of 1918, members of the Industrial Workers of the World [I.W.W.] constituted the largest single group incarcerated at the country's principal penitentiary located in Leavenworth, Kansas.[51]

Once the United States became a belligerent, most German-American sources denounced the Kaiser, but others, such as the *Unsere Zeit* of Chillicothe, Ohio, that refused to adopt a pro-Entente line, soon went bankrupt from the loss of postal privileges. Indeed, the application of this penalty, or the burdensome translation costs placed upon these usually small publications, played fundamental roles in accounting for 47 per cent of the U.S. Teutonic press disappearing from the marketplace between April 1917 and the end of 1918. Nevertheless, it is important to recognize that First Amendment rights prevented Congress—despite widespread pressure spearheaded by notables such as ex-President Theodore Roosevelt—from passing legislation similar to PC 2381 that prohibited various languages from print.[52]

With considerable vigour, the Espionage and Sedition Acts were applied to control socialist thought.[53] In fact, while America was at war, each of its major left-wing sources was denied mailing rights for at least one issue. To stay in business, many softened their tone, while those who balked, such as Max Eastman's *Masses* magazine, often went bankrupt as a result of not being able to reach their subscribers by mail.[54] Still, when compared to Canada, First Amendment rights seemed to establish more confining parameters for repressive action. Rather than instituting an outright ban against a newspaper, U.S. censorship authorities stuck by the policy of denying individual editions access to the postal system. This strategy enabled the government to ruin a number of sources without having to face the constitutionally difficult position of defending attempts to deny the right of a newspaper to publish, especially where their contents straddled acceptability. But it also meant that socialist editors and publishers willing to risk a jail term if their paper proved a "clear and present danger" could still legally distribute copies. This was the case with the Canadian-banned *International Socialist Review* that survived a few months through the capacity of its wealthy and well-connected publisher, Charles H. Kerr, to use private railway express companies along with the "cooperation of…friends in many cities." In some situations, foreign-language socialist tracts, such as in New York, survived through street sales in ethnic enclaves.[55]

Perhaps given its common cultural and legal roots, one might have anticipated Canada's standard of repression to more closely resemble that in Great Britain. No doubt, a healthy dose of intolerance existed in the mother country. Within the general population were those who, in venting their hatred against Germans, stoned daschunds in London streets. In the supposedly more broad-minded scholarly world, Trinity College Council fired the famed philosopher, Bertrand Russell, for his pacifist beliefs.[56] And at the political level, by early 1916, British authorities had accumulated over 38,000 personal dossiers on potential malcontents, particularly Irish Republicans and conscientious objectors.[57]

When it came to the press, however, dissent in England remained relatively notable. There, battles for free expression had transpired over centuries, a struggle during which many a writer had perished in the Tower of London. Such a protracted fight, while not making Britain's fourth estate strikingly less partisan nor more professional than Canada's, did however apparently instill within a substantial number of its members a lower threshold of tolerance for official control. This should not be confused with disloyalty; in 1912, for example, English press representatives joined a standing committee of military personnel to set down guidelines on war reporting, one result of which was a voluntary news blackout on British troop movements between 27 July and 18 August 1914 so that all soldiers might arrive safely in France.[58] But the Great War also generated rigid legislation from Westminster, namely the Defence of the Realm Act, prohibiting stories "jeopardizing the success of...His Majesty's troops...assisting the enemy...[or] likely to cause disaffection...."[59] Responding, Fleet Street insisted that it knew full well what was suitable and patriotic to print, an interpretation that soon brought some disputes.

To urge more men into service during the opening weeks of the war, the London *Times* carried headlines about "Broken British Regiments Battling Against All Odds" at Mons—an episode that precipitated Kitchener's failed effort at banning correspondents from the front, and led to the resignation of the government's Press Bureau Chairman, F.E. Smith. His replacement, Sir Stanley Buckmaster, proved incapable of exerting more control.[60] Although most editors concurred with Press Bureau D notices emphasizing the need to downplay monumental disasters, which became especially apparent following the July 1916 Somme offensive, they also realized that their readers had heard at least some disconcerting scuttlebutt about the war's progress from troops on leave. Therefore, to maintain credibility, and, as they claimed, to raise resolve and help win the war, newspapers continued to provide some coverage of setbacks along with what was perceived as ineffective military tactics. Such practices, for example, incensed the First Lord of the Admiralty, Winston Churchill, whose strategic abilities came under fire in 1915 after the Royal Navy suffered a series of defeats near Antwerp.[61]

Churchill demanded official retribution, but nothing transpired. In possessing a total daily circulation exceeding 11 million in 1915, a figure that, due to Britain's denser population, tripled the Canadian total on a per capita basis, many politicians appreciated, if not cowered before, Fleet Street's strength.[62] Already that year, the Conservative press was well advanced in its campaign to discredit the Asquith government, charging it with negligence by failing to adequately prepare Britain for war.[63] The might of England's fourth estate was also acknowledged by Field Marshal Haig. Following the Somme fiasco, he made special efforts to provide visiting correspondents with interviews in order to enhance the potential for positive coverage—a policy that, though working in July 1916, did not dissuade several newspapers the next year from describing the encounter at Cambrai as "one of the most ghastly stories in English history."[64]

In only a few instances did the British government openly challenge the press, a cautious approach determined as well by England's courts. Although far from monolithic, nevertheless, in a majority of cases, judges seemed loath to undermine Common Law press rights won through long battles against arbitrary authority. As long as newspaper copy was not libelous nor of direct benefit to the enemy, editors and publishers were by and large exonerated of wrongful action. Even when found guilty of misconduct, the penalties imposed—the largest during the war being £ 200 against the *Morning Post* for revealing details of a general reserve scheme[65]—hardly proved capable of securing submissive behaviour. By contrast, Canadian censorship regulations and practices became severe enough to catch the attention of and elicit derisive commentary from a few English newspapermen. "The public shall be allowed to know and…think only what happens to suit the purpose of a small group of individuals," contended the Manchester *Guardian* just prior to the passage of PC 1241. "It surpasses in strictness anything we know here."[66]

The *Guardian*'s critique also seemed to apply to the treatment of publications serving those presumed as or even openly unenthusiastic towards the war effort. Despite public antipathy towards Germans and other enemy aliens, Westminster, perhaps recognizing the commitment of most courts to defend legal expression, did not, like Canada's Parliament, pass legislation banning certain languages from print. Moreover, difficulties before the courts in curbing the religious freedom of Quakers to espouse pacifism, prompted the Crown in 1917 to suspend all proceedings against the group despite their decision to ignore Regulation 27c of the Defence of the Realm Act requiring that they submit all printed material in advance to censors.[67] Just against some minor and viciously anti-war sources—such as Rose Allatini's pacifist polemic, *Despised and Rejected*[68]—were English authorities able to obtain temporary prohibition orders. As a result, in most circumstances, British officials, if unable to affect content changes, acted only to deny the export of dubious tracts, an initiative that, besides being applied against sources promoting the creed of conscientious objectors, also curtailed the distribution of publications supporting Irish Republicans and the radical left.[69]

Yet other considerations behind Chambers's stern methodology emerge through comparisons with British and American wartime mobilization networks. In those countries, huge campaigns were promptly mounted to mould the mass psyche. Whereas Chambers's operations cost approximately $100,000 to run over four-and-a-half years and did not include machinery for the infusion of information, forays by London into the realm of domestic propaganda amounted to more than £2,000,000 while Washington's Committee on Public Information spent about $10 million over nineteen months.[70]

Following extensive casualties at Mons and the Marne River in late 1914, the British War Office hired professional advertisers such as Henry Le Bas to design broadsides for what became a massive nationwide recruitment campaign.[71] Of even greater consequence was the near simultaneous creation of Wellington House. Run by the former *Daily Mail* literary editor and prominent M.P., Charles Masterman, this agency furnished, among other things, posters, banners, movies and even cigarette cards for distribution at home and in neutral countries depicting images such as the Hun shooting, knifing, beating or mutilating helpless victims.[72]

As the pressures of war mounted, British propaganda continued to intensify. Controversial compulsory service introduced in early 1916, soon followed by Republican uprisings in Ireland and massive casualties at the Somme, generated demands (particularly from the War Office, which received extra powers that year over the production of newsreels) for a more consolidated and better funded system. Masterman and Foreign Office Secretary Lord Balfour, whose department helped distribute propaganda overseas, expressed concern about any changes introduced under the new Prime Minister, Lloyd George, whose last cabinet posts were in Munitions and the War Office. However, the result, did not, as they feared, turn out as a coup for the military. In February 1917, author John Buchan was selected to run a new Department of Information. As a former liaison officer with General Headquarters in France, he proved acceptable to the War Office; but Masterman was permitted to retain some control over the production of books, pamphlets, photographs and war art, while the Foreign Office continued its work abroad. More propaganda resulted, but many, including Buchan, soon concluded further improvements were necessary. Despite being directly answerable to Lloyd George, Buchan did not enjoy ministerial clout and hence lacked the power to press home the need for massive morale-building material as weariness grew and coupon food rationing appeared. The subsequent creation of a streamlined and well-financed Ministry of Information filled the propaganda bill, and led to Maxwell Aitken's greatest wartime coup, for in February 1918, he was named to cabinet in order to direct its operations. Opposition was heard over a Canadian assuming such a high position, but his C.W.R.O. and Cinematograph Committee experience, as well as his links to the War Office where he had formed a personal friendship with Lloyd George (for whom he helped line up Parliamentary support against Asquith), made him, in the words of the King's Private Secretary, Lord Stamfordham, "the best man available." The Foreign Office retained some supervision over propaganda disseminated abroad, but all other activity was centralized and escalated. Indeed, despite its administrative rivalries over the years, Britain's forays into information infusion always remained substantive — impressive enough, in fact, for the Nazi Propaganda Minister, Joseph Goebbels, to comment 20 years after the armistice that London's efforts at mass mobilization proved a key factor in producing an Allied victory.[73]

By contrast, as long as flag-waving patriotism continued to supply adequate recruits, Ottawa refused to create a large publicly-funded propaganda network. No doubt the system introduced after 1917 became significant, but was always run by several departments and for the most part remained geared to particular causes (viz. food, fuel, and Victory Bond drives), thus not affording Chambers the opportunity to direct material against specific targets. On several occasions during the war, the Chief Censor discussed the need for more "effective counter-propaganda,"[74] and even after Nichols's Department of Public Information appeared, at times he still felt compelled to supplement efforts at infusing ideas within the populace. In late 1918, Chambers wrote the presidents of several universities to advise that faculty members be recruited to deliver "a few well thought out exposures of the fallacies of the Bolshevist idea."[75] And, clearly, as a corollary to his conclusion about the government lacking adequate machinery to drown out dissenting voices was the (perhaps convenient, and, after 1917, probably unwarranted) belief that he needed to fully exploit what repressive powers he possessed as a compensatory devise in order to promote conformity and ensure the triumph of democracy over tyranny.

Canada's model of wartime information control demonstrated most commonality with Australia's, a country that shared colonial status; manifested comparable constitution rights and limitations; and possessed many of the same ideological, logistical and social factors that encouraged and permitted those moulding public opinion to exert exceptional impact. Like Canadians, those down under were, before 1914, intellectually preconditioned towards jingoism. Besides inexperience with costly battles, the presence of a strong imperialist ethos (demonstrate by Canberra's leading support among the Dominions at several Imperial Conferences for an Empire Federation) also acted to reinforce the notion of war as a rather glorious enterprise through which the colony could help Britain spread liberty, and, in the process, eventually obtain an equal footing in directing the Crown's worldwide affairs.[76] Acting, however, to retain the power of these, and other, optimistic views was the nature of information conveyed to Australia from the fray. Geographic isolation ensured that those down under, similar to Canadians, had little or no direct contact with grim realities. All news, including letters from soldiers, was filtered through overseas censorship, or manipulated by the desire of troops not to cause worry nor lose face by displaying unmanly weakness in their correspondence.

Much of what Australians read about their sons in action came from the country's official *eye-witness*, Charles Bean. In fact, while at Gallipoli in 1915, this former Sydney *Herald* reporter formed the basis of what became, and to this day still persists as, the "Anzac legend"—namely, the physically powerful, independent-minded and adaptable product of the outback who always prevailed in combat no matter the odds. Besides censorship rules, Bean's imperialist faith and desire "not to spread distress at home," produced a succession of reports from the Dardenelles downplaying 7,600 dead out of a force of 50,000, and emphasizing the towering presence of Australian manhood (that "totally fearless, flawless fighting machine") who struggled and sacrificed not in what today historians often cast as a bungled and confused military exercise, but in clash of momentous "national importance" that catapulted the colony into a leading force within the Empire—sentiments that, upon the first anniversary of the Gallipoli landings, were consecrated, and thereafter forever celebrated as Anzac Day.[77]

These despatches, when left unchallenged by conflicting evidence, apparently delayed, as in Canada, the need for large-scale domestic propaganda. Not until late 1916, when Prime Minister William Hughes launched a referendum campaign on overseas conscription, did government-sponsored information became notable. And even after voters rejected the draft—something attributable as much to naive optimism as anti-war sentiment—voluntary recruitment in a still-jingoistic Australia remained above Canadian and South African levels. Not until 22 August 1918, did Canberra finally believe it necessary to establish a formal Directorate of War Propaganda whose task was to encourage unity in a land where, besides ongoing conscription debates, inflationary trends precipitated some weariness and class-based dissent.[78]

Further to imperialist ideology, distance from the carnage, and the romanticized quality of front-line reports, a strict domestic censorship system also helped form the Australian mind set. Stationed at military head-quarters in Melbourne was a Chief Censor who issued guidelines to six directors coordinating state-level efforts in a network extending surveillance and state control to every means of domestic and international communication. In determining legal commentary, Australian censors derived their powers from the 1914 War Precautions Act. Initially it provided a top penalty of £100 and/or six months' imprisonment, but after the costly and potentially morale-destroying Gallipoli campaign, along with an expanding need for reinforcements, amendments stipulated that those who "spread false reports…public alarm…or prejudice[d] His Majesty's relations with foreign powers" could face an unlimited fine or jail term.[79]

Out of patriotism and without complaint, many members of Australia's fourth estate cooperated with this and other decrees. Also apparent, however, is that not one of those running the country's 30 daily newspapers had anything approaching the power or confidence of their British counterparts to openly oppose censorship policy.[80] Even though the War Precautions Act was never applied to its full effect, several editors—especially of labour publications that had previously demonstrated some opposition to large numbers of reinforcements—discovered that one transgression required them to submit page proofs for three to six month intervals to censors placed at their premises, an order often renewed for the duration of the conflict. By December 1918, this ruling had been applied 84 times, and, in order to avoid outright prohibition, most affected parties altered their conduct rather than defy officials, either directly in print or by leaving blank spaces to indicate censored copy.[81]

In justifying the severity of this system, some Australian authorities, including Prime Minister Hughes, argued, just like Chambers, that distance from the front made civilians "especially vulnerable" in the sense that gruesome or depressing material carried a huge capacity to shock and consequently prompt people to reconsider a commitment based primarily upon idealism as opposed to the realistic risk of an invasion.[82] Therefore, news wire reports passed in Britain were rechecked by censors down under who regularly removed references to Allied setbacks or anything reflecting negatively upon the Anzac's performance. Suppressed were despatches from Britain's correspondent at Gallipoli, Ellis Ashmead-Bartlett, who, though not offering graphic details, still told readers in England about "brave but dispirited" Anzacs being "sacrificed needlessly because of muddled staff work."[83]

The impact of information control upon Australians was evident during the October 1916 conscription referendum, playing, according to some historians, the ironic role of having helped to produce a narrow defeat—51 to 49 per cent—for the pro-draft government. This is not to dismiss the importance of several other factors. From the outset of hostilities, organized labour insisted upon the conscription of wealth before men. Many among Australia's large Irish-Catholic population were first-generation migrants, and, in still feeling strong emotional attachment to their homeland, loudly opposed fighting alongside the British following London's brutal suppression of the Easter 1916 Republican uprising in Dublin. There also existed a wide cross-section of people who realized that Australia had, on a per capita basis, provided more recruits than several other Dominions; and besides they had no identifiable group, such as French-Canada, upon which to focus as *slackers* requiring a legal obligation to serve. As well, nativism played a part with opponents to conscription arguing that with more Australians shipped overseas, foreign workers would increase their presence and soon undermine the country's whiteness—a fear confirmed in the minds of many by the arrival of 98 Maltese labourers just weeks before the referendum.

But also tipping the balance was censorship. After an endless stream of sugar-coated front-line reports, and with authorities unwilling to jolt people towards their perspective via graphic propaganda, many Australians, perhaps enough to decide the tight outcome, simply failed to appreciate the need for more recruits and thus gave issues such as the Maltese scare equal if not greater importance. One Brigadier General returning to the country to help the pro-draft campaign was "so distressed by the rosy picture given in the papers," that he visited the New South Wales premier urging him to use his influence to reverse the tone.[84] Furthermore, because so many citizens failed to comprehend the situation from the same perspective as the government, some anger was expressed when word leaked that the Prime Minister had ordered the censorship of anti-draft articles to manipulate what many, from their sheltered perspective, still deemed as a purely political if not personal crusade by Hughes as opposed to a bona fide crisis.[85] Rather than symbolizing a populace having gone sour on the war, certainly it is just as feasible to characterize the defeat of conscription in October 1916, and again 14 months later, as linked to Australia's disconnection from depressing information. With little evidence to convince them otherwise, most people down under never questioned the Allies' eventual triumph. As a result, many joined core oppositionist forces, including organized labour, to reject a policy that they envisaged as not changing the outcome abroad, but that at home held out the potential to undermine the caucasian character of the country. Such a pattern also explains why in the face of compulsion being rejected, a forceful war policy based upon voluntarism remained enthusiastically endorsed. Indeed, in the 1917 election, the jingoistic William Hughes, having broken from more moderate Labour party to form a new Nationalist bloc, actually increased his share in the Commonwealth Parliament, winning 54 per cent of the popular vote and taking 46 of 65 seats.[86]

Australia's imperialist and nativist leanings, along with its relatively blunt application of censorship, also produced a pattern mirroring Canada's handling of sources serving less-favoured ethnic and political groups. Prior to August 1914, among the newcomers to Australia, Irish-Catholics, Russians and Italians, were most vehemently denounced as compromising the country's racial standards. Hostilities with Germany expanded such loathing and distrust to the country's 100,000 inhabitants of Teutonic birth or descent. In late 1914, Canberra passed legislation prohibiting Germans—even those born in Australia—from voting, while under its Aliens Restrictions Order, 6,890 Teutons were interned, many of whom were naturalized.[87] Meanwhile, the German press, along with other newspapers printed in enemy languages, succumbed before Section 28b of the War Precautions Act. Under this provision, introduced in February 1916, Australia's Chief Censor, without proof of disloyalty, ordered the country's six secular German tracts to publish in English. By the end of 1917, the order was extended to a wide array of religious publications serving enemy aliens, and, as part of Australia's anti-radical campaign, Russian texts, and remained in effect until 1921.[88]

When it came to the leftist threat, the Hughes government, rather than focusing upon deteriorating economic conditions and the ongoing refusal of employers to recognize unions, interpreted events such as the 1917 New South Wales General Strike as the work of alien agitators whose actions served, and numerous parliamentarians erroneously assumed, were financially underwritten by Germany. Determined to hold the line against such treasonous forces, legislators not only banned the Russian language from print and at public gatherings, but also, under the 1917 Unlawful Associations Act, groups such as the Union of Russian Workers and I.W.W., many of whose members were deported after the war. Finally, for good measure, the Unlawful Associations Act joined the War Precautions Act in remaining on the books until 1921, only to be replaced by a Commonwealth Crimes Act that established a 20-year jail term against those involved with the production or distribution of material exhibiting a "seditious" character or intent.[89]

In Canada and Australia, well-entrenched imperialism and nativism, a desire to bolster naivete in part supplied by geography, as well as the presence of a patriotic and apparently more pliant press corps, all provided the impetus for and perseverance of comparatively severe, albeit effective, censorship networks. Those such as Chambers both fed off and reinforced a fervently jingoistic and exceptionally repressive social atmosphere, as a majority of people, including most members of the country's fourth estate, accepted to some degree the need of placing collective security over individual liberty. This was especially apparent when involving enemy aliens and other foreigners who were suspected of plotting invasions, sabotage or the creation of a Bolshevist state.

In some respects, it is wrong to denounce Chambers as a martinet; that is to judge him against ideological standards not relevant to his time. His strategy exemplified the belief, still in fact shared by many, that war requires quick and decisive action; such people emphasize that to equivocate or err on the side of leniency is to court lost lives if not military disaster. For instance, Chambers was made aware of German U-Boats near Canada that in October 1916 translated into five destroyed cargo vessels only miles off Nantucket.[90] Furthermore, secret service personnel and detective agencies provided reports about possible troubles from German-Americans, as well as from Canadian East Indians, Chinese and Socialists. Although inexperienced, or perhaps exaggerating matters to demonstrate the worth of their employment, these operatives still represented the most reliable means through which one could gauge potential threats.

To buoy morale and ensure that nefarious influences would not damage Canada's war effort, Chambers was asked to fulfil the paradoxical task of protecting democracy by curtailing free expression. This involved creating an efficient, yet relatively low-profile system capable of catching subversives while not raising concerns from the wider community over the emergence of a police state. Therefore, with little funding, he and his small staff laboured long hours to serve King and country. His ingenuity and skill proved impressive. To monitor private correspondence and prevent the dissemination of material considered dangerous, Chambers, through personal diplomacy, established links with newspaper editors, telegraph and telephone company directors, film distributors and others involved with spreading ideas and information. Realizing that they, like most Canadians, were favourably disposed towards the war, he cultivated good feelings by couching many a request and even reprimands in tactful tones and patriotic appeals, practices that produced compliance with minimal protest. But also understood by those who proved recalcitrant was that there existed the very real possibility of harsh retribution. Such tireless and effective management, significant legislative and *de facto* authority, not to mention the propitious restraints sometimes imposed upon Chambers by more expedient elected politicians, resulted in a censorship system that effectively curtailed the leakage of potentially hazardous military information, reinforced the legitimacy of romanticized front-line reports, and helped retain among most Anglo-Canadians the belief that their country symbolized democracy in a life-and-death struggle against Prussian authoritarianism and the Red hordes.

But by performing his duties with such uncompromising diligence — often to the point of overstepping the bounds of repressive legislation — the Chief Censor contributed directly and indirectly to considerable and often unjust suffering, both during the war and for generations to come. Giving form to long-pervasive and war-heightened nativism, Chambers, with no solid proof, treated Canada's German press as odious and helped set the stage for PC 2381; spearheaded an unswerving crusade against East Indians that, while perhaps initially understandable, eventually even produced reservations from the Chief of the Dominion Police; and always Chambers remained in the forefront among those advocating a heavy-handed approach to crush any revolutionary nuance, especially if involving distrusted foreigners. Even if one was inclined to justify such actions as an unfortunate by-product of the need to win the war and defeat an unprecedented post-armistice socialist challenge, the draconian approach Chambers established certainly becomes less commendable in light of the painful and largely racist-based legacies it helped forge for ethnic and political minorities. From tireless efforts that ultimately identified a few pockets of radical aliens, the Chief Censor, as well as Cahan and various secret service personnel, supplied much of the evidence that, once buoyed by post-war labour militancy culminating in the Winnipeg General Strike, supposedly verified the necessity for new and terribly oppressive amendments to the Immigration Act and Criminal Code, as well as the amalgamation of all those involved with security matters into a permanent peacetime spy network. Lieutenant-Colonel Charles Frederick Hamilton, the former cable censor, became Security Board Commissioner for the newly-created Royal Canadian Mounted Police [R.C.M.P.], and by 1922, its Chief Liaison and Intelligence Officer responsible for compiling weekly reports from agents on "Revolutionary Organizations and Agitators."[91] Moreover, until his death, Chambers persisted in the battle against those he perceived as traitors to Canada, counselling the Mounties as an informal advisor on "dangerous" left-wing tendencies in publications such as the B.C. Federationist and Calgary Searchlight.[92]

Besides laying some groundwork for the ongoing suppression of minorities and political dissidents, information control played a key part in exacerbating bitter legacies for practically all Canadian civilians and soldiers. This is because for nearly five years, those at home remained both physically and intellectually dissociated from the intensity and suffering wrought by war. Despite confronting conscription, inflation and sometimes the loss of a loved one, on a day-to-day basis, those in the Dominion, unlike many Europeans civilians, perceived or experienced little to discredit idealized versions of combat. Such a condition came courtesy of geographic location, but was also bolstered by a partisan and relatively weak press neither ideologically averse to nor professionally offended by demands for patriotic copy, and who, even if inclined to expose gritty truths, proved technologically incapable and/or lacked the influence to effectively challenge censorship authorities. Without instantaneous means of communication capable of by-passing censors, press correspondents, photographers and filmmakers had all their material checked, not only near the fray, but again in Canada where Chambers applied terribly demanding standards in order to retain the ardour of people he regarded as attached to war more by emotion than imminent concerns about survival. Throughout years of horror and butchery, therefore, Canadians consistently read about and saw pictures confirming a tremendous tale of victory and heroism, especially when involving their gallant sons who, it was proclaimed, won on the battlefield ever-lasting worldwide renown and sowed the seeds for a proud and strong nationalism.

Admittedly, after 60,000 dead, as well as the domestic socio-economic strains caused by the war and the draft, people were not anxious for another major struggle. Still, among most civilians, repugnance towards combat itself was not widespread. With the exception of certain religious minorities whose pacifist convictions predated this conflagration, the anti-war sentiment in Quebec, among organized labour, and in the rural sector, remained primarily based upon anti-imperialism, the supposedly unfair sacrifices demanded of the working class, or an inability under aggressive recruitment and/or conscription to retain decent levels of agricultural output. Among most Canadian civilians in November 1918, romantic imagery about the Great War and the role played by Johnny Canuck still swirled, thus making for many a traumatic reunion with those who left what was essentially an ideological cocoon. Press copy, motion pictures, war trophies as well as other forms of information, made those at home expect the return of a valiant and strong conquering hero. Even if not falling for such a caricature, precious few were intellectually prepared to greet men upon whom the strains of conflict often showed for years. In passing judgment upon this situation, Desmond Morton speculated that perhaps exceeding the regional, class, and ethnic cleavages exacerbated by the Great War was that "division…[between] those who had spent the…years in Canada and those who would return from months and years overseas."[93] Indeed, so unchallenged did quixotic accounts remain throughout practically a half decade of slaughter, that in those circumstances where post-armistice events provided surface legitimacy, idealized notions persisted within Canada's "modern memory"[94]—thus always retaining a perceptual gap between participants who experienced unvarnished verity and outsiders whose ideas derived in part from the capacity of the Dominion's censors and propagandists to help construct a *fire-proof house*. In fact, to this day in the collective consciousness, alongside that world of dirt and death, are sacred names such as Ypres and Vimy Ridge that invoke romanticized images of heroic warriors whose unparalleled exploits almost single-handedly transformed Canada from *colony to nation*.

5

Newspapers for the Fighting Man

In donning khaki with near-giddy enthusiasm, countless Canadians were, as studies on the *spirit of 1914* reveal[1], not that different from multitudes elsewhere. Young men waxed chimerically about defending democracy from Hun barbarism, a contention that, among Anglo-Canadians, was further strengthened by imperialist beliefs casting the Empire as synonymous with liberty and Christian standards. Moreover, in coming from a land where censorship, propaganda, and geography cocooned people so completely, many in the Dominion, even after years of bloodshed, thought in terms of a grand trans-Atlantic ocean voyage to a place where, as the current literary fashion promised, "lightening quick charges" would alter "the destinies of empires and nations… overnight."[2] Notwithstanding hostilities dragging on longer than projected, newspaper reports detailing a succession of Allied triumphs always had many prospective recruits talking anxiously about getting overseas before the excitement ended. Lengthy casualty lists were counteracted by claims that only German losses were truly frightening, and besides, citizens were never enlightened as to the indiscriminate slaughter often accompanying advances nor the gruesomeness so often associated with death. Consequently, throughout the conflict, notions continued circulate about a *field of honour* from which heroes emerged, and where death was clean, quick, painless and saintly—the small bullet hole in the left breast, while the victim, with arms outstretched, urged his comrades on to victory.

There seemed something for everyone in this struggle; even the less quixotic, many of whom were unemployed, could obtain steady pay and three square meals. But bolstering all these convictions and motivations, including the pragmatic considerations of the jobless, was a growing feeling throughout the late nineteenth and early twentieth centuries that military life and war constituted one of the few remaining routes through which men could offset the emasculating aspects of an urbanizing world perceived as increasingly soft, vice-ridden and alienating.

Critics said that in cities an expanding number of middle-class male youths confronted fewer physical chores than their fathers likely raised in a rural setting. Also, in the urban environment, some people perceived a dangerous growth of female influence over boys, not just in newly-compulsory schools, but also at home where fathers, more than ever before, left the family each day to attend work. In order to counteract the potential for physical and emotional enfeeblement, several popular and professional sources endorsed rugged games like *War* or *Cowboys and Indians* during which, it was hoped, boys would develop such manly traits as courage and the ability to deal stoically with pain.[3] Such were characteristics promoted as well in the emerging Scout and Cadet movements. The former, started for British youth in 1907 by Lord Baden-Powell had, by 1910, 10,000 Canadian members.[4] Through emphasizing outdoor pursuits, along with good deeds and Christian conduct, the Scouts aimed to "provide an environment in which boys could become red blooded virile men."[5] Such a lifestyle, proponents argued, was just as crucial for impoverished minors in city slums as pampered middle-class youth, for unless periodically removed from what was cast as a diseased milieu, it was predicted that lower class lads would not only grow weak in body, but also in soul, soon succumbing to the supposedly pervasive vice in their locale. Meanwhile, the Cadets, through whose ranks nearly 45,000 Canadians passed by 1914,[6] also endeavoured to mould a loyal, moral, muscular and mentally-disciplined adolescent possessing the physical and spiritual attributes to rise above the potentially destructive aspects of the modern city.

The new emphasis placed upon honing masculinity did not just focus upon youth. Increasingly, urban males found themselves in sedentary professional positions, bureaucratized offices or large factories where jobs were broken down into constituent parts, leaving many feeling like cogs in a giant machine. In contrast to tilling the soil, planting seed and harvesting crops, many jobs required comparatively less exertion; some pointed out that even in factories, machines were making it possible for women to perform tasks previously requiring brawn.[7] Furthermore, in the midst of taking orders from seemingly endless managers, or performing assembly-line work perhaps under new "time and motion" studies, a number of workers found it difficult to think of themselves as doing a man's job when compared to their forbearers who, whether on farms or in small shops, exerted substantial control over the productive process and saw the fruits of their labours.

One way men fought back against such debilitating influences was to follow the prescription advised for boys—rough play. In the late nineteenth century, sports across North America and Britain transformed in public consciousness from a gentlemanly pastime into a central aspect of national life with relatively tame activities such as running and jumping giving way in preference to competitions involving contact that, besides enhancing one's physique, were also said to develop manly will. In America, baseball, which began professionalising in 1869, continued its steady climb towards becoming that country's pastime, but the most stunning gains in popularity during these years were enjoyed by gridiron football, a game that, many stressed, required bravery, grit, and prowess.[8] In Canada, besides these activities, there occurred significant growth of participation in soccer and ice hockey, each of which spawned amateur and even some semi-professional leagues.[9]

On the playing field or ice rink, men could enhance their physique, display their prowess, experience excitement, and rise to notoriety in an environment where more jobs became routinized and where ever-larger communities seemed to reduce people to anonymity. And not lost among middle- and upper-class advocates of sport was its role in helping to ease growing class tensions by teaching that "success went to those who earned it through determination and disciplined skill," instead of people who reacted to unsatisfactory circumstances with "violent outbursts."[10] During these years, the Muscular Christian became the new ideal—a man who obtained noble "spiritual ends through bodily means."[11] In celebrating and promoting those in whose hands perhaps lay the continuing vigour of society, magazine biographies shifted from an idealization of passive traits such as "piety [and] thrift" to emphasize the virtues of "vigour, forcefulness, and mastery." In real life, those filling such a bill included American President Theodore Roosevelt who, in the Spanish-American war, led U.S. "Rough Riders" up San Juan Hill[12]; while, in fiction, Zane Grey's reverential treatment of the cowboy—"a man's man, violent but honourable...defending women without being dominated by them"—sold books by the millions.[13]

An active lifestyle was not only advanced as a tonic against the feminizing and increasingly fractious aspects of modern urban society, but also as an antidote for the medical and moral ailments for which city life seemed responsible. Those engaged in sports would be better able to resist the diseases that festered in grimy cities; and since the prevailing wisdom of the day linked unhealthy bodies with mental illness and errant behaviour, the physically robust, it was figured, would commit less crime. Larger and denser agglomerations of people appeared to bring more vice in the form of rising intemperance, prostitution and venereal disease. From clerics, urban reformers,[14] the press, and other public figures and/or forums, came stronger and more vocal efforts to break the connection long made between manliness and unruly behaviour, especially the notion about the need for males to drink hard and sow their wild oats. The new emphasis, building upon the ethos of Muscular Christianity, professed that only the weak were ruled by the bottle or their libido. Physical exertion was believed to be the key in helping men reach a new and higher standard, the theory being that it would cleanse the mind by channelling surplus energy away from degenerate activities.[15]

In Canada, this prevailing emphasis upon masculinity drew yet more power from imperialist ideology. In order to stand effectively alongside Britain in its various campaigns to spread democracy and other qualities associated with Anglo-Saxondom, leading Canadian imperialists promoted the need for men of strong bodies and possessing a martial spirit, such as acquired through militia service. They believed these characteristics would preserve a tough, disciplined and self-reliant manhood once forged by a harsh environment, but perceived as imperilled by the various negative manifestations of urbanization and modernization.[16] Moreover, besides imperialist entreaties to support England based upon Canada's legal colonial status, its British heritage, or the promise that wartime participation would earn the Dominion a major share in developing the policies of Pax Britanniaca, the power of this philosophy also derived from its ability to tap

His Greatest Victory.   By Ripley.

» *The connections between sport, war, and, in this case, everlasting glory, are*
  made by the Halifax Morning Chronicle *in reporting upon the death of the*
  American track and field star, Lt. Johnny Overton, during a dash across No
  Man's Land near Château Thierry. Said the paper: "He put all he had into
  this race—his life; and won all there is—the glory of God and man."
  30 August 1918, p. 4.

into the theme of "manly adventure"—namely the idea that imperial
expansion allowed men a chance to flee the mundane aspects of civilian
life for rousing exploits in far-off lands.[17]

Clearly, military life offered much to assuage an early twentieth century
and predominantly male angst. Like sports, but on a far grander scale, it
would supply a healthy outdoor life; build a bold physique; presumably
encourage a stronger moral code by exhausting surplus energy; and allow
escape from what many saw as a stultifying civilian existence for travel,
high adventure and even, should one display their mettle, fame. Moreover,

military life, insisted many, could very well represent Canada's best hope for continued progress both within the Empire and in facing some its own troubling socio-economic trends. For even among the most wretched civilians, it was maintained, a sharp uniform, army discipline and clean living would create a more handsome, chivalrous and gentlemanly Christian motivated by praiseworthy concerns such as destroying evil, promoting freedom and protecting the sanctity of women.

Guided by this faith as well as ubiquitous homefront naivete, many recruits foresaw combat as little more than an intense sporting contest. In this *game*, as many called the Great War, a few might get hurt or killed, but the potential rewards more than compensated. Besides serving in a righteous cause, building a glorious Empire and re-establishing the greatness of Canadian society, combat would, it was thought, provide each participant with an opportunity to develop that which was inherent and best in their gender: physical strength, bravery and natural aggressiveness. Like those on the football field or hockey rink, a number heading towards the battlefield aspired to re-assert the relevance of individual power and will that they saw as juxtaposing sharply against a civilian world apparently ruled by plutocrats in whose colossal and impersonal concerns, an endless array of machines, routines and managers sapped vigour and, like the expanding urban environment in general, blended all into the mass. Certainly it is noteworthy that up until 1 March 1916, at a time when just over half of Canada's population was classified as rural, 64.8 per cent of the country's volunteers were manual workers, 18.5 per cent left clerical occupations, while only 6.5 per cent were farmers or ranchers.[18] By the end of the war, after conscription was implemented, 85.4 per cent of office workers and 86.1 per cent of labourers were volunteers, but only 55.9 per cent of farmers.[19] Although rising food demand and record farm profits enticed many to stay on the land, urban jobs also became more plentiful and better-paying during the war. No doubt multitudinous motivations existed among those enlisting, but it is evident that for both physical and psychological reasons, a number felt a special need to try to cultivate their *manly* attributes. Even among many of the unemployed who played an important role in filling numerous regiments during the war's early stages, concerns about manliness probably played at least an indirect part in their decision to volunteer. In addition to providing work, the war presented them with an opportunity to fulfil the male breadwinner role, a consideration undoubtedly important to a portion among the one-fifth of Canadian soldiers who were married.[20]

The problem was that those who participated in the Great War all-too-often confronted an abundance of brutal and depressing incongruities. Many who sought escape from an overly-regulated, mechanized and flacci-fying homefront environment, discovered a military life that carried far more potential for repression than any previous civilian job; a conflict where *elan* paled in importance to battlefield technology; clashes during which the exalted male physique was often literally ripped to shreds; and artillery duels that frequently prompted the most muscular into releasing so-called weak emotions bottled up since childhood. Soon enough, count-less volunteers expunged, or at least tempered, the idealism that had propelled them into combat to acquire that proverbial sense of disillusion-ment so associated with this conflagration. Yet, the masculine impulse, besides driving so many into battle and helping them endure unspeakable travails, determined as well what feelings and observations they shared with those they left behind. Beyond instructions from military authorities, or any practical incentive to encourage a healthy flow of needed reinforce-ments, countless recruits resolved on their own that it was the soldiers' lot to bear the brunt like men in order to allay homefront consternation and promote that tough image from which they derived respect. Such a creed confined most disquieting commentary to sources deigned only for the eyes of combatants and thus, in the process, increased the ability of official censorship and propaganda to keep civilians contained within a world of blissful ignorance.

Military newspapers constituted one source with little or no civilian distrib-ution where a darker version of the Great War appeared. Few copies were mailed home as most men figured that pages containing minutia on battal-ion affairs would hold little interest for outsiders, or that their often satirical prose and poetry made them inappropriate for keeping the home fires burn-ing. Such tracts, which emerged within most armed forces during the Great

War, were designed to entertain, and, to a lesser extent, inform troops. The British began the *Wiper's Times*—reflecting the sardonic nickname soldiers gave to muddy Ypres—which was printed in London and circulated throughout the ranks. Canadian production proved more decentralized and limited, a fact traceable to the stingy support that the Militia Department under Hughes adopted towards propaganda or morale matters among men that the Minister considered unyielding in their loyalty. Not until late 1917 did the federal government, through the Canadian War Records Office [C.W.R.O.], fund a paper for Johnny Canuck. Before then, various battalions usually took up the slack, producing, perhaps every week or month (depending on their financial position or access to presses), a thousand or so copies of predominantly eight- to ten-page tracts containing a little war-related and Canadian-based news, along with orders of the day, and, most appealing of all to readers, a healthy dose of lighthearted fare designed to divert attention from the strains and fierceness of military life.

In Canada and Britain, local printing shops and newspaper plants, as a patriotic gesture, provided battalions or regiments with the necessary equipment and services for a modest sum. Closer to the fray, presses were available in Paris and in several towns, some of which, a frugal military happily discovered, were abandoned. Trainees obtained their copies at bases, while at the front, issues accompanied the delivery of mail, food or ammunition.[21]

Day-to-day operations were usually handled by officers possessing some journalistic background, or, on occasion, a demonstrated flair for writing. While they provided some editorial commentary, the majority of material came via contributions from countless soldiers, a fact that, along with a dearth of other reading matter, accounted for the enormous popularity of these tracts. But to ensure that rank and file candour not cripple morale, commanding officers often joined editors in perusing page proofs for unsuitable copy. Still, when compared to the contents of civilian newspapers, these is no disputing that these publications enjoyed far wider latitude. Clearly, those in charge understood that in a setting where reality forked so dramatically from expectations, spirits were best bolstered through paradoxical means; in other words, military papers attempted to use, rather than deny, the depressing discrepancies of this *Great* War. Although issuing patriotic calls to service, they also included black humour submitted by servicemen that not only amused troops but also helped them vent frustrations and fears so the adversity of military life and the ever-present possibility of death could be more easily endured. One colonel postulated that without the presence of such psychological escape valves at the Western Front, insubordination or even mutiny became possibilities. "It's a very good thing for soldiers to grumble," he reasoned. "Officers are very leery if there is no grumbling going on because they think there is something afoot."[22] What military authorities ensured, however, was that this healing role of satire never extended to the point of countenancing disobedience to superiors or allowing basic or dangerous questions—such as whether participation in this conflict was just?—to appear in print. Moreover, in the pages of these publications readers also encountered inspirational reminders about the noble cause for which the Allies battled, the heinous nature of the enemy, as well as the manly qualities that war had kindled in many of their comrades.

In analyzing these newspapers there are limitations. While a decent run remains of some sources, far too frequently only a few tracts have survived to the present, thus imposing restrictions upon comparative analysis, such as between papers serving different types of battalions. Nonetheless, by scouring and contrasting available copies printed at home and abroad, one can still demonstrate, even in these censored publications, how the outlook and attitudes of trainees and combatants progressively grew more distant from those who remained in Canada—for in their columns, there appears a direct correlation between the level of satire and proximity to the front. Despite ever-mounting casualties, jingoistic rhetoric and talk of glory remained a prominent feature in those papers printed for fresh recruits. Like their civilian counterparts in Canada, for whom death in battle, even of a family member, represented an abstract concept shrouded by patriotic imagery, most reinforcements exhibited guilelessness about what lay across the ocean. Even their grousing related to romantic expectations; they wished to escape the tedium of training and test themselves as men in the *real show*. Similar in tone were those tracts printed for Canadian trainees in Britain. Sarcastic references multiplied over a seemingly eternal preparation process, but contributions still exuded determination to participate in *the game*. Only at the front, where most men finally accepted war as a series of disheartening ironies, did the beneficial role performed by this sophisticated system of information management come fully to the fore.

As long as soldiers remained in Canada, military papers suggested that they, like their kinfolk, perceived the majesty of battle. Invariably, stories about combat ignored suffering, blood and death to concentrate upon the thrill and dash. After nearly three years of conflict and casualties, *Breath o' the Heather* (236th Battalion, Fredericton) trumpeted the "feats of arms and the valour of men in battle,"[23] while the *Clansman*, distributed among trainees in the Niagara region, emphasized those who "grasp[ed] their rifles...and blaze[d] way" at the foe.[24] In this momentous struggle, promised the Morrisey *Mention* to members of the 107th Battalion, anyone could rise from the mass to achieve renown. "Men we have all known of no great physique, nor any apparent very special strength of mind," it declared, "emerge from the ordeal like heroes."[25] Even the wounded, said the Lethbridge *Highlander*, were devastated when removed from action and "wept like children if rejected by physicians for a new battalion."[26] Those who refused to join the fight were contemptuously dismissed as cowardly. Parroting a pillar of homefront propaganda and the manliness theme — that those in uniform got the girls — the *Clansman* depicted a young civilian asking a pretty maiden if he should play a song for her on the piano. "Oh, yes, Mr. Slacker," she replied, "sing *Let Me Like a Soldier Fall.*"[27]

Such an idealistic pattern harkened to imperialist-based affirmations about defending the mother country and the high values for which it stood. Proclaimed the Morrisey *Mention*: "It is a fight between...ideals of a balanced and representative democracy, as opposed to an insensate and automatic autocracy."[28] Equally common were caricatures of the enemy mirroring those found in the civilian press. One entry read that the Kaiser was "Fit to rank with murderous vile/ For what you've done on Belgian soil."[29] Of Nurse Cavell's execution, the Victoria-based *Western Scot* chivalrously asserted that "if it's vengeance they want, and if they are men, they will go where they can get it — at the front."[30]

While trainees realized that preparation was essential to their ultimate performance, they were anxious for adventure and soon expressed dismay over apparently never-ending parades, inspections and exercise, which some probably saw as paralleling the deadening aspects of a civilian life from which they had sought escape. Those managing sources such as the *Kilt* responded by arguing to members of the 72nd Battalion that such a regimen transformed citizens who "used to lie in bed to nurse a headache," into "rather more of men."[31] The *Whizz Bang*, published by the 207th Battalion in Leamington, Ontario, agreed, asserting that physical activity proved especially beneficial for city youth who, once exposed to outdoor life, "fe[lt] a new vigour."[32] Even supposed trivialities like shining shoes, it contended, were all part of a disciplinary process sure to forge a "powerful, effective and unstoppable fighting force."[33] To develop such vigour, military newspapers tried to encourage *esprit de corps*. Summaries appeared of inter- and intra- battalion sporting events and even which company commanding officers said marched the best.[34] Unit gossip and good-natured ribbing were also printed to create a positive atmosphere. Typical was the *Kiltie*'s quip to members of the 134th asking "who were the girls Frankie Leonard was sporting around with the other Sunday and not inviting his chums?"[35]

Nevertheless, even to maintain the morale of jingoistic trainees, battalion newspapers had to do more than rely on pre-war concerns about masculinity or reveal the latest juicy rumour. Certainly many recruits took pride in a firmer physique, but other aspirations they carried into enlistment booths, such as fleeing mind-numbing routines, were clearly lacking in a military machine designed to eliminate any deviance from the norm. In helping men cope with such disappointment, a number of tracts permitted biting commentary upon the source of so much grief, the drill sergeant, a figure who, as one understandably unsigned article claimed, frequently appeared as a "rather fat...taskmaster."[36] Meanwhile, *Action Front* carried what one member of the horse artillery sarcastically cast as a typical day's training, a description that hardly conveyed the excitement so many anticipated when signing their induction papers.

The reveille — in the middle of the night. The smothered words. The sock you can't find. The shivery parade ground. The stables. The grooming. The bed making. The breakfast....The million or so buttons to shine. The morning parade. The gun drill and laying. The noon. The dinner. The not being able to buy anything to help out dinner. The afternoon parade. The exercise ride — bare back. The supper which we don't wait for. The look at tomorrow's orders to see if it can be true. The horrible truth. The likely knowledge that you'll most likely be doing the same damned things, tomorrow.[37]

Following next for recruits was a two-week trans-Atlantic ocean voyage that usually took place in an overcrowded converted passenger liner often stinking from the consequences of seasickness. Still, most men remained upbeat. Military publications printed for Canadian trainees in Britain and western France demonstrated that months of tedious drill made them all the more intent on seeing *the show*. "Fourteen months have elapsed since we discarded the garments and conventions of civilian life," read an entry in *Action Front*, a publication that followed troops from Canada to France. "We…are more than ready to meet the Hun."[38]

The odd Zeppelin or airplane raid upon London or the distant echo of artillery fire in France did not muffle the bravado of fresh reinforcements, a tendency aided by relatively clean practice trenches and the reluctance of numerous frontliners on leave to discuss their experiences (they'll find out soon enough, represented the attitude of many veterans). *Chevrons to Stars*, a publication printed for officer trainees in Britain, showed that even in mid 1917, many remained convinced that a wonderful experience lay across the Channel. Without intending to convey a negative or gruesome connotation, one soldier, in exemplifying submissions from several others, told of his earnest desire to depart what he regarded as a "tame" world for "excitement, blood, thunder and flame!"[39]

As the preparation process lengthened among such eager and unsuspecting men, sarcasm intensified and articles booning the benefits of training dwindled. In attempting to put a positive face upon an increasingly unbearable regimen, one piece, with unforeseen irony, declared that "when all the parades and 'jerks' are done, and forgotten are all the days of weary stress," soldiers would reflect "affectionately" upon this time, and even with "favour on their instructors" who were "always willing to offer friendly 'tips'." But rather than accept the drill sergeant as a fatherly figure, cartoonists frequently depicted him as resembling the archetypal and presumably tyrannical *squarehead*.[40] Also mocked in publications such as in the *Kilt* were infinite army regulations that, as the following story suggests, appeared to eventually get everyone in trouble.

> "Button up that tunic! Did you ever hear of by-law 217, subsection D? I'm Sergeant Winterbottom!"
> A gentleman in the seat behind tapped the sergeant sternly on the shoulder. "How dare you issue orders with a pipe in your mouth....Go home and read paragraph 174, section N, part IX. I'm Major Eustice Carroll."
> Here a gentleman with a drooping white moustache interposed from the other side of the aisle.
> "If Major Carroll," he said coldly, "will consult by-law 31 of section K, he will learn that to reprimand a sergeant in the presence of a private is an offence not lightly to be overlooked."[41]

In spite of such wisecracks, military publications, whether written in 1915 or 1918, made clear that so long as reinforcements were spared from direct contact with the war, by and large they retained a cheerful disposition on their decision to volunteer. In most cases, men believed or convinced themselves that an exhilarating experience awaited where finally they could abandon a drab and/or structured existence to demonstrate their individual capabilities. Only the odd glib comment emerged about the possibility of being killed. The *C.A.S.C. [Canadian Army Service Corps] News*, whose readers ultimately served behind the front- lines, jokingly advised other recruits to "transfer at once to the Postal Corps before it is too late."[42] Perhaps such trepidation was more pervasive, but it was something few soldiers admitted for fear of being labelled cowardly, and that, undoubtedly for morale purposes, military editors curtailed. In any case, no substitute existed for first-hand combat experience. Before that point, satire assisted a number of recruits in enduring what appeared as an interminable training process, but not until they confronted the terror of battle and misery of trench life did the real service performed by these sources in helping them cope with disheartening realities truly become evident.

» *Catching up on news from Canada. (National Archives of Canada, PA 2403)*

Among the myriad revelations upon which front-line military newspapers offered sarcastic commentary was that those in the midst of this maelstrom knew surprisingly little about the general progress of the war. Unlike popular literature where men could view the battlefield, or at least sense the general course of events, this conflict saw soldiers herded into trenches and cut off from incidents beyond their immediate locale. In getting them to accept such an upsetting situation, the *C.C.S. Review* (which ironically, yet also somehow fittingly, came from the Communications Squadron) turned to the well-proven method of satire—describing a meeting between a young woman and a soldier on leave who, when asked how things were going in France, replied, "I haven't the least idea. I haven't seen a newspaper for weeks."[43]

For much of the war, Johnny Canuck found himself in just such an information vacuum. Besides some civilian newspapers and magazines mailed from Canada, in December 1915 the Militia Department funded a measly 50-word daily communique summarizing war-related events at home and abroad.[44] Moreover, at its height, only 2,000 copies of British newspapers were distributed among all Canadian soldiers in action. Finally, in 1917, the C.W.R.O. started circulating in France 25,000 free copies of the *Canadian Daily Record*, which provided a 1,000 word summary of domestic and international news, along with a quarterly magazine entitled *Canada in Khaki*.[45] However, because these sources also disseminated in England, and often found their way back to the Dominion, their version of front-line life remained rather unrealistic. On the front page of each *Daily Record* issue was a C.W.R.O. photograph projecting images such as "a trio of happy Canadian soldiers…bespattered with mud but brisk and jovial as ever,"[46] while stories emphasized things like the respect enlisted men extended to officers who always proved "daring, quick-thinking, self-reliant, [and] hard-hitting…."[47]

Canadian troops read these sources for general information and diversion, but as military newspapers showed, they ridiculed and demonstrated resentment over descriptions trivializing the torment of warfare. On this subject, soldiers drew a clear distinction: for them to hide grittiness or make light of suffering symbolized manly stoicism, but when practised by supposedly pampered outsiders from a civilian agency, such a pattern, though understandable for homefront morale purposes, was nevertheless viewed as distasteful. Therefore, while the *Fortyniner* was one of several front-line publications advising soldiers to write cheery correspondence to their loved ones, it also carried an illustration depicting one member of the 49th [Edmonton Regiment] Battalion from carrying a copy of the *Record* trudging through muddy Flanders as shells and bullets buzzed around and muttering to himself in exasperation over "that Beaverbrook [Aitken]."[48] Far more preferred by those in action were tracts written by and exclusively for soldiers. In their pages servicemen acknowledged, as far as possible under the guidance of military editors, that once exposed to the desolation of No Man's Land, shell fire, or perhaps the death of a comrade, idealism frequently waned in favour of cynicism and despair.

Some commentary reflected gripes first heard during training. After enduring approximately a year's preparation, it was clear that precious little less patience remained among those at the front for the enforcement of trivialities. In conveying such a feeling, the 27th Battalion's *Trench Echo* depicted a general speaking on a field telephone with a sector under severe bombardment and asking the lieutenant "if all your men shaved this morning?"[49] Also providing the basis for biting, and, military editors hoped, tension-relieving critiques, was the courage of those in the rear planning battles. The *Sapper*, a product of the Engineers, mused that "one afternoon the colonel of an infantry battalion went up to the firing line (No, no, that's not the joke. Wait.)" Concerned about a German sniper, he sent for a marksman. "There," he said after the enemy was shot, "that'll learn you to mess with me."[50] Meanwhile, through humorous verse, one member of the 7th Battalion told the *Listening Post* that yet another reason for resentment between the ranks was that when it came to leaves, "Privates pray for one/ Corporals crawl for one/ Sergeants scheme for one/ Officers often get one."[51]

Never far from the thoughts of men, these tracts revealed, was the apparently endless nasty weather and all-consuming mud. One entry observed that "it was a beautiful spring morning in Flanders, that is to say it was merely drizzling and not raining with that silent persistence."[52] A member of the 58th Battalion wrote *O.Pip.* that the trenches were really "Panama Canals in miniature," while another wit said the only good thing about front-line life was that he would never have to hear his nagging wife telling him to wipe his feet before coming inside.[53]

Hardly mentioned in the homefront press were encounters between soldiers and rats. But "here," noted the *Trench Echo*, "the Belgian rat attains his full dignity and...amuses himself by contentedly chewing the ears of sleepers."[54] Military newspapers dwelt as well upon the acquaintance that all men made with lice. For readers who hardly needed reminding, the *Canadian Machine Gunner* printed the stinging *Ode to a Louse*: "They bite and the red blood rushes/ For they fear no human foe/ With curses, groans and flushes/ We scratch but still the legions grow...."[55]

Sometimes in these publications romanticized imagery of individuals perishing in a bold thrust was replaced with macabre humour about indiscriminate slaughter. The *Shell-Hole Advance* told members of the 11th

Infantry Brigade that by the time hostilities ceased, French and Belgian farmers would already be more than amply compensated for any damage by well churned and fertilized fields.[56] More hard-hitting was the *Ontario Stretcher*, which was distributed among the wounded at the Orpington military hospital outside London. Describing the remnants of one convoy it pointed to "an arm gone from this one, a leg off another…every part of the human body—battered, mangled and badly smashed."[57]

Contrasting with civilian newspapers in Canada, which heaped praise upon soldiers who never wavered in battle and always bore their lot stout-heartedly, the military press conceded that the dangers and discomforts of warfare sometimes transformed once ardent trainees into veterans desperate to depart the madness. Coveted by countless troops was the *Blighty*, a wound serious enough to send one back to England but that did not result in amputation nor permanent disfigurement. Thus, the *Canadian Hospital News*, printed for those recuperating at Ramsgate and Buxton, undoubtedly mirrored the feelings of more than a few of its readers by telling about a soldier who "many a time had cursed the German shells, but now he was grateful for the one that sent him back to spend Christmas out of the mud."[58]

It was not only from putrid trenches, costly human wave attacks or unnerving artillery duels that men sought to flee. For weeks that stretched into months, if not years in some sectors, a near-maddening stasis prevailed. While those at home read of tremendous Allied victories and an imminent German collapse, the fact was that between the Battle of the Marne in September 1914 and the last 100 days of the war, countless soldiers remained mired along a relatively immobile 400-mile front stretching from the mouth of the Yser to the Swiss frontier. To press correspondents, military commanders may have spoken with confidence about an imminent great breakthrough to be achieved by their men of supreme *elan,* but military tracts divulged that from the worm's-eye perspective, things appeared less promising. "Honours for inches" is how a writer from the Second Division described "active service,"[59] while another soldier made the same point by setting his story "somewhere in France" a half century later where the "officer commanding strokes his flowing beard and inspects his troops from his bath chair."[60]

Besides such stagnation there often came considerable tedium as each side waited for the other to initiate something. Men who were promised excitement habitually found themselves languishing in wet ditches with no opportunity to look over the parapet for fear of snipers, a predicament that generated jokes about the "cosmopolitan rat" who travelled freely across No Man's Land to feed off corpses from both sides.[61] At night, troops, some of whom enlisted to leave behind the drudgery of factories, frequently found themselves performing industrial-type duties: trench repairs, ferrying supplies and other uninspiring tasks during which they ran the risk of becoming the unfortunate victim of a stray bullet. Noting the irony, one critic told the *Listening Post* that "We work at a job that is endless/ Till the sight of a shovel's enough/ To make you curse at the training/ That at home was all a bluff."[62]

Admitted as well in military sources was that boredom, when interspersed with terrors and pressures, produced an environment that, rather than steeling the soul against moral decay, provided greater stimuli towards debased conduct than anything faced in civilian life. Each sundown, troops waited anxiously for their tot of Service Rum that provided momentary escape, warmth, and, many hoped, the courage to face death or kill the enemy. The presence of Salvation Army and Y.M.C.A. temperance advocates near the trenches who ran dry canteens had practically no effect in abating what became a near-obsessive and ubiquitous demand. In fact, such teetotalling civilians were condemned as ignorant busy bodies. The *Listening Post* argued that "Till they come and share the scrapping/ At the side of fighting men/ They should stop their yapping/ Never to commence again."[63] Moreover, rather than draining surplus energy, some papers acknowledged that the frontliner's plight convinced more than a few participants to experience life while it lasted. Some poetry went as far as to praise prostitutes and so-called loose women soldiers met while at rest stations or on leave. A member of the 7th Battalion noted that "Ev'ry little while they [women] go out scouting/ Ev'ry little while they catch a boy in blue/ They're always lonely/ They want us only/ And in these hard times we want them too...."[64]

In fact, a few entries, while by no means condoning desertion, admitted that many men had had enough adventure and now were ready to accept that sedate lifestyle against which they had once rebelled. That newspaper released by the Machine Gun Service wrote: "When your shirt begins to walk and your socks begin to talk/ And you've grown a beard on which you need a comb/ When the cold rain gives you shivers, makes your trenches blooming rivers/ 'Tis the time you long for 'home, sweet home'."[65] Revulsion toward squalor and death also no doubt played a role in producing the odd piece humanizing enemy soldiers whom some men probably came to see as victims like themselves. In civilian newspapers, fraternization received no mention since it held out the potential to subvert a rallying cry based in part upon the Hun's satanic disposition. Military publications, however, could not deny to fighting men that a few friendly encounters transpired. The *Garland from the Front*, which was printed by the 5th Battalion, noted that when the 1st Division took up its position in the Fleurbaix district, the Germans sent over a small wooden horse into which a hole was "promptly drilled by a ready Canadian marksman." In response, the "humorous Hun hauled in his toy," wrapped a bandage around its neck, and put it over again "amid much laughter from both sides."[66]

Satire and black humour, while getting many men to laugh at rather than rebel against their dreadful predicament, did not represent the only formula by which military newspapers buttressed morale. As during training, those in charge of these sources also ensured that soldiers in action received other, more positive, messages. For instance, the *Twentieth Gazette* declined to release a pure "grouser's edition," reasoning that without the input of something inspirational, "such a thing would demoralize us." Therefore, newspapers printed for soldiers at the front carried on the practice of reporting upon battalion athletic competitions, unit gossip, plus other news men might want to know and that advanced good spirits. The *Iodine Chronicle*, a product of several field ambulance units, took this practice to the point of writing about a mustache contest with winners announced for "Charlie Chaplin," "ferocious," and "non-descript" classes.[67]

The most prominent means used to counterbalance the potentially negative effects of sarcasm were articles claiming that volunteers, despite some
disenchantment, still possessed the desire to demonstrate manly courage as
well respect for duty—attributes that not only enhanced their individual
reputation, but also, it was contended, Canada's status and the triumph of
democracy. Without doubt, this mix of cynicism and patriotic purple
prose, that remained a fixture in front-line military papers between 1915 and
1918, represented a rational strategy; it permitted soldiers to release anger
but also reminded them that important, if not sacred, purposes lay behind
their travails. Therefore, the same newspapers that admitted that troops suffered from war weariness also implored them to display pluck and endure
for victory. "You're sick of the game? Well that's a shame!" wrote the
Sapper. "You're young, and you're brave and you're bright/ You've had a
raw deal? I know, but don't squeal/ Buck up, do your darndest, and
fight…."[68] The *Hospital News*, in whose pages one found joking references
to men anxious for injuries, nevertheless declared with confidence that at
their crux, all Canadian troops, despite years of anguish, remained loyal to
their high-principled task. "Whether the [fight] ends in 1918 or 1928," it
asserted, such men would continue to "face death day and night" until "liberty r[a]ng along the borders of France and Belgium…to finally reach the
ears of the autocrats in Berlin."[69]

Military editors also likely figured that it was easier for soldiers to bear
hardships and confront dangers if their accomplishments were celebrated.
For this reason, and also to arouse troops to a truly manly performance, all
battalion newspapers listed the medals won by and commonly emphasized
the prowess of those to whom their pages were primarily directed. "When
history is written," read a standard account, "it will be found that the great
work accomplished by the lads from Bruce County will have aided in no
small degree in the consummation of a victory that will lead to the
unshackling of righteousness and liberty."[70] In a similar vein, the *Mail
Slingers' Gazette* wrote that though noncombatants such as postmen did
not carry rifles, always, it stressed, they too performed their duties "bravely
within the inferno."[71] Battlefield victories, whether or not legitimately
claimed, furnished further opportunities for these sources to bluster on a
par with the civilian press. Ypres, Sanctuary Wood, Vimy Ridge, and several other encounters that have become celebrated episodes in Canadian
history, produced copious material promoting the glory that Johnny

Canuck had bestowed upon the Dominion. Contended the *Iodine Chronicle*: "Their splendid conduct in holding back the German onslaught [at Ypres] in the face of terrific fire and then 'saving the day', as General Sir John French termed it, place[d] the Canadians in the first rank of heroic men."[72] And in offering tribute to those who captured Vimy Ridge, the *Canadian Hospital News* proudly proclaimed that "the lads whose valiance forged the way…emblazoned the Maple Leaf…."[73]

Although some articles tried to alleviate agitation by providing disarming humour about massive casualties, the approach changed dramatically when involving someone from the regiment or battalion. To soldiers whose faces were not mere abstractions, respect, often approaching the level of reverence, was directed. These were sentiments also displayed by the considerable efforts made by frontliners to provide fallen comrades with a decent burial even if it meant gathering up a paybook or a few remaining chunks of flesh.[74] Prose and verse often spoke of courageous and even saintly men, a trend that perhaps provided comfort to those still facing enemy guns by assuring that they too, if meeting a similar fate, would not slip into oblivion but remain a source of inspiration. Among other sources, the *Trench Echo* talked of "the chivalry which lies deep at the breast of those who died for Empire, liberty and right," while *N.Y.D.*, a product of the Number 3 Ambulance Corps, dwelt upon the "spirit of self-abnegation" that dead comrades exemplified, a characteristic that, it insisted, not only assured them the "reward of just Providence," but also "serve[d] as an example [for] those who are yet to come."[75]

Those running military newspapers understood the futility of presenting the idealistic and sanitized portrayal of training and hostilities dominating civilian publications. "Of necessity, our humour must be rather blunt to appeal to men spending their days and nights in wet and muddy trenches…." explained the *R.M.R. Growler*, a product of the 14th Battalion. "If we can manage to take their minds off the unpleasant surroundings for an hour every two weeks, we will feel we have achieved our aim."[76] In pursuing this goal, a rather subtle form of information management was applied. Satirical observations and black humour were allowed to punctuate the pages of battalion newspapers in order to help soldiers deal with depressing conditions. Officers managing the *Vic's Patrol* realized that "simple grousing" did "not constitute disloyalty," but rather could exert a "positive effect"[77] if enabling men to vent and in the process cope with their anxieties and anger. However, so that cynicism not give way to disobedience or desertion, limits were established. Mixed in with commentary about muddy trenches and high casualties were references to loyalty, duty and adoration for those who sacrificed, beliefs that reassured troops that meaning lay behind the madness in France and Flanders.

But beyond serving as another valuable, and more innovative system of wartime information control, the satirical disposition of military publications, which grew in direct proportion to their front-line proximity, also highlighted a progressively widening rift between Canadians in khaki and civilians in a *fireproof house*. In contrast to the comically cheerful version of events delivered to and seemingly holding considerable legitimacy within Canada's geographically-removed and meticulously censored homefront, battalion newspapers, even under direction of military managers, conveyed attitudes approaching what historian Paul Fussell identified as the "ironic mode."[78] In other words, to brace the morale of men operating within a setting so discordant from romantic expectations, military tracts curtailed reliance upon high diction and permitted troops to express satire that mirrored, but would also hopefully contain, their growing sense of disillusionment. Significantly, for the most part, this cynicism remained disconnected from Canadian civilians, a pattern attributable not only to official censorship. Submissions to these newspapers demonstrated that numerous soldiers possessed the literary competence to send home a less than uplifting rendition of events. Yet, often without guidance from military officials, more than a few who enlisted in order to prove their manhood responded, where rational in this conflict, to the goal of meeting such a challenge. While rarely launching suicidal single-handed forays against the enemy, many did at least voluntarily assume the responsibility of protecting their loved ones, not to mention their own image, by choosing to grouse in sources, such as the military press, meant solely for the eyes of combatants—a pattern that becomes even more evident from the dissimilar renditions of this tumultuous time relayed home in letters as opposed to that revealed in personal diaries. Therefore, along with the influence exerted by censorship, propaganda and geography, Canadian soldiers helped fashion yet another painful irony to their Great War experience. Specifically, they played a fundamental role in authenticating naive notions about this conflict circulating within the Dominion, and hence ultimately exacerbated what became a distressing post-war breach between participants and outsiders that in some ways never quite healed.

SOLDIERS

6

Hidden Truths: Letters and Diaries from Canadian Soldiers

As one scholar aptly stated, "any[one] …would err badly who relied on letters for factual testimony about the war."[1] Although it is impossible to present a picture totally encompassing the images transmitted home by soldiers, most troops reinforced rather than undermined idealistic notions. In part, this was a product of censorship that was initially justified by military authorities due to the Boer War experience where a few letters printed by newspapers mentioned the location of British battalions and how some troops looted and burned enemy homes where only women and children remained.[2] Just as significant as official controls in curtailing the flow of disturbing information was the desire of soldiers to project those manly attributes that had proven so central in prompting multitudes to take up arms. To whine, many believed, would project a weak and womanly disposition, as well as depress and worry their loved ones. Even though soldiers resented the falsehoods spread by outsiders such as Aitken who did not share their suffering, most still determined that it was their burden to bear the brunt stoically and, as dictated by the social construction of gender, to protect the weak, especially females, not just in the physical sense, but also from suffering psychological torment.

Senior officers realized that not every participant was capable of keeping military secrets or a stiff upper lip, so formal rules were established and publicized throughout the ranks. When training in Canada, troops received orders to mail all correspondence from camps where, they were informed, random sampling was applied to ensure that information useful to the saboteur, such as the precise location of arsenals, not be leaked. Once in England, officers were told by General Headquarters [G.H.Q.] to "impress" upon men "the necessity for keeping silence regarding all information which may be of use to the enemy."[3] As well, Regulation #453, passed by the Department of Militia and Defence just as the Canadian Expeditionary Force [C.E.F.] landed in France, classified as secret: the position of units; their plans "whether rumoured, surmised or known"; the organization, strength and movement of troops; the location of any bridge, road, railway or defensive work; the "physical and moral" condition of soldiers; casualties; the "effect of enemy fire"; any "criticism of operations"; and "statements calculated to bring the army or individuals into disrepute."[4]

Each company, while overseas, designated an officer as a field censor who stamped all acceptable correspondence with his particular number. Such a practice reinforced the reluctance of men to complain, especially about an immediate superior whom, it was figured, would be shown such a letter, and possibly mete out punishment like an assignment to a particularly dangerous mission. Moreover, to prevent needling from the unit's censor with whom most soldiers were personally acquainted, many messages expunged emotional or heartfelt matter that was crucial in helping to keep families and particularly couples in touch. Claude Williams, who served as a field censor, observed that most personal correspondence simply "acknowledg[ed] a parcel...said they are well, [and] commented on the weather...."[5] Much preferred by troops were the *green* or *blue* envelopes—

solely for "personal and family matters"—that were opened by strangers at bases. Officially, each man was designated one per week, but often this quota went unfulfilled after authorities noted a greater propensity here by soldiers to reveal their positions to curious family members.[6]

Illegal information and offending passages were blotted out with printer's ink or excised with a razor blade. For troops, however, the consequences often extended beyond damaged correspondence. Near the front, Private R.D. Nelson received 14 days in a field prison for complaining that senior officers appeared more interested in continuing parades than preparing men for action, while a Captain G.H. Holton had his leave cancelled for a year after attempting to divulge his whereabouts.[7] Although regulations were somewhat ambiguous on the matter of sending home grisly information, one soldier, no doubt summing up the conclusion made by countless others, remarked in his diary that "in writing [home] we were supposed to be very cheerful...[and] only tell the people...how well pleased we were."[8]

Yet, in spite of fairly extensive efforts by the military, this phase of censorship was, in actual fact, far from air-tight. Officers, often working in dimly-lit trench dugouts, examined hundreds of letters. Fatigue, boredom or distractions such as shell fire produced mistakes. G.H.Q. also understood that some field censors, if not sharing the despair that came to overwhelm many a frontliner, sometimes passed gruesome correspondence as a result of becoming desensitized to such matter. Therefore, perhaps more critical than the formal controls established over soldiers were self-imposed beliefs and exogenous factors. Some men convinced themselves that there was no point in trying to describe the Great War in their correspondence, the magnitude and inhumanity of which those in Canada could never really comprehend. Even if inclined to try and transmit ugly truths, many faced the obstacle of poor education. In most cases, Johnny Canuck had not gone beyond grade six.[9] Some of the more literate, in fact, commented upon what they perceived as the impossibility of adequately describing their reactions to battle. "You give me too large an order in asking for reflections," said C.M. Butler to his wife just before Second Ypres. "I simply live....Thoughts seem suppressed."[10] A number of men also probably felt silly about admitting that they had been duped by propagandists, a situation that, they realized, even if disclosed, those at home could not rectify. But most powerful as a motivating force and shining

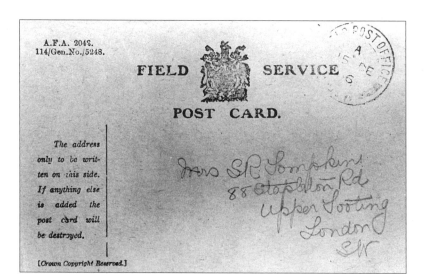

A.F.A. 2042.
114/Gen.No./5248.

FIELD SERVICE

POST CARD.

The address only to be written on this side. If anything else is added the post card will be destroyed.

[Crown Copyright Reserved.]

Mrs SR Tompkins
88 Stapleton Rd
Upper Tooting
London
SW

NOTHING is to be written on this side except the date and signature of the sender. Sentences not required may be erased. If anything else is added the post card will be destroyed.

I am quite well.

I ~~have been admitted into hospital~~
{ ~~sick~~ } ~~and am going on well.~~
{ ~~wounded~~ } ~~and hope to be discharged soon.~~

I ~~am being sent down to the base.~~

I have received your { letter dated _13th_
{ ~~telegram~~ „ _____
{ ~~parcel~~ „ _6th_

Letter follows at first opportunity.

I have received ~~no letter from you~~
{ ~~lately.~~
{ ~~for a long time.~~

Signature }
only } SR Tompkins Lieut

Date _13/12/16_.

[Postage must be prepaid on any letter or post card addressed to the sender of this card.]

W: W3497/293 29248. 609m. 9/16. C. & Co., Grange Mills, S.W.

» "The Field Service Post Card was a staple of communication during the Great War, and it embodied near perfect censorship." (Reprinted from Stuart Ramsay Tompkins, A Canadian's Road to Russia: Letters from the Great War Decade, edited by Doris Pieroth. Edmonton: University of Alberta Press, 1989.)

through in many letters, both directly and by virtue of what was omitted, was the conviction that to remain a true man, it was crucial that participants, even if not choosing to promote their courageous conduct, at least bear the physical and emotional pain of war with quiet resolve.

Consequently, it was usually without intent that private correspondence betrayed that troops were holding back. Civilians might have found it peculiar that letters frequently avoided describing the great adventure, choosing instead to discuss any tidbit of information received from home.[11] More revealing were designations at the top of letters such as "somewhere in France," along with stationary supplied by the Y.M.C.A. to soldiers bearing the printed letterhead warning not to "mention your rank, battalion, brigade, or the names of places, expected operations, movements, or number of troops...." Furthermore, Field Service Cards, sent home by the millions as a quick way to demonstrate one was still alive and to prevent trouble with censors, probably appeared suspicious to many recipients since they only contained pre-printed messages like "I am quite well," or, if wounded, "hope to be discharged soon."[12]

Certainly, a few troops were forthright about the muzzle applied by authorities. One private joked to his family that "we don't lead a very letter writing existence here because anything that might be interesting is tabooed by the censor."[13] As well, a minority, being unable to bottle up their anguish or desiring to protect their loved ones, took a chance in communicating disheartening information. One infantryman told his enthusiastic teenaged brother that "I have seen a lot of life since I joined and more than I hope you will ever have to see."[14] While spreading some unpleasant rumours via word of mouth, such appeals were on the whole uncommon, overwhelmed by lighthearted correspondence, and, as Ernest Chambers ensured, not publicized in the homefront press.

Worth noting as well is that correspondence mailed from Canada failed to alleviate and/or actually contributed to the intellectual divide between soldiers and civilians. Cognizant of servicemen who longed for contact with those they left behind, the military established a massive Postal Corps, with branches in Canada, Britain and at the front. Once arriving in England, Canadian mail destined for the trenches was separated alphabetically and matched with the soldier's last reported battalion affiliation. This proved a colossal task and added to already excruciating delays produced by a trans-Atlantic voyage. For example, in the case of Australia, whose military postal system was identical to Canada's, 57 per cent of letters and 62 per cent of parcels were, at some point in the war, redirected and, unfortunately, sometimes lost.[15] In trying to retain some normality in what often became a haphazard dialogue, people numbered their correspondence and answered letters in sequence. However, a sunken ship or a front-line postman killed by a shell could throw off a conversation for months.

Besides logistically-related problems, some wives and fiancees, no doubt reflecting current codes of propriety, felt uncomfortable about writing overly sentimental messages, figuring that they might be, like the soldier's correspondence, read by another party. Many such letters, therefore, while going into considerable detail about day-to-day activities in order to keep the absent soldier a part of one's life, remained simplistic and artificially cheery. Such an approach was also actively encouraged by the media that claimed that distressing news would only distract servicemen from the performance of their duty.[16] For example, guided by an illustration carried in several newspapers of a trench-bound soldier writing his spouse that "it relieves me of much worry to know you are so well cared for," numerous wives, in their correspondence, downplayed unsatisfactory support—$500 maximum per annum—received from the Canadian Patriotic Fund that, even when supplemented in 1915 by dependants' allowances, caused thousands of women to seek help from regimental auxiliaries, church groups or enter the workforce.[17] And among those entering the paid employment market, such as the 35,000 females who helped make munitions—approximately 20 per cent of whom were married—a substantial proportion, in reflecting current conceptions regarding the woman's sphere and/or out of consideration for the feelings of their husbands or fiances, purposefully made few noises in their letters about enjoying a greater sense of financial independence, self-confidence or the fact that they now realized themselves more than capable of performing a *man's* job.[18]

Personal messages consciously composed with an eye towards confirming gender-based expectations, allaying worry, or bolstering morale, helped numerous couples and families endure years of absence with few serious and/or disheartening trans-Atlantic spats. However, ultimately there came costs. When combined with official censorship and propaganda, such contrived correspondence aided in the creation of two solitudes that, when eventually called upon to re-unite, all-too-often proved ill-prepared to deal with the troubling changes inevitably created within people by wartime strains and demands.

Starting right from basic training, the bulk of letters from soldiers downplayed the dehumanizing facets of this preparation process, choosing instead to stress such masculine attributes as their growing physical strength. Private Haultain boasted that his regiment was composed of "big husky fellows keen as mustard," who could "handle three or four times our number of Germans."[19] Rather than chastise the drill instructor, officer trainee Leonard Youell said to his family that by enduring a tough regimen, he would "become a man with a capital M…."[20] To his mother a member of the Princess Patricia's Regiment insisted that he enjoyed "good health, good grub, good sleep, good company and good pay," and claimed the only thing that could improve matters was if she would "stop fretting."[21]

Personal diaries divulged that much of this ardour was genuine. Knowing little more about combat than what appeared in censored civilian newspapers, trainees were anxious to get overseas and display their grit. Undeniably, many joined up to find work, but by mid 1915 this became less necessary as the Canadian economy shifted to a war footing. Exuded by countless young men, therefore, were those Victorian era beliefs in duty, honour and patriotism; the desire to enter the celebrated cult of masculinity; along with the wish to flee the routines of everyday life to see places read about since boyhood. "I was excited," recalled C.B. Cockburn. "I liked it because it was a change from the peacetime routine." Once enlisting, S. Ellis looked forward to "travelling the world."[22] Brooke Claxton, who became a key member in Mackenzie King's cabinet during a later war, volunteered in 1917 as soon as he reached the required age and even resigned his commission in order to get overseas faster and thus reveal his leadership abilities.[23]

Diaries and post-war recollections disclosed that soldiers proved rather less forthcoming in their letters about the more mundane and unpleasant aspects of an up to eight-month training stint in Canada. Soon after signing their induction papers, recruits were assembled at depots and processed in an assembly line-type procedure. Scores of enlistees lined up naked — some said like meat on hooks — for medical examinations that included inoculations that always left a number ill for days.[24] Soon enough, gripes mounted over frequent inspections, 12 to 15 mile route marches, apparently endless calisthenics, and blind obedience to barking drill sergeants whose job, it seemed, was to forge automatons as opposed to men who would hopefully rise to great acts of individual heroism. Articulating the feelings of innumerable comrades, Pierre Van Paasen claimed that "the moment an apparently good natured farm yokel received his first pair of stripes he turned into an arrogant brute."[25]

Moreover, the harshness and strict discipline of military life, instead of draining excess energy and encouraging a higher moral code, frequently had troops turning to unsavoury tension-easing conduct, especially since most camps provided inadequate after-hours' entertainment — such as a movie often playing for weeks or the odd battalion concert. So rampant was drunkenness that in most cases first-time offenders received only a verbal reprimand.[26] During leave time, it was common for boisterous and inebriated soldiers to swagger through nearby towns or cities in an effort to blow off steam and demonstrate their toughness. Some restaurateurs, in fact, barred troops from their establishments. Furthermore, the bonding process between recruits usually encouraged coarseness. As a rite of passage into a rough male club whose members would soon be required to demonstrate an uninhibited fighting spirit, Canada's Christian soldiers, without exception, felt pressures to "drink, smoke, swear, and gamble,"[27] or, especially in the case of younger and innocent enlistees, to make a trip to the local brothel in order to fully establish their maleness and just in case they were destined to join the unfortunate few who would not return.

More often than not, descriptions mailed home of the trans-Atlantic voyage brushed aside the tedium of a two-week trip, as well as cramped quarters, poor food, frequent lifeboat drills and the stench often caused by widespread seasickness. Once again, men were aware that their correspondence was examined to ensure that details about the route taken, in case it was used in future, or the vessel itself (weaknesses, firepower and so forth) were not disclosed. However, those such as Private Fournier, who recalled a reprimand being given to a soldier for telling his parents about the rotten food on board, realized that the definition of unacceptable information extended beyond security matters. The vast majority of letters, therefore, reinforced images of a rather grand trip or vacation, maintaining that everyone on board was in "good spirits."[28]

Confidentially, considerable unhappiness was commonly expressed. "The ventilation was poor—very stuffy—then the first thing you knew, someone would get sick," recalled one private. "Well, the only thing they could do was to reach over the hammock and vomit on the tables below where we were to eat breakfast the next morning." Resentment between the ranks festered because officers received private or semi-private quarters while enlisted men slept on hammocks strung closely together down below in the hold. As for the food, typical was John Brophy's sally about officers on his vessel being lucky that its quality did not produce a mutiny. Furthermore, like several others, he wished "to see a 'sub'" in order to break the boredom that lifeboat drills, physical exercise and the rare battalion concert failed to assuage.[29] In this atmosphere, disciplinary problems sometimes resulted. On the *Francona*, a ship carrying part of First Contingent as well as 100 nurses, Colonel J.J. Creelman, commanding the 2nd Field Artillery Brigade, observed "dozens of hugging couples." In fact, it became necessary to place the upper deck where the women were stationed out of bounds after one marriage of convenience was performed during the voyage.[30]

Photographs and letters mailed from England perpetuated the theme of the soldier as a sort of tourist.[31] Soon after embarkation each man was given one week's furlough. Those of British birth, who comprised about two-thirds of the First Division, described heartwarming reunions with relatives. From Canadian-born troops came snapshots or descriptions of places such as Tower Bridge, Buckingham Palace and St. Paul's Cathedral, along with, quite often, commentary about a show seen in one of London's famous west end theatres. Imagery was also conveyed across the Atlantic in the form of postcards, a relatively new but instantly popular form of communication reflecting the recent surge in leisure travel. With the war, England's approximately 300 postcard companies faced a potentially catastrophic situation; the German U-Boat threat and confiscation of most passenger liners by the military cut off practically all tourism.[32] In response these firms targeted a new clientele in uniform, particularly the hundreds of thousands arriving from the various British dominions who, in serving, they were also able to perform patriotic work by disseminating some morale-boosting messages across the Empire. Besides famous landmarks, Canada's homefront received postcards showing things such as No Man's Land littered with German dead, or, at the other extreme, humorous cartoons trivializing the dangers of combat.[33]

In other Canadian-bound correspondence, England's damp cold along with further adversities particular to British-based training, received comparatively short shrift. At Salisbury Plain, where it rained for 89 of 123 days following the First Division's arrival (resulting in a massive influenza rate and an outbreak of cerebo-spinal meningitis), one officer assured his wife that "notwithstanding what some people might call our hardships, we remain cheerful." Commenting upon the relatively skimpy rations that Canadians often discovered at English training facilities, another letter insisted that "everybody gets just what he actually needs to keep fit...." As well, few complaints were made about a generally tougher training regimen than that administered back in Canada. In fact, several men, in attempting to boost homefront confidence by promoting a picture of their growing prowess, claimed that a more demanding programme would ultimately yield a superior warrior. "The troops they are sending over [to France] now are the most fit and well trained that have ever left here," proclaimed one recruit. "Our standard is rising while the German is lowering."[34]

To those in Canada, optimism and excitement was usually professed when news came about postings across the English Channel. T.D. Johnson, who received his orders to ship out soon after 6,000 of his countrymen became casualties at Second Ypres, wrote to his family with relief that "at last...I have been given the opportunity of going across and I hope to stay until the end of the war...." Private Lester McKenzie explained to his minister, Archdeacon H.J. Cody of Toronto, that those in Blighty felt "like...spare[s] on a football team—not really satisfied unless...in the game."[35] Some worried that a cowardly reputation would result if they failed to participate. While waiting in England as Ottawa decided whether or not to put a fifth division in the field, Robert Correll complained to his family that "there are enough cold-footed N.C.O.s around in this district and I don't want to be classed with that bunch."[36]

Much of the enthusiasm transmitted home was sincere. However, diaries and post-war testimony also divulged a number of contrasts, starting with the fact that Canadian-born soldiers often had negative reactions towards the revered mother country—enough, in fact, argued R.G. Moyles and Doug Owram, to cause many, as veterans, to eventually play a major role in establishing within Canada a post-war intellectual environment expediting the decline of imperialism as a philosophical force.[37] Certainly, there were plenty of men such as Private Ernest Nelson who revelled in the opportunity of seeing "Westminster Abbey…Blackfriars…and one hundred and one other places" that, one assumes, confirmed to him that England was indeed the greatest of all nations. But when it came to British social customs and behaviour, Johnny Canuck sometimes soured. One rather pious soldier was shocked to discover that "here saloons as well as the moving picture shows" remained open on Sunday.[38] And like many others, Captain W.J. O'Brien focused his disapproval upon "the shop keepers [who] found the boys from Canada very fine pickings." At "every turn," he said, "they…[tried to] soak us in the manner of prices."[39]

Also filling the pages of numerous diaries was terribly caustic commentary upon Britain's climate. Although the situation at Salisbury Plain was extreme, always there remained some dismay among Canadians over what at times appeared as an endemically inhospitable environment. At Shoreham, a volunteer with the 13th Battalion recalled that for days on end "soldiers had to…crawl into damp, frost-laden tents and lie stiff and shivering, trying to sleep in wet clothing."[40] Far more bitterness than that revealed in letters was also expressed over the portions of food that were supposed to sustain hard-working trainees. At Salisbury Plain, Canadian troops lobbied for 1.5 pounds of meat per day but had to settle for one pound that included the bone.[41] Compounding the situation was that many could not adapt to an English diet heavy on mutton, sausages, suet, margarine and other such stodge. When trays were returned with unfinished food, those in charge conveniently concluded that the portions were more than adequate.[42]

Newspaper reports and a majority of personal correspondence from soldiers may have told of "enthusiastic" recruits in England "keen to learn," but realities such as 5:30 a.m. route marches, entrenching lessons, drill,

P.T, along with endless rounds of cleaning rifles, polishing buttons and shining shoes, had one officer trainee wishing in his diary for a "visit of a Zeppelin to break things up."[43] Largely hidden as well from those at home was the fact that British instructors often thought of newly arrived Canadians as soft greenhorns who required an especially tough and, needless to say, unappreciated regimen. Yet the English had a point. As a firm believer in the militia system and an opponent of professional staff schools, Sam Hughes argued that citizen-soldiers, once taught to shoot straight and inculcated with a sense of mission, would emerge as unstoppable. As a result, Canadian-based training, while reaching beyond such rudiments, still too often was conducted by older and out-of-shape ex-British N.C.O.s, and failed, until perhaps the final year of the war, to incorporate any lessons learned at the front.[44] Perhaps such troops should have thanked instructors in England for increasing their ability to contend with the hardships and hazards of trench-life, but instead, many saw themselves as the victims of sadists possessing a superiority complex towards colonials. For example, noting the prohibition against wearing gloves while on parade no matter how far the temperature plunged, one member of the First Canadian Siege Battery confided to his diary that the British consistently displayed a propensity to treat those from the Dominion "like dogs."[45]

In trying to relieve the monotony, strain and bitterness left by a seemingly eternal and increasingly resented preparation process, more drunkenness and problems with discipline resulted. During the first six months of 1917, 1,465 charges were laid by British authorities against Johnny Canuck for drunk and disorderly behaviour—a figure upon which Canadian military officials attempted to put a positive spin by pointing out that it represented less than one per cent of those stationed in the U.K.[46] Still, it became necessary at places such as Camp Whitley to issue orders banning Canadian soldiers from neighbourhood bars after Mayor Iona Davey of nearby Godalming complained to the Adjutant-General about "attacks on elderly ladies walking or even driving home at night."[47]

A minority of volunteers, while still in Britain, looked with trepidation beyond the well groomed practice trenches to notice the wounded who filled up hospital beds. As well, some talked with those on leave willing to share their experiences. John Brophy met two men who expressed a desire to never return—"Great life," said one, "you occasionally find a foot or half a man up a tree."[48] Nevertheless, in the vast majority of cases, private thoughts continued to reflect publicly-expressed bravado. Travelling so far and putting up with the hardships and humiliations of training made men all the more determined to participate in that event where finally, it was believed, they could validate their masculinity, rise from anonymity, and experience a level of excitement unattainable in civilian life. Even John Brophy, who came face to face with disillusioned veterans, said that "I couldn't help envying them for having been through it." Such naivete was especially apparent to battle-hardened soldiers like Courtney Tower who, while on his way to a leave in England, observed that "the new men are cheering and shouting and waving their arms, but the old fellows aren't....They know what it's like and the others don't...."[49]

At the front, most letters, if not emphasizing valiant conduct, downplayed dangers to satisfy censors, ease family concerns and to act out the manly role. "Be sure to know that I'm all right even if there be gaps in the correspondence," went a standard message from an infantryman to his mother. "Every time an Atlantic liner sinks take it for granted that it carries...my letters."[50] Usually, what civilians might have assumed as the discomforts of front-line life were dismissed as minor inconveniences. Sure some soldiers tipped off those at home about unappetizing rations by going on about their desire to receive a food package from Canada, but just as many, it seemed, were like Leonard Youell who, perhaps somewhat cagily, insisted that the provisions supplied at the front were "fine considering the conditions under which they are cooked."[51] Furthermore, though troops often slept in fetid funk holes dredged from the sides of trenches, typical was the comment of one man who assured his kinfolk that "if you could only see me...I'm sure, [you would] think life in France is not so bad after all."[52] Another soldier, while admitting that things could sometimes get a little spartan, nonetheless insisted that rough conditions, like the frontier at home, broke down artificial barriers and provided new opportunities for real men to forge better personal destinies. Unlike the class-divided civilian

» *(National Archives of Canada, PA 1326)*

world, explained R.H. Neil to his brother, those at the front got "to know" their comrades not as "draindigger[s] or... bricklayer[s]" but as "m[e]n and for what [they] really [are]."[53]

Comforting or exciting metaphors such as a "symphony orchestra" or a "fireworks display" described to Canadian civilians the artillery duels often responsible for smashing countless bodies into unrecognizable pulp and driving many men to the point of insanity.[54] Some soldiers insisted that it was possible to minimize the dangers posed by shells. Those who "ke[pt] their nerves cool," wrote one soldier to his family, could gauge the incoming trajectory and "run and fall in time."[55] Meanwhile, John Symmons, in attempting to boost homefront morale, not to mention his own image, assured his parents that "there is no such thing as fear in this land."[56] One of his comrades, also exemplifying such machismo, as well as a popular portrayal of combat, depicted war as the greatest of all competitive sport. "Just like before a football or hockey match," read this rendition of a charge towards enemy lines, "my nerves were very jumpy, but soon it wore off and was replaced by a sort of exhilaration."[57]

Most soldiers spoke optimistically about a triumphant return; but, after witnessing the carnage, some also desired to prepare their families for the possibility of bad news. In doing so, they re-asserted the often genuine conviction that it was a privilege to sacrifice oneself in such a righteous cause.[58] Yet, even if they had proven reluctant to convey their willingness to die for King and country, letters written by army chaplains or commanding officers always expressed such sympathies after the fact. In such correspondence, death always came with honour; never was there talk about an indiscriminate demise from shell fire nor allusions made to grisly details. "Your husband," read one of many such accounts, "died a noble death and there are few better deaths than dying for one's country on the field of battle."[59] Commanding officers were even known to tell the families of those shot for desertion or cowardice that the victim perished in the fight with honour—though eventually the truth surfaced because the Militia Department had to explain why no widow's pension was forthcoming.[60]

In letters, the vast majority of men made no mention about the almost desperate longing for a *Blighty* admitted in some regimental tracts. More often came bold rhetoric such as from one colonel who cursed the "rotten luck" that landed him in a hospital just days before the attack on Passchendaele. Also emphasized was that Canada's wounded never cried out in self-pity. Describing the casualties of Germany's gas attack at Ypres, one soldier visiting the hospital at West Sandling called attention to the fact that "though some lost both legs, some blind…everyone looked happy."[61] If forced to recuperate for any length of time, emphasis shifted to outlining the first-rate care provided. A nursing sister in England whose personal correspondence appeared in *Saturday Night* wrote that "hotels and many beautiful chateaux are turned into hospitals." Newly advanced prostheses and retraining methods, she also contended, insured that everyone would return as a productive member of society. Among the cases she highlighted was that of "a man…[with] two artificial arms below the elbow" who could, through shoulder movements, even sign his name.[62]

Virtually ignored in most messages to Canada were the thousands of troops who would have survived if prompt medical care was administered.[63] Sometimes for hours or even days following battles, wounded soldiers languished in No Man's Land until the shooting subsided. Once recovered by stretcher-bearers, the injured were ferried through communication trenches to a forward aid station. After being stabilized, they were loaded into ambulances for a bumpy ride to the rear. Casualty Clearing Stations, where triage and most operations occurred, were commonly set up in drafty and leaky tents where, after major encounters, men often waited for life-draining hours before seeing besieged doctors. Back in England, where recuperation took place, the conversion of many stately buildings and the construction of new hospitals (such as that erected at Orpington through the monetary contributions of Canadians) provided pleasant surroundings and decent facilities. Nevertheless, there remained a number of cases, such as that of a Captain Charles Rutherford who, in a December 1916 diary entry, recorded that at the Hastings, 200-300 Canadians waited for treatment on concrete floors in an unheated building.[64]

On the positive side, substantial advances made in medical procedures during the Great War ultimately accounted for a 93 per cent survival rate among those who made it to Canadian medical facilities.[65] Counterbalancing, however, was that in several circumstances the suffering among men was compounded as doctors bled patients and used chloroform that caused liver damage as an anaesthetic. Blood typing and antibiotics had yet to appear. Thus, to prevent infection, damaged tissue was removed through a debriding process that widened wounds. Furthermore, the prothesis technology so celebrated in *Saturday Night* was actually still quite crude, producing ill-fitting limbs that soon prompted many recipients to opt instead for empty shirtsleeves.

War weariness and battle fatigue, ailments that sent thousands to hospitals—either as psychiatric cases or as a result of deliberately soliciting wounds—were aspects of combat few men shared with those at home. A rare admission by one soldier that "this four days up [at the firing line] and four days down makes me...want to get clear away from it all," also included a disclaimer for his family not to take such "blue letters...seriously."[66] A majority at the Western Front insisted that their "spirit...[was] excellent" and that everyone was willing to "fight on for 10 years if necessary."[67] Battlefield setbacks were rarely admitted and most men never wavered from the prediction of an ultimate triumph over Germany. During the carnage of the July 1916 Somme offensive, Robin Haultain confidently proclaimed that "we are starting on the final stages of hammering the Hun into submission—he will be a sick man by the time we are finished with him…."[68]

Despite the bluster of letters, and the fact that for some the Great War with manly comradeship and mammoth battles turned out to be a positive experience, the majority of participants quickly came to the depressing conclusion that months of gruelling training did not involve them in a glorious or uplifting contest. Instead, once-eager recruits discovered a conflict characterized more by stalemate, incessant artillery duels, a mole-like existence, as well as shell holes filled with a mixture of mud, blood and body parts. Such observations, and the sense of despair accompanying them, dominated the pages of many a frontliner's diary. Officially, these journals were illegal in the war zone because military authorities believed that their contents, if obtained by the enemy, could furnish valuable information. Yet, men from all ranks showed a determination to record for posterity their impressions of an event that in numerous cases was foreseen as a critical life juncture when they would finally and fully develop their masculine capabilities. Unfortunately, all-too-often, the diary—reflecting in essence the bitter ironies faced by men during the Great War—chronicled not a record of courage and renown, but instead, an emotional catharsis, for in its very private pages countless soldiers were moved to express anxieties, anger, and *effeminate* weakness.

One of the first nasty shocks was that despite enduring a relatively intense British-based training regimen, Canadian soldiers still frequently discovered themselves inadequately prepared for action. They had graduated through a demanding programme that included some lessons in rapid rifle fire, machine-gun use, and silent patrols; but the readiness of many had still been compromised in some respects as a consequence of the 1914 patronage appointments by Sam Hughes of J.C. MacDougall and Sam Steele to direct the British-based training of the First and Second Divisions respectively. Both were given considerable autonomy and, in order to protect their turf, refused to cooperate with one another down to the level of retaining separate and equally outdated training programmes. In addition, senior Canadian militia officers who accompanied their regiments to England but proved unsuitable for front-line duty, were permitted, with Hughes's approval, to help the British prepare Johnny Canuck for action despite being too aged, unfit and inexperienced with modern warfare to properly perform this task.[69]

The products of this politicized system boarded vessels for a rough five-hour voyage across the English Channel. A final gruelling and far-too-brief training routine—appropriately called the bull-ring—greeted them at French depots before 40 soldiers crammed into boxcars for a slow and bumpy two-day ride to a point near the front. Finally at the end of their long expedition, many promptly concluded themselves technically and psychologically ill-prepared, not to mention improperly and poorly equipped. "When I think of it," said one Canadian private, "our training was decidedly amateurish and impractical," consisting mainly of "route marches and alignment movements."[70] A lieutenant, writing just before the attack on Vimy Ridge, charged that training instructors had placed far too much emphasis upon using bayonets. With few soldiers ever getting close to the enemy, just 0.03 per cent of wounds recorded by British physicians during the Great War came from this weapon.[71] Frequently, newcomers were bewildered by the devastation, cannonading noise and first signs of death. The initial reaction of many to shell fire was typified by R.W. Rigsby's admission that "I nearly dropped my breakfast when the…'heavies' began to bark just outside our hut."[72] If towns transformed into rubble or frightening explosions failed to unnerve, news of the first casualty often did the trick. "There was a rumour going around to-day that a man in the 4th Brigade had been killed," wrote Lieutenant-Colonel D.E. McIntyre. "It made quite an impression…[for] one always thinks that no matter who may get hurt it won't be him, but here was a fellow who probably had that idea and now he was dead."[73]

Kit bags, containing equipment weighing approximately 80 pounds, hardly proved suitable to a life of marching through mud, manoeuvring in trenches, or charging across No Man's Land. Much to the pleasure of French civilians, "one by one the unnecessary articles were flung to the side of the road." What was left, said an infantryman, "was done up in a couple of sandbags, and consisted mainly of two blankets and a waterproof sheet."[74] Anger was also vented, especially during the war's early stages, over binoculars "of poor quality, low range, and inferior efficiency"; shortages of shells and maps; as well as the Ross Rifle whose bolt jammed when subjected to rapid fire or the slightest contact with dirt. Neglected in press accounts of Second Ypres, for instance, were stories about the approximately 1,500 desperate Canadians who tossed aside this weapon to gather up Lee Enfields from dead British soldiers.[75] However, because the Ross was Hughes's personal choice, its limitations, which also included a muzzle too long for easy manoueverability in the trenches, plagued Canadian troops for yet another year.

Notwithstanding the rough introduction, it was not true, as sometimes stated in press reports, that troops appreciated the need for and responded well to continued training near the fray.[76] Diaries revealed that such activities, along with front-line inspections, were frequently condemned as the brainchild of the pretentious and overly officious. At least one captain sympathized by accusing some fellow junior officers of "boot-licking" for insisting upon presentable uniforms in the trenches when word circulated that someone important might be making the rounds.[77] Regardless, troops submitted to such minutia for fear of savage and humiliating penalties such as Field Punishment #1 that involved being tied spread-eagle to a cart wheel for two hours daily no matter the climatic conditions.

In releasing anger against those who imposed petty regulations, one member of the 13th Battalion told his diary that it was such people who invariably "lost their nerve" when shells began to fly.[78] Of course, Canada possessed plenty of truly courageous leaders who inspired their underlings. Indeed, since officers led men into battle with nothing more than a pistol, they met with an approximately 47 per cent casualty rate compared to 37 per cent among noncommissioned ranks.[79] Nevertheless, many enlisted personnel, particularly during the first half of the conflict when inadequate central control was exerted over the selection of officers, found it difficult to respect their superiors whom they quite rightly alleged often obtained their commissions through high-ranking connections. Unfortunately, not until Hughes's departure as Militia Minister were those such as General Arthur Currie able exert enough influence to insist that the most competent be promoted from the ranks and sent to tactical schools such as that started in 1917 by the newly organized Canadian Corps at Bexhill-on-Sea.

Despite Canada's officer corps improving over time, the pervasive muck and misery of the Western Front always motivated many a common foot-soldier to focus upon every snobbish nuance—such as the use of walking sticks—and privilege enjoyed by their superiors.[80] More than a few enlisted personnel noted that even the most incompetent lieutenant collected greater pay than the highest ranking and most proficient N.C.O., received the best living quarters, enjoyed better access to alcohol, had batmen to lug around his gear, and was granted three to four times more leave. Therefore, while several men hesitated to complain about their superiors in letters home, and press copy commonly talked of brave and effective combat leadership, another, and perhaps more revealing tendency was the wilful neglect of frontliners to salute junior officers, a form of protest that became so widespread that the punishment usually applied was a simple admonishment.[81]

Special disdain was reserved for senior staff officers at G.H.Q. responsible for devising battle plans. Visits to the trenches by such personnel brought snide mutterings about uniforms too clean and girths too large. As casualties mounted and German defences refused to break, those formulating strategy were increasingly cast by men in the *poor bloody infantry* as "authority-crazed, overfed...old fogies with a tragic lack of imagination and a criminal ignorance of actual warfare."[82] When later transcribed into veterans' memoirs, such anger created the still-prevalent image of the bumbling Great War general who regarded his underlings as little more than pawns on a chess board. Although not entirely bereft of legitimacy, such a view primarily reflected the fury of men forced to endure a virtual hell and thus understandably ignored the fact that prevailing military technology made it easier to devise defensive strategy while the Allies confronted the task of removing the Kaiser's army from Belgium and France. Still, one must concede that for far too long, the British high command thought rather myopically in terms of a great breakthrough. Their typical plan of attack was to massively shell opposing trenches and then let up for the charge, the belief being that the enemy would not have adequate opportunity to get out of their dugouts and properly man defences by the time Allied soldiers dashed across No Man's Land. One of many problems with this scheme, however, was that the barbed wire placed in front of German trenches remained intact because "shell fuses were not sensitive enough to detonate… just when they hit the ground," thus leaving attackers as easy prey for machine-gunners.[83] By the end of 1915, some generals suggested to Field Marshal Haig that enemy targets be kept under artillery fire while troops advanced, advice that he, to the detriment of 60,000 men, ignored the following July at the Somme. In fact, the ultra-sensitive Haig resented suggestions from his subordinates. As well, both he and his principal advisors, having been inculcated with the elitism of British staff schools, seemed to regard common footsoldiers as a sort of *lumpenproletariat*, capable only of following simplistic and always costly massed linear assaults.[84]

Most of Canada's generals, only 40 per cent of whom possessed any pre-1914 battle experience, did not question the Field Marshal's wisdom.[85] Indeed, the front-line performance of some suggested that their appointment came as the result of a personal friendship with Hughes as opposed to actual abilities. Certainly this appeared the case following the St. Eloi debacle where the British-connected Canadian commander, E.A.H. Alderson, was dismissed, but Richard Turner and H.B.D. Ketchen, both loyalists of the Militia Minister, were retained despite having been equally involved in planning and overseeing this blunder.

Notable improvements came after the Overseas Military Ministry assumed control from Hughes of troops outside Canada. Its successive directors—Sir George Perley, Sydney Mewburn and Sir Edward Kemp— permitted proven commanders, principally Arthur Currie, to make major decisions with little interference.[86] A superior strategist who proved less steeped in orthodoxy than Britain's high command, Currie immediately discarded the linear attack scheme for Canadian troops in favour of platoon formations, fire and movement tactics and rolling artillery barrages. Its first test produced the victory at Vimy Ridge. After becoming Corps Commander in June 1917, Currie also effectively integrated Mark IV tanks into attack formations, as well as innovations developed by the former McGill chemistry professor, Colonel A.G.L. McNaughton, such as that enabling artillery personnel to factor in wind speed and shell velocity, and, through observing muzzle flashes in the distance, to locate enemy guns.[87] While many in the ranks carped about Currie's insistence upon spit and polish, few realized that when compared to most generals, he proved far more concerned about enhancing their chances for survival. In fact, if Haig had not respected his abilities, Currie might well have lost his command for so strenuously opposing what he envisaged as an unjustifiably costly assault upon Passchendaele.[88] Moreover, telling was the fact that while 37 per cent of Canadians became casualties at Second Ypres, this dropped to 14 per cent three years later at major battles fought by the Corps at Amiens and Arras.[89]

But regardless of whether the forays were linear- or platoon-based, to men in the field suffering to execute the plans, those such as Currie safely sheltered in the rear always remained a target of derision. Newspaper correspondents may have written of generals who gave orders within "close proximity of the firing line," yet privately, numerous soldiers spoke about cowards who "sprinkled D.S.O.'s among themselves like water,"[90] or, as Charles Yale Harrison's post-war memoir bitterly contended, "died in bed."[91] While about a quarter of Canadian generals were wounded in the "theatre of action," the fact that only one was killed over more than four years of hostilities seemed to legitimize caustic quips from the ranks about their duty tours as having been arranged by the Thomas Cook travel company.[92] Even during the final 100 days of the war, when the Canadian Corps won a series of impressive battles, countless infantrymen focused upon fallen comrades—44,887 in all—and grew desperate about their own chances of survival. "We hear he [Currie] has said that he will have Cambrai tho' he will lose 75% of his corps," said Albert West of Winnipeg's 43rd Battalion. "If so he is a fool and a murderer." The objective, West insisted, "can be taken but we do not need to be slaughtered to capture it."[93]

When it came to day-to-day life at the front, diaries, as one might expect, projected a far different picture than that revealed to Canadian civilians. During the first two years of the conflict, the Germans held virtually all the high ground in Flanders and were able to flood Allied trenches by breaking several dikes. "Mud, mud, mud, again to-day," wrote one private. "About all we do is to wallow through it." Sometimes, commented Bugler Vic Syrett, it became virtually impossible for soldiers to walk because the "half-frozen mud" that caked uniforms, boots and puttees weighed as much as 120 lbs.[94] Until Canadian soldiers were ordered to change their socks frequently and apply whale oil to their feet, 4,987 fell victim to trench foot, a

» *Keeping clean near the front. (National Archives of Canada, PA 1464)*

condition that often resulted in amputation and in two cases death. Moreover, wet, dank conditions helped account for 45,960 cases of influenza that, in 776 circumstances, proved fatal.[95]

In the summer there usually came some relief as the trenches dried out, and with time, the appearance of duckboards, bath mats, gasoline-powered water pumps, and corrugated iron walls also improved conditions. Furthermore, following the dismal July 1916 Somme campaign, the Allies adopted a more defensive strategy and transformed a number of rough and temporary trenches into a more elaborate network where, for instance, dugouts replaced most funk holes. Still, the front never became a place that one could characterize as providing decent living conditions. Even motorized pumps were incapable of controlling water seepage after rain storms, while dugouts, almost all of which lacked proper ventilation, "reek[ed] of unwashed bodies, wet serge, rotting food, and stale urine."[96] Trench latrines often only consisted of poles suspended over pits. Sometimes, close to the action, men were forced to relieve themselves in pails or helmets and toss the contents onto No Man's Land.[97]

This attracted rodents that also fed off corpses and army rations and left behind a litany of diseases. Private Leonard Wood recollected that they were "great, podgy brutes with fiendish, ghoulishly gleaming eyes," that, because of their size, combined with fatigue among the troops, were sometimes mistaken for the enemy.[98] As well, practically every soldier came to curse the fact that not until 1918 did the military develop an effective anti-lice powder for use in laundries. Solutions improvised by frontliners such as creosote, Keating's mustard powder, or cheesecloth underwear brought at best only marginal and fleeting relief. Equally ineffectual were matches or cigarettes run along the seams of uniforms where the vermin laid eggs. "We used to play poker for lice," joked Tom Bovey. "If you won, [you] put it back in your shirt."[99] Despite some men managing to keep a lighthearted attitude, the official history of the Canadian Army Medical Corps [C.A.M.C.] noted that lice caused many to "pass through all stages of mental disturbance from dislike and disgust to hatred and frenzy."[100] In fact, high influenza and tuberculosis rates were partly attributable to lice-ridden soldiers stripping off uniforms in a vain attempt to rid their clothes of the pest.[101] Often expressed, therefore, was a rather desperate desire for the baths or showers provided at rest stations. One infantryman explained that "after, say, twelve days of filth and slush, of fecundence and slime…a bath is somewhat of a glorious affair." Unfortunately, the facilities commonly proved far from adequate. For about one minute, wrote a soldier, "the patient or should I say the victim, stands under a sprinkler spout and receives small streams [of tepid or cold water] from six holes."[102] Therefore, men often settled for less formal settings. Common was the occurrence described by one corporal whose unit had a bath in a rain-filled shell hole—"A shallow muddy bit of water," he admitted, "but it was enough to swim in & felt mighty good."[103]

Both the quantity and quality of food delivered to the front enhanced despondency. Rarely shared in any detail with Canadian civilians was that coal braziers, or, towards the end of the war, primus stoves, heated up a pitiful repast almost always consisting of tea, one tin of pork and beans, bully (corned) beef or Maconochie stew (primarily carrots and turnips) between two or three men; a can of jam (invariably apple and plum flavour) or butter between five; a few hardtack biscuits; and on rare occasions, mutton or beef. It was a diet that historian Denis Winter noted, "left men hungry, flatulent, and afflicted with boils."[104] Moreover, the drums used to transport water often retained traces of petrol or the lime chloride used to toss over corpses to prevent the spread of disease.[105] Although countless men asked their loved ones for food packages, military censors still at times established controls over the nature of such correspondence. One dejected soldier was stopped from telling his family that Christmas dinner did not consist of "turkey and all fixings" as described in a Canadian newspaper he received from home, but rather, cold pudding, a few biscuits and tea.[106] Behind the lines, much-appreciated Salvation Army huts offered free soup or stew, but many men longed for a little more variety. Private Donald Fraser went as far as to state that the most important reason a soldier needed pay was to supplement the army diet.[107] Assuming that officers had not purchased all the supplies, chocolate or tinned salmon was available from Y.M.C.A. personnel, or, if that failed, many turned to the staple of eggs, chips and cheap wine sold at *estaminets* run out of numerous French farmhouses.

Perhaps men could have accepted such discomforts with fewer complaints if they had indeed discovered a Great War of quick and decisive clashes where individual will made a difference to the outcome of events. But that inspirational contest described in newspapers and that most recruits anticipated was, until practically the final year of hostilities, revealed in diaries to be an uninspiring, largely immovable, battle of attrition. For the most part, troops adhered to a pattern of four-day revolving shifts in the firing line (usually about 100 yards from the enemy), followed by service in the support and reserve trenches (respectfully located a few hundred yards and then perhaps a mile further back from where artillery was fired). During the day, those near the front stood sentry, sniped at the enemy, waited for meals or the rum ration, tried to catch a nap, and repaired trench interiors. At each dawn and dusk, they *stood to* and went through the motions of preparing for a German attack. Some likened this "troglodyte" world to a common grave. Such detached conditions also helped give rise to a number of bizarre rumours like the existence of a deserters' army comprised of men from both sides that emerged nightly to ravage corpses for supplies.[108] Between battles, boredom often manifested that in attempting to counteract some men adapted baseball to the confines of trenches, calling the game *scrub*.[109] Also emerging as popular in this atmosphere was the "rat shoot." Ross Cameron remembered many days being spent spearing "fat and overfed" rodents with bayonets and then lining them up like a regiment.[110]

With the onset of darkness some men were assigned to unnerving patrols or trench raiding parties, tasks at which the press cast Johnny Canuck as particularly adept given his supposed backwoods' heritage. Maybe this was so in some cases, but it was also evident that many men selected for such jobs were simply not up to the test of blindly skulking towards the enemy. Things even got to the point where several commanders asked for evidence, such as a piece of German equipment, to prove that the trench raiders had not just camped out for a few hours near Allied lines.[111] Ironically, however, a number of troops envied the trench raiders. This was because throughout much of the war, tens of thousands saw themselves as little more than a glorified workforce. Nightfall had them bolstering parapets, laying or fixing barbed wire, and collecting the dead — their major challenge being to freeze quickly enough when star shells were fired in order to avoid detection.

However, when action did intensify for the multitudes, few, it appears, revelled in the type of excitement usually provided. Technological domination, which in civilian life men had often condemned as robbing them of autonomy and masculinity, appeared at the front more hegemonic than ever. Such was especially evident during enemy artillery salvos that, prior to a major thrust, could go on incessantly for days. Before such bombardments, troops could only hunker down and hope, as the popular front-line saying went, that a shell did not have their *number on it*. One soldier told of his "difficult[y] in realiz[ing] that this is the Great War of which we read so much." Rather than bold and effective thrusts against the foe, he discovered himself reduced to "playing a game at hide and seek."[112]

Shell-fire, which accounted for 59 per cent of British casualties, tested and broke the manly will of thousands. No previous conflict approached the Great War conflict in terms of intensity; in March 1915, during one 35 minute artillery barrage at Neuve Chapelle, where Canadian forces received their baptism of fire, more shells fell than during the entire Boer War.[113] Those reassuring terms used in many letters home such as a *fireworks* display were, in diaries, replaced with more menacing metaphors like "wall of fire" and "running locomotive."[114] One man, in his diary, even remarked that "to get up over the parapet and rush to certain death at the hands of machine gunners or riflemen [was] a welcome mental relief as opposed to remaining stoically in a trench with an avalanche of shells smashing and burying everything."[115] While some troops leaped into action in order to relieve maddening tension, or perhaps in their final act to earn a hero's grave, many others were forced into battle under threat of death. Prior to an offensive it was made known to all men that officers had appointed battle police whose job was to shoot anyone who hid or purposefully lagged behind.[116]

Concluding that they were no longer masters of their own fate, some soldiers, in attempting to increase their chances of survival, turned to lucky charms or ritualistic behaviour.[117] At the other extreme were those who, in surrendering to the strain of ever-looming death, opted out by committing suicide. Others chose to risk the firing squad by going AWL. Of the 25 Canadians executed during the Great War, 22 were charged with desertion and one with cowardice—a number that far understates the problem since capital punishment was applied only to repeat offenders.[118] Diaries also confirmed commentary in battalion newspapers that many men longed for a wound that, while not permanently disfiguring, would provide an honourable exit from hostilities. "Nice clean ones they were," commented an envious Colonel D.E. McIntyre about a private shot in the leg. "He will have two months in England, lucky beggar."[119] A few tried not to leave things to chance. "One of our original draft," recalled a soldier, "came to me…holding a large jagged piece of shrapnel in an old handkerchief, begging me to strike the back of his hand." During the war, 729 Canadians were arrested for self-inflicting wounds, a problem that, in exhibiting an upward curve over time, prompted G.H.Q. in 1917 to issue warnings that such a charge would even be levied against those acquiring trench foot or who failed to promptly don a respirator when gas alarms sounded.[120]

An even more common reaction to the cacophony of noise, orgy of death and apparent impotence of men before machines, was shell shock, neurasthenia or, as sneeringly labelled by some military authorities, "hysterical sympathy with the enemy." The fact that so many suffered mental anguish did not surprise one colonel who said "it is very trying…to stand in a wet trench and hear shells all about and see…chums getting knocked out."[121] In attempting to discourage soldiers from succumbing to psychological strain, headquarters utilized masculine stereotypes, claiming that such a condition afflicted only those with an "inborn disposition to emotivity." As well, to uncover suspected fakers and to force so-called cowards to regain their self-respect, medical personnel ignored emerging psychoanalytic theory and instead implemented cures such as excruciating electro-shock therapy. Yet, despite harbouring such cynicism, the C.A.M.C. was still compelled to recognize 8,513 Canadian soldiers as having legitimately developed various "nervous diseases," a figure that should have been much higher in light of recent psychiatric studies concluding that troops can bear the strain of war for perhaps 200 days.[122]

In letters, therefore, civilians were not just sheltered from the hideous aspects of combat, but also, quite frequently, from the myriad ways in which battle mentally altered many participants. Indeed, to retain sanity, or to avoid neurasthenia, many soldiers developed a blasé attitude toward death and suffering. One man remarked that "in civilian life when I saw an accident, I felt the horror of it, but in the attack, I thought no more of falling men than of flicking the ash off a cigarette." Others came to accept and reflect their environment in a more direct and troubling manner. George Bell remembered one man returning from battle carrying a carving knife dripping blood along with a human head—"His face glow[ed] with a fierce light...his fingers entwined in the blond hair as he swung his grisly trophy."[123]

Probably more disturbing to G.H.Q. than the brutalization of thousands, was that in some, the presence of such widespread suffering helped generate a more compassionate type of transmutation. To those at home, men usually denied and denounced fraternization not only to retain morale, but also because specific instances, if uncovered by censors, could bring disciplinary consequences.[124] But to see first-hand an enemy demonized by propagandists left a number of soldiers astonished. "We could not believe [it]," recalled one man after encountering a German prisoner. "He was not a squarehead with a double chin on the back of his neck...[but] just an average young man, who would have been one of us."[125] Admittedly, the tendency towards re-evaluation did not undermine the general will to defeat those believed responsible for atrocities such as the rumoured crucifixion of a Canadian soldier; but it did at times encourage a degree of cordiality with a foe whom more than a few Canadian servicemen realized negotiated mud as deep, endured cold as penetrating, and spilled blood just as freely. Fraternization was far more extensive than the famous Christmas truce of 1914 where British and German forces played a football match. For instance, despite orders to shoot those attempting to reenact the event, one Canadian serving at the Somme noted that Christmas

1916 brought a "friendly exchange of greetings." There also existed more subtle forms of cooperation: it was considered bad style to launch artillery during meal hours, and in some sectors informal truces prevailed so long as one side did not start something.[126]

Beyond conjuring the extremes of brutalization and empathy, it seemed that most men, in order to cope with unprecedented pressures and a good deal of despondency, loosened in some manner their sense of propriety. Civilians who expected disciplined, chivalrous and Christian soldiers to return triumphant from God's battle against the pagan Hun frequently faced the shock of confronting those who still showed some effects of having developed while overseas a *live for the day* attitude. Such a jolt must have, for example, greeted more than a few Methodists in Canada whose clergymen assured them that all troops—even those terribly unruly during their civilian days—"learned to pray in the trenches."[127] Maybe such a tendency did surface during the thick of battle, but soldiers also developed other less savory means to handle tension and privations. There were the multitudes who developed a linguistic reliance upon expletives. One captain "urged the boys not to take back to Canada…the dirty filthy adjective which everyone here uses to describe everything under the sun." He referred "to the word which men use the world over to mean sexual intercourse…although it may have started from the word fecundate."[128] Thriving as well among soldiers who in many cases foresaw few tomorrows were high-stakes poker, crown and anchor, and floating crap games. Another telltale of military morality was the savoured daily issue of rum. Attempts by teetotalling commanders such as Brigadier-General Odlum to distribute cocoa instead was wisely vetoed by divisional headquarters. Indeed, prior to an offensive, several extra rations of rum were commonly provided to prepare men for the possibility of death or the need to kill. One soldier explained that "under the spell of this all-powerful stuff, one almost felt that he could eat a German, dead or alive, steel helmet and all."[129]

Without doubt, those in the Dominion would have been left incredulous had they known the degree to which their sons threw civility to the wayside; for still considered scandalous in wartime Canada was entertainment provided by the Naughty Nine, a group of young women from Ottawa who put on a Ziegfeld Follies-type benefit show. Yet even in England the more visible strains of war eased Victorian moral codes, a development that Johnny Canuck was more than happy to exploit. For

those on leave who wanted to the banish horrors of combat from their consciousness, not only was there booze, but also, especially in London's west
end, chloroform and cocaine. One can only assume that the problem was
serious since the usually sanitized and upbeat C.W.R.O. publication,
Canada in Khaki, carried a fictionalized account about how a soldier was
nearly enticed into this shadowy world. "A pinch or two of cocaine snuff,"
promised a young temptress, "will make you happy as a king." In this story,
however, the conversation was overheard by a nursing sister who saved
Canada's pristine hero from becoming a drug fiend.[130]

Troops also craved sexual release, something that the realities of life and
death during the Great War convinced many to satisfy while still having
the chance. Rather than developing self-discipline and a code of courtly
conduct, more telling was the fact that 66,346 Canadians in uniform were
diagnosed with venereal disease, a figure that topped all other noncombat
injuries acquired by Dominion soldiers during this conflict.[131]
Approximately 75 per cent of cases were contracted in England. Besides
lonely wives, Johnny Canuck discovered adolescent girls whose parents
and older brothers were occupied with military duties or civilian jobs.
Moreover, a small army of prostitutes milled around leave centres such as
the Maple Leaf Club and filled London's alleys, sometimes plying their
trade outdoors under the cover of darkness. For those who desired more
discretion and safety, there were places such as the Cavendish Hotel where
proprietor Rosa Lewis promised "clean tarts."[132] Military authorities, perhaps in a nod to Victorian taboos, balked at authorizing formal lectures to
troops on sexual matters, but in 1916, the C.A.M.C., of its own volition,
established a department in England to produce literature warning soldiers
about venereal disease. As well, in cooperation with the London National
Guard Volunteer Corps, it set up a few Early Treatment Centres where
men might go after sexual contact.[133]

Meanwhile, from across the Channel, a number of soldiers assured
wives and girlfriends that they had no interest in "unattractive" French
peasant women. However, regardless of appearances and promises, a number decided to capitalize upon the desperation of civilians who were
sometimes forced to sell their bodies for food. In meeting the demand from
servicemen, one private observed that in practically every town, "little boys
would be out there touting for their sisters."[134] And while orders stipulated
that France's renowned brothels be placed out of bounds, instances

occurred where scores of men, with a ten franc note in hand, queued up while Military Police kept order. Although commanders publicly condemned loose behaviour and fined those whom it became necessary to hospitalize because of V.D., they tolerated, and often partook in, such stress-relieving conduct. In most cases, it seemed the rule of thumb was that so long as one's fighting ability was not adversely affected, a blind eye was turned.

Apart from fears over incurring savage punishment or the label of coward, there is no denying that innumerable men drew sustenance to carry on through the muck and misery of the Great War from their undying attachment to concepts of duty and national honour, as well as the belief that Allied aims were laudable. W.J. O'Brien, though distraught after his participation at St. Eloi, still wrote that his year at the front was "worthwhile" because "authoritarianism was being brought to an end."[135] But while many remained unyielding in such convictions, a substantial proportion, desperate for the guns to fall silent, eventually softened their position on the need to completely crush the German beast. "If the people…knew half of what the men have to go through," went a typical diary entry, "they would try to get peace as quickly as possible." In expressing despair over the war's apparent interminability, many a participant even grew pessimistic about its eventual outcome. Following the much-touted Somme offensive, one captain, in his diary, contended that "we simply can not win…." At best, he claimed, the Allies could "force down a little bit" Germany's conditions for accepting peace.[136]

When an armistice was finally declared, troops often reacted with disbelief. A few, in fact, viewed the accord as just one more rumour circulating within their information vacuum. Recalling the news, V.E. Goodwin wrote: "Surely in a few days Col. Mearling would order us to load up and move out for yet another bloody engagement." Soon everyone accepted the treaty's authenticity, but amidst the resulting euphoria was a concern from one frontliner soon to echo loudly: "What to do? So quiet one could hear one's hair growing. The change was too sudden."[137]

For the moment, however, almost everybody savoured the silence and focused upon getting home. Therefore, delays resulting from a combination of ship shortages and dockyard strikes in England; a Canadian train service capable of handling only 20,000 passengers per month from Halifax; General Currie's plan of sending back men as battalions, rather than by individual length of service, to maintain administrative order and for homecoming celebration purposes; plus the federal government's desire not to flood the employment market, aroused impatient troops towards violence. At the depot in Estaples, France, angry Canadians made their way past a British guard detachment, entered the town, got drunk, then stormed brothels and "toss[ed] naked whores high on blankets."[138] In England, riots involving Johnny Canuck occurred at Pirbright, Shoreham, Folkestone, Dover, Fairlop, Grove Park, Kempton Park, Park Royal, Sydenham, Whitley, Bramshott, Guildford and Aldershot, and culminated in March 1919, when the prospect of yet more holdups caused by the decommissioning of the decrepid passenger liner *Northland* precipitated an uprising at Kinmel Park leaving five dead, 25 wounded, and 59 under arrest.[139] To prevent another such occurrence extra efforts were made to expedite the repatriation process, and by that summer all Canadian troops scheduled to depart Europe were finally home.

Then, in what perhaps emerged as the bitterest irony of their Great War experience, many soldiers came to regret the haste with which they cast off uniforms. This was because those who finally returned from France and Flanders were not the same people who left Canada, a metamorphosis that, to their consternation, was often duplicated among their kith and kin. To Canadians on both sides of the Atlantic who transcended physical distance and endured lengthy separations through cheery correspondence there came a series of unsettling shocks. In the case of soldiers, within whom the changes were usually more extreme, manly letters designed to bolster self-image, ease homefront anxiety and satisfy censors, were obviously incapable of preparing civilians for the often embittered and damaged products emerging from that bloody and soul-destroying experience conveyed in diaries and later relayed in oral reminiscences and memoirs. For while once-eager recruits searched for excitement, too often they discovered tedium; having anticipated the fulfilment of their masculine potential, they instead found a military machine endeavouring to break down individuality; expecting to find pomp, gallantry and heroism, they encountered mud, rats, lice, dismembered bodies and indiscriminate death; and while hoping to come home as redeemed and better people, in many cases they returned as callous, sadistic, disillusioned and morally debauched.

A painful post-war pattern was now ready to commence, one in fact partly created by Johnny Canuck. For in the process of acting out the role of a real man in his messages home, he further legitimized that absurdly clean and appealing depiction of combat and its participants promoted by official opinion-makers. Although undeserved after having suffered through so much, nevertheless it was predictable that soon after returning to Canada, it did not take long for many veterans to discover yet another, and even longer, struggle—namely to re-integrate within a society conditioned to greet valiant warriors improved by their great adventure overseas as opposed to ordinary men frequently left maladjusted by what, unfortunately, they alone understood as a trip to Hades.

» *Returning Canadian soldiers celebrate their impending homecoming.*
  (National Archives of Canada, PA 6341)

7

Johnny Canuck Returns to Civilian Life

Those charged with the task of manipulating Canadian public opinion during the Great War faced a population well primed for the struggle. Celebrations across the land in August 1914 demonstrated that most people endorsed some contribution to promote liberty's triumph over autocracy, and perceived combat in terms presented by romanticized paintings or popular adventure stories. Outside Quebec, further encouragement came from an imperialist faith that had thousands responding to help a revered mother country, while at the same time hopefully boosting Canada's status to full partnership within the Empire.

Contributing to the perseverance of this optimism was the Dominion's physical location that went a long way towards ensuring that the potential power of the communication media remained geared towards providing a favourable portrayal of warfare. Had overseas journalists, photographers and filmmakers been inclined to disseminate unpleasantries, none enjoyed the technological means to easily by-pass censors. Copy was filtered through a jingoistic sieve applied at G.H.Q., by those watching the one trans-Atlantic cable linking North America to England, or perhaps by the British Board of Film Censors. But to a large extent, such controls were superfluous. Canadians received news through official *eye-witnesses* and correspondents anxious to pitch in for victory—a situation reflecting a journalistic profession where the aim of objectivity was still far from conventional. What logistics did, however, was retain the credibility of their largely dream-like front-line despatches by sheltering Canadians from contradictory first-hand evidence such as air raids or distressed soldiers on leave. Also important in this context was the pattern of the country's battlefield participation, which peaked after Vimy Ridge, thus bringing comparatively few wounded men home before 1917. To citizens, therefore, the Great War remained a distant event about which truths were conveyed through patriotic purple prose and film versions that servicemen no doubt found laughable. In describing that rendition of the *Battle of the Somme* censored in Canada, one soldier on leave in Britain said: "It was nothing compared to the real thing."[1]

Long casualty lists certainly saddened thousands, but with romanticized copy bombarding civilians through every conceivable mass medium, it remained possible for most people to think of brave men cleanly cut down in a cause for which they happily sacrificed all. So influential were such views outside French-Canada, that despite a haphazard and penurious recruitment scheme imposed by Militia Minister Hughes, ongoing jingoism and naivete (though supported as well by high unemployment) allowed Ottawa to delay for more than two years before initiating a major domestic propaganda effort. When finally forced to launch campaigns to meet the challenges of national registration, conscription, along with food, fuel and Victory Bond drives, politicians still encountered a majority ready to respond fervently to shibboleths about duty, defending freedom and promoting national honour.

Another critical force in forging the homefront consensus was the country's Chief Censor, Lieutenant-Colonel Ernest J. Chambers. To identify and suppress subversive sources and ensure that Canadians remained staunch in their loyalty, he regularly sent instruction sheets to newspaper editors, cable and phone company personnel, book sellers, provincial movie censors, theatre owners, record firms, as well as to federal, provincial and local law enforcement authorities. In addition to such efficient management, Chambers also attained impact through herculean work habits that connected to his longstanding desire to serve the Empire. Never did he relent in the effort to crush those he perceived as compromising Canada's commitment to the war and the mother country. A dearth of permanent staff also made suppression his preferred method instead of straining over-burdened employees by constantly monitoring sources that appeared unacceptable. In executing this rigid regimen he was well-equipped by oppressive legislation reflecting a Canadian legal tradition placing "peace, order and good government" over individual liberties. Although Chambers exaggerated the power of America's Bill of Rights in protecting expression, it did at least provide a modicum of flexibility to filmmakers that he perceived as imprudent; prevented Congress from out-lawing entire language groups; and apparently prompted U.S. censorship authorities to deny mailing rights rather than quash sources completely and in perpetuity, that, once arriving in Canada, usually constituted their fate.

The imperialist philosophy to which the Chief Censor subscribed dove-tailed with the well-established ethos of Anglo-conformity where those judged as foreigners were depicted as inferior and as a threat to Canada's British way of life. During the war and the Red Scare, this belief was inten-sified to near-hysteria as Canadians, including the country's neophyte secret service, fretted over a German-American invasion and a multitude of other traitors in their midst. In sharing and feeding off these ideas, Chambers adopted an uncompromisingly harsh approach toward scores of foreign-language and socialist tracts. A number were indeed inflammatory, but the vigour with which he harassed Sikhs, Chinese, Germans, Finns and Ukrainians in Canada often appeared as motivated more by nativism rather than any concrete proof of disloyalty. Furthermore, such rigidity, even if partly absolved by the intolerance invariably bred by the war or anx-ieties over a significant leftist surge, still played a part in establishing controversial patterns. By helping to spearhead a largely nativistically-motivated campaign that identified a few unpatriotic elements and radical aliens, Chambers, as well as those like C.H. Cahan, assumed a pioneering role in establishing the supposed need for rather draconian legislation as well as a permanent peacetime surveillance network.

Moreover, on a wider front, while the Chief Censor performed valuable work in helping to keep the home fires burning brightly, his extraordinary determination and ability to coddle Canadians helped produce, along with propagandists, painful legacies for society-at-large by contributing to the creation of two distinct ideological solitudes. Besides his resolve to com-pensate for supposed laxity in America derived from First Amendment rights, Chambers's exceptionally strict approach was also guided by the contention that British citizens, because of their nearness to action, possessed a better understanding of and more tolerance for the less palatable aspects of combat. Banned in the Dominion, therefore, were a number of books, photographs, etchings, movies, as well as newspaper reports that circulated in the mother country.

Augmenting Chambers's ability to maintain widespread idealism was that most Canadians did not perceive themselves as overly manipulated. Most mainstream newspapers refrained from mentioning censorship, either directly or by inserting blank spaces. Certainly, it was not much of a stretch for a pre-war partisan fourth estate to accept propagandistic copy and censorship decrees in order to rally behind the standard. Cleverly, Chambers appealed to their patriotic inclinations. Furthermore, three decades of experience as a newspaperman undoubtedly helped him gain compliance from those running publications, some of whom must have been personal friends. There was also Chambers's "genial" disposition that became apparent in the tactfully phrased admonitions he gave to editors and publishers he presumed as loyal. Indeed, upon his retirement as Chief Censor, the Kingston *British Whig* commented that "he went at the job with an earnestness and fidelity that resulted in success," while the Calgary *Herald* said "it is a tribute to his efficiency that he carried on during the war with so little friction."[2]

However, in addition to favourable professional and ideological factors, as well as an appreciated diplomatic approach, Chambers also secured submissive behaviour because Canadian newspaper proprietors and editors apparently realized that they had limited leverage. The humble contrition expressed by many after being told that they transgressed the censorship rules demonstrated that Canada's fourth estate, though politically connected, did not possess the confidence nor clout of Fleet Street press barons. Admittedly, there were occasions where, in order to avoid creating martyrs, the Secretary of State intervened to curb Chambers's fervour; nevertheless, the Chief Censor enjoyed enough legislative and political power to affect the editorial decisions of major publications such as *Maclean's* and even *Le Devoir*.

Finally, the ability of censors and propagandists to shape opinion also derived from the fact that their unrealistic depictions were usually confirmed by soldiers. In hiding from their family and friends the grim realities of front-line life, some men feared the consequences of challenging military censors; others could not find words to express their feelings; while a number believed that there was no point in trying to enlighten people who could never comprehend their predicament. But probably the most salient reason in explaining self-censorship derived from the desire of participants to fulfil the masculine role that had prompted so many to enlist. While the aspirations of countless soldiers for physical and moral improvement, greater autonomy and rousing adventures were dashed in the trenches, many still decided to act out the manly stereotype in correspondence home. By talking about their brave conduct and/or by downplaying the undesirable aspects of the Western Front, they hoped to spare loved ones from worry and not lose the respect of those at home by *whining like women*. In most circumstances, it was only in sources deigned for the eyes of combatants, such as battalion newspapers or diaries, that a more sombre version of the Great War appeared.

As a result, the concocted correspondence from Johnny Canuck ultimately intensified a clash with a society well sheltered from the torment he endured. To be sure, a period of awkward social readjustment was evident in every nation that had sent men into battle. British civilians expressed dismay over impatient Tommies awaiting discharge in Leeds who precipitated a riot leaving 100 injured. Meanwhile, much to the consternation of Yale University students, veterans of the 102nd Infantry Battalion conducted patrols to reap vengeance against those they deemed as slackers.[3] But the Americans were abroad for a maximum of two years, while it was possible for British civilians to see their kin during leave time, thus affording an opportunity to adapt to personality transformations. When it came to Canadians, however, separation between civilians and soldiers may have persisted for five years, and troops returned to a land where geographic, legal, ideological, and social factors affecting the press and citizens in general helped propagandists and censors exert a colossal effect. In particular, never were civilians made aware about a war capable of psychologically devastating men; indeed, to the contrary, newspapers, movies and other forms of mass communication, told of an adventure that had called forth and honed the innate prowess and heroism of its participants. In short order, countless civilians grew impatient with Canadians returning from overseas who could not promptly re-adapt and thrive by displaying those manly qualities that, it was said, had brought a succession of stupendous victories and glory to the country.

Keshon
see, big home/front divide (a little Granel)

This is not to cast Canada's civilian population as wholly unaffected by nearly a half decade of unprecedented sacrifice. Hundreds of thousands were distraught over the loss of family members and friends; conscription and inflation had intensified class- and racial-based divisions; and, by the end of 1918, the country faced the daunting task of reducing a national debt that had, over the previous four years, nearly quadrupled to $1.33 billion.[4] People remained cautious about future commitments. Few complained when both Prime Ministers Arthur Meighen and William Lyon Mackenzie King refused to endorse Article X of the League of Nations' Covenant promoting collective security, and, in 1922, support was not widespread for despatching men to help the British fend off a possible Turkish attack at Chanak. Moreover, within two years of the armistice, Canada's full-time military was scaled down to 4,125 personnel, a measure undertaken not just to save money, but also to improve the chances of achieving a lasting peace since the arms' race was seen as having been a major factor behind the Great War.[5]

Still, in no manner did civilians approach the level of disillusionment, or several other disturbing war-related emotions, that they discovered prevailed among repatriated soldiers. For while domestic opposition to the Great War mounted with time and called for stricter codes of censorship as well as more Canadian-based propaganda, at its essence, the bulk of antipathy did not derive support from some new-found abhorrence towards combat _per se_. Besides certain religious sects whose pacifism existed before the conflict, resistance grew most among Quebecois, as well as factions within organized labour and the rural sector—groups who rallied against measures such as conscription on the basis of pre-1914 anti-imperialism, the impression of unequal sacrifices being made by different social classes, or due to an inability with less farm help to provide increased food production.

In fact, several barometers of public opinion strongly suggest that among most civilians in 1919, the Great War in general, and the part played by Canada in particular, still constituted causes for celebration as opposed to sadness. Democracy had triumphed, and, as the Vancouver _Sun_ predicted, "a new dawn for humanity" now beckoned.[6] The Dominion, proclaimed several sources, had supposedly obtained worldwide respect, something evident by its separate signature on the Versailles Treaty along with a seat in the League of Nations. "This country is 'on the map' so to speak as never before," said the Calgary *Herald*, "and nations which all but ignored us in the past are now almost certain to look our way."[7] Deemed as the cause of such progress was the superhuman Johnny Canuck. While not intending to belittle his conduct in battle nor role in creating national pride, nevertheless, after the war, embellished portrayals continued to characterize his exploits and legacies. Typical was the Hamilton *Spectator* that, in reporting the 19th Battalion's return, dwelt upon a "path of glory...across the craters of St. Eloi, over the shell-swept areas of the Somme basin, up the scarred heights of Vimy Ridge and the slopes of Hill 70, through Passchendaele's slough and mud and blood to the epic days of 1918...which released the world from the yoke of Prussian militarism."[8]

The post-war acceptance of such pumped up renditions was evident as well from the ongoing love affair that civilians displayed for battle trophies. Instead of demonstrating disgust towards instruments of mass destruction, tens of thousands continued to flock to a series of shows arranged by Dominion Archivist, Sir Arthur Doughty, during the autumn of 1919 to see those items that in capturing, it was stressed, many of the country's courageous lads made the supreme sacrifice. At the Canadian National Exhibition, the best attended pavilion, attracting over 200,000 people in ten days, was a war trophy display billed by the Toronto *Star* as "living evidence of Canadian valour in France and Flanders."[9] From hundreds of towns, schools, militia regiments and patriotic associations, Doughty received appeals for artifacts to commemorate the country's glorious dead. Competition was fierce. Communities staked their claim by asserting that on a per capita basis, they had lost more men than the national average. Exploiting such sentimentality, the Dominion Publicity Committee, in its most successful strategy for the 1919 Victory Loan, offered 36 captured guns to that place attaining the highest per capita subscription rate—a dispute never settled between Redcliffe and Monitor, Alberta.[10]

Many artifacts, particularly large guns, were used to help build war memorials that emerged in practically every hamlet that had lost one of its own men.[11] With such monuments, melancholy over the enormous loss of life was not a prominent theme; more typical was a romanticized commemoration of those who had, through their "heroic sacrifice" and "saintly deaths," earned the eternal gratitude of their countrymen for having saved democracy and creating a nation whose battlefield exploits generated worldwide respect. The tribute erected in Preston, Ontario, portrayed a warrior with arms outstretched in the crucifixion position suggesting that he too had died for the salvation of civilization, and in the process, achieved ever-lasting life. In commissioning a National War Memorial in 1925, Ottawa wished to promote "the spirit of heroism...exemplified in the lives of those [who] sacrificed." The result depicted 22 figures from all service branches symbolizing the "great response," while the arch through which they passed represented "peace and freedom."[12] That same year, construction commenced on an edifice at Vimy Ridge to honour those men who, it was contended, had not just won a battle, but changed the course of the Great War and laid the seeds of modern Canadian nationalism. On 250 acres provided by the French government, the structure (not completed until 1936 due to funding problems during the Depression) had two pillars signifying Canada's European founding races soar 226 feet from a 40,000 square foot platform set upon the ground's highest point so that those for miles around could appreciate the significance of the triumph. To ensure that generations to come would not forget the astounding feat, for the columns Ottawa went to the expense of re-opening a Croatian quarry that had supplied stones for a still-standing third century Roman palace.[13]

Besides such concrete tributes, soon after the war ended, the C.W.R.O. art collection commissioned by Maxwell Aitken reached Canada. While hostilities raged, it was considered too risky to transport the originals across the Atlantic, but sometimes Canadian magazines and newspapers carried sketch-like reprints. Viewed by millions, was Richard Jacks's romanticized rendering of muscular and bronzed *Canadian Gunners in Action* at Ypres. However, courtesy of Ernest Chambers, who outlawed illustrations "showing trenches littered with the dead," and other such "gruesomeness,"[14] never during the war did those in the Dominion confront sombre entries such as C.W.R. Nevinson's ironically-titled *Paths of Glory* that circulated before tens of thousands in a series of C.W.R.O. displays across Britain.[15] That which was finally repatriated to Canada ranged from *The Conquerors*, by Eric Kennington, that depicted a triumphantly marching Canadian Highland Regiment, to Frank Varley's chilling picture of corpses heaped onto a cart in the ominously titled *For What?*[16] Overall, the impact of the collection upon public opinion was marginal as art was viewed as elite entertainment. Following poorly attended exhibitions in Montreal and Toronto, the pictures were placed in storage. However, among those who went or offered critiques, there appeared a propensity to place an upbeat interpretation upon the collection and not to dwell upon, nor often even mention, the more disturbing entries. A few newspapers stressed, perhaps with a measure of euphemism, that the paintings were "educational" and as something in which citizens could take great pride.[17] Less ambiguous was the Toronto *Telegram*'s reviewer who chose to devote almost all his attention to the portraits of Canada's Victoria Cross winners, the inspirational depiction of the C.E.F.'s landing in France, and of Dominion troops liberating Courcelette. In fact, at both 1919 displays, audiences selected *The Flag* by John Byam as their favourite entry where a saintly-looking fallen Canadian soldier lay upon a Union Jack-draped pedestal also bearing a statue of the symbolically proud and powerful British lion.[18]

Until the late 1920s, Canadians retained an overwhelming preference for literature celebrating the courage of their fighting men. H. Napier Moore, a literary reviewer for *Maclean's*, went as far as to advise the Canadian Authors Association that citizens were not interested in "gloom" but continued to desire "stories of romance and adventure."[19] This recommendation was made easier to meet since disenchanted veterans usually wished to expel the horrors of war from their consciousness rather than rehash them before an audience they believed psychologically ill-equipped for compassionate comprehension. Typical of the initial post-war novel was Ralph Conner's 1919 epic, *The Sky Pilot in No Man's Land*. Here, the protagonist, Henry Dunbar, perished on the battlefield where, like a true man, he told his comrades "to carry on." The gallantry of Canadian warriors was also celebrated the following year in J. Murray Gibbon's *The Conquering Hero* where the author described the exploits of Donald Macdonald of the "fighting 42nd" who, in the process of displaying his unswerving "respect to tradition, King and Country," won the Distinguished Service Medal.[20]

Clearly, the Canadian homefront was far more disposed to welcome back heroes enhanced by combat rather than ordinary men often left physically and mentally scarred by their experiences overseas. Telling was the fact that just before the armistice, *Saturday Night* postulated that a returning Johnny Canuck might at first appear "a bit rough," but in practically no time, such "Christian" soldiers would mellow, and, by applying their battlefield grit and skill, conquer any post-war obstacle.[21] Certainly not every veteran stepping off the boat in Halifax harbour in 1919 was embittered and/or maladjusted. Countless men quickly found a job and got on with their lives. Many even recalled their military careers with fondness. "I wouldn't take anything in the world for the experience that I had," commented a veteran of the 5th Battalion. "I learned much about human nature...." Some also talked about having acquired self-confidence while in uniform—men such as Corporal Curll of the Nova Scotia Highlanders who credited that which he was forced to overcome while in combat as instilling within him the requisite drive and aplomb to ultimately attain an executive position with the Royal Bank.[22]

Yet for thousands it was literally frightening to think about rejoining a society that, they felt, possessed no conception of the ordeals that they had endured nor the torment still often dominating their thoughts. "Prisoners! We were prisoners, prisoners who could never escape," said Will Bird as his troopship approached Canada. "I had been trying to imagine how I would express my feelings when I got home, and I knew I never could...."[23] Countless men realized that the war, contrary to popular belief, had proven a disjunctive rather than a constructive experience, trapping their minds within a reality where civilian norms did not apply. Making this point in a extreme manner was Captain H.S. Murton who, soon after the conflict, wrote an unpublished short story exonerating a veteran charged with murder because after "four years of being ordered to kill for his country...it became a habit with him to take the lives of others...."[24]

In a matter of moments, and without any preparatory lectures, soldiers went from a situation where almost every aspect of their lives were regulated to the widespread freedoms of civvy street. Despite having longed for emancipation from seemingly endless military rules, more than a few men discovered that they had actually grown accustomed to regimentation and still needed someone to provide them with direction. One veteran noted that at the 1919 Canadian National Exhibition, ex-soldiers "clung together as if afraid to break up and face life individually."[25] These men also often talked about having lost the feel of things. Many discovered their old stomping grounds virtually unrecognizable as war industry had drawn multitudes from rural to urban Canada. Indeed, between 1915 and 1918, if the presence of military trainees are also factored in, both the populations of Montreal and Toronto had doubled.[26] Further surprises included record inflation and a far more militant labour movement. As well, those who had left wet districts, or became accustomed to English pubs and the rum ration, now faced a homeland that had opted for prohibition.

If such factors failed to unsettle or anger, there were always the clichéd visions of combat still swirling among civilians. "Friends wanted to hear [glorious] stories of the battlefield," wrote one soldier about his homecoming, "and you felt like vomiting when the subject was mentioned."[27] Instead of reliving the butchery in what more than a few perceived as a vain attempt to enlighten the naive, many ex-soldiers magnified their estrangement from citizens by expressing their feelings only to those who had also seen action, such as in Great War Veterans' Association [G.W.V.A.] halls. Others did respond more forthrightly, but frequently it was in order to berate civilians, especially those who, in demonstrating their innocence about trench warfare, began complaining over having made some measly sacrifices such as a few meatless and fuelless days. To many veterans, it appeared that civilians had done quite well—in fact, too well—while they had endured unspeakable travails. Some returnees noted that despite inflation, relatively high paying war industry jobs had permitted Canadian automobile ownership to double between 1915 and 1919.[28] Harbouring considerable resentment, it was even common for ex-soldiers to publicly denounce well-dressed citizens as profiteers. Soon enough, more than a few civilians began talking about "self-righteous" veterans, or men who had perhaps become "polluted" by the killing overseas.[29]

Apprehension also mounted over the apparent inability of repatriated men to dissociate themselves from violent behaviour. While nativistic civilians had no problem with veterans ransacking the offices of German newspapers or bodily removing *disloyal* minorities and Bolsheviks from workplaces in order to claim their jobs, too often the outbursts appeared uncontrolled. A perceived slight by an ex-serviceman frequently resulted in a verbal or physical assault. In Quebec City, troops used walking sticks given to them as presents before their final discharge to attack civilians. In part, the action was revenge for poor French-Canadian recruitment, but even English-speaking bystanders were disgusted by a event that left three veterans dead from alcohol poisoning (having procured supplies from moonshiners), and caused the destruction of the local police station as a result of soldiers liberating some of their drunken comrades.[30]

Despite having longed for a tranquil setting while part of the fracas, numerous men simply found it impossible to settle down once home. Often lads who returned to rural roots were soon packing their bags and heading off for the bright lights and supposed excitement of the big city. They, and veterans from all walks of life, drifted between jobs. Work-related problems flourished not only because of edginess, but also because many men returned to mundane tasks that, through enlisting, they had aspired to escape. Like others, Pierre Van Paasen desperately hoped that something better awaited after having endured so much for his country, but found only the "same petty, monotonous, joyless, suffocating world of three years before...."[31] As a patriotic gesture, numerous employers kept jobs open for former workers who volunteered. However, even if the tasks were interesting, the prospect of reassuming junior positions (which one presumes was the case in numerous circumstances since most recruits were under 25 years old) appeared insulting, particularly to officers who had held responsibility for scores of lives. To little avail, ex-soldiers asserted to bosses and managers, whom, they sometimes noted with disdain, had spent the war years in Canada, that the discipline and harsh demands of military life had prepared them for important positions.[32] Refusing to accept that the skills they learned while in uniform were often inappropriate for civilian work, many veterans displayed animosity when asked to prove their worthiness for advancement. Thus, among numerous employers who for the most part did not fully appreciate the deep-seated reasons for such resentment, a tendency developed to write off ex-soldiers as a spoiled and unreliable lot who considered themselves entitled to special treatment. Indeed, circumstances became so bad that at one point the

G.W.V.A. threatened to publicize the names of companies that refused to hire those who had served overseas.[33]

In addition to the challenge of re-establishing themselves economically, veterans also faced the matter of reconstituting their family life. Following the excitement of the initial reunion, many experiences turned sour. Indeed, though few grounds existed for divorce and spouses usually had to go to the trouble of obtaining a Parliamentary decree to have their marriage annulled, the number of separations across Canada jumped from 70 in 1914 to 373 five years later, and by 1921, topped 500.[34] Long absences tested and defeated the commitment of many couples, a process that did not always wait for the termination of hostilities to culminate. Ignoring advice to keep the spirits of recipients high, a few people composed *Dear John* or *Jane* letters. More common was that upon returning home, some men discovered that the loneliness of their partner produced unfaithfulness, something that, if not admitted by the wife or girlfriend, was often relayed by a morally outraged relative or neighbour. On the other side of the ledger, while Canada's Army Medical Corps verified that soldiers were free of venereal disease at the time of their discharge, the names of those infected were forwarded to Provincial Boards of Health. They periodically sent notices in plain brown envelopes with no return address advising on the need for check-ups, thus disclosing, in spite of such discretion, the moral transgression to numerous spouses and sweethearts.[35]

Letters helped tremendously in maintaining emotional ties between loved ones through years of separation. But while keeping many couples faithful to one another during the melee, their proclivity to expunge potentially disturbing information nevertheless produced a number of individuals unprepared to cope with those who, besides having aged rather shockingly on occasion, were no longer, psychologically-speaking, the same people once known and still anticipated. Men who endured bombs and bullets by thinking wistfully about returning to the archetypal hearth replete with a dutiful spouse, sometimes confronted a resentful wife who had been left behind with little money while he experienced, according to countless reports received in Canada, a pretty thrilling, if not enjoyable, time overseas. Potentially more problematic was the post-war family situation among men who returned to children as well as wives. Often youngsters perceived the father as an intruder who competed for the mother's attention. For some veterans, there were even more extreme behaviourial problems with which to cope. Between 1914 and 1918, prosecutions in Canada of those under 16 climbed from 2,628 to 4,104, a fact that some wives, out of exasperation in being forced to contend with the situation on their own, were known to blame on the husband for having abandoned his disciplinary responsibilities in order to seek out adventure.[36]

Also often unbeknown among men overseas was that in their absence, thousands of women, as a result of running all aspects of the home, including finances and repairs, or by expanding their endeavours from the domestic sphere to undertake and/or organize volunteer patriotic activities, grew tremendously in confidence. Among many women who entered the workplace, there was, despite the lower wage paid to female employees, an unprecedented feeling of independence as well as demystification of the *man's* job. With the armistice, it is true that many single women thought less about continuing such liberating trends and instead sought to catch a husband among the now expanded stock of men; a good portion of married women eagerly abdicated the double bind of home-based and outside work for sole custody over the domestic sphere; and countless females, in conforming to current mores, accepted that their first priority related to family life and thus voluntarily and patriotically moved aside to make room in the workplace for those who had sacrificed most. Nonetheless, among some women, the conscious and unconscious changes caused by new activities and responsibilities, even if purposefully downplayed in wartime correspondence, must have manifested to some degree after the conflict. Besides veterans who returned to less submissive spouses and sweethearts, some women reported that their "passion for their husbands was utterly quenched when they appeared in civilian clothes, garbed again in the costume that signalled the[ir] resumption of domestic roles."[37] As well, the war years, in helping to at least engender some social acceptance of female work before marriage, gave way to the "new girl" of the 1920s who, in some cases, aspired towards "mak[ing] life-long careers for themselves."[38] Such alterations, when combined with new female voting rights, no doubt produced difficulties in many domiciles, especially since more than a few men went overseas to re-assert masculine dominance over the feminizing aspects of modern society.

Nevertheless, the upsetting changes discovered by veterans paled in comparison to the unpleasant surprises that awaited families who remembered ardent young men marching off to battle, and who, during the intervening years, received manly letters from overseas along with quixotic media reports. All-too-often, civilians discovered not a gallant conquering hero on a white horse returning triumphant from God's crusade, but an ordinary man who, even if not physically scarred, had somehow transformed for the worst. Among high-strung returnees, a loud noise could trigger memories of an artillery duel; a red rose images of ghastly wounds. Concern was unquestionably expressed in a number of households when Canada's Christian soldiers proved incapable of purging obscenities from their vocabulary that, while in uniform, became second nature. Common as well were those such as Lieutenant-Colonel Agar Adamson who, before dying in 1929 from alcoholism, barked out orders to his sons as if they were batmen. Desperately some veterans tried to submerge the anguish of trench warfare from their thoughts, but still it surfaced in a variety of ways. According to medical reports, extreme and persistent nervousness caused more than a few ex-soldiers to experience sexual dysfunctions like premature ejaculation or the inability to achieve an erection.[39] Even those capable of keeping their emotions in check while awake sometimes released the torment at night. "'They're coming over'," said a veteran in describing a recurring dream. "I jumped out of bed…[and] reached to catch my rifle. It wasn't there and I swung around…and hit [the wife] who was black for two weeks afterwards."[40]

The chasm between soldiers and civilians grew yet more intense after the repatriated discovered that while the homefront seemed anxious to canonize those who had perished overseas, it appeared far less eager to extend generosity to troops who had survived the carnage, suggesting that such manly men, by applying their wartime pluck, could, with relatively little assistance, prosper in the peacetime world. To help underwrite reintegration programmes, federal authorities allocated a substantial proportion of funds raised from the 1919 Victory Loan. The fact that all veterans were getting at least some help represented a significant departure from a penurious pattern of public welfare that was normally distributed only to the *deserving*

poor.[41] Moreover, with only about one-fifth of federal revenue coming from income and corporate taxes prior to 1930 (compared to approximately 60 per cent by 1945), on the surface, the various benefits extended to veterans, which averaged some $60 million per annum over the initial post-war decade, appeared impressive.[42] Counterbalancing any beneficence, however, was Ottawa's desire to eliminate a national debt acquired during wartime. This was not going to occur through hefty direct taxation due to the still prevailing wisdom of classical (pre-Keynesian) economic theory. Moreover, the power to implement taxes partly remained with the provinces that, only because of wartime exigencies, had accepted Ottawa's limited foray into this area.

By focusing upon perceived liberal trends with welfare, and being relatively incognizant of the ways in which the war had affected participants, most citizens concluded that veterans were aptly rewarded. Carrying the contention further and echoing the feelings of numerous readers, the Montreal *Star* said that though some compensation was deserved, it was crucial that Canadian veterans, after having displayed such fortitude in action, not be weakened by a programme making it possible for them to become "unlimited creditors of the state to be supported in idleness."[43] Not surprisingly, among many of those liberated from the trenches who insisted that rarely did any link exist among soldiers between the need for assistance and indolence, the government's package was condemned as contemptuous of their sacrifices and as breaking a solemn wartime vow to adequately reward those who gave the best years of their lives to defend democracy. Thus, in addition to providing veterans with a venue to reminisce and commiserate, clubs such as the Returned Soldiers' Association, the Army and Navy Veterans' League, the Imperial Veterans of Canada, and especially the G.W.V.A. (whose membership peaked at around 200,000 in 1919), emerged as pressure groups for a more generous approach. While a War Service Gratuity tided veterans over for awhile, the G.W.V.A. soon led a charge for a $2,000 bonus citing high post-war unemployment and inflation, along with the fact that many men did not qualify for the maximum gratuity. The Liberals made vague commitments about fulfilling this demand at their 1919 national convention, but this was conveniently forgotten when they formed a government two years later.

In their newspapers, civilians encountered letters from ex-soldiers complaining about parsimonious government support, as well as back page reports on demands issued by veteran associations. Neutralizing this material was propaganda issued by the Military Hospitals Commission [M.H.C.] and Department of Soldiers' Civil Re-Establishment [D.S.C.R.]. Through press releases, pamphlets, posters, movies and live demonstrations, citizens were assured that generous pensions, gratuities, employment opportunities and first-rate retraining methods were made available. Accentuated, for instance, was the fact that over 80 per cent of physically handicapped veterans who began a government-sponsored retraining course eventually finished; but neglected were the more than 34,000 rejected applicants (78.7 per cent of the total) whom officials insisted were physically capable of returning to their old jobs. Official communiques also disregarded the inadequate state of several rehabilitation facilities. In early 1919, the *Veteran*, the G.W.V.A.'s literary organ, complained about "a lack of equipment in the vocational schools" that "forc[ed] students to stand round watching others use whatever…is available," a situation that, along with the dubious qualifications of many instructors, prompted some trade unions and employers to reject the validity of M.H.C. and D.S.C.R. certificates.[44]

As far as pensions were concerned, Ottawa feared a repetition of an American experience where, in order to gain votes from Civil War veterans, President Rutherford B. Hayes implemented a permissive programme that soon drained 20 per cent from the U.S. Treasury Department budget.[45] To control costs, Canadian pension commissioners, acting upon orders from their elected superiors, went to the other extreme, commonly denying compensation to Great War veterans unless their injuries were directly related to military service. This doctrine, known as *attributability*, produced no shortage of injustices. F.R. Phillips, though returning from France with multiple fractures of the arm, was denied benefits because he had broken the same bone in 1908.[46] Meanwhile, a sliding pension scale relating to the extent of a soldier's disability, far from extending appropriate aid to every applicant, resulted in about five per cent of claimants collecting the highest possible rate (approximately $600 per annum) while 80 per cent received under 50 per cent of the maximum. A low award, it was reasoned, would encourage men to triumph over their handicaps and not become permanent public charges, a trend also encouraged by high post-war inflation that forced men to seek supplementary income and the periodic rechecking of recipients to see if their benefits could be reduced.[47]

With practically every programme for veterans there proved significant discrepancies between upbeat government claims and the experiences of ex-servicemen. Literature about the Soldier Settlement scheme proudly pointed out that as of 31 March 1921, 25,433 veterans had harvested over 2.6 million bushels of wheat and nearly three times as much oats. Unpublicized, however, was the complaint of many would-be farmers that despite promises to let any veteran try his hand at this occupation touted as suitable for the manly and robust, Ottawa minimized its risks by handing out loans primarily to those who before the war had led an agricultural exis-tence. Applications were also rejected because D.S.C.R. bureaucrats, frequently without ever having seen the property in question, determined that ex-soldiers had offered previous owners too much for their land, thus effectively forcing them to commence operations on remote homesteads purchased by the government upon which 80 per cent of men went broke within five years.[48]

An equally unsatisfactory situation prevailed with civil service jobs promised to veterans. In 1919, when the average annual salary paid to a pub-lic servant stood at $1,071, veterans were assigned jobs, such as in the Post Office, where their earnings failed to reach $800.[49] Employment obtained through government labour bureaus invariably proved low paying and con-tributed to high turnover rates. By 1923, about 20 per cent of veterans—a number significantly higher than the national average—were jobless. Throughout the decade, a multitude of hard luck stories flooded into the federal government, such as that relayed from the disgruntled leader of the Imperial Veterans of Canada who told Prime Minister Borden that he was forced to pawn several "war decorations and a beautiful gold watch and chain presented to me by my Commander…to procure the common nec-essaries of life for my family."[50]

In expressing anger over government repatriation programmes, the inequities of post-war society, and perhaps drawing some inspiration from the wartime goal of improving civilization, some veterans, at least a consid-erable proportion belonging to the G.W.V.A., became leading advocates for a welfare state. Besides passing self-serving proposals for a $2,000 bonus and access to better civil service posts at its 1919 national convention, the association also endorsed a public housing programme; a minimum wage; old age, sickness and unemployment insurance; profit controls and stronger anti-trust legislation; progressive income and corporate taxes; the nationalization of key primary resources; and labour's right to an "adequate voice" in industrial management.[51] Caution must be shown, however, in pushing this left-wing characterisation too far. Soldier organizations went on record as strongly denouncing Bolshevism since most members considered themselves as defenders of constituted authority, and, like a majority of Canadians, linked socialism with disloyal foreigners. Still, those returning from battle were not a monolithic lot. Tens of thousands came from working-class backgrounds and undoubtedly looked askance at a land more than ever plagued by high unemployment and inflation. Moreover, while in uniform, some soldiers may well have developed a proto-class consciousness against authority whom they saw as providing a succession of lies and/or misery: whether it be the propagandists who promised a wonderful war experience; the general staff who planned criminally costly campaigns; or, after the contest, federal politicians with their talk of generous reintegration programmes.

In fact, cynicism was expressed by many veterans over the official explanations given for heightened post-war socio-economic disturbances. Much to the consternation of the federal government, some ex-soldiers in Winnipeg rejected the idea of the 1919 General Strike as representing a revolution, and instead cast the dispute in terms of "three or four stiff-necked iron masters…[who] defied and denied working men their common rights."[52] Fearing radical tendencies among their former comrades, a number of veterans in Winnipeg joined Captain F.G. Thompson's Returned Soldiers' Loyalist Association that organized anti-strike parades and created a special police force to maintain order. By most accounts, veterans in Winnipeg split evenly in their sympathies. On the first day of the strike, the local G.W.V.A. branch passed a motion proposed by labour leader, R.A. Rigg, declaring solidarity with the workers. Two weeks later, such support reached a crescendo when several thousand veterans heeded a call from the G.W.V.A.'s Manitoba commander, former Sergeant Roger Bray, to march upon the Provincial Legislature and City Hall to demand collective bargaining rights for labour.[53]

Vocal disenchantment continued to emanate from ex-servicemen throughout the 1920s. In particular, with the physical and psychological effects of battle persisting within thousands, the government's cautious approach towards pensions remained a bitter bone of contention. Not until 1930, in an era when literature from soldiers began enlightening people about how the horrors of the Great War could still linger with such debilitating effect, did the governing Liberals strike a Royal Commission under the sympathetic veteran and then Minister of National Defense, J.L. Ralston. Finally assuaging some anger was a War Veterans Allowance Act. Starting that year, it replaced partial pension awards for many ex-soldiers with monthly payments of $40 to married and $20 to impoverished single veterans over the age of 60 (thereby alleviating their need to wait for Old Age Pensions then starting at age 70), or sustained during the Depression younger veterans unable to obtain employment because of bodily or emotional damage related to their military service.[54]

Helping to produce the milieu that encouraged the War Veterans Allowance Act were those writers whom the American author and social commentator Gertrude Stein labelled as the *Lost Generation*. It took about a decade for veterans such as Ernest Hemingway, Robert Graves, Erich Maria Remarque and Siegfried Sassoon to understand and confront their outrage over the Great War. Soon, their eloquent, yet unnerving, testimonials about the waste and bloodshed of combat also began affecting mediums such as film. Of greatest consequence was the 1930 Academy Award winner, *All Quiet on the Western Front*. So persuasive was this adaptation of Remarque's classic novel with its anti-war message that it was banned in Fascist Italy and subsequently in Nazi Germany.[55]

For these writers, the passage of time was required not only to fully fathom how the Great War affected the generation that fought, but also to produce a civilian population that they perceived as psychologically disposed to extend some empathy. In the case of Canada, which also produced its own Lost Generation of writers, one witnessed, besides pride over growing post-war autonomy, a fading sense of idealism once citizens realized that in most respects the 1914–18 struggle was not going to generate a new and higher order. On the economic front, class divisions remained sharp; moreover, an initial peacetime buying frenzy, followed by over-production and deflation, produced a severe recession lasting until 1924. Meanwhile, confronting those who had previously envisaged the conflagra-tion as a progressive social force, was large-scale bootlegging that, by 1926, forced most provinces to discontinue prohibition; a new and loose *flapper* morality; and what a number of people condemned as a more pronounced materialist ethos. Finally, the end of the decade brought the Wall Street Crash, an event that, in all belligerent nations, further closed the intellec-tual rift between once-optimistic civilians and disgruntled veterans. As Eric Leed explained, "population[s] as a whole w[ere] victimized, reduced to a level of abjectness and dependence with which the former footsoldier could immediately identify."[56]

It was in this atmosphere that Canada's most notable anti-war novels emerged. Peregrine Acland, who wrote *All Else Is Folly* in 1929, served as a major with the First Contingent; Charles Yale Harrison, previously a machine gunner with the Royal Montreal Regiment followed the next year with *Generals Die in Bed*; and in 1937, Philip Child, formerly a subaltern with a howitzer battery, produced *God's Sparrows*.[57] Worth noting, how-ever, is that even when addressing an apparently more sympathetic audience, not one of these books became a best-seller. In fact, Harrison's novel, arguable the most shocking, was first published and primarily dis-tributed in the United States. Admittedly, he was an American citizen, but certainly it is still reasonable to expect that an account set within the Canadian army would have enjoyed its greatest appeal north of the border.

For those ready to put aside stories of romance and adventure—and their numbers had increased—the new imagery was jarring. Acland demonstrated little respect for his fellow officers, writing, for example, about an inebriated major blindly leading his men into a bloodbath.[58] Meanwhile, Harrison, in attempting to communicate the dehumanizing nature of military life and war, decided to leave his narrator nameless. Most soldiers, observed his anonymous voice from the mass, threw aside notions about "camaraderie...and *esprit de corps*," and only concerned themselves with survival and maintaining sanity. During an artillery duel, he said, men "hug[ed] the earth, digging...[their] fingers into every crevice," while many a "bowel liquif[ied]."[59] In Child's story, the hero, Quentin, was a pacifist who died not in a blaze of glory, but because his convictions pre-vented him from bayoneting the enemy. Moreover, his supposed opposite,

Daniel, who at first talked ardently about making his mark in battle, soon found himself tortured by images of "Sergeant West lying beheaded at Passchendaele [and] the infantry officer who liked fishing disembowelled before his eyes."[60]

A rather jaundiced view of the Great War also came to dominate non-fiction narratives from veterans. In *A Rifleman Went to War*, a former member of the Canadian Expeditionary Force, Herbert McBride, said that for countless soldiers the 1914–18 struggle did not encompass much more than making continual trench repairs. Death, he added, usually came with little fanfare or the proverbial inspirational last words to one's comrades. "Just as we were about to start into the trench," he recalled, "a man from the 'Buffs' came over to talk…when sput—he looked around in a vague, questioning sort of manner and dropped to the ground, groped around with his hands, then straightened out—and died."[61] Then there was Pierre van Paasen's *Days of Our Years* that appeared just months before hostilities commenced against the Nazis. When dealing with the training regimen, this author, far from fixating upon vigourous exercise transforming soft civilians into real men, told about "a boy, who was a piano teacher in civil life, [who] taught me how to twist a long butcher knife…into the soft part of an adversary's body, [and] a gentleman who once sold…stamps who introduced me to the gentle art of crawling up stealthily behind an enemy and strangling him to death with bare hands…." In an outcome perhaps manipulated for dramatic impact, readers, instead of encountering a heroic journey ultimately improving both participants and civilization, discovered the descent of men into a hellish world that mercilessly consumed thousands—including the piano teacher who Van Paasen saw decapitated at Abbeville, as well as the postal employee who "later coughed up his lungs, filled with poison gas, at a hospital in Bethune…."[62]

It was no wonder, therefore, that between 1919 and the mid 1930s, Canadian pacifist associations expanded from a small cadre of Social Gospellers and labour radicals, to include those belonging to farm, women, student, church and mainstream labour organizations, as well as members of the new Co-operative Commonwealth Federation and League for Social Reconstruction. In 1932, 500,000 signatures were collected by the Canadian branch of the Women's International League for Peace and Freedom to support the upcoming Geneva conference on disarmament. Two years later, polls conducted by the Students' Christian Movement discovered that of 497 respondents at McGill and 275 at McMaster University, only 16.7 and 2.9 per cent respectively declared unqualified support for Canada in the event of war.[63] Such sentiments, when combined with the economic ravages of the Great Depression, precipitated further cutbacks to the country's already beleaguered military. In 1933, expenditures upon the Royal Canadian Navy plummeted to $422,000 and only the threat of resignation by Commodore Hose brought about a marginal budgetary improvement.[64]

Undoubtedly, the reaction of Canadians to the outbreak of hostilities in September 1939 illustrated such increased public comprehension of what combat actually entailed. Largely absent was the jingoistic euphoria prevalent in August 1914. Robert England, a veteran of the Great War and an architect of Canada's far more liberal post-1945 repatriation programmes, explained that those who marched off to fight Hitler were "less naive than we were," having read, seen or heard about "soggy sand bags, squelchy corpses... rats, lice [and] the smell of...sewerage."[65] While a number of young men still emitted heady idealism about helping the Mother Country, saving democracy, and seeking adventure, just as many, if not more, simply desired to escape grim economic conditions and/or perform what they accepted as a unpleasant but ultimately necessary task.[66]

A case for the enduring influence of Canadian information management might also be made by examining the comparable Australian experience. There too citizens were favourably pre-conditioned towards war by imperialism and romanticism, sentiments that were sustained throughout the conflict by a strict censorship system whose impact was augmented by geographic isolation and a relatively malleable press (see chapter 4). It therefore emerges as significant that Australia's post-war story, both in the short- and long-run, bears striking similarity to its northern sister Dominion. Those down under, though brimming with new-found pride and confidence in 1919 over their role in helping to achieve the Allied victory, were also, after sacrificing 60,000 men, apprehensive about making future commitments. Following the armistice, Canberra initiated a policy of military retrenchment, chopping its armed services approximately 90 percent by 1922 both to eliminate an £80 million war debt and to express opposition to any future arms' race. Yet, regardless of their reluctance to enter another major conflict, Australian citizens did not appear, in distinction to countless Anzacs, repelled by the idea of warfare itself. For years, they had seen few unpleasantries and heard endless tales of triumph, such as that provided by Australia's *eye-witness*, Charles Bean, or from the Anzacs who, if not inclined towards bravado and/or stoicism in their letters, were told by military authorities that all their correspondence would be scrutinized for "harmful criticism."[67]

Given such inspiring information, as well as years of complete separation from an army that actually endured the highest percentage of field casualties among imperial forces, many an Australian on armistice day stood prepared to greet "strong, heroic [and] undefeated" veterans now ready to thrive in civilian life, as opposed to "real men who needed the support of their society."[68] As in Canada, financially *prudent* policies were introduced to facilitate the post-war reintegration of soldiers. Although constituting an expansion of Australian social welfare, they appeared designed in expectation of the country welcoming home the self-reliant and manly.[69] Quickly emerging as a political force, therefore, was the Australian Returned Soldiers' and Sailors' Imperial League that demanded, among other things, a major increase to the post-war gratuity, especially in light of a 1919 unemployment rate climbing to approximately 14 per cent.[70] However, given the government's response, and a public often stressing the importance of not enfeebling the Anzac through massive welfare, it was with disdain that more than a few veterans soon concluded that "when the war ended, [the] soldier [was] little more than a pest to his country."[71]

Notwithstanding what many civilians must have perceived as the selfish demands issued by ex-servicemen, their sometimes violent outbursts,[72] and the eventual appearance of sobering soldier memoirs, the "Anzac legend"—created by Bean's reports from Gallipoli—crediting these men with transforming Australia from colony to nation refused to die. Remaining prominent in the national psyche was the picture of warriors whose deeds exceeded "those done on the field of Troy," a rendition that, in echoing over the "long-run," contended Deborah Hull, produced an ongoing "division" between civilians and the reality of "often crude" Anzacs.[73]

Australia's celebration of soldierdom, as Canada's, soon produced a near-obsession with war memorials—something built, said Patsy Adams-Smith "at every crossroads where it was difficult to imagine a squad of men having lived at any time."[74] To provide the Anzac with a fitting tribute, in the early 1920s, the ever-present Charles Bean initiated a campaign to construct a national testimonial without rival. "We planned," he said in later years, "that just as one had to go to Florence or Dresden to see the finest picture galleries, so people would have to come to Australia to see the finest war memorial." In 1925, Canberra allotted a little over £250,000 for the project, then a record for a public building. Financial constraints slowed construction during the 1930s, but when finally completed 1941, commemorative addresses invoked images of brave Anzacs to raise resolve in the face of a possible Japanese invasion. The monument's centrepiece, the domed Hall of Memory, reproduced Will Longstaff's painting, *Menim Gate at Midnight*, where valiant and saintly Australian soldiers rose from graves overseas to make their final journey home. Finishing touches in 1955 included stained glass windows detailing the country's Great War achievements, as well as a mammoth bronzed statue of a soldier exemplifying "young Australia proudly and courageously giving her all in the cause of freedom and honour."[75]

It was also through post-war literary endeavours that Bean strengthened the *Anzac Legend*. In 1919, he commenced what became a 23-year task to write and edit a 12-volume official Australian war history. Along with meticulous research and comprehensive battlefield accounts for which he won a number of awards—including the prestigious Chesney Gold Medal—was a laudatory depiction of the Anzac who, through his courage, established the "consciousness of...nationhood."[76] This picture, along with the muck and gore, has come to dominate Australia's modern memory of the Great War. In 1958, Russell Ward wrote of Anzacs who, in glorious victories, showed themselves as "spiritual descendants" of bushmen who conquered an unforgiving terrain.[77] A generation later, W.F. Mandle, also playing upon this frontier or environmentalist theme, characterized the country's soldiers "as tough and inventive...a bit undisciplined...[but also] chivalrous and gallant."[78] And in describing the accomplishments of these men at Gallipoli, Patsy Adam-Smith made comparisons with "the three hundred [Spartans] at Thermopylae" who stemmed the tide against several thousand Persian invaders.[79] Indeed, as long as Australia's Great War veterans proved physically able, their drunken and disorderly conduct on Anzac Day was tolerated, as a sign of respect for and acknowledgement of those cast as having embodied the best of the country's independent and rugged manhood.[80]

Although time healed many old wounds between soldiers and civilians, the rapprochement was never quite complete. Despite growing social cognizance of war, to some extent and to their dying day, many veterans remained as outsiders in those societies that managed to retain a few idealistic notions about this conflagration. In present-day Canada, like Australia, there persists a dichotomous popular perspective on the Great War. Alongside the world of mud and massive slaughter is a romanticized rendering of courageous men who, by winning the toughest and most important battles, forged a proud and esteemed country. Whereas the British or Americans might play up the pluck of Tommy Atkins or the doughboy, in neither country does the reverence approach the historical portrayal of, say, the Canadian Corps, a group still often depicted in their homeland as single-handedly sealing Germany's fate during the last hundred days of the war, and, in the process, raising the colony to nationhood and worldwide renown.

Granted, much of this interpretation derives from pre-war conditions. In the early twentieth century, neither Britain nor the United States felt the need to prove themselves as nations, so it naturally followed that both their wartime and historical accounts did not infuse their troops with such a transcendent purpose. Nonetheless, it remains significant that in accounting for the post-war growth of Canadian autonomy, the popular explanation among citizens continues to place relatively little emphasis upon England's declining strength nor the coinciding rise of America to superpower status; instead there persists an almost homeric tale, told with all the trappings of high diction, of bold men who bequeathed an unparalleled future through the crucible of combat. In the face of post-armistice realities, it was impossible for civilians to sustain the full range of romanticized notions fostered by wartime opinion makers, such as the conflict ushering in a new era of Christian brotherhood. But milestones ranging from the 1923 Halibut Treaty to the 1931 Statute of Westminster seemed to make the correlation between the highest of masculine qualities displayed on the battlefield and national greatness ring true, despite the presence of men who often returned from the trenches as unruly and soon resented. To what extent this interpretation relates to reality is debatable. Its pervasiveness was a cumulative process, being constructed upon a succession of post-war events, the extent of their actual relevance to the role played by Canadian soldiers becoming more clouded with time. However, making it easier for this magnified portrayal of Johnny Canuck to emerge as the dominant explanation for mounting post-war independence, and become a part of national folklore, was that in spite of multitudes of bodies and minds being mangled overseas, wartime censors and propagandists, with their particular Canadian-based advantages, ensured that those at home constantly heard tales heralding only the stupendous qualities of such men.

Even during the anti-war 1930s, as shown by the nationalistic fervour accompanying the dedication of the Vimy memorial, the superior attributes of Canada's fighting men remained a prominent theme. Secluded in popular consciousness from the grisly war that most people now realized had been fought was the still-strong belief that those whose uniforms emblazoned the maple leaf had emerged, through the boldest of exploits, as among the most important progenitors of national progress. Tapping into this theme, Edward VIII, before a throng of 6,400, many of whom made a trans-Atlantic pilgrimage to this former battle site, proclaimed that Vimy was "a feat of arms that history will long remember and Canada," with its total independence recently conferred, "[could] never forget."[81]

Such a conviction still resounded strongly in a number of popular works written during the 1960s about those Canadians who fought in France and Flanders. In such accounts, the unparalleled vigour of Dominion soldiers was acclaimed as having forged that self-assured nation about to experience its one-hundredth anniversary. Impossible to "overstress," wrote John Swettenham in his 1965 work, *To Seize the Victory*, was "the quality of the human material making up the [Canadian] Corps."[82] That same year,

Kenneth Macksey emphasized the "martial manhood" of those who "saved the day" at Ypres and captured Vimy Ridge.[83] H.F. Wood's narrative, written during Canada's centenary year, made much of the fact that the clash at Vimy Ridge occurred during the Dominion's half century point, thus symbolizing a watershed where heroic men thrust the country from its colonial roots to full national status—it was, he declared, Canada's "Agincourt, no more, and no less."[84]

Only the lasting influence exerted by this romanticized cult of the Canadian soldier can explain the reaction to the 1986 National Film Board production of *The Kid Who Couldn't Miss*. So offended were thousands by its suggestion that Billy Bishop was psychologically unstable and exaggerated his war record that Canada's Senate launched an official inquiry that ultimately, but unsuccessfully, attempted to pressure the director into labelling the film a "docudrama."[85] Revealing as well was that the same year, Pierre Berton, in *Vimy*, believed it necessary to inform his readers that Canadian soldiers did not in this battle forever turn the tide against Germany; he noted, for instance, that the British historian, Liddell Hart, "in his definitive history of the Great War...gave [the encounter] no more than a paragraph."[86]

Over the last generation, the historical portrayal of Johnny Canuck has shown signs of losing its romanticized edge. No doubt this trend obtained intellectual encouragement from anti-war attitudes growing out of America's unpopular escapade in Vietnam; but a more fundamental reason relates to the explosion of graduate level studies over the past quarter century. Besides producing a greater quantity of works on the era, from graduate history programmes came scholars trained to question long-held assumptions, and instructed, like modern-day journalists, to avoid polemicized prose in an effort to attain more objective conclusions—factors that produced several critical studies of Canadian tactics and performances upon land, at sea, and in the air during the Great War.[87] But compensating, if not outshining such academic inquiries in terms of exerting general influence, are a number of recent popular accounts reasserting traditional beliefs. Daniel Dancocks, in a best-selling war trilogy written during the late 1980s, commented not only upon muddy trenches and costly battlefield strategy, but also upon "noble" sacrifice "not [undertaken] in vain."[88] While the experiences of ten Canadians permitted Sandra Gwyn's 1992 work, *Tapestry of War*, to reveal much heartache and suffering, there also reverberated that declaration about Johnny Canuck whose roots clearly run deep in the national psyche: "Thrust for the first time upon the world stage [h]e performed at all times credibly and often brilliantly—holding the line under gas attacks at second Ypres in 1915, capturing Vimy Ridge in 1917 and…performing in the vanguard in 1918 during the hundred days of the astonishing counter-attack…."[89]

In Canada and Australia, more so than England or America, the Great War still calls forth high diction, and demonstrates a modern memory not only of muddy ditches and massive death, but also of gallant men scaling the heights at Vimy Ridge or persevering at Gallipoli to endow the foundations of modern-day nationalism. The fact that both countries entered the Great War as colonies intent upon demonstrating their worthiness no doubt pre-determined that monumental significance would be attached to each of their battlefield encounters. However, in addition to pre-war desires, there also existed a series factors, ranging from geography, to press corps' compliance, to the manly stoicism often displayed in the letters of soldiers home, making it easier for authorities to mould the views of civilians.

As a result, the sarcasm expressed in military publications or the bitterness permeating the diaries of servicemen remained alien sentiments to these citizens who never encountered reports of battlefield setbacks, the still mud-caked uniforms of men on leave, the terror of bombing raids, nor the pangs of hunger. Under such conditions, censors and propagandists maintained romanticism at a level where citizens became virtually predestined to apply a rather idealized interpretation in those circumstances where post-war events furnished some rationality. Such it seems became the case with the *cult of the superior soldier* who, despite his often errant behaviour after repatriation, was (and still to a large extent remains) esteemed as the valiant and critical catalyst behind the growth in post-war autonomy. No doubt this was a flattering and, in many respects, deserved image for those who had suffered through so much. Yet, it was also a picture deriving its birth from opinion-makers who shaped the image of muscular and always victorious soldiers; thus downplaying and in some respects forever alienating countless mere mortals sent to a land where *no man* belonged, and from which few escaped unscathed.

Abbreviations

AG	Attorney-General records
AO	Archives of Ontario
AR	Department of Agriculture, Ottawa, Main Library
BB	Lord Beaverbrook papers
BP	Sir Robert Borden papers
BR	Metropolitan Toronto Library, Baldwin Room
CPC	Chief Press Censor records
CWM	Canadian War Museum
DE	Department of Education records
DND	Department of National Defence records
GG	Governor-General records
EA	Department of External Affairs records
FN	Department of Finance records
IB	Immigration Branch records
JD	Department of Justice records
HL	House of Lords Record Office
MD	Militia and Defence records
NAC	National Archives of Canada
NFTSA	National Film, Television, and Sound Archives
OPP	Ontario Provincial Police records
PM	Parliamentary records
PR	Privy Council records

RCMP	Royal Canadian Mounted Police records
SS	Secretary of State records
UC	United Church Archives
UT	University of Toronto, St. Michael's Archives

Notes

Introduction

1. Denis Winter, *Death's Men: Soldiers of the Great War* (Toronto: Penguin, 1979), 23.
2. Walter Lippmann, *Public Opinion* (New York: Macmillan, 1960 ed.). For the British experience see Cate Haste, *Keep the Home Fires Burning* (London: Lane, 1977), and M.L. Saunders and Philip Taylor, *British Propaganda During the First World War* (London: Macmillan, 1982). The most significant works on the United States are James Mock and Cedric Larson, *Words that Won the War* (New York: Russell & Russell, 1968); Stephen Vaughn, *Holding Fast the Inner Lines: Democracy, Nationalism and the Committee on Public Information* (Chapel Hill: University of North Carolina Press, 1980); and Alfred E. Cornebise, *War as Advertised: The Four Minute Men and America's Crusade* (Philadelphia: American Philosophical Society, 1984). On Australia consult Kevin Fewster, "Expression and Suppression: Aspects of Military Censorship in Australia during the Great War," unpublished Ph.D. Thesis, University of New South Wales, 1980.
3. Among the better accounts describing enthusiasm in wartime Canada are Robert Craig Brown and Ramsay Cook, *Canada 1896–1921: A Nation Transformed* (Toronto: McClelland and Stewart Ltd., 1974); John Herd Thompson, *The Harvests of War* (Toronto: McClelland and Stewart, 1978); Desmond Morton and J.L. Granatstein, *Marching to Armageddon: Canadians and the First World War* (Toronto: Lester & Orpen Dennys, 1989);

and Robert Matthew Bray, "The English Canadian Patriotic Response to the Great War," unpublished Ph.D. Thesis, York University, 1977.

4. Despite its title, Peter Buitenhuis's *The Great War of Words: British, American and Canadian Propaganda, 1914–1933* (Vancouver: University of British Columbia Press, 1987) offers no description of the publicly-funded network established within the Dominion. Its Canadian connection relates to work done by Maxwell Aitken as Dominion eye-witness overseas, along with the efforts of expatriate author, Sir Gilbert Parker, to mobilize some major British writers on behalf of Wellington House in order to inundate a neutral United States with Entente justifications for the war. Information on the Victory Loan campaigns is contained in Robert Allain, "Sir Thomas White and Canadian Wartime Financial Policy," unpublished M.A. Thesis, Queen's University, 1975, and Robert Fyfe, "Sir Thomas White, the Victory Loans and the Canadian Financial Community, 1917–1919," unpublished M.A. Thesis, Carleton University, 1986. On fuel conservation see Andrew Pateman, "Keeping the Home Fires Burning: Fuel Regulation in Toronto During the Great War," unpublished M.A. Thesis, University of Western Ontario, 1988.

5. See Peter Rider's brief overview, "The Administrative Policy of the Chief Press Censor of Canada," unpublished B.A. Thesis, Carleton University, 1966. Alan Steinhardt's *Civil Censorship in Canada During World War I* (Toronto: Unitrade Press, 1986) is of marginal use since its primary purpose is to inform philatelists how to recognize examples of censorship stamps used by military and postal authorities. Some scholars exploring the plight of particular ethnic groups mention Ernest Chambers. See Werner A. Bausenhart, "The Ontario German Language Press and Its Suppression by Order in Council in 1918," *Canadian Ethnic Studies* 4 (1972): 35–48; W. Entz, "The Suppression of the German Language Press in September 1918 (with a special emphasis to the secular German-language papers in Western Canada)," *ibid.*, 8 (1976): 56–70; and Arja Pilli, *The Finnish Press in Canada, 1900–1939* (Turku, 1982). The harsh treatment extended towards several socialist tracts is discussed in Gregory Kealey, "State Repression of Labour and the Left in Canada, 1914–20: The Impact of the First World War," *Canadian Historical Review* 78, 3 (September, 1992): 281–314.

6. For this theory in a "global context" see Marshall McLuhan, *The Gutenberg Galaxy: The Making of Typographic Man* (Toronto: University of Toronto Press, 1962), 31.

7. Carl Berger, *The Writing of Canadian History, Aspects of English-Canadian Historical Writing: 1900 to 1970* (Toronto: Oxford University Press, 1976), 189–92.

8. Gladys Engel Lang and Kurt Lang, "Mass Communication and Public Opinion Strategies for Research," in Morris Rosenberg and Ralph Turner, eds., *Social Psychology: Sociological Perspectives* (New York: Basic Books, 1981), 653–82.

9. See for example Carl Berger, *The Sense of Power: Studies in the Ideas of Canadian Imperialism, 1867–1914* (Toronto: University of Toronto Press, 1970).

10. *Ibid.*, 235–36.

11. Tom Kent *et al.*, *Royal Commission on Newspapers* (Ottawa: Ministry of Supplies and Services, 1981), 65.

12. See Howard Palmer, *Patterns of Prejudice: A History of Nativism in Alberta* (Toronto: McClelland and Stewart, 1982), chapter 1.

13. This dichotomy has yet to receive systematic examination in studies of Canadian soldiers who served in France and Flanders, the best of which are Desmond Morton, *When Your Number's Up: The Canadian Soldier in the First World War* (Toronto: Random House, 1993); Sandra Gwyn, *Tapestry of War: A Private View of Canadians in the Great War* (Toronto: HarperCollins, 1992); and Bill Rawling, *Surviving Trench Warfare: Technology and the Canadian Corps, 1914–1918* (Toronto: University of Toronto Press, 1992). Published diaries include David Pierce Beatty, ed., *Memories of a Forgotten War: The World War I Diary of Private V.E. Goodwin* (Port Elgin: Baie Verte Editions, 1988); Reginald Roy, ed., *The Journal of Private Fraser* (Victoria: Sono Nis Press, 1985); and Brereton Greenhous, ed., *A Rattle of Pebbles: The First World War Diaries of Two Canadian Airmen* (Ottawa: Department of National Defence, 1987). The letters written home from France to one family are traced in Grace Morris Craig, *But This Is Our War* (Toronto: University of Toronto Press, 1981). Oral reminiscences are recorded in Heather Robertson, *A Terrible Beauty* (Toronto: James Lorimer & Company, 1977); Daphne Read, *The Great War and Canadian Society* (Toronto: New Hogtown Press, 1978); and William Mathieson, *My Grandfather's War* (Toronto: Macmillan, 1981).

14. Paul Fussell, *The Great War and Modern Memory* (Toronto: Oxford University Books, 1975), 22.

1 A Nation Rallies to the Cause

1. J.M. Bliss, "The Methodist Church and World War One," in Carl Berger, ed., *Conscription 1917* (Toronto: University of Toronto Press, 1970), 53.
2. On this point about war offering renewal for society see Eric J. Leed, *No Man's Land: Combat and Identity in World War I* (Cambridge: Cambridge University Press, 1979), 45.
3. He was released in June 1915. Melvyn Lubek, "The Uncaring Blind: Or Freedom of Expression in Canada during World War One," unpublished LL.M. Thesis, Osgoode Hall Law School, 1980, 43.
4. Alexander M. Lindsay, "The Effect of Public Opinion on the Borden Administration During World War I, 1914–1918," unpublished M.A. Thesis, Acadia University, 1953, 12.
5. Morton and Granatstein, *Marching to Armageddon*, 28.
6. V.R. Porter, "The English-Speaking Labour Press and the Great War," unpublished M.A. Thesis, Memorial University, 1981, 16.
7. Col. A. Fortescue Duguid, *Official History of the Canadian Forces in the Great War 1914–1919: Chronology, Appendices and Maps*, Vol. 1 (Ottawa: King's Printer, 1938), 34–35; Sir Robert Borden, *Memoirs*, Vol. 1 (Toronto: Macmillan, 1938), 452.
8. National Archives of Canada [NAC], MG26 H, Sir Robert Borden papers [BP], OC208 (1), Memo, 11 Aug. 1914, 21,065; Toronto *Globe*, 10 Aug. 1914, 13.
9. BP, RLB 709, Ames to Borden, 11 Aug. 1914; John Castell Hopkins, *The Canadian Annual Review, 1916* (Toronto: The Canadian Annual Review Publishing Company, 1917), 440–44.
10. Raymond Evans, *Loyalty and Disloyalty: Social Conflict on the Queensland Homefront, 1914–1918* (Sydney: Allen & Unwin, 1987), 55.
11. Toronto *Star*, 8 Feb. 1916, 6.
12. House of Commons, *Sessional Papers*, 1917, Paper #59, 2.
13. NAC, RG25, Department of External Affairs records [EA], Vol. 1057, Sir Joseph Pope to Harcourt, 18 Aug. 1914.
14. See note 12.
15. EA, Vol. 1057, Pope to Borden, 8 Aug. 1914. Duguid, *Official History*, 11, 16.
16. Archives of Ontario [AO], RG4, Attorney-General records [AG], Series 4–32, 1915, No. 1, Hughes to I. Lucas, 12 Jan. 1915.
17. NAC, RG24, Department of National Defence records [DND], Vol. 2524, File C-1648, Sherwood to Gwatkin, 12 Nov. 1915; NAC, MG27 III D9, Sir Edward Kemp papers, Vol. 76, File 122, Lt.-Colonel C.H. Carrington to Kemp, 30 Aug. 1916.

18. See note 12.

19. See Martin Kitchen, "The German Invasion of Canada in the First World War," *International History Review* 7, 2 (1985): 245–60, and Michael Boyko, "The First World War and the Threat of Invasion," unpublished Ms., York University, n.d.; Duguid, *Official History*, 19.

20. Mark Sullivan, *Our Times: The United States, 1900–1925*, Vol. 5, *Over Here, 1914–1918* (New York: Charles Scribner's Sons, 1933), 190; Ottawa *Evening Journal*, 4 Feb. 1916, 1.

21. AO, RG20, Ministry of Correctional Services, Series E-4, Vols. 1–2 (Burwash), Series E-18, Vol. 3 (Ontario Central Prison), Series F-43, Vol. A-31 (Toronto Jail), Series F-19, Vols. 5–6 (Kitchener [Berlin] Jail). These records constitute all surviving Ontario jail registers for the World War One period. As well, court records for Perth, Pembroke, and Waterloo, all areas containing substantial German settlements, divulge no prosecutions between 1914 and 1918 for crimes of a traitorous nature. AO, RG22, Court Records, Series 13, Vol. 14, Police Court records for Waterloo, and Clerk of the Peace papers for Perth and Pembroke.

22. Patricia Roy McKegney, "Germanism, Industrialism and Propaganda in Berlin, Ontario, during World War One," unpublished M.A. Thesis, University of Waterloo, 1979, 116, 236–37.

23. Multicultural History Society of Ontario, Interview with J.H. Baetz, Acc # Ger. 350.

24. Barbara Wilson, *Ontario and the First World War* (Toronto: Champlain Society, 1977), LXXIX.

25. Palmer, *Patterns of Prejudice*, 27, 29.

26. NAC, MG30 E79, W. O'Connor papers, Vol. 10, Proclamation, 7 Aug. 1914.

27. NAC, RG6 E1, Chief Press Censor records [CPC], File 104–5, PC 2283, 3 Sept. 1914; *ibid.*, PC 341, 28 Feb. 1916. Also see Brown and Cook, *Canada, 1896–1921*, 225.

28. Lubomyr Luciuk, "Internal Security and an Ethnic Minority," *Signum* 4, 2 (1984): 37.

29. Joseph Boudreau, "The Enemy Alien Problem in Canada, 1914–1921," unpublished Ph.D. Thesis, University of California, Berkeley, 1965, 45–46; Curtis Johnson Cole, "The War Measures Act, 1914: Aspects of the Emergency Limitation of Freedom of Speech and Personal Liberties in Canada, 1914–1919," unpublished M.A. Thesis, University of Western Ontario, 1980, 70.

30. Moreover, after the war, Immigration Branch officer W. Scott, who became Deputy Minister in 1923, admitted that from the time Budka issued the

second communique "his attitude ha[d] been absolutely correct as testified to by the authorities of the Dominion Police who…kept him under careful surveillance." NAC, RG13, Justice Department records [JD], Vol. 234, File 1919–753, W. Scott to Meighen, 20 May 1919.

31. Luciuk, "Internal Security," 40, 44; Peter Melnycky, "The Internment of Ukrainians in Canada," in John Herd Thompson and Francis Swyripa, eds., *Loyalties in Conflict* (Edmonton: Canadian Institute for Ukrainian Studies, 1982), 8, 10.

32. BP, Vol. 208, Meighen to Borden, 28 Aug. 1914, 105, 951–52. Also see Andrij Makuch, "Ukrainian Canadians and the Wartime Economy," in Thompson and Swyripa, eds., *Loyalties in Conflict*, 69–77.

33. BP, Vol. 21, T. Crothers to J.S. Willison, 8 Aug. 1914, 7, 279–80; Brown and Cook, *Canada, 1896–1921*, 240.

34. Of the twenty-four internment camps established in Canada during the Great War, thirteen were closed by the end of 1916. Luciuk, "Internal Security," 35.

35. Donald Avery, *Dangerous Foreigners: European Immigrant Workers and Labour Radicalism in Canada* (Toronto: McClelland and Stewart, 1979), 67–68; Melnycky, "The Internment of Ukrainians in Canada," 14.

36. AG, 4–32, 1918, No. 2399, M. Boland to I. Lucas, 19 Nov. 1918; AO, RG23, Ontario Provincial Police records [OPP], E-83, File 1.2, Crown Attorney in Stratford to OPP Superintendent Joseph Rogers, 13 March 1919.

37. NAC, RG76, Immigration Branch records [IB], Vol. 30, Part 682, Memo, 20 March 1920. The legislation remained in place until 1923.

38. David J. Bercuson and J.L. Granatstein, *Collins Dictionary of Canadian History: 1867 to the Present* (Toronto: Collins, 1987), 248. Although most students did not proceed beyond elementary school, still, between 1891 and 1923, total enrolment in all Canadian public educational institutions grew from 942,500 to 1,939,700. Neil Sutherland, *Children in English-Speaking Society: Framing the Twentieth-Century Consensus* (Toronto: University of Toronto Press, 1976), 164.

39. Paul Rutherford, *The Making of the Canadian Media* (Toronto: McGraw-Hill Ryerson, 1978), 45–54; W.H. Kesterton, *A History of Journalism in Canada* (Ottawa: Carleton University Press, 1984 ed.), 131.

40. For example, J.S. Willison, proprietor of the Toronto *News*, periodically acted as an advisory for Borden. Rutherford, *Making of the Canadian Media*, 69–70, 95–96.

41. Kesterton, *History of Canadian Journalism*, 133–35.

42. Metropolitan Toronto Library, Baldwin Room [BR], World War One Broadside Catalogue, n.p.; Toronto *News*, 23 Jan. 1917, 6.

43. NAC, MG30 D14, J.S. Willison papers, Willison to J.M. MacDonald, 21 July 1915, 26,401–3; Robert Craig Brown, *Robert Laird Borden: A Biography*, Vol. 2 (Toronto: Macmillan, 1980), 26–30.
44. Manitoba *Free Press*, 3 May 1915, 5.
45. Winnipeg *Tribune*, 12 April 1917, 9; Keith Robbins, *The First World War* (Toronto: Oxford University Press, 1984), 66.
46. Toronto *Star*, 3 Dec. 1915, 5; Manitoba *Free Press*, 17 Jan. 1917, 9.
47. Toronto *Star*, 7 June 1917, 6.
48. Ramsay Cook, "Laurier, Dafoe, and the Formation of the Union Government," *Canadian Historical Review* 42, 3 (1961): 185–208.
49. *Saturday Night*, 3 Oct. 1914, 14.
50. Halifax *Herald*, 18 May 1915, 9.
51. See *National Geographic Magazine* 185, 4 (April 1994): 68–85.
52. Manitoba *Free Press*, 8 May 1915, 11; Winnipeg *Tribune*, 23 Oct. 1915, 9.
53. *Saturday Night*, 13 July 1918, 8.
54. Hamilton *Spectator*, 3 Nov. 1917, 1.
55. James Playsted Wood, *The Story of Advertising* (New York: The Ronald Press Company, 1958), 287–357. Also see Edward K. Strong, "Psychological Methods as Applied to Advertising," in *Journal of Educational Psychology* 4 (1913): 393–404.
56. *Maclean's*, Nov. 1915, 59; *ibid.*, April 1917, 78.
57. Hugh S. Eayrs, "Canadian Publishers and War Propaganda," *Canadian Bookman* 1 (Jan. 1919): 47–48.
58. Harry M. Woodson, *Private Warwick: Musings of a Canuck in Khaki* (Toronto: Sovereign Press, 1915), 10, 45.
59. Linda Rae Steward, "A Canadian Perspective: The Fictional and Historical Portrayal of World War One," unpublished M.A. Thesis, University of Waterloo, 1983, 12–13.
60. Crawford Killian, "The Great War and the Canadian Novel, 1915–1926," unpublished M.A. Thesis, Simon Fraser University, 1972, 17; Dagmar Novak, "The Canadian Novel and the Two World Wars," unpublished Ph.D. Thesis, University of Toronto, 1988, 24–27, 45.
61. Corningsby Dawson, *The Glory of the Trenches* (Toronto: S.B. Gundy, 1918), 103, 112.
62. During the Great War, ten Canadian pilots achieved thirty or more kills. Col. G.W.L. Nicholson, *Canadian Expeditionary Force 1914–1919* (Ottawa: Queen's Printer, 1962), 504.
63. Major W.A. Bishop, *Winged Warfare* (Toronto: McClelland, Goodchild and Stewart, 1918), 76–77, 95, 109.

64. Robbins, *The First World War*, 100.

65. F. McKelvey Bell, *The First Canadians in France* (Toronto: McClelland, Goodchild and Stewart, 1917), 122, 133–34.

66. George G. Nasmith, *On the Fringe of the Great Fight* (Toronto: McClelland, Goodchild and Stewart, 1917), 100–102.

67. Lieut. J. Harvey Douglas, *Captured* (Toronto: McClelland, Goodchild and Stewart, 1918), 95, 117.

68. George Pearson, *Escape of a Princess Pat* (Toronto: George H. Doran, 1918), 42–43.

69. Robert Fisher, "Film Censorship and Progressive Reform: The National Board of Censorship of Motion Pictures, 1909–22," *Journal of Popular Film* 4 (1975): 144; Garth S. Jowett, "The First Motion Picture Audiences," *ibid.* 3 (1974): 40–54.

70. Toronto *Star*, 15 Nov. 1915, 7; *Maclean's*, April 1916, 21–23.

71. CPC, *Final Report of the Chief Press Censor for Canada*, 123–24.

72. NAC, National Film, Television, and Sound Archives [NFTSA], *204th Battalion Sham Battle*, NFA #6471. Also see Peter Morris, *Embattled Shadows: A History of the Canadian Cinema, 1895–1939* (Montreal: McGill-Queen's University Press, 1978), chapters 2, 3.

73. John Turner, ed., *Canadian Feature Film Index* (Ottawa: National Archives of Canada, 1987), n.p.

74. Ron Van Dopperen, "Shooting the Great War," *Film History* 4, 2 (1990): 123–29; David H. Mould, *American Newsfilm, 1914–1919: The Underground War* (New York: Garland Publishing Company, 1983), 79.

75. Charles Roetter, *Psychological Warfare* (London: B.T. Batsford, 1974), 52; Timothy L. Lyons, "Hollywood and World War One, 1914–1918," *Journal of Popular Film* 1, 1 (1972): 18.

76. Vaughn, *Holding Fast the Inner Lines*, 204.

77. *Canadian Motion Picture Journal*, 30 March 1918, 17; *ibid.*, 18 May 1918, 16.

78. Michael Issenberg, "The Mirror of Democracy: Reflections on the War Films of World War I, 1917–1919," *Journal of Popular Culture* 9, 4 (1976): 882–83; *Canadian Motion Picture Journal*, 5 Jan. 1918, 10.

79. *Ibid.*, 3 July 1918, 18.

80. *Ibid.*, 25 May 1918, 16.

81. Manitoba *Free Press*, 3 March 1918, 27. The live theatre, though not nearly as influential as motion pictures (because it was considered far less adaptable for the production of war scenes), still contributed some jingoistic fare. Toronto's Royal Alexandra staged *The Man Who Stayed Home* and *The White Feather*, both of which were scathing indictments of pacifism. The Princess Theatre, also of the Queen City, put on *Over There* that followed the struggle of a

London tenement girl "who longs to help and rises to heroism…behind the fighting lines in France." Patriotic passions were also stimulated through productions of *King Henry V*, arguably Shakespeare's most rousing tribute to Britain's battlefield prowess, as well as Gilbert and Sullivan's *H.M.S. Pinafore* with its songs like *For He's an Englishman*. As well, on a number of occasions, vaudeville stars such as Al Jolson, William Faversham, De Wolfe Hopper and Harry Lauder gave benefit concerts on behalf of assorted war charities. See Mora O'Neill, "A Partial History of the Royal Alexandra Theatre, Toronto, Canada, 1907–1939," unpublished Ph.D. Thesis, Louisiana State University and Agricultural and Mechanical College, 1976, Vol. 1, 166; Nancy Jane Haynes, "A History of the Royal Alexandra Theatre, Toronto, Ontario, Canada, 1914–1918," unpublished Ph.D. Thesis, University of Colorado, 1973, 44–50, 109, 169–70.

82. *Maclean's*, March 1915, 100; Helmut Kallmann, Gilles Potvin and Kenneth Winters, eds., *Encyclopedia of Music in Canada* (Toronto: University of Toronto Press, 1981): 486–87.

83. Muriel Bruce, *Kitchener's Question* (Toronto: Empire Music and Travel Club Limited, 1915); Harry Taylor, *We'll Love You More When You Come Back Than When You Went Away* (Toronto: Lee Grove & Harry Taylor, 1915).

84. Keith Hardyside, *The World Is Simply Mad on Uniform* (Toronto: W.R. Draper, 1918).

85. See for example, Morris Manley, *When They Come Back* (Toronto: Morris Manley, 1916).

86. Bomber H. Rose, *His Name's on the Roll of Honour* (Toronto: Anglo-Canadian, 1917).

87. H. Keane, *The Colonials and the Flag* (Toronto: Anglo-Canadian, 1914).

88. Marion Templeton, *Canada's Brave Boys* (Toronto: Empire Music and Travel Club Limited, 1916); J.B. Spurr, *Canada, Star of the Empire* (Aurora: J.B. Spurr, 1919).

89. United Church Archives [UC], Pamphlet Collection, T.B. Kirkpatrick, *The War and the Christian Church*, 6; UC, P.P. Pedley papers, Box 2, File 71, sermon, n.d.

90. Bliss, "The Methodist Church," 41. On the jingoistic response from Anglicans see Duff Crerar, "The Church in the Furnace: Canadian Anglican Chaplains Respond to the Great War," *Journal of the Canadian Church Historical Society* 35, 2 (1993): 75–104.

91. David Patterson, "Loyalty, Ontario and the First World War," unpublished M.A. Thesis, McGill University, 1986, 86, 98.

92. According to the 1911 census, Methodists had almost 1.08 million adherents while there were 1.1 million followers of the Presbyterian faith. F.H. Leacy,

ed., *Historical Statistics of Canada*, 2nd edition (Ottawa: Statistics Canada, 1983), series A–164–184.

93. Bliss, "The Methodist Church," 42–49. For an analysis of the Social Gospel doctrine see Richard Allen, *The Social Passion: Religion and Social Reform in Canada, 1914–1928* (Toronto: University of Toronto Press, 1970).

94. UC, Pamphlet Collection, Rev. George Coulson Workman, *Armageddon, or, The World Movement* (Toronto: William Briggs, 1917), 68.

95. The three were I. Benzinger (Professor of Oriental languages), P.M. Meuller (Associate Professor of German), and B. Tapper (Instructor in German). University of Toronto Archives, Office of the Registrar, Acc# A73/0051/219, File 8; *University Magazine* 13 (1914): 375.

96. AO, MU2083, #18, *Varsity Magazine*, Dec. 1916, 26.

97. AO, Pamphlet Collection, 1915, No. 95, George Wrong, *The War Spirit of Germany*, 17.

98. AO, RG2, Department of Education records [DE], Series P–3, Box 4, Miscellaneous material.

99. Sir Edward Parrot, *The Children's History of the War*, Vol. 29 (Toronto: Thomas Nelson and Sons Limited, 1916–18), 80.

100. Sue Malvern, "'War As It Is': The Art of Muirhead Bone, C.R.W. Nevinson and Paul Nash, 1916–1917," *Art History* 9, 4 (1986): 491; note 95.

101. Robert Stamp, *The Schools of Ontario* (Toronto: University of Toronto Press, 1976), 95.

2 Official Propaganda

1. NAC, RG7 G21, Governor-General records [GG], Vol. 435, File 14,071, Item 154, Harcourt to Devonshire, 18 Aug. 1914.

2. Fewster, "Expression and Suppression," 88.

3. Robbins, *The First World War*, 33; Toronto *Globe*, 31 Aug. 1914, 1.

4. Phillip Knightley, *The First Casualty From Crimea to Vietnam: The War Correspondent as Hero, Propagandist, and Myth-Maker* (New York: Harcourt Brace Jovanovich, 1975), 94; Nicholas Reeves, *Official British Film Propaganda During the First World War* (London: Croom Helm, 1986), 48.

5. Fewster, "Expression and Suppression," 90–91; NAC, RG25, EA, Vol. 272, "Regulations for Press Correspondents Accompanying a Force in the Field," n.d.

6. House of Lords Record Office [HL], Lord Beaverbrook papers [BB], BBK E/1/16, Beckles Willson to Aitken, 28 June 1916. Indeed, after the war, each of Britain's principal front-line correspondents received a knighthood. Malvern, "'War As It Is,'" 505.

7. Nicholson, *Canadian Expeditionary Force*, 144; Toronto *Star*, 7 July 1916, 1.

8. Fussell, *The Great War and Modern Memory*, 176.

9. NAC, RG2, Privy Council records [PR], Vol. 1106, #3117, 6 Jan. 1915; NAC, RG9, Militia and Defence records [MD], D1, Vol. 45, File 8–5–15, J.G. Ross to Paymaster, Militia Headquarters, London, 26 April 1916.

10. A.J.P. Taylor, *Beaverbrook* (New York: Simon and Schuster, 1972), 87.

11. *Ibid.*, 91; Anne Chisholm and Michael Davie, *Beaverbrook: A Life* (London: Hutchinson, 1992), 127.

12. NAC, RG24, Department of National Defence records [DND], Vol. 1749, File D.H.S. 7–1, C.W.R.O. Report, 31 Dec. 1919.

13. Major J.E. Hahn, *The Intelligence Service Within the Canadian Corps, 1914–1918* (Toronto: The Macmillan Company of Canada, Limited, 1930), 4–19.

14. MD, Vol. 4676, File 4–5, Operation Report, 17 April 1916.

15. *Ibid.*, File H.S. 27–1–2, Despatch, 29 March 1916.

16. HL, BB, BBK/E/1/19, Aitken to Manley-Sims, 27 June 1916.

17. *Ibid*, BBK E/1/32, Manley-Sims to Aitken, 3 July 1916.

18. Chisholm and Davie, *Beaverbrook*, 127.

19. *Saturday Night*, 22 May 1916, 8; Ken Ramstead, "The 'Eye-Witness': Lord Beaverbrook and Canada in Flanders," *The Register* 12 (1984): 309–10.

20. BP, Vol. 76, Aitken to Borden, 30 Oct. 1916, 39,563.

21. BB, BBK E/1/20, Undated Report on *Canada in Flanders, Vol. 2*.

22. *Ibid.*, BBK E/1/42, The Censor and Vol. 2 of *Canada in Flanders*, n.d.; Buitenhuis, *The Great War of Words*, 99–100.

23. Toronto *Star*, 12 Aug. 1916, 6; BB, BBK E/1/16, Beckles Willson to Aitken, 28 June 1916.

24. *Ibid.*, BBK E/2/11, Robinson to Beckles Willson, 29 April 1916. Instructive as well was the case of the Toronto *Mail and Empire*'s correspondent, H.A. Gwynne, who in October 1916 sent back reports about Dominion soldiers "splendid in courage…and keen to beat the Germans." Once home, however, he alerted Borden about ranks rife with discontent over supposedly incompetent officers whom many enlisted personnel concluded were "appointed by virtue of political influence…." BP, Vol. 58, H. Gwynne to Borden, 9 Oct. 1916, 28, 968–74.

25. EA, Vol. 262, File P-6/73, C.F. Crandall to Lt.-Col. Hugh Clark, 7 Feb. 1917.

26. MD, Vol. 354, File 17, Lyon to Manley-Sims, 5 March 1917.

27. *Ibid.*, Vol. 4688, File 42–21, Operations Report, 30 Nov. 1917; A.M.J. Hyatt, "Corps Commander: Arthur Currie," in Marc Milner, ed., *Canadian Military History: Selected Readings* (Toronto: Copp Clark Pitman Ltd., 1993), 109.

28. MD, Vol. 4725, File 186–1, Despatch, 6 Dec. 1917.

29. Knightley, *First Casualty*, 99.

30. Maria Tippett, *Art at the Service of War* (Toronto: University of Toronto Press, 1984), 19; MD, Vol. 4728, File 127–5, Memo, 19 Sept. 1917.

31. Tippett, *Art at the Service*, 22; NFTSA, Interview with William Rider-Rider, V-28007.

32. BB, BBK E/1/20, undated memorandum.

33. MD, Vol. 1921, File 124–4; *ibid.*, Vol. 4732, File 138–10.

34. *Ibid.*, Vol. 4772, File CIF-40, W. Watkins to Manley-Sims, 14 July 1916.

35. John MacKenzie, *Propaganda and Empire: The Manipulation of British Public Opinion, 1880–1960* (Manchester: Manchester University Press, 1984), 70–71.

36. Nicholas Reeves, "Film Propaganda and Its Audience: The Example of Britain's Official Films During the First World War," *Journal of Contemporary History* 18, 3 (1983): 465.

37. MD, Vol. 4772, File CIF-42, B.B. Cubitt to G.O.C., War Office, 15 Dec. 1915; *ibid.*, Aitken to Lieut-Col. B. de Panet, 6 Aug. 1916.

38. Taylor, *Beaverbrook*, 89–95.

39. BB, BBK, E/2/11, Memorandum re War Office Cinematograph Committee, n.d. It is not surprising, therefore, that to promote the product, its major Canadian distributor, the Montreal-based Specialty Film Import Company, appealed to the pocket books as well as the patriotism of theatre owners. "Get this family business," read its advertisement in the *Canadian Motion Picture Journal*. "It is with…fond eyes and yearning hearts that the loved ones at home will look on the screen at our boys 'over there'." *Canadian Motion Picture Journal*, 4 May 1918, 11.

40. Reeves, *Official British Film Propaganda*, 100–105; BB, BBK E/1/10, Memo, 22 May 1916.

41. *Ibid.*, BBK E/1/30, Memo, 3 July 1916; NFTSA, 13–0981, Dawson City Collection, Catalogue, Nos. 1266, 1918.

42. Rawling, *Surviving Trench Warfare*, 83.

43. NAC, RG37, Dominion Archivist records [DA], Vol. 366, Copies of Memoranda by the Dominion Archivist, 1916–1922, 51–52, 84–85.

44. Sandra Gwyn, *Tapestry of War: A Private View of Canadians in the Great War* (Toronto: HarperCollins, 1992), 286; DA, Vol. 363, Montreal *Gazette* article dated 10 Oct. 1917.

45. *Ibid.*, E.W. Farrell to Doughty, 23 Aug. 1918.

46. *Ibid.*, Warson to Doughty, 17 Sept. 1918; Halifax *Herald*, 24 Oct. 1917, 6. Initially, many Canadian artifacts shipped from Europe were, along with

contributions from other Allied nations, loaned to the United States for more than a year to help boost preparedness, and later Liberty Bond campaigns. DND, Vol. 1025, File 157–4, D. Hopper to Doughty, 25 May 1917.

47. DA, Vol. 366, 59–60.

48. By January 1917, total Canadian enlistment as a percentage of the population was only one per cent less than Australia and two per cent less than New Zealand. Meanwhile, Quebecois, despite constituting about one-quarter of the population, provided only about five per cent of Canadians in uniform. Public Records Office, Cab 23/1, War Cabinet Minutes, Min. 5 to Min. 41, 23 Jan. 1917.

49. DND, Vol. 856, File 54–21–12–5, Extract from House of Commons Debates, 25 Feb. 1915.

50. Ronald Haycock, "Recruiting," in Milner, ed., *Canadian Military History*, 60–61, 65; Department of National Defence, Directorate of History, L4, "Recruiting in Canada, 1914 to 1917," 16.

51. Morton, *When Your Number's Up*, 63.

52. Robert Craig Brown and Donald Loveridge, "Unrequited Faith: Recruiting the C.E.F., 1914–1918," *Revue internationale d'histoire militaire* 54 (1982): 62; Directorate of History, 34.

53. Nicholson, *Canadian Expeditionary Force*, 12.

54. Haycock, "Recruiting," 58.

55. For example, in the spring of 1915, the Hon. F.J. Robidoux informed Hughes that practically no enlistment activity had occurred in Kent County, New Brunswick; yet, only months later, the Brantford Board of Trade wrote military officials that "if another 1,200 men are taken…we will have to face the closing down of our factories." MD, Vol. 856, File 54–21–12–10, F.J. Robidoux to Sam Hughes, 5 May 1915; BP, RLB 709, Frank Stanfield to Borden, 25 Feb. 1916.

56. Morton, *When Your Number's Up*, 60.

57. Haycock, "Recruiting," 59.

58. Brown and Loveridge, "Unrequited Faith," 57; BP, RLB 709, W.E. Springfield to Sam Hughes, 24 Jan. 1916.

59. DND, Vol. 4479, File 25–1–20, Secretary of the Montreal Citizens' Recruiting League to O.C. of M.D. #4, n.d.

60. Metropolitan Toronto Library, Baldwin Room [BR], World War One Broadside Catalogue, n.p.; NAC, Photographic Division, #C95723, # C95748.

61. Haycock, "Recruiting," 70.

62. J.L. Granatstein and J.M. Hitsman, *Broken Promises: A History of Conscription in Canada* (Toronto: Oxford University Press, 1977), 25–26.

63. Haycock, "Recruiting," 73.

64. *Ibid.*, 67; Stephen J. Harris, *Canadian Brass: The Making of a Professional Army* (Toronto: University of Toronto Press, 1988), 117.

65. DND, Vol. 4431, File 26–6–1, Memo from O.C. of M.D. #3, 21 Aug. 1916.

66. Brown, *Robert Laird Borden*, Vol. 2, 63.

67. DND, Vol. 4428, File 26–5–64–3, Chief Recruiting Officer for M.D. #3 to D.A.A. for M.D. #3, 18 Oct. 1916.

68. Duguid, *Official History of the Canadian Forces*, Vol. 1, 173.

69. DND, Vol. 6600, File 1982–1–87, Mignault to A.G. at Militia Headquarters, 5 Feb. 1917; *ibid.*, Mignault to O.C. of M.D. #4, 7 Feb. 1917.

70. *Ibid.*, Vol. 6600, File 1982–1–87, parish priests in Rawdon, St. Marie and St. Honore to Mignault, 25 Jan. 1917 and 28 Jan. 1917.

71. *Ibid.*, Memorandum, n.d.; Vol. 4479, File 25–1–2, Mignault to O.C. for M.D. #4, 19 Feb. 1917.

72. In 1912, Ontario passed Regulation XVII that severely restricted French-language instruction for those beyond the first form. It was repealed in 1927. See Robert Choquette, *Language and Religion: A History of English-French Conflict in Ontario* (Ottawa: University of Ottawa Press, 1975), part 3.

73. Granatstein and Hitsman, *Broken Promises*, 30.

74. DND, Vol. 5, File HQ 94–8, A.R. Alloway to Kemp, 21 March 1917; Kemp Papers, Vol. 74, File 94, Major-General Mewburn to Kemp, 23 July 1917.

75. Morton, *When Your Number's Up*, 61.

76. Tait resigned over his inability to appoint Canadian Manufacturers' Association Secretary, G.M. Murray, a Borden critic, as his assistant. Brown, *Robert Laird Borden*, Vol. 2, 63–64.

77. Maurice F.V. Doll, *The Poster War: Allied Propaganda Art of the First World War* (Alberta: Historic Sites and Archives Services, 1993), 28; Granatstein and Hitsman, *Broken Promises*, 45.

78. Directorate of History, 33.

79. A.M. Willms, "Conscription: A Brief for the Defence," in Carl Berger, ed., *Conscription 1917* (Toronto: University of Toronto Press, 1970), 1–2.

80. See note 48.

81. Granatstein and Hitsman, *Broken Promises*, 46.

82. Brown, *Robert Laird Borden*, 87.

83. Fewster, "Expression and Suppression," 138–50.

84. While 24,132 Canadian conscripts made it to France, only 838 furloughs were granted. Wilson, *Ontario and the First World War*, LXXIX.

85. Morton, *When Your Number's Up*, 66; Brown, *Robert Laird Borden*, Vol. 2, 125.

86. *Ibid.*, 111.

87. BP, Vol. 41, Union Government Publicity Committee Pamphlets; Morton and Granatstein, *Marching to Armageddon*, 183.
88. Brown and Cook, *Canada 1896–1914*, 273; Granatstein and Hitsman, *Broken Promises*, 97–98.
89. Brown, *Robert Laird Borden*, 101.
90. On this theme see John English, *The Decline of Politics: The Conservatives and the Party System, 1901–20* (Toronto: University of Toronto Press, 1977), chapters 7–10.
91. A sapper was one who tunnelled towards enemy lines to plant explosives underneath their trenches. Rawling, *Surviving Trench Warfare*, 53.
92. Palmer, *Patterns of Prejudice*, 30; NAC, MG27 II D18, Sir T. White papers, Vol. 7, File 28, Final Report of the Fuel Controller, March 1919, 32.
93. Pateman, "Keeping the Home Fires Burning," 126–27; Brown and Cook, *Canada, 1896–1921*, 237.
94. BP, RLB 1536, Fuel Controller Bulletin #1; Thompson, *The Harvests of War*, 160.
95. *Canadian Food Bulletin*, 17 Nov. 1917, 13; NAC, RG36, Boards, Offices and Committees [BOC], Vol. 5, File 36/15/2, PC 1460, 16 June 1917.
96. NAC, RG17, Department of Agriculture, Vol. 1987, Report of the Food Controller, 26 Oct. 1917; BOC, Vol. 5, File 36/15/2, Memo, 18 March 1918.
97. Department of Agriculture, Ottawa, Main Library [AR], *What Canada has Done to Feed the Armies and Civilian Population of the Allies* (Ottawa: 1917), n.p.
98. *Canadian Motion Picture Journal*, 20 April 1918, 1; AR, Report of the Canada Food Board, 31 Dec. 1918, 62.
99. White papers, Vol. 7, File 26, Report of the Food Controller, 24 Jan. 1918; *Canadian Food Bulletin*, 12 Jan. 1918, 11, 13 April 1918, 2, 1 June 1918, 17.
100. Note 95; AR, Pamphlet entitled "Recipes for Bread"; BR, Broadside Catalogue, n.p.
101. NAC, RG19, Department of Finance records [FN], Vol. 4008, St. John's *Telegram*, 25 April 1918; Toronto *Star*, 21 March 1918, 8.
102. Morton and Granatstein, *Marching to Armageddon*, 84–85; Bernard Sandwell, "Financial Measures," in *Canada in the Great War: An Authentic Account of the Military History of Canada From the Earliest Days to the Close of the War of Nations*, Vol. 2 (Toronto: United Publishers of Canada Ltd., 1921), 98, 116, 154–57. All told, new income and corporate taxes covered less than ten per cent of 1917 war costs. Brown, *Robert Laird Borden*, Vol. 2, 95.
103. Allain, "Sir Thomas White," 86–97, 140.
104. *Ibid.*, 124–25; FN, Vol. 4010, White to T. Kelly Dickinson, 16 Jan. 1917.
105. Allain, "Sir Thomas White," 157.

106. FN, Vol. 4008, Memorandum, 25 April 1918.

107. NAC, RG14 D2, Parliamentary records [PM], Vol. 46, No. 131, Memo, 7 July 1919; FN, Vol. 4006, Stephenson to Muirhead, 25 April 1918, Memorandum, 6 June 1919.

108. *Ibid.*, Vol. 4005, Aces to White, 5 Sept. 1918.

109. For instance, through the offices of department store owner Sir John Eaton or Toronto *Star* President J.E. Atkinson, directors in Ottawa issued instructions to thousands of volunteers in the Queen city. During the fourth loan, such people were directed to prime the populace by asking church leaders to stress 'thrift' in their sermons, to plaster city streets with posters, and to turn on town lights at midnight to commemorate the formal inauguration of the campaign. FN, Vol. 4008, Roberts to Aces, 14 Nov. 1917; *ibid.*, J.W. Mitchell to White, 21 Nov. 1917.

110. *Ibid.*, Vol. 4005, E.A. MacNutt to White, 26 Sept. 1918; PM, Vol. 136, No. 120, 24 April 1918.

111. Representative was the archetypal woman in white robes bearing a shield symbolizing "militant democracy" in the fight for freedom against "*kultur* which is striving to subdue the world." Dominion Publicity Committee, *Press Publicity for Canada's Victory Loan* (Ottawa: King's Printer, 1918), n.p.

112. *Ibid.*

113. FN, Vol. 4005, Form letter from White dated 1 Oct. 1918.

114. *Ibid.*, Dominion Publicity Committee *Bulletin*, 10 Oct. 1917; *ibid.*, Vol. 4013, F. Kerr to Roberts, 14 Dec. 1917.

115. Doll, *The Poster War*, 32.

116. FN, Vol. 4005, Aces to White, 5 Sept. 1918; *ibid.*, Vancouver *Sun*, 14 Sept. 1918.

117. *Canadian Motion Picture Journal*, 9 November 1918, 9.

118. DND, Vol. 1761, File D.H.S. 10–65, unidentified newspaper clipping dated 31 Dec. 1919.

119. NAC, RG6, Secretary of State records [SS], H–3, Vol. 600, File 1393, Nichols to Mulvey, 20 Sept. 1918; *Canadian Official Record*, 18 Oct. 1918, 10.

120. *Canadian Motion Picture Journal*, 3 July 1918, 9; *ibid.*, 3 Aug. 1918, 20.

121. Department of Public Information, *Bolshevism in Russia* (Ottawa: 1919), n.p.

122. Bray, "The Canadian Patriotic Response," 518; McKegney, "Germanism, Industrialism and Propaganda," 151.

123. PM, Vol. 45, No. 56, 7 July 1919; SS, Vol. 600, War Lecture Bureau Bulletin, 18 April 1918, 5.

124. Department of Public Information, *What Canada Does for Her Wounded Soldiers* (Ottawa: 1919), 24–26; *Military Hospital Commission Bulletin*, Dec. 1917, 2.

125. *Back to Mufti*, Feb. 1918, 31.

126. Department of Public Information, *What Canada Does*, 7–13; Calgary *Herald*, 18 Jan. 1919, 2.

127. *Reconstruction*, Jan. 1918, 8; *ibid.*, March 1918, 15.

128. Desmond Morton and Glenn Wright, *Winning the Second Battle: Canadian Veterans Return to Civilian Life* (Toronto: University of Toronto Press, 1987), 43.

3 A Loyal or Muzzled Press?

1. Morton and Granatstein, *Marching to Armageddon*, 6–7.

2. House of Commons, *Statutes*, 5 George V, Chapter 2, 22 Aug. 1914.

3. *Canadian Military Gazette*, 21 Nov. 1899, 15; Duguid, *Official History of the Canadian Forces*, Vol. 1, 14.

4. PC 1330, 10 June 1915.

5. PC 2073, 10 Sept. 1915.

6. CPC, File 104–1, Privy Council Memorandum, 23 June 1916.

7. PC 146, 17 Jan. 1917.

8. PC 1241, 18 May 1918.

9. PC 2381, 25 Sept. 1918.

10. PC 2733, 7 Nov. 1918; PC 703, 2 April 1919.

11. The original order banned the Industrial Workers of the World, Russian Social Democratic Party, Russian Revolutionary Group, Russian Social Revolutionists, Russian Workers Union, Ukrainian Social Democratic Party, Social Democratic Party, Social Labour Party, Group of Social Democrats of Bolsheviki, Group of Social Democrats of Anarchists, Workers International Industrial Union, Chinese Nationalist League, and the Chinese National Reform Association. PC 2384, 28 Sept. 1918. PC 2786 was passed within days to correct the names of some organizations and add others to the list such as the Finnish Socialist Organization of Canada. Barbara Roberts, *Whence They Came: Deportation from Canada 1900–1935* (Ottawa: University of Ottawa Press, 1988), 72.

12. Cole, "The War Measures Act, 1914," 24.

13. Phyllis Keller, "German-America and the First World War," unpublished Ph.D. Thesis, Kent State University, 1969, 326–27.

14. Kesterton, *A History of Canadian Journalism*, 119; CPC, File 104, Memorandum on the Duties of the Press in War, 17 Aug. 1914.

15. *Ibid.*, Memorandum, June 1915. Besides addressing this deficiency, the timing

of Chambers's appointment in June 1915 also suggests Ottawa might have been growing concerned about public reaction to unprecedented casualties overseas and thus desired to clamp down upon information possibly fostering despondency. Despite rhapsodic press accounts, long casualty lists from Second Ypres, wrote Robert Borden that May in his diary, had "greatly excited" public opinion. Indeed, two months later, in order to maintain a satisfactory flow of recruits, the Militia Department reduced both height and chest measurement requirements. BP, Diary, 3 May 1915; Jean Bruce, "The Toronto *Globe* and the Manpower Problem, 1914–1917," unpublished M.A. Thesis, Queen's University, 1967, 5.

16. CPC, File 104, Toronto *Globe*, 7 Aug. 1914, 7; *ibid.*, Montreal *Gazette*, 5 Oct. 1914.

17. NAC, RG7 G21, Governor-General records [GG], Vol. 438, File 14,071, Item 1910.5, Admiral R.N. Stephens to Lt.-Col. E.A. Stanton, 25 Feb. 1915.

18. CPC, File 104, Doherty to Deputy Minister of Militia and Defence, 15 Feb. 1915; *ibid.*, Memo from Governor-General's office to Canadian newspaper editors, 31 May 1915.

19. GG, Vol. 435, File 14,071, Item 1769.

20. Lubek, "The Uncaring Blind," 84; CPC, File 104, Miller to C.F. Hamilton, 22 April 1915.

21. See note 19.

22. London *Times, Who's Who in Canada* (London: 1910), 41.

23. W. Stewart Wallace, ed., *The Macmillan Dictionary of Canadian Biography* (Toronto: Macmillan, 1976), 145.

24. CPC, File 205, Address to Canadian Press Association, 26 Aug. 1915.

25. The degree to which imperialist and militarist ideals guided Chambers was also evident from his many works as a regimental historian. For example, the *Origin and Services of the 3rd (Montreal) Field Battery of Artillery* presented a unit which he proclaimed was proud to display its "determination to keep the Union Jack flying for all time over this broad Dominion," while in *The Montreal Highland Cadets* he even expressed approval for boys attempting to deceive military recruiters about their age so they could join those bound for Pretoria. Ernest Chambers, *The Origin and Services of the 3rd (Montreal) Field Battery of Artillery* (Montreal: E.L. Ruddy, 1898), 80; *The Montreal Highland Cadets* (Montreal: Desbarats & Co., 1901), 85. Other books written by Chambers expressing an imperialist and militarist philosophy include *The Queen's Own Rifles of Canada* (Toronto: E.L. Ruddy, 1901); *The Governor-General's Horse Guard* (Toronto: E.L. Ruddy, 1902); *The Duke of Cornwall's Own Rifles* (Ottawa: E.L. Ruddy, 1903); *The 5th Regiment: Royal Scots of Canada* (Montreal: E.L. Ruddy, 1904); *The Royal Grenadiers* (Toronto: E.L.

Ruddy, 1904); *The Royal North-West Mounted Police: A Corps History* (Ottawa: Mortimer Press, 1905); and *A History of the Canadian Militia* (Montreal: L.M. Fresno, 1909).

26. Wallace, *Macmillan Dictionary*, 145; Entz, "The Suppression of the German Language Press," 58.

27. William Banks, "The Press Censorship," *The Canadian Magazine*, Dec. 1915, 152; CPC, File 104, Hamilton to Sladen, 16 March 1915.

28. *Ibid.*, File 144–C, Chambers to Sir William Otter, 20 Dec. 1915; *ibid.*, File 107, Chambers to W. Foran, 20 June 1918.

29. *Ibid.*, Chambers to Wilson, 24 Aug. 1918; *ibid.*, Chambers to Colson, 31 Jan. 1918; NAC, RG14 D2, Parliamentary records [PM], Vol. 54, No. 179, 7 July 1919.

30. CPC, File 279–2, Chambers to Williams, 26 Nov. 1919.

31. Steinhardt, *Civil Censorship in Canada*, 17–25, 46–47; NAC, RG3, Post Office records, Vol. 617, File 1686–C.

32. CPC, File 141, Post Office Memorandum, 22 Sept. 1915; *ibid.*, File 103, Post Office Circular to employees, 29 Feb. 1916.

33. *Ibid.*, File 107, Chambers to Colson, 29 Aug. 1916; *ibid.*, Chambers to Tartak, 12 May 1916; *ibid.*, Chambers to Reid, 8 May 1916.

34. *Ibid.*, *Final Report of the Chief Press Censor for Canada*, 83.

35. *Ibid.*, File 205, Chambers to Young, 26 Aug. 1915.

36. *Ibid.*, Address to Canadian Press Association, 4 Sept. 1915; *ibid.*, File 104–5–1, Chambers to T.T. Shaw, 26 July 1916.

37. *Ibid.*, File 162, Chambers to McNab, 16 Aug. 1915.

38. In fact, out of fear and respect, Lloyd George, soon after becoming Prime Minister, tried to win over Northcliffe by making him a special envoy to America to organize counter-propaganda against Berlin. Philip Taylor, "The Foreign Office and British Propaganda During the First World War," *The Historical Journal* 23, 4 (1980): 875.

39. JD, Vol. 219, File 1918–294.

40. NAC, RG2, Privy Council records [PC], Vol. 1207, Memo, 28 Sept. 1918; CPC, *Final Report of the Chief Press Censor for Canada*, 90–93.

41. AO, MU56, Maclean-Hunter records, Series B–1–2–A, Box 50, Article entitled "The Unthinking Chatter of our Rag-Tag Press"; *ibid.*, Costain to Maclean, 27 March 1918.

42. See for example CPC, File 252, Chambers to Ewart, 2 Nov. 1915, Chambers to Blondin, 10 April 1916, Chambers to Patenaude, 8 Feb. 1917.

43. BP, Dairy, 30 May 1915.

44. CPC, File 252, Vancouver *Sun* article, n.d.

45. *Ibid.*, File 104–5–1, Press release by Bourassa, May 1918.

46. *Ibid.*, File 197, Lewis to Chambers, 26 Aug. 1915.

47. *Ibid.*, Chambers to Vanderhoof, 11 May 1916; *ibid.*, File 107, Chambers to Meighen, 20 May 1918.

48. *Ibid.*, File 142–8, Chambers to J. Bohn, 24 July 1916.

49. *Ibid.*, File 142, Chambers to Walker, 19 Oct. 1915.

50. *Ibid.*, File 207–5, Chambers to Ross, 25 Jan. 1916.

51. *Ibid.*, Chambers to Field, 23 Sept. 1915.

52. *Ibid.*, File 112–8, Fitzgerald to Chambers, 1 Feb. 1916; *ibid.*, Chambers to the editors of the Ottawa *Journal*, Ottawa *Citizen*, Manitoba *Free Press*, Montreal *Star* and Quebec *Chronicle*, 2 Feb. 1916.

53. *Ibid.*, *Final Report of the Chief Press Censor for Canada*, 82.

54. *Ibid.*, File 206–B–6; *Saturday Night*, 9 March 1918, 2.

55. *Ibid.*, File 206–A–4, Chambers to Patenaude, 9 April 1917.

56. On Canadian press reaction see *Ibid.*, File 153–J–1, Ottawa *Evening Telegram*, 12 Nov. 1916, Montreal *Mail*, 26 May 1916.

57. Yuvaraj D. Prasad, "William Randolph Hearst and Pro-Germanism During World War I," *Indian Journal of American Studies* 17, 1–2 (1987): 94.

58. GG, Vol. 464, File 14,071, Part 31, Item 1660, Law to Devonshire, 26 Oct. 1916; CPC, File 153–J–1, Chambers to Blondin, 10 Nov. 1916.

59. GG, Vol. 501, File 14,071, Part 83, Pope to the Governor-General, 3 May 1918; CPC, File 206–H–1, Chambers to Burrell, 29 May 1918.

60. See for example the case of the New York *Staatszeitung. Ibid.*, File 116–S–5.

61. *Ibid.*, *Final Report of the Chief Press Censor for Canada*, 83.

62. *Ibid.*, File 116–B–3, Chambers to Burrell, 16 May 1917.

63. Maureen Brandstaetter, "Deutschtum on the Prairies: A Study of German-Canadian Newspapers during the Great War," unpublished M.A. Thesis, University of Calgary, 1986, 3, 30.

64. CPC, File 144–F, Chambers to Livesay, n.d.

65. Herbert Karl Kalbfleisch, "History of the German Newspapers of Ontario, Canada, 1835–1918," unpublished Ph.D. Thesis, University of Michigan, 1953, 56, 120–21.

66. CPC, File 158, Weichel to Chambers, 18 Aug. 1915; *ibid.*, Chambers to Motz, 23 Aug. 1915.

67. Morton and Wright, *Winning the Second Battle*, 82; Roz Uisikin, "'The Alien and Bolshevist in Our Midst': The 1919 Winnipeg General Strike," *Jewish Life and Times* 5 (1983): 29.

68. NAC, MG27 II D7, Sir George Foster papers, Vol. 42, R.M. Stewart to Doherty, 22 Aug. 1918; Morton and Wright, *Winning the Second Battle*, 83, 123.

69. BP, Vol. 92, Calder to Borden, 20 Sept. 1918, 48, 143.

70. Entz, "The Suppression," 61; CPC, File 119–N–1, Maron to Chambers, 29 Sept. 1918.

71. *Ibid.*, File 370–GA–9, Chambers to Burrell, 2 Aug. 1919.

72. EA, Vol. 1149, File 1871, Pope to Borden, 3 April 1915.

73. Kealey, "State Repression of Labour," 283, 308. Also see Gregory Kealey, "1919: The Canadian Labour Revolt," *Labour/Le Travail* 13 (1984): 11–44.

74. William Rodney, *Soldiers of the International: A History of the Communist Party of Canada, 1919–1929* (Toronto: University of Toronto Press, 1968), 18; Gregory Kealey, "The State, the Foreign-Language Press and the Canadian Labour Revolt of 1917–1920," in Christiane Harzig and Dirk Hoerder, eds., *Labor Migration Project: Labor Newspaper Preservation Project* (Bromen, 1985), 320.

75. BP, RLB 559, Borden to White, 2 Dec. 1918.

76. Pierre Van Paasen, *Days of Our Years* (New York: Hillman-Carl Inc., 1939), 79.

77. For example, in Winnipeg, newspapers blamed enemy aliens for a 1917 construction sector walkout, as well as for the 1918 civic strike. See Avery, *Dangerous Foreigners*, 73.

78. T.C. Baxter, "Selected Aspects of Canadian Public Opinion on the Russian Revolution," unpublished M.A Thesis, University of Western Ontario, 1973, 18, 21–33; Morris K. Mott, "The 'Foreign Peril': Nativism in Winnipeg, 1916–23," unpublished M.A. Thesis, University of Manitoba, 1970, 16. Although little evidence existed at the time to authenticate this conspiracy theory, and though labour radicals in North America had no connection whatsoever to German interests (by and large considering the Kaiser as an authoritarian ruler of a capitalist and imperialist state), nevertheless, recently released Russian documents do suggest that Lenin, in order to increase his chances for success in the revolution, accepted funding from Germany. See Dmitri Volkogonov, *Lenin: A New Biography* (New York: Free Press, 1995).

79. *MacLean's*, Aug. 1919, 34–35.

80. CPC, File 358, CPC Circular, 26 Nov. 1918; Cole, "The War Measures Act," 137–62.

81. *Ibid.*, File 260–A–3, Chambers to Burrell, 30 Sept. 1918; Allen Ruff, "Repression of the Press in the World War I Era: The Case of Charles H. Kerr & Company," *Journal of Newspaper and Periodical History* 5, 2 (1989): 8.

82. Kealey, "The State, the Foreign-Language Press, and the Canadian Labour Revolt," 320.

83. Donald Avery, "European Immigrant Workers in Western Canada, 1900–1930: A Case Study of the Ukrainian Labour Press," in Christiane

Harzig and Dirk Hoerder, eds., *Labor Migration Project: Labor Newspaper Preservation Project*, (Bromen, 1985), 290.

84. Peter Krawchuk, *The Ukrainian Socialist Movement in Canada, 1907–1918* (Toronto: Progress Books, 1979), 46.

85. Orest Martynowych, "The Ukrainian Socialist Movement in Canada, 1900–1918," *Journal of Ukrainian Graduate Studies* 1 (1976): 27–30; Nestor Makuch, "Influence of the Ukrainian Revolution on Ukrainians in Canada, 1917–1922," *ibid.*, 6 (1979): 42–61.

86. Edward W. Laine, "Finnish Canadian Radicalism and Canadian Politics: The First Forty Years, 1900–1940," in Jorgen Dahlie and Tissa Fernando, eds., *Ethnicity, Power and Politics in Canada* (Toronto: Methuen, 1981), 94–112; Avery, *Dangerous Foreigners*, 290.

87. Also helping the paper reappear was the renaming of the F.S.O.C. to the Finnish Organization of Canada. Arja Pilli, *The Finnish Press in Canada, 1900–1939* (Turku, 1982), 95–129.

88. CPC, File 279–1, Coulter to Chambers, 23 Nov. 1917. Perhaps those like Burrell were aware that the censorship of anti-draft articles in Australia's left-wing press the previous year further alienated organized labour and its supporters from a government condemned as attempting to stifle democratic debate on what many perceived as a still politically partisan issue rather than a matter of law. Kevin Fewster, "The Operation of State Apparatuses in Times of Crisis: Censorship and Conscription, 1916," *War & Society* 3, 1 (1985): 37–54.

89. CPC, File 279–1, Memorandum, 13 Sept. 1918; *ibid.*, Chambers to Burrell, 25 Oct. 1918.

90. *Ibid.*, Chambers to Burrell, 14 Jan. 1919; *ibid.*, Reid to Chambers, 20 Oct. 1919.

91. *Ibid.*, Chambers to Burrell, 7 Nov. 1919; *ibid.*, Chambers to Hamilton, 26 Nov. 1919.

92. W.L. Morton, *The Progressive Party in Canada* (Toronto: University of Toronto Press, 1950) 300–301; William R. Young, "Conscription, Rural Depopulation and the Farmers of Ontario," *Canadian Historical Review* 53, 3 (1972): 307, 311.

93. CPC, File 279–39, Buchanan to Chambers, 18 April 1918.

94. *Ibid.*, Chambers to Campbell, 26 Jan. 1919.

95. Kealey, "State Repression," 301.

96. Avery, *Dangerous Foreigners*, 76.

97. Also instructive was the case of Isaac Bainbridge, leader of the Social Democratic Party, who, in November 1917, was sentenced to nine months for distributing copies of the pacifistic publication, *Brockway's Defence*. However, protests by several unions, including the threat of a city-wide strike

organized by the Toronto District Labor Council, prompted Ottawa to back off. The following January, Senator Gideon Robertson, a former T.L.C. executive and acting Minister of Labour, advised Justice Minister Charles Doherty, that in order "to solicit the cooperation of labour...it would be wise to err on the side of leniency." An appeal by Bainbridge went unopposed by the Crown, and the government accepted without complaint the new verdict of a suspended sentence. JD, Vol. 216, File 1918–1724, Robertson to Doherty, 19 Jan. 1918; *ibid.*, Vol. 231, File 1919–132, Cahan to Doherty, n.d.

98. Avery, "European Immigrant Workers," 296; Gregory Kealey, "The Surveillance State: The Origins of Domestic Intelligence and Counter-Subversion in Canada," *Intelligence and National Security* 7, 3 (1992): 189.

99. *Ibid.*, 186; DND, Vol. 2543, File 2051, Cahan to Doherty, 8 Jan. 1919.

100. C.H. Cahan, "A Pernicious Propaganda," *Empire Club of Canada Addresses, 1919* (Toronto: Warwick Bros. & Rutter, 1920), 206. For a more detailed account of Cahan's role and disputes with Ottawa see Gregory Kealey, "The Early Years of State Surveillance of Labour and the Left in Canada: The Institutional Framework of the Royal Canadian Mounted Police Security and Intelligence Apparatus, 1918–26," *Intelligence and National Security* 8, 3, (1993): 129–48.

101. DND, Vol. 2543, File 2051, Rogers to Cawdron, 8 Jan. 1919.

102. IB, Vol. 627, File 961162; Roberts, *Whence They Came*, 84–85, 88.

103. *Revised Statutes of Canada*, 10 George V, Chapter 146, 7 July 1919.

104. See Kealey, "The Surveillance State."

105. Kealey, "The State, the Foreign-Language Press, and the Canadian Labour Revolt," 315.

4 The Censor's Extended Scope

1. House of Commons, *Debates*, CXXV, 6 Feb. 1917, 576; BP, Vol. 82, Spence to Borden, 16 July 1917, 42, 150.

2. Bliss, "The Methodist Church," 51, 52, ft. 64; CPC, File 269–45, Chambers to Christie, 18 July 1917.

3. PM, Vol. 52, No. 113, Doherty to Lucas, 10 April 1918; *ibid.*, Raney to Lucas, 29 April 1918.

4. CPC, File 371–U–3.

5. SS, Vol. 600, File 2030, Chambers to Mulvey, 24 June 1918.

6. CPC, File 269–16, Chambers to Hughes, 29 July 1916.

7. GG, Vol. 422, File 14,071, Item 13, Order in Council, 2 Aug. 1914; Duguid, *Official History of the Canadian Forces*, Vol. 1, 13–14.

8. For example, such efforts in Britain led to the interception of 400 revolvers bound for Germany via Amsterdam. Fewster, "Expression and Suppression," 256.

9. DND, Vol. 3880, File 1029–5–8, Regulations for Censorship of Wireless Telegraph Messages, 20 Nov. 1914.

10. CPC, File 150–F, Mathieson to Chambers, 17 Feb. 1916.

11. *Ibid.*, File 150–11, Memorandum, 20 March 1916.

12. *Ibid., Final Report of the Chief Press Censor for Canada*, 83.

13. W.P. Ward, *White Canada Forever: Attitudes and Public Policy Towards Orientals in British Columbia* (Vancouver: University of British Columbia Press, 1978), 79, 82, 87.

14. IB, Vol. 385, Part 9, Reid to Mitchell, 14 Sept. 1914; Hugh Johnston, "The Surveillance of Indian Nationalists in North America, 1900–1918," *B.C. Studies* 78 (Summer 1988): 5–15.

15. Norman Buchignani and Doreen Indra, "The Political Organization of South Asians in Canada, 1904–1920," in Dahlie and Fernando, eds., *Ethnicity, Power and Politics in Canada*, 210–24.

16. CPC, File 150–D–4, Chambers to Sherwood, 14 Feb. 1916; *ibid.*, Sherwood to Chambers, 6 Aug. 1916.

17. Ward, *White Canada*, 7–10, 42, 61; Palmer, *Patterns of Prejudice*, 34; Allan Sears, "Immigration Controls as Social Policy: The Case of Canadian Medical Inspection, 1900–1920," *Studies in Political Economy* 33 (1990): 91–112.

18. JD, Vol. 183, File 1914–124, Tang Shu Wen to Borden, 19 Jan. 1914.

19. CPC, File 168, Chambers to Stephens, 12 Oct. 1917; *ibid.*, Chambers to Perry, 10 April 1917.

20. Undaunted, Chambers shifted his focus to Vice-Consul David Lew who, he said, was rumoured in April 1917 to have contacted Viscount Di Villa of Seattle, a man the Pinkerton Detective Agency accused of espionage. This avenue of investigation proved fruitless, as did efforts centring upon the Edmonton branch of the Nationalist League in response to local (and undoubtedly racist-inspired) gossip accusing members of using the opium trade to finance the training of a battalion. *Ibid.*, Reid to Chambers, 10 July 1918; NAC, RG18, Royal Canadian Mounted Police records [RCMP], A–1, Vol. 509, File 203, Det-Sgt. W. MacBrayne to the Officer Commanding 'G' Division, 23 March 1917.

21. CPC, File 168, Sherwood to Chambers, 25 Sept. 1918.

22. *Ibid.*, File 150–70, Chambers to Pope, 18 Feb. 1918.

23. Cable and wireless censorship formally ended on 24 July 1919. PC, Vol. 1229, PC 1661, 7 Aug. 1919; CPC, File 150–70, Chambers to Coolican, 26 Jan. 1919.

24. *Ibid.*, File 150–50–3, Memo, April 1917.

25. *Ibid.*, File 150–2, Chambers to Chamberlain, 17 May 1917.

26. *Ibid.*, File 231, Chambers to A.C. Batten, 2 Feb. 1917; *ibid.*, Chambers to Abbott, 22 Jan. 1916.

27. *Ibid.*, File 231, Chambers to Crandall, 25 April 1917; Peter Robertson, "Canadian Photojournalism During the First World War," *History of Photography* 2 (1978): 40.

28. CPC, File 231–13, Chambers to Yorbston and Bohn, 3 April 1917.

29. *Ibid.*, Yorbston to Chambers, 5 April 1917.

30. David H. Mould, *American Newsfilm, 1914–1919: The Underground War* (New York: Garland Publishing, 1983), 79; *Saturday Night*, 28 Aug. 1915, 1.

31. CPC, File 228, Chambers to Gwatkin, 29 Jan. 1918.

32. *Ibid.*, *Final Report of the Chief Press Censor for Canada*, 120, 123–24; AO, RG56, Theatre Branch records, A–1, Box 1, File 6, Memo, n.d.

33. CPC, File 228–1, Chambers to Armstrong, 9 Feb. 1917.

34. *Ibid.*, File 228, Chambers to President of Superfeatures Inc., 28 Jan. 1918; *New York Times Film Reviews, 1913–68*, Vol. 1 (New York: Arno Press, 1970), 42. Also see Craig W. Campbell, *Reel America and World War One* (Jefferson: McFarland & Company, 1985), 168, 206–12.

35. Reeves, *Official British Film Propaganda*, 217; GG, Vol. 472, File 14,071, Part 56, Item 1735, Devonshire to Long, 30 April 1917.

36. Reeves, *Official British Film*, 238.

37. HL, BB, BBK E/2/11, Sir Edward Kemp to Beaverbrook, 23 July 1917; CPC, *Final Report of the Chief Press Censor for Canada*, 131.

38. For this production, Maxwell Aitken obtained soldiers for battlefield scenes, while the Canadian military provided shells. Chisholm and Davie, *Beaverbrook*, 152.

39. *Canadian Motion Picture Journal*, 9 Feb. 1918, 14; CPC, File 228, Chambers to Pierce, 12 July 1918.

40. See chapter one, note 78.

41. *Saturday Night*, 25 May 1918, 3; CPC, File 228–11, Chambers to Manager of Russell Theatre, 22 Nov. 1917.

42. *Ibid.*, File 228, Chambers to Banks, 8 May 1918.

43. *Ibid.*, *Final Report of the Chief Press Censor for Canada*, 137.

44. *Saturday Night*, 25 May 1918, 3; DND, Vol. 3884, File 1029–6–24, CPC Circular, 10 June 1918.

45. Among the pro-Republican Irish publications banned in Canada during the war were the New York-based *Irish World* and *Freeman's Journal*, as well as the *Hibernian* of Camden, New Jersey. See *Ibid.*, Files 153, 153–J–1, and 206–M–1.

46. Robert Graves, *Goodbye to All That* (London: Penguin ed., 1976) 120; Christopher Hibbert, *The English: A Social History, 1066–1945* (London: Grafton Books, 1987), 708.

47. Fussell, *The Great War and Modern Memory*, 68.

48. EA, Vol. 1221, File 49, Chambers to Pope, 9 June 1918.

49. Wayne A. Weigand, "In Service to the State: Wisconsin Public Libraries During World War I," *Wisconsin Magazine of History* 72, 3 (1989): 206–7, 220–21; Keller, "German America and World War One," 42. Also see Frederick C. Luebke, *Bonds of Loyalty: German Americans and World War One* (De Kalb: Northern Illinois University Press, 1974).

50. John Sayer, "Art and Politics: Dissent and Repression," *American Journal of Legal History* 32, 1 (1988): 45.

51. Robert K. Murray, *Red Scare: A Study in National Hysteria, 1919–1920* (Minneapolis: University of Minnesota Press, 1955), 50.

52. *Ibid.*, 50–54; John Arkas Hawgood, *The Tragedy of German America* (New York: Arno Press, 1970), 82–86.

53. Indeed, the post-war surveillance of leftists was a major factor in accounting for the appearance of the F.B.I. See David Williams, "The Bureau of Investigation and its Critics, 1919–1921: The Origins of Federal Political Surveillance," *Journal of American History* 68 (1981–82): 560–89.

54. Sayer, "Art and Politics," 55.

55. Ruff, "Repression of the Press in the World War I Era," 9–10; Murray, *Red Scare*, 233–36.

56. Charles F. Howlett, "Academic Freedom Versus Loyalty at Columbia University During World War I: A Case Study," *War & Society* 2, 1 (1984): 51.

57. Malvern, "'War As It Is,'" 498; John Rae, *Conscience and Politics: The British Government and the Conscientious Objector to Military Service, 1916–1919* (London: Oxford, 1970), 226–27. For instance, some 1,200 conscientious objectors were imprisoned.

58. Colin Lovelace, "Press Censorship During the First World War," in George Boyce, James Curran, and Pauline Wingate, eds., *Newspaper History from the Seventeenth Century to the Present Day* (London: Sage, 1978), 309.

59. CPC, File 104–A–1, Great Britain, House of Commons, *Statutes*, 4 & 5 George V, Chapter 29, 27 Nov. 1914.

60. Philip Howard, *We Thundered Out: 200 Years of the Times* (London: Times Books Limited, 1985), 88; Lovelace, "Press Censorship," 311.

61. John M. McEwan, "'Brass Hats' and the British Press During the First World War," *Canadian Journal of History* 18, 1 (1983): 47.

62. John M. McEwan, "The National Press During the First World War: Ownership and Circulation," *Journal of Contemporary History* 17, 4 (1982): 459–68.

63. Philip Taylor, "The Foreign Office and British Propaganda During the First World War," *The Historical Journal*, 23, 4 (1980): 875.

64. Lovelace, "Press Censorship," 314; McEwan, "Brass Hats," 53.

65. Lovelace, "Press Censorship," 312–13.

66. CPC, File 104–5–A, Manchester *Guardian*, 24 April 1918.

67. Leigh Tucker, "English Friends and Censorship, World War I," *Quaker History* 71, 2 (1982): 118–23.

68. Claire M. Tylee, "'Maleness Run Riot'—The Great War and Women's Resistance to Militarism," *Women's Studies International Forum* 14, 3 (1988): 209, ft. 19.

69. M.L. Saunders and Philip Taylor, *British Propaganda during the First World War* (London: Macmillan, 1982), 42; Deian Hopkins, "Domestic Censorship in the First War," *Journal of Contemporary History* 4, 4 (1970): 160.

70. House of Commons, *Debates*, CXLI, 18 March 1920, 541; Robert Lutz, "Studies of World War Propaganda," *Journal of Modern History* 5, 4 (1933): 496-98. On England also see James Squires, *British Propaganda at Home and in the United States from 1914 to 1917* (Cambridge: Harvard University Press, 1935). Robert H. Ferrell, *Woodrow Wilson and World War I, 1917–1921* (New York: Harper and Row, 1985), 289–90. Indicative of America's commitment to propaganda was the fact that it produced some 20 million war posters of more than 2,500 different designs, an amount which exceeded all other Allied nations combined. See Walton Rawls, "Wake Up America," *American History Illustrated* 23, 5 (1988): 32–35.

71. Nicholas Hiley, "Sir Henry Le Bas and the Origins of Domestic Propaganda in Britain," *Journal of Advertising History* 10, 2 (1987): 32–33.

72. Prior to directing Wellington House, Masterman headed the British Parliament's National Insurance Commission. Taylor, *Beaverbrook*, 876–77; Buitenhuis, *The Great War of Words*, xvi, 71.

73. Chisholm and Davie, *Beaverbrook*, 154–59.

74. CPC, *Final Report of the Chief Press Censor for Canada*, 152–54.

75. *Ibid.*, Vol. 2543, File 2051, Chambers to the Presidents of Queen's, Dalhousie, McMaster, Mount Allison, King's College, and the Universities of Saskatchewan, Manitoba, Alberta, New Brunswick and Toronto, 3 Feb. 1919.

76. Gavin Souter, *Lion and Kangaroo: The Initiation of Australia, 1901–1919* (Sydney: Collins, 1976), 245.

77. Kevin Fewster, ed., *Gallipoli Correspondent: The Frontline Diary of C.E.W. Bean* (Sydney: George Allen & Unwin, 1983), 9–20; Deborah Hull, "'The Old Lie': Teaching Children about War, 1914–1939," *Melbourne Historical Journal* 20, 1 (1990): 90, 98.

78. Fewster, "Expression and Suppression," 223.

79. *Ibid.*, 27–28.

80. *Ibid.*, 223.

81. *Ibid.*, 131.

82. *Ibid.*, 239.

83. A few months after Australia's withdrawal from the Dardenelles, Ashmead-Bartlett applied to enter the colony to lecture on his wartime observations, permission for which was granted only after he promised not to utter anything disheartening. So that he remained true to his word, Australian censorship authorities arranged for two guards to attend each talk and pull him off stage should he deviate from the pledge. *Ibid.*, 122.

84. *Ibid.*, 108.

85. Fewster, "The Operation of State Apparatuses," 37–54.

86. Souter, *Lion and Kangaroo*, 258.

87. Evans, *Loyalty and Disloyalty*, 149; Fewster, "Expression and Suppression," 244, 258, 263–64.

88. *Ibid.*, 131–32, 267–69.

89. *Ibid.*, 328; Evans, *Loyalty and Disloyalty*, 129–32, 164, 171–72.

90. Michael Hadley and Roger Sarty, *Tin-Pots and Pirate Ships: Canadian Naval Forces and German Sea Raiders, 1880–1918* (Montreal: McGill-Queen's University Press, 1991), 163–67.

91. Kealey, "The Early Years of State Surveillance," 132–33.

92. Kealey, "The State, the Foreign-Language Press, and the Canadian Labour Revolt," 328.

93. Desmond Morton, *Canada and War* (Toronto: Butterworths, 1981), 81.

94. This concept is discussed in Fussell, *The Great War and Modern Memory*.

5 Newspapers for the Fighting Man

1. See Modris Eksteins, *Rites of Spring: The Great War and the Birth of the Modern Age* (Toronto: Lester & Orpen Dennys, 1989), and Lyn Macdonald, *1914* (London: Penguin Books, 1987).

2. Gordon Martel, "'Generals Die in Bed': Modern Warfare and the Origins of Modernist Culture," *Journal of Canadian Studies* 16, 3–4 (1981): 2–3.

3. E. Anthony Rotundo, *American Manhood: Transformations in Masculinity from the Revolution to the Modern Era* (New York: Basic Books, 1993), 33–34.

4. Berger, *The Sense of Power*, 255.

5. Jeffrey P. Hantover, "The Boy Scouts and the Validation of Masculinity," in Elizabeth H. Pleck and Joseph H. Pleck, eds., *The American Man* (Englewood Cliffs: Prentice-Hall, 1980), 290.

6. Morton, *When Your Number's Up*, 4.
7. Peter N. Stearns, *Be a Man! Males in Modern Society* (New York: Holmes and Meier Publishing Inc., 1979), 71–73.
8. John R. Belts, *America's Sporting Heritage: 1850–1950* (Reading: Addison-Wesley Publishing Company, 1974), 124; Stearns, *Be a Man*, 76.
9. Morris Mott, "One Solution to the Urban Crisis: Manly Sports and Winnipeggers, 1900–1914," *Urban History Review* 12, 2 (1983): 59. Also see Alan Metcalfe, *Canada Learns to Play: The Emergence of Organized Sports, 1807–1914* (Toronto: McClelland and Stewart, 1987), and Colin Howell, *Northern Sandlots: A Social History of Baseball in the Maritimes* (Toronto: University of Toronto Press, 1994).
10. Mott, "One Solution to the Urban Crisis," 66.
11. Peter G. Filene, *Him/Her/Self: Sex Roles in Modern America* (Baltimore: John Hopkins University Press, 1974), 75.
12. Joe L. Dubbert, *A Man's Place: Masculinity in Transition* (New York: Prentice-Hall Inc., 1979), 166; Hantover, "The Boy Scouts," 289.
13. Filene, *Him/Her/Self*, 94.
14. Especially so-called "maternal feminists" who saw women and children as the principal victims of errant male conduct. See for example Wendy Mitchinson, "The WCTU: 'For God, Home and Native Land': A Study in Nineteenth-Century Feminism," in Linda Kealey, ed., *Not an Unreasonable Claim: Women and Reform in Canada, 1880s–1920* (Toronto: The Women's Press, 1979), 151–67, and Mariana Valverde, "'When the Mother of the Race is Free': Race, Reproduction, and Sexuality in First Wave Feminism," in Franca Iacovetta and Mariana Valverde, eds., *Gender Conflicts: New Essays in Women's History* (Toronto: University of Toronto Press, 1992), 13–20.
15. Rotundo, *American Manhood*, 120–26.
16. Berger, *The Sense of Power*, 233–34, 251–52.
17. See Martin Green, *The Adventurous Male: Chapters in the History of the White Male Mind* (University Park: Pennsylvania State University Press, 1993), 185.
18. Morton, *When Your Number's Up*, 278.
19. Granatstein and Hitsman, *Broken Promises*, 97.
20. Morton, *When Your Number's Up*, 279.
21. Essentially, the system of production and distribution in World War Two, though more centralized and sophisticated, strongly resembled that established during the 1914–18 conflict. See DND, Vol. 10,315, File 63/12, Brown to P&S, Sub-Depot, London, 23 July 1945.
22. NFSTA, C.B.C., Flanders' Field Series, Reel #7, Testimony by John MacKenzie.

23. MD, III, Vol. 5077, June 1917, 5.

24. *Ibid.*, Vol. 5078, 24 Feb. 1917, 5.

25. *Ibid.*, Vol. 5080, 26 Oct. 1916, 3.

26. *Ibid.*, Vol. 5079, 14 April 1916, 2.

27. *Ibid.*, Vol. 5078, 1 July 1916, 13.

28. *Ibid.*, Vol. 5080, 26 Oct. 1916, 3.

29. *Ibid.*, Vol. 5078, *Clansman*, 1 Oct. 1916, 14.

30. *Ibid.*, Vol. 5080, 18 Dec. 1915, 5.

31. *Ibid.*, Vol. 5079, 27 Nov 1916, 2.

32. *Ibid.*, Vol. 5080, 8 July 1916, 4.

33. *Ibid.*, *Whizz Bang*, 3 Dec. 1916, 2.

34. *Ibid.*, Vol. 5078, *Clansman*, 1 July 1916, 14.

35. *Ibid.*, Vol. 5079, Dec. 1917, 10.

36. *Ibid.*, Vol. 5078, *Clansman*, 1 Aug. 1916, 10.

37. *Ibid.*, Vol. 5077, April 1916, 24.

38. *Ibid.*, May 1917, 4.

39. *Ibid.*, Vol. 5078, Aug. 1917, 10.

40. *Ibid.*, *Chevrons to Stars*, Aug. 1917, 10, 24.

41. *Ibid.*, Vol. 5079, No. 11, 30.

42. *Ibid.*, Dec. 1916, 1.

43. *Ibid.*, March 1918, 8.

44. HL, BB, BBK E/1/20, undated memorandum.

45. MD, Vol. 4737, File 143–7; *ibid.*, Vol. 4732, File 140–5, C.W.R.O. Report, 1918.

46. *Ibid.*, Vol. 5077, 16 Jan. 1917, 1.

47. *Ibid.*, 6 Feb. 1917, 3.

48. *Ibid.*, Vol. 5078, no. 4, 8.

49. *Ibid.*, Vol. 5080, Christmas 1915, 13.

50. *Ibid.*, June 1918, 130.

51. *Ibid.*, Vol. 5079, 10 Dec. 1917, 22.

52. *Ibid.*, *Listening Post*, 29 April 1916, 29.

53. *Ibid.*, no. 1, 4.

54. *Ibid.*, Vol. 5080, Easter 1916, 7.

55. *Ibid.*, Vol. 5079, Jan. 1917, 10.

56. *Ibid.*, Feb. 1916, 48.

57. AO, MU2055, #21, 21 July 1916, 3.

58. MD, Vol. 5078, Christmas 1917, 6.

59. *Ibid.*, Vol. 5080, *Vic's Patrol*, 3 June 1916, 3.

60. *Ibid.*, Vol. 5079, *Listening Post*, 15 March 1916, 61.

61. Fussell, *The Great War and Modern Memory*, 250.

62. MD, Vol. 5079, 10 Aug. 1916, 124.

63. *Ibid.*, Dec. 1916, 25.

64. *Ibid.*, *Listening Post*, 23 Feb. 1918, 4.

65. *Ibid.*, Vol. 5078, *Canadian Machine Gunner*, June 1917, 22.

66. *Ibid.*, 16 March 1918, 82.

67. *Ibid.*, Vol. 5080, March 1916, 48; *ibid.*, Vol. 5079, 25 Oct. 1915, 4.

68. *Ibid.*, Vol. 5078, April 1918, 81.

69. *Ibid.*, 5 Jan. 1918, 1.

70. *Ibid.*, Vol. 5079, *Listening Post*, 18 June 1916, 6.

71. *Ibid.*, Vol. 5078, 18 Aug. 1917, 4.

72. *Ibid.*, Vol. 5078, 30 Nov. 1915, 4.

73. *Ibid.*, 14 July 1917, 8.

74. Morton, *When Your Number's Up*, 231.

75. MD, Vol. 5080, 16 March 1918, 85; *ibid.*, 10 May 1916, 2.

76. *Ibid.*, Vol. 5077, Dec. 1916, 8.

77. *Ibid.*, Vol. 5080, 3 June 1916, 3.

78. Fussell, *Great War and Modern Memory*, 12.

6 Hidden Truths

1. Fussell, *Great War and Modern Memory*, 183.

2. Gwynne Dyer and Tina Viljoen, *The Defence of Canada: In the Arms of the Empire* (Toronto: McClelland and Stewart, 1990), 170–71.

3. NAC, MG30 E439, Hugh MacDonald Dunlop papers, officer's order book, 1.

4. CPC, File 112–14, Militia and Defence Memo, 13 Feb. 1915.

5. NAC, MG30 E400, C. Williams papers, Williams to his family, 27 April 1917.

6. Fewster, "Expression and Suppression," 62, 64.

7. MD, Vol. 919, File C–74–3, Williams to G.H.Q., 1st Echelon, 20 July 1917; *ibid*, Vol. 1221, File C–49–5, Ferguson to H.Q., Shorncliffe, 27 June 1917.

8. BR, Series A, J.A. Fournier papers, Diary, 52.

9. Morton, *When Your Number's Up*, 278.

10. NAC, MG30 E114, C.M. Butler papers, Butler to Cecile, 2 April 1915.

11. See for example AO, MU7151, C.S. Haultain papers, File 8, R. Haultain to his mother, 22 May 1918.

12. BR, Series 137, Neil Family papers, R.H. Neil to his mother, 5 July 1915; *ibid.*, Neil to his aunt and uncle, 21 March 1916; *ibid.*, Neil to his parents, 15 Sept. 1915.

13. NAC, MG30 E304, Kenneth Duggan papers, Duggan to his brother, 11 Nov. 1915.

14. Gwyn, *Tapestry of War*, 160–63; NAC, MG30 E441, Russell Bradley papers, Diary, 61.

15. Fewster, "Expression and Suppression," 70.

16. *Saturday Night*, 2 Sept. 1916, 21.

17. BR, World War One Broadside Catalogue, n.p.; Hopkins, *Canadian Annual Review*, 1916, 440. On the financial and moral support provided by regimental auxiliaries see NAC, MG28 I 331, Montreal Soldiers Wives League papers.

18. Allison Prentice, Paula Bourne, Gail Cuthbert Brandt, Beth Light, Wendy Mitchinson, and Naomi Black, *Canadian Women: A History* (Toronto: Harcourt Brace Jovanovich, 1988), 139. This point about some women developing, but not publicizing, a new sense of independence is suggested in Leed, *No Man's Land*, 47.

19. Haultain papers, File 4, Haultain to his mother, 7 Nov. 1914.

20. BR, Series 241, Youell Family papers, Box 1, Leonard Youell to his mother, 13 Nov. 1915.

21. BR, Series L44, Norman Keys papers, Keys to his family, 13 June 1915.

22. Mathieson, *My Grandfather's War*, 11, 13.

23. Gwyn, *Tapestry of War*, 463–64.

24. Morton, *When Your Number's Up*, 70.

25. Van Paasen, *Days of Our Years*, 67.

26. Brown and Loveridge, "Unrequited Faith," 58; Leslie Frost, *Fighting Men* (Toronto: Clark, Irwin & Company, 1967), 75–76.

27. Morton, *When Your Number's Up*, 73–74.

28. Fournier papers, Diary, 52–53.

29. Mathieson, *My Grandfather's War*, 24; NAC, MG30 E370, J. Brophy papers, Diary, 19 Dec. 1915.

30. Greenhous, ed., *A Rattle of Pebbles*, 4; NAC, MG30 E8, J.J. Creelman papers, Diary, 14 Oct. 1914.

31. On this theme see Richard White, "The Soldier as Tourist: The Australian Experience of the Great War," *War & Society* 5, 1 (1987): 63–77.

32. MacKenzie, *Propaganda and Empire*, 17.

33. See BR, Series 209, T. Fisher papers, postcard collection; George L. Mosse, *Fallen Soldiers: Reshaping Memory of the World Wars* (New York: Oxford, 1990), 70.

34. Creelman papers, Creelman to his wife, 18 Feb. 1915; Williams papers, Williams to his family, 20 May 1916, 7 July 1916.

35. NAC, MG30 E429, J. Johnson papers, T.D. Johnson to his mother, 5 Nov. 1915; AO, MU4970, H.J. Cody papers, Vol. 1, L. McKenzie to Cody, 26 Oct. 1917.

36. Morton, *When Your Number's Up*, 91.

37. R.G. Moyles and Douglas Owram, *Imperial Dreams and Colonial Realities: British Views of Canada, 1880–1914* (Toronto: University of Toronto Press, 1988), 239–40.
38. NAC, MG30 E459, E. Nelson papers, Diary, 13 Oct. 1916; Neil Family papers, R. Neil to his aunt and uncle, 10 July 1915.
39. NAC, MG30 E389, W. O'Brien papers, Vol. 1, Diary, 20 Jan. 1916.
40. Frost, *Fighting Men*, 74; Beatty, ed., *Memories of a Forgotten War*, 90.
41. Duguid, *Official History of the Canadian Forces*, 125.
42. Morton, *When Your Number's Up*, 87.
43. MD, Vol. 4734, File 144–1, Press Despatch, 6 Nov. 1917; NAC, MG30 E450, F. Paull papers, Diary, 30 Jan. 1917.
44. Rawling, *Surviving Trench Warfare*, 16–17.
45. Morton and Granatstein, *Marching to Armageddon*, 51; University of Toronto, St. Michael's Archives [UT], W. O'Brien papers, Diary, 1.
46. MD, Vol. 29, File 25–1–1, H.C. McLeod to Borden, 1 Aug. 1917; Duguid, *Official History*, 136.
47. MD, Vol. 29, File 25–1–1, Iona Davey to O.C. of Whitley Camp, 14 Oct. 1916.
48. Greenhous, ed., *Rattle of Pebbles*, 12–13.
49. *Ibid*, 11; Canadian War Museum [CWM], Acc #19800745, C. Tower papers, Diary, 29 June 1916.
50. Keys papers, Keys to his mother, 18 July 1915, 5 Oct. 1915.
51. Youell Family papers, Box 1, L. Youell to his mother, 12 Nov. 1916.
52. AO, MU906, M. Ellis papers, Ellis to his mother, 19 Feb. 1917.
53. Neil Family papers, Neil to his brother, 23 Nov. 1915.
54. See for example NAC, MG30 E170, F. Hazlewood papers, Hazlewood to his mother, 6 May 1917; NAC, MG30 E277, F. Maheaux papers, Maheaux to his wife, 7 Jan. 1916.
55. York University Archives, Jack Lawrence Granatstein papers, Box 6, File 95, A.P. Menzies to his parents, 29 July 1916.
56. NAC, MG30 E456, J. Symmons papers, Symmons to his parents, 21 Nov. 1915.
57. NAC, MG30 E335, F. Matthews papers, F. Matthews to his father, 17 June 1916.
58. Talbot Papineau told his parents "that if I do get killed I was completely happy and content to the last minute." Heather Robertson, ed., *A Terrible Beauty* (Toronto: James Lorimer & Company, 1977), 91.
59. Lt. A. Anderson to Mrs. Jim Irvine, 12 Dec. 1917. Private collection held by Bill Irvine, Mewburn Veterans' Hospital, Edmonton, Alberta.
60. Desmond Morton, "The Supreme Penalty: Canadian Deaths by Firing Squad in the First World War," *Queen's Quarterly* 79, 3 (1972): 350.
61. AO, MU8230, E. Grier papers, Box B–2–A, File 8, C. Grier to his brother, 15 Nov. 1917; Maheaux papers, Maheaux to his wife, 19 May 1915.

62. Grier papers, File 8, undated clipping from *Saturday Night*.

63. For instance, John Keegan postulated that up to one-third of British soldiers who died on the opening day of the Somme offensive could have survived if medical care had been available more quickly. See *The Face of Battle: A Study of Agincourt, Waterloo and the Somme* (Toronto: Penguin, 1976), 274.

64. AO, MU134, C. Rutherford papers, Diary, 8.

65. Morton, *When Your Number's Up*, 181.

66. Craig, *But This Is Our War*, 74.

67. NAC, MG30 E521, K. Wright papers, Wright to Martin, 13 Nov. 1916.

68. Haultain papers, File 4, Haultain to his mother, 5 July 1916.

69. Rawling, *Surviving Trench Warfare*, 68–69; Harris, *Canadian Brass*, 113.

70. Roy, ed., *The Journal of Private Fraser*, 23.

71. E.L.M. Burns, *General Mud* (Toronto: Clarke, Irwin & Co, 1970), 44; Winter, *Death's Men*, 40.

72. NAC, MG30 E450, R.W. Rigsby papers, Diary, 13 June 1918.

73. NAC, MG30 E241, D.E. McIntyre papers, Diary, 24 Sept. 1915.

74. NAC, MG30 E351, C. Craig papers, Diary, 16 Feb. 1917.

75. NAC, MG26 K, R.B. Bennett papers, Reel m–907, "War Scandals of the Borden Government," 806–8; Daniel Dancocks, *Welcome to Flanders' Field: The First Canadian Battle of the Great War, Ypres, 1915* (Toronto: McClelland and Stewart, 1988, 340.

76. MD, Vol. 4327, File H.S. 27–1–4, Press Despatch, 20 Jan. 1917.

77. UT, O'Brien papers, Diary, 4 Aug. 1916.

78. Beatty, *Memories of a Forgotten War*, 102.

79. Granatstein and Morton, *Marching to Armageddon*, 279.

80. Lieutenant John Teahan diary quoted in the Toronto *Globe & Mail*, 6 Nov. 1993, D3.

81. NFTSA, C.B.C., Flanders' Field series, Tape #1, testimony by Tom Bovey.

82. Molly Unger, "A Subtle Reshaping: Effects of World War I on Canadian Soldiers Who Fought in It," unpublished Ms., McMaster University, August 1987, 9. In fact, the frequency of such remarks lends some credence to the contention made by a few scholars that the physical distance among enlisted personnel from and their disenchantment with senior officers forged within the lower ranks a degree of proto-class consciousness. It seems that a number of frontliners came to regard the General Staff as an elite group harbouring diametrically opposed interests. Like the left-wing or progressive critics of that era who talked of 'fat-cat plutocrats' sweating 'expendible' labour of surplus value, many a *grunt* perceived their most prominent leaders as leeches who, in the context of war, enriched themselves by obtaining personal glory at the

expense of the infantryman's blood. See Martel, "'Generals Die in Bed,'" 4.

83. Rawling, *Surviving Trench Warfare*, 15, 71.

84. Tim Travers, "Learning and Decision-Making on the Western Front, 1915–1916: The British Example," *Canadian Journal of History* 18, 1 (1983): 87–97.

85. A.M.J. Hyatt, "Canadian Generals of the First World War and the Popular View of Military Leadership," *Histoire Sociale/Social History* 12, 24 (1979): 424.

86. Harris, *Canadian Brass*, 137.

87. Pierre Berton, *Vimy* (Toronto: McClelland and Steward Ltd., 1986), 93–94, 110.

88. A.M.J. Hyatt, "Arthur Currie: Corps Commander," in Milner, ed., *Canadian Military History*, 107.

89. Rawling, *Surviving Trench Warfare*, 221.

90. MD, Vol. 4734, File 145–1, Press Despatch, 12 Sept. 1918; Roy, *Journals*, 39, 87.

91. Charles Yale Harrison, *Generals Die in Bed* (Owen Sound: Richardson, Bond and Wright, 1976 ed.).

92. Hyatt, "Canadian Generals of the First World War," 421.

93. NAC, MG30 E32, A. West papers, Diary, 9 Sept. 1918.

94. NAC, MG30 E447, Roy Family papers, A.C. Roy, Diary, 1 May 1918; Roger Sarty and Brereton Greenhous, "The Great War," in R. Douglas Francis and Donald B. Smith, eds., *Readings in Canadian History: Post Confederation*, 3rd ed. (Toronto: Holt, Rinehart and Winston, 1990), 329.

95. Sir Andrew Macphail, *Official History of the Canadian Forces in the Great War 1914–1919: The Medical Services* (Ottawa: King's Printer, 1925), 270–71.

96. Morton, *When Your Number's Up*, 136.

97. CWM, Acc #19650038–016, W. Coleman papers, Diary, 2 Nov. 1915; Dancocks, *Welcome to Flanders' Field*, 127.

98. Robertson, *Terrible Beauty*, 67.

99. MD, Vol. 10, File 4–2–43, A.E. Ross to D.A.Q.M.G. 1st Division, 9 May 1916; NFTSA, Reel #1, testimony by Tom Bovey.

100. Macphail, *Official History*, 279.

101. DND, Vol. 134, File 8994–1, Walter S. Woods to Norman Rogers, 20 Dec. 1939.

102. Mathieson, *My Grandfather's War*, 71; Rigsby papers, Diary, 6 March 1918.

103. CWM, Acc # 19750196–001, G. Greenwood papers, Diary, 20 May 1915.

104. Morton and Granatstein, *Marching to Armageddon*, 54; Duguid, *Official History*, 196.

105. Winter, *Death's Men*, 102.

106. Coleman papers, Diary, 22 Dec. 1915, 100.

107. Roy, ed., *Journal of Private Fraser*, 37.

108. Fussell, *Great War and Modern Memory*, 36, 123–4.

109. CWM, Acc #19890200–018, F. Tidy papers, Diary, 26 April 1915.

110. NFTSA, Reel #3, testimony by Ross Cameron.

111. Morton, *When Your Number's Up*, 140–41.

112. BR, Series A, W. Rattle papers, Diary, 21; NFTSA, Reel #2, testimony by Ian Sinclair.

113. Winter, *Death's Men*, 79.

114. CWM, Acc #19860259–001, F. Bolton papers, Diary, 6 April 1917; CWM, Acc # 19890275–028, A. Anderson papers, Diary, 24 Oct. 1916.

115. Roy, ed., *Journal of Private Fraser*, 151.

116. Morton, "The Supreme Penalty," 345–52.

117. Fussell, *Great War and Modern Memory*, 114–15.

118. Morton, "The Supreme Penalty," 348.

119. McIntyre papers, Diary, 20 Nov. 1915.

120. Macphail, *Official History*, 279; Mathieson, *My Grandfather's War*, 127.

121. McIntyre papers, Diary, 19 Nov. 1915; *Ibid*, 5 April 1916.

122. Macphail, *Official History*, 274; Keegan, *The Face of Battle*, 275–76, 281.

123. Mathieson, *My Grandfather's War*, 113, 127.

124. See for example Williams papers, Williams to his parents, 22 Oct. 1916.

125. Robertson, *Terrible Beauty*, 47.

126. Robert Hanks, "The Humane Dimension of War: Fraternization and Community on the Western Front," unpublished Ms., University of Toronto, March, 1989, 1–20, 35.

127. Bliss, "The Methodist Church," 46.

128. NAC, MG30 E392, F. Lacey papers, Diary, 12 Oct. 1916.

129. Burns, *General*, 14; Fournier papers, Diary, 65.

130. Gwyn, *Tapestry of War*, 194; *Canada in Khaki*, No. 1, 1917, 151–53.

131. Morton, *When Your Number's Up*, 200.

132. Read, ed., *The Great War and Canadian Society*, 146; Gwyn, *Tapestry of War*, 221–24.

133. Jay Cassel, *The Secret Plague: Venereal Disease in Canada, 1838–1939* (Toronto: University of Toronto Press, 1987), 122.

134. Beatty, *Memories of a Forgotten War*, 199–200.

135. UT, O'Brien papers, Diary, 4 Aug. 1916.

136. BR, Series 138, D. Fraser papers, Diary, 54, 62.

137. Robertson, *Terrible Beauty*, 99–100.

138. Van Paasen, *Days of Our Years*, 89.

139. Desmond Morton, "'Kicking and Complaining': Demobilization Riots and

the Canadian Expeditionary Force, 1918–1919," *Canadian Historical Review* 61, 3 (1980): 334–60; Dave Lamb, *Mutinies, 1917–20* (Leeds: Solidarity Press, 1977), 9–12.

7 Johnny Canuck Returns to Civilian Life

1. AO, MU7662, J. Mould Papers, Diary, Vol. 5, 65.
2. NAC, RG6 E1, CPC, File 104–5–A, Kingston *British Whig*, 31 Dec. 1919, Calgary *Herald*, 2 Jan. 1920.
3. Leed, *No Man's Land*, 203.
4. J.C. Hopkins, *Canada and War: A Record of Heroism and Achievement, 1914–1918* (Toronto: The Canadian Annual Review Limited, 1919), 214.
5. James Eayrs, *In Defence of Canada: From The Great War to the Great Depression* (Toronto: University of Toronto Press, 1965), 66.
6. Vancouver *Sun*, 29 May 1919, 6.
7. Calgary *Herald*, 25 March 1919, 8.
8. Hamilton *Spectator*, 9 May 1919, 1.
9. Toronto *Star*, 3 Sept. 1919, 3.
10. Doll, *The Poster War*, 33–34.
11. Berton, *Vimy*, 296.
12. Allan R. Young, "'We Throw the Torch': Canadian Memorials of the Great War and the Mythology of Heroic Sacrifice," *Journal of Canadian Studies* 26, 4 (1990): 13, 16, 18.
13. Brereton Greenhous and Stephen Harris, *Canada and the Battle of Vimy Ridge, 9–12 April 1917* (Ottawa: Minister of Supply and Services, 1992), 139.
14. DND, Vol. 3884, File 1029–6–24, CPC Circular, 5 May 1917.
15. Malvern, "'War As It Is,'" 504–5.
16. Tippett, *Art at the Service of War*, 65; Canadian War Museum, C.W.R.O. Art Collection.
17. *Canadian Courier*, Nov. 1919, 12; *The Canadian Magazine*, Nov. 1919, 3.
18. Toronto *Telegram*, 20 Oct. 1919, 20; Tippett, *Art at the Service*, 80.
19. John Herd Thompson and Allen Seager, *Canada 1922–1939: Decades of Discord* (Toronto: McClelland and Stewart, 1985), 166.
20. Steward, "A Canadian Perspective," 10, 22–23; Novak, "The Canadian Novel," 22.
21. *Saturday Night*, 14 Sept. 1918, 9.
22. NFTSA, C.B.C., Flanders' Field Series, Tape #2, Interview with R.L. Christopher; Berton, *Vimy*, 300.
23. Robertson, ed., *A Terrible Beauty*, 100.

24. BR, Series S219, H.S. Murton Papers, Diary, 6–8.

25. Van Paasen, *Days of Our Years*, 90.

26. Greenhous and Harris, *Canada and the Battle*, 146.

27. Van Paasen, *Days of Our Years*, 91.

28. Morton, *When Your Number's Up*, 268.

29. Leed, *No Man's Land*, 13.

30. Van Paasen, *Days of our Years*, 90.

31. *Ibid.*

32. Robert England, *Discharged: A Comment on Civil Re-establishment of Veterans in Canada* (Toronto: Macmillan, 1943), 19.

33. In Germany and France, the government passed laws requiring employers to hire a certain number of veterans. See Desmond Morton, "'Noblest and Best': Retraining Canada's War Disabled, 1915–1923," *Journal of Canadian Studies* 16, 3&4 (1981): 83.

34. James G. Snell, *In the Shadow of the Law: Divorce in Canada, 1900–1939* (Toronto: University of Toronto Press, 1991), 10–11.

35. On the post-war campaign against venereal disease see Cassel, *The Secret Plague*, chapters 8 and 9.

36. *Canada Year Book*, 1919, 616–17.

37. Leed, *No Man's Land*, 47.

38. Prentice *et al.*, *Canadian Women*, 141. Also see Ceta Ramkhalawansingh, "Women during the Great War," in Janice Acton, ed., *Women at Work: Ontario, 1850–1930* (Toronto: Women's Press, 1974), 261–307.

39. Gwyn, *Tapestry of War*, 431; Leed, *No Man's Land*, 184.

40. NFTSA, Tape #2, Interview with J. Bold.

41. Desmond Morton argues that the programmes initiated for veterans established the roots of federal welfare measures such as health care, as well as various individual and family pension benefits. See "'Noblest and Best,'" 75.

42. M.C. Urquhart and K.A.H. Buckley, eds., *Historical Statistics on Canada* (Toronto: Macmillan, 1965), series G1–25, G26–44.

43. Morton, *When Your Number's Up*, 263–64.

44. Morton and Wright, *Winning the Second Battle*, 94, 134; *Veteran*, Feb. 1919, 20.

45. Morton, *When Your Number's Up*, 255.

46. House of Commons, *Journals*, LIX, No. 2, 115.

47. Morton and Wright, *Winning the Second Battle*, 153, 220; Morton, "'Noblest and Best,'" 77.

48. Morton and Wright, *Winning the Second Battle*, 148, 204.

49. *Veteran*, July 1920, 17.

50. BP, Vol. 240, Captain Charles A. Weaver to Borden, 17 Dec. 1919, 134,256–59; Morton and Wright, *Winning the Second Battle*, 153.
51. *Veteran*, March 1919, 12, 19; BP, Vol. 240, 134,008–10.
52. *Veteran*, July 1919, 16.
53. David Jay Bercuson, *Fools and Wise Men: The Rise and Fall of the One Big Union* (Toronto: McGraw-Hill Ryerson, 1978), 91; D.C. Masters, *The Winnipeg General Strike* (Toronto: University of Toronto Press, 1950), 61, 142–44.
54. England, *Discharged*, 29–30.
55. Michael T. Issenberg, "An Ambiguous Pacifism: A Retrospective on World War I Films, 1930–1938," *Journal of Popular Film* 4, 2 (1975): 106.
56. Leed, *No Man's Land*, 191–92.
57. Novak, "The Canadian Novel," 37, 69, 92; Steward, "A Canadian Perspective," 80.
58. Peregrine Acland, *All Else Is Folly* (Toronto: McClelland and Stewart, 1929), 245–46.
59. Harrison, *Generals Die in Bed*, 91, 110–12.
60. Philip Child, *God's Sparrows* (London: Thornton Butterworths, 1937), 251, 311.
61. Herbert McBride, *A Rifleman Went to War* (Onslow: Small-Arms Technical Publishing Company, 1935), Preface and 49.
62. Van Paasen, *Days of Our Years*, 66.
63. Thomas Socknat, *Witness Against War: Pacifism in Canada, 1900–1945* (Toronto: University of Toronto Press, 1987), 147–55.
64. Eayrs, *In Defence of Canada*, 275.
65. England, *Discharged*, 15.
66. J.L. Granatstein and Desmond Morton, *A Nation Forged in Fire: Canadians and the Second World War, 1939–1945* (Toronto: Lester & Orpen Dennys, 1989), 11.
67. Paul Twomey, "Small Power Security Through Great Arms Control? Australian Perceptions of Disarmament, 1919–1930," *War & Society* 8, 1 (1990): 74; Fewster, "Expression and Suppression," 60.
68. Hull, "'The Old Lie,'" 95.
69. See for example, Ken Fry, "Soldier Settlement," *Labour History* 48 (1983): 29–43.
70. Souter, *Lion and Kangaroo*, 286.
71. Patsy Adams-Smith, *The Anzacs* (London: Hamish-Hamilton, 1978), 354.
72. See Raymond Evans, "Some Furious Outbreaks of Riot: Returned Soldiers and Queensland's 'Red Flag' Disturbances, 1918–1919," *War & Society* 3, 2 (1985): 75–95.

73. Hull, "The Old Lie," 92, 95, 100.

74. Adams-Smith, *The Anzacs*, 316.

75. K.S. Inglis, "A Sacred Place: The Making of the Australian War Memorial," *War & Society* 3, 2 (1985): 100–101, 109.

76. C.E.W. Bean, *The Australian Imperial Force in France, 1916* (London: University of Queensland Press, 1982), xviii; *The Story of the Anzac* (Sydney: Argus & Robertson, 1924), 110.

77. Russell Ward, *The Australian Legend* (Melbourne: Oxford University Press, 1958), 212.

78. W.F. Mandle, *Going it Alone: Australia's National Identity in the Twentieth Century* (Victoria: Penguin, 1977), 4.

79. Adams-Smith, *The Anzacs*, ix.

80. Evans, *Loyalty and Disloyalty*, 2.

81. Berton, *Vimy*, 304.

82. John Swettenham, *To Seize the Victory: The Canadian Corps in World War I* (Toronto: Ryerson Press, 1965), 247.

83. Kenneth Macksey, *The Shadow of Vimy Ridge* (Toronto: Ryerson Press, 1965), 189.

84. Herbert Fairlee Wood, *Vimy!* (Toronto: Macmillan of Canada, 1967), 170.

85. Senate Standing Committee on Social Affairs, Science and Technology, *Production and Distribution of the National Film Board Production, "The Kid Who Couldn't Miss"* (Ottawa: Supply and Services, 1986); "Bishop Disclaimer Rejected," *Winnipeg Free Press*, 16 April 1986, 33.

86. Berton, *Vimy*, 295.

87. See Morton, *When Your Number's Up*; Granatstein and Morton, *Marching to Armageddon*; Rawling, *Surviving Trench Warfare*; Michael Hadley and Roger Sarty, *Tin-Pots and Pirate Ships: Canadian Naval Forces and German Sea Raiders, 1880–1918* (Montreal: McGill-Queen's University Press, 1991); Harris, *Canadian Brass*; and S.F. Wise, *Canadian Airmen and the First World War: The Official History of the Royal Canadian Air Force*, Vol. 1 (Toronto: University of Toronto Press, 1980).

88. Daniel Dancocks, *Spearhead to Victory: Canada and the Great War* (Edmonton: Hurtig Publishers, 1987), 240. Also see *Legacy of Valour: The Canadians at Passchendaele* (Edmonton: Hurtig Publishers, 1986), and *Welcome to Flanders' Field: The First Canadian Battle of the War, Ypres, 1915* (Toronto: McClelland and Stewart, 1988).

89. Gwyn, *Tapestry of War*, xvii.

Bibliography

Primary Sources

1 Departmental Records

PUBLIC RECORDS OFFICE, LONDON, ENGLAND

War Cabinet Minutes

NATIONAL ARCHIVES OF CANADA, OTTAWA, ONTARIO

Agriculture
Boards, Offices and Committees
Chief Press Censor
Dominion Archivist
External Affairs
Finance
Governor General
Immigration
Justice
Militia and Defence
Naval Service
Parliament
Post Office

Privy Council
Royal Canadian Mounted Police
Secretary of State
Trade and Commerce
Veterans' Affairs

ARCHIVES OF ONTARIO, TORONTO, ONTARIO

Attorney General
Correctional Services
Court Records
Education
Ontario Provincial Police
Theatre Branch

2 Private Papers

HOUSE OF LORDS RECORDS OFFICE, LONDON, ENGLAND

Lord Beaverbrook

NATIONAL ARCHIVES OF CANADA, OTTAWA, ONTARIO

Peregrine Acland
W.A. Alldritt
Harold V. Ardaugh
W.G. Barker
Lord Beaverbrook
R.B. Bennett
Sir Robert Borden
Russell Bradley
John B. Brophy
C.M. Buller
Canadian Press Association
Claude G. Craig
J.J. Creelman
W. Crisford
Felix Cullen
Sir Arthur Currie
William Howard Curtis
J.W. Dafoe

Charles Doherty
Kenneth Duggan
Hugh Macdonald Dunlop
W.E. Edwards
Robert L. Ferrie
Sir George Foster
L.A. Gamble
George Grant
Charles Frederick Hamilton
Frank Hazlewood
W.H. Hewgill
Sophie Hoerner
J. Johnson
Sir Edward Kemp
William Lyon Mackenzie King
F. Lacey
Sir Wilfrid Laurier
R.G.E. Leckie
William S. Lighthall
T.S. Lyon
D.E. McIntyre
George P. MacLaren
G.L. Magann
Charles Magrath
Frank Maheaux
Frank G. Matthews
John P. McNab
Arthur Meighen
William C. Morgan
Ernest Nelson
E.F. Newcombe
W.J. O'Brien
T.F. O'Kelly
Francis H. Paull
Sir George Perley
James Roy Pond
Ernest F. Pullen
Hugh C. Pullen
R.W. Rigsby
P.D. Ross

Sir N. Rowell
Roy Family
E.W. Russell
Sir Percy Sherwood
A.L. Sifton
Sir Clifford Sifton
Alexander G. Sinclair
Ian Sinclair
T.B. Smythe
Ernest J. Spilett
John H. Symmons
Russell Tubman
A. West
Sir Thomas White
Claude V. Williams
J.S. Willison
K. Wright

ARCHIVES OF ONTARIO, TORONTO, ONTARIO

H. Arbuckle
H.J. Cody
L. Duncan
M. Ellis
Fielde-Sefton Family
C.S. Haultain
C. Jennings
R. Luxton
A.C. Macdonnell
Maclean-Hunter
D.H. Mendies
J.F. Mould
C. Rutherford
L.V. Shier

CANADIAN WAR MUSEUM, OTTAWA, ONTARIO

A. Anderson
F. Bolton

F. Brangwyn
W. Coleman
R. Fogerty
G. Greenwood
J. Holmes
A. Lismer
A. Mackay
H.M. May
A. McNally
J.E. Sharman
F. Tidy
C. Tower
S. Turner

METROPOLITAN TORONTO LIBRARY BALDWIN ROOM, TORONTO, ONTARIO

J.J. Dolman
J.A. Duncan
T.E. Fisher
J.A. Fournier
D. Fraser
Harman Family
W.M. Johnson
N. Keys
Merriman Family
E.H. Mitchener
H.S. Murton
Neil Family
W.F. Rattle
Shanly Family
Youell Family

UNIVERSITY OF TORONTO, TORONTO, ONTARIO

Mrs. H.J. Cody
Sir Robert Falconer
H.A. Innis
James Mavor
Office of the Registrar

W.J. O'Brien
Rankin Family
William Rattle
Sir Edmund Walker

UNITED CHURCH, TORONTO, ONTARIO

Salem Bland
S.D. Chown
W.T. Herridge
T.J. Jewitt
P.P. Pedley
George Workman

YORK UNIVERSITY, TORONTO, ONTARIO

Jack Lawrence Granatstein

3 Newspapers and Magazines

B.C. Federationist
Calgary Herald
Canadian Bookman
Canadian Courier
Canadian Forum
Canadian Hospital News
Canadian Magazine
Canadian Military Gazette
Canadian Motion Picture Journal
Canadian Official Record
Canadian War Pictorial
Financial Post
Globe and Mail
Grain Grower's Guide
Halifax Herald
Hamilton Spectator
Kingston Whig-Standard
La Presse
Le Devoir
London Free Press

Maclean's
Manitoba Free Press
Maple Leaf Magazine
Military Hospitals Commission Bulletin
Montreal Gazette
National Geographic Magazine
Ottawa Citizen
Ottawa Evening Journal
Quebec Chronicle
Queen's Quarterly
Reconstruction
Regina Leader Post
Saturday Night
Sudbury Star
Toronto Globe
Toronto Mail and Empire
Toronto News
Toronto Star
Toronto Telegram
University Magazine
Vancouver Sun
Victoria Daily Colonist
Windsor Evening Record
Winnipeg Tribune

4   Military Newspapers

Action Front (53rd Battery, C.F.A)
Blister, later the *Convoy Call* (5th Cdn. Gen. Hosp.)
Barrage (Cdn. Reserve Artillery)
Beaver (Khaki University)
Bramshott Souvenir Magazine (Bramshott Camp)
Brazier (16th Battalion)
Breath o' the Heather (236th Battalion)
Bruce in Khaki (160th Battalion)
Busy Beaver (Cdn. Engineers)
C.R.O. Bulletin (C.W.R.O.)
C.A.S.C. News (Cdn. Army Service Corps)
C.C.S. Review (No. 3 Casualty Clearing Station)

Canada in Khaki (C.W.R.O.)

Canadian Daily Record (C.W.R.O.)

Canadian Sapper (Cdn. Engineers)

Chevrons to Stars (Cdn. Training School, Bexhill)

Clansman (17th Cdn. Reserve Battalion)

Clearings (No. 4 Casualty Clearing Station)

Dead Horse Corner Gazette (4th Battalion)

Field Comforts (Field Comforts Commission)

From Camp to Hammock (Camp Borden)

Fortyniner (49th Battalion)

Frontiersman (Legion of Frontiersmen)

Garland From the Front (5th Battalion)

Growler (14th Battalion)

Hospital News (Hospitals in Ramsgate and Buxton)

Iodine Chronicle (Nos. 1,2,3, Cdn. Field Ambulance)

Khaki Life (Camp Borden)

Kilt (72nd Battalion)

Kiltie (134th Battalion)

La Vie Canadienne (G.H.Q., 3rd Echelon)

Lethbridge Highlander (113th Battalion)

Listening Post (7th Battalion)

Mail Slingers' Gazette (Cdn. Postal Corps)

Message From Mars (4th Cdn. Division)

Canadian Machine Gunner (C.M.G. Service)

McGilliken (No. 3 Cdn. General Hosp.)

Morrisey Mention (107th Battalion)

Now and Then (No. 3, Cdn Field Ambulance)

N.Y.D. (Nos. 1,2,3, Cdn. Field Ambulance)

O.Pip. (58th Battery, C.F.A.)

Ontario Stretcher (Ont. Military Hosp., Orpington)

Princess Patricia's Post (Princess Patricia's Hosp.)

Roulles Camp Magazine (Cdn. Base Depot, Le Havre)

Shell Hole Advance (11th Cdn. Infantry Brigade)

Stand Easy, Chronicles of Cliveden (No. 15, Cdn. General Hosp.)

Strafer (66th Field Artillery)

Tank Tattler (1st Cdn. Tank Battalion)

'Tchun (Cdn. Corps Training School, Fr.)

Timber Wolf (103rd Battalion)

Trench Echo (27th Battalion)

Twentieth Gazette (20th Battalion)

Vic's Patrol (24th Battalion)
Weekly Chronicle (Central Mobilization Camp, Vernon, B.C.)
Western Scot (67th Battalion, later Pioneer Battalion)
Whizz Bang (207th Battalion)

5 Photographs and Broadsides

NATIONAL ARCHIVES OF CANADA, OTTAWA, ONTARIO

Department of National Defence Collection
Horace Brown Collection
William Rider-Rider Collection
World War One Broadside Collection

METROPOLITAN TORONTO LIBRARY, TORONTO, ONTARIO

D. Fraser Collection
World War One Broadside Collection

Secondary Sources

1 Printed Government Sources

NATIONAL LIBRARY, OTTAWA, ONTARIO

Beland, H. *Summary of Activities of the Government of Canada in ConnectionWith
    the Demobilization and Re-establishment of Members of the Canadian
    Expeditionary Force to 31st
December, 1923.* Ottawa: King's Printer, 1924.
Canada Food Board. *Report.* Ottawa: King's Printer, 1919.
Canada. House of Commons. *Debates.*
_____. House of Commons. *Journals.*
_____. House of Commons. *Sessional Papers.*
_____. House of Commons. *Statutes.*
_____. Privy Council Office. *Orders-in-Council.*
_____. Dominion Bureau of Statistics. *Canada Year Book, 1919.*
Department of Public Information. *Sacrifice—The Price of Victory.* Ottawa: King's
    Printer, 1918.

_____. *The Sinking of the H.M.H.S. Llandovery Castle*. Ottawa: King's Printer, 1918.

_____. *To the Members of the Great War Veterans' Association*. Ottawa: King's Printer, 1918.

_____. *Canada's War Work, 1914–1918*. Ottawa: King's Printer, 1919.

_____. *War Lecture Bureau — Bulletins*. Ottawa: King's Printer, 1917–19.

_____. *What Canada Does For Her Soldiers*. Ottawa: King's Printer, 1919.

Department of Soldiers' Civil Re-establishment. *Canada's Work For Disabled Soldiers*. Ottawa: King's Printer, 1919.

_____. *The Programme of Repatriation*. Ottawa: King's Printer, 1919.

_____. *War to Peace*. Ottawa: King's Printer, 1919.

Dominion Publicity Committee. *Press Publicity for Canada's Victory Loan, 1918*. Ottawa: King's Printer, 1918.

_____. *Toronto's Victory Loan Campaign*. Ottawa: King's Printer, 1918.

_____. *Advertisements for the Victory Loan 1919*. Ottawa: King's Printer, 1919.

_____. *Bulletins*. Ottawa: King's Printer, 1917–19.

_____. *The Victory Loan 1919, Its Message to Speakers*. Ottawa: King's Printer, 1919.

Final Report of the Food Controller. Ottawa: King's Printer, 1919.

Final Report of the Fuel Controller. Ottawa: King's Printer, 1919.

Military Hospitals Commission. *Provision of Employment for Members of the Canadian Expeditionary Force on Their Return to Canada and the Re-Education of Those Who Are Unable to Follow Their Previous Occupations Because of Disability*. Ottawa: King's Printer, 1915.

National Service Board. *How To Live in Wartime*. Ottawa: King's Printer, 1917.

Ontario. *Sessional Papers*.

Quebec. *Sessional Papers*.

Library of Congress, Washington, D.C., U.S.A.

Committee on Public Information. *Complete Report of the Chairman*. Washington: Government Printing Office, 1920.

Division of Exposition. *Catalogue*. Washington: Government Printing Office, 1918.

Division of Four Minute Men. *Bulletins*. Washington: Government Printing Office, 1917–19.

Division of Industrial Relations. *Special Bulletin for Employers*. Washington: Government Printing Office, 1918.

Division of Still Photography. *Photography in Time of War*. Washington: Government Printing Office, 1917.

Division of Women's Work. *Women's Committees of the Council of National Defence*. Washington, Government Printing Office, 1918.

Munro, Dana. *German Treatment of Conquered Territory*. Washington: Government Printing Office, 1918.

Wilson, Woodrow. *Labour and the War*. Washington: Government Printing Office, 1917.

2 Books

Acland, Pergrine. *All Else Is Folly*. Toronto: McClelland and Stewart, 1929.

Adami, J.G. *The War Story of the C.A.M.C., 1914–1915*. Toronto: Musson Book Company, 1918.

Adams-Smith, Patsy. *The Anzacs*. London: Hamish-Hamilton, 1978.

Aitken, Sir Maxwell. *Canada in Flanders*. Vols. 1 & 2. Toronto: Hodder and Stoughton, 1915, 1916.

Aldrich, Mildrid. *A Hilltop on the Marne*. Toronto: Musson Book Company, 1915.

———. *The Peak of the Load*. Toronto: Musson Book Company, 1918.

Allen, Ralph. *Ordeal by Fire*. Toronto: Doubleday, 1961.

Allen, Richard. *The Social Passion: Religion and Social Reform in Canada, 1914–1928*. Toronto: University of Toronto Press, 1970.

Archer, William. *The Thirteen Days: July 23-August 4, 1914*. Toronto: Oxford University Press, 1915.

Armstrong, Elizabeth. *The Crisis of Quebec, 1914–1918*. New York: Columbia University Press, 1938.

Avery, Donald. *Dangerous Foreigners: European Immigrant Workers and Labour Radicalism in Canada*. Toronto: McClelland and Stewart, 1979.

Avakumovic, Ivan. *The Communist Party of Canada: A History*. Toronto: McClelland and Stewart, 1975.

Bairnsfather, Bruce. *Bullets and Billets*. Toronto: Gordon & Gotch, 1916.

Bean, C.E.W. *The Story of Anzac*. Sydney: Argus & Robertson, 1924.

———. *The Australian Imperial Force in France 1916*. London: University of Queensland Press, 1982.

Beatty, David Pearce, ed. *Memories of a Forgotten War: The World War I Diary of Private V.E. Goodwin*. Port Elgin: Baie Verte Editions, 1988.

Bell, F. McKelvey. *The First Canadians in France*. Toronto: McClelland, Goodchild and Stewart, 1917.

Bell, Ralph. *Canada in War Paint*. Toronto: J.M. Dent & Sons, 1917.

Belts, John R. *America's Sporting Heritage: 1850–1950*. Reading: Addison-Wesley Publishing Company, 1974.

Bennett, S.G. *The 4th Canadian Mounted Rifles, 1914–1919*. Toronto: Murray Printing Company Limited, 1926.

Bercuson, David Jay. *Fools and Wise Men: The Rise and Fall of the One Big Union*. Toronto: McGraw-Hill Ryerson, 1978.

_____, and J.L. Granatstein. *The Collins Dictionary of Canadian History: 1867 to the Present*. Toronto: Collins, 1988.

Berger, Carl. *The Sense of Power: Studies in the Ideas of Canadian Imperialism, 1867–1914*. Toronto: University of Toronto Press, 1970.

_____. *The Writing of Canadian History, Aspects of English-Canadian Historical Writing: 1900 to 1970*. Toronto: Oxford University Press, 1976.

Berger, Thomas. *Fragile Freedoms: Human Rights and Dissent in Canada*. Toronto: Clarke, Irwin & Company, 1981.

Berton, Pierre. *Vimy*. Toronto: McClelland and Stewart, 1986.

Bird, Will. *Ghosts Have Warm Hands*. Toronto: Clarke, Irwin & Co., 1968.

Bishop, W.A. *Winged Warfare*. Toronto: McClelland, Goodchild & Stewart, 1918.

Bly, Robert. *Iron John: A Book About Men*. Reading: Addison-Wesley Publishing Company, 1990.

Borden, Robert Laird. *Memoirs*. 2 vols. Toronto: Macmillan, 1938.

Breen, William J. *Uncle Sam at Home*. Westport: Greenwood Press, 1983.

Brown, Robert Craig. *Robert Laird Borden: A Biography*. 2 vols. Toronto: University of Toronto Press, 1975, 1980.

_____, and Ramsay Cook. *Canada 1896–1914: A Nation Transformed*. Toronto: McClelland and Stewart, 1974.

Bruce, Constance. *Humour in Tragedy: Hospital Life Behind Three Fronts by a Canadian Nursing Sister*. London: Skeffington & Son, 1917.

Bruce, Herbert A. *Politics and the C.A.M.C.* Toronto: William Briggs, 1919.

Buitenhuis, Peter. *The Great War of Words: British, American and Canadian Propaganda and Fiction, 1914–1933*. Vancouver: University of British Columbia Press, 1987.

Burns, E.L.M. *General Mud*. Toronto: Clarke, Irwin & Co., 1970.

Campbell, Craig W. *Reel America and World War One*. Jefferson: McFarland & Company, 1985.

Carter, David J. *Behind Canadian Barbed Wire*. Calgary: Tumbleweed Press, 1980.

Cassel, Jay. *The Secret Plague: Venereal Disease in Canada, 1838–1939*. Toronto: University of Toronto Press, 1987.

Chafetz, Janet Saltzman. *Masculine/Feminine or Human? An Overview of Sex Roles*. Ithaca: F.E. Peacock Publishers, Inc., 1974.

Chaffee, Zechariah Jr. *Free Speech in the United States.* Cambridge: Harvard
University Press, 1954.

Chambers, Ernest J. *The Origin and Services of the 3rd (Montreal) Field Battery of
Artillery.* Montreal: E.L. Ruddy, 1898.

_____. *The Montreal Highland Cadets.* Montreal: Desbarats, 1901.

_____. *The Queen's Own Rifles of Canada.* Toronto: E.L. Ruddy, 1901.

_____. *The Royal Grenadiers.* Toronto: E.L. Ruddy, 1904.

_____. *The Governor-General's Body Guard.* Toronto: E.L. Ruddy, 1902.

_____. *The Duke of Cornwall's Own Rifles.* Toronto: E.L. Ruddy, 1903.

_____. *The Book of Canada: Illustrating the Great Dominion.* Montreal: Book of
Canada Company, 1904.

_____. *The 5th Regiment: Royal Scots of Canada.* Montreal: Guertin Print
Company, 1904.

_____. *The Royal North-West Mounted Police: A Corps History.* Montreal:
Mortimer Press, 1905.

_____. *The Canadian Militia: A History of the Origin and Development of the
Force.* Montreal: L.M. Fresno, 1907.

_____, ed. *Canada's Fertile Northland.* Ottawa: King's Printer, 1907.

_____, ed. *The Great Mackenzie Basin.* Ottawa: King's Printer, 1908.

_____. *A History of the Canadian Militia.* Montreal: L.M. Fresno, 1909.

_____, ed. *The Unexploited West.* Ottawa: King's Printer, 1914.

Child, Phillip. *God's Sparrows.* London: Thornton Butterworths, 1937.

Chisholm, Anne and Michael Davie. *Beaverbrook: A Life.* London: Hutchinson,
1992.

Choquette, Robert. *Language and Religion: A History of English-French Conflict
in Ontario.* Ottawa: University of Ottawa Press, 1975.

Coe, Brian and Paul Gates. *The Snapshot Photograph: The Rise of Popular
Photography, 1888–1939.* London: Ash and Grant, 1977.

Cole, W.S. *Roosevelt and the Isolationists.* Lincoln: University of Nebraska Press,
1983.

Colombo, John Robert and Michael Richardson, eds. *We Stand on Guard: Poems
and Songs of Canadians in Battle.* Toronto: Doubleday, 1985.

Cornebise, Alfred E. *War as Advertised: The Four Minute Men and America's
Crusade, 1917–1918.* Philadelphia: American Philosophical Society, 1984.

Craig, Grace Morris. *But This Is Our War.* Toronto: University of Toronto Press,
1981.

Craig, Terence. *Racial Attitudes in English-Canadian Fiction, 1905–1980.*
Waterloo: Wilfrid Laurier University Press, 1987.

Creed, Catherine. *Whose Debtors Are We*. Niagara: Niagara Falls Historical Society, 1922.

Creel, George. *How We Advertised America*. New York: Harper & Brothers, 1920.

Curry, Frederic C. *From the St. Lawrence to the Yser*. Toronto: McClelland, Goodchild & Stewart, 1916.

Dahlie, Jorgen, and Tissa Fernando, eds. *Ethnicity, Power & Politics in Canada*. Toronto: Metheun, 1981.

Dancocks, Daniel. *Legacy of Valour: The Canadians at Passchendaele*. Edmonton: Hurtig Publishers, 1986.

_____. *Welcome to Flanders' Field: The First Canadian Bettle of the Great War, Ypres, 1915*. Toronto: McClelland and Stewart, 1988.

_____. *Spearhead to Victory: Canadians and the Great War*. Edmonton: Hurtig Publishers, 1987.

_____. *Welcome to Flanders' Field: The First Canadian Battle of the War, Ypres, 1915*. Toronto: McClelland and Stewart, 1989.

_____. *Gallant Canadians: The Story of the Tenth Canadian Infantry Battalion, 1914–1919*. Calgary: Calgary Regimental Fund Foundation, 1990.

Dawson, Corningsby. *The Glory of the Trenches*. Toronto: S.B. Gundy, 1918.

Desjardins, L.G. *England, Canada and the Great War*. Quebec City: Chronicle Print, 1918.

Doll, Maurice F.V. *The Poster War: Allied Propaganda Art of the First World War*. Alberta: Historic Sites and Archives Services, 1993.

Douglas, J. Harvey. *Captured*. Toronto: McClelland, Goodchild & Stewart, 1916.

Doyle, Arthur Conan. *The British Campaign in France and Flanders, 1914*. Toronto: Hodder and Stoughton, 1916.

Drew, George. *Canada's Fighting Airmen*. Toronto: Maclean Publishing, 1930.

_____. *Truth About the War*. Toronto: Maclean Publishing, 1931.

_____. *Salesmen of Death*. Toronto: Maclean Publishing, 1931.

Dubbert, Joe L. *A Man's Place: Masculinity in Transition*. New York: Prentice-Hall Inc., 1979.

Duguid, A. Fortescue. *Official History of the Canadian Forces in the Great War 1914–1919: Chronology, Appendices and Maps*. Vol. 1. Ottawa: King's Printer, 1938.

Durkin, Douglas Leader, ed. *The Fighting Men of Canada*. London: Erskine Macdonald Limited, 1918.

Dyer, Gwynne and Tina Viljoen. *The Defence of Canada: In the Arms of the Empire*. Toronto: McClelland and Stewart, 1990.

Eayrs, James. *In Defence of Canada: From The Great War to the Great Depression*. Toronto: University of Toronto Press, 1965.

Ecksteins, Modris. *Rites of Spring: The Great War and the Birth of the Modern Age.* Toronto: Lester & Orpen Dennys, 1989.

Ellis, John. *Eye-Deep in Hell: Trench Warfare in World War I.* New York: Pantheon, 1976.

Empey, Arthur Guy. *Over the Top.* Toronto: William Briggs, 1917.

England, Robert. *Discharged: A Comment on Civil Re-establishment of Veterans in Canada.* Toronto: Macmillan, 1943.

English, John. *The Decline of Politics: The Conservatives and the Party System, 1901–20.* Toronto: University of Toronto Press, 1977.

_____. *Shadow of Heaven: The Life of Lester Pearson.* Vol. 1. London: Vintage, 1990.

Epp, Frank. *The Mennonites in Canada: History of a Separate People.* Vol. 1. Toronto: Macmillan, 1974.

Evans, Raymond. *Loyalty and Disloyalty: Social Conflict on the Queensland Homefront, 1914–1918.* Sydney: Allen & Unwin, 1987.

Falconer, R.A. *The German Tragedy and Its Meaning for Canada.* Toronto: University of Toronto Press, 1915.

Ferrell, Robert H. *Woodrow Wilson and World War I, 1917–1921.* New York: Harper and Row, 1985.

Fewster, Kevin, ed. *Gallipoli Correspondent: The Frontline Diary of C.E.W. Bean.* Sydney: George Allen & Unwin, 1983.

Filene, Peter G. *Him/Her/Self: Sex Roles in Modern America.* Baltimore: John Hopkins' University Press, 1974.

Frobenius, H. *The German Empire's Hour of Destiny.* Toronto: Macmillan, 1914.

Frost, Leslie. *Fighting Men.* Toronto: Clarke, Irwin & Company, 1967.

Fussell, Paul. *The Great War and Modern Memory.* Toronto: Oxford University Press, 1975.

_____. *Wartime: Understanding and Behavior in the Second World War.* Toronto: Oxford, 1989.

Gallishaw, John. *Trenching at Gallipoli.* Toronto: S.B. Gundy, 1916.

Gammage, Bill. *The Broken Years.* London: Penguin, 1974.

Garvin, John W., ed. *Canadian Poets.* Toronto: McClelland, Goodchild and Stewart, 1916.

_____, ed. *Canadian Poems of the Great War.* Toronto: McClelland and Stewart, 1918.

Gerard, James W. *My Four Years in Germany.* Toronto: Hodder & Stoughton, 1917.

_____. *Face to Face With Kaiserism.* Toronto: McClelland, Goodchild & Stewart, 1918.

Gibbs, Philip. *The Soul of War*. Toronto: McClelland, Goodchild & Stewart, 1916.

_____. *The Battle of the Somme*. London: William Heinemann, 1917.

_____. *From Bapaume to Passchendaele*. Toronto: William Briggs, 1918.

_____. *Now It Can Be Told*. New York: Harper & Brothers, 1920.

Goodspeed, D.J. *The Road Past Vimy: The Canadian Corps, 1914–1918*. Toronto: Macmillan, 1969.

Graham, W.R. *Arthur Meighen: The Door of Opportunity*. Toronto: Clarke, Irwin and Company, 1960.

Granatstein, J.L. and J.M. Hitsman. *Broken Promises: A History of Conscription in Canada*. Toronto: Oxford University Press, 1977.

_____, and Desmond Morton. *A Nation Forged in Fire: Canadians and the Second World War, 1939–1945*. Toronto: Lester & Orpen Dennys, 1989.

Graves, Robert. *Goodbye to All That*. London: Penguin ed., 1976.

Great Advance: Tales From the Somme Battlefield Told By Wounded Officers and Men on Their Arrival at Southampton From the Front. Toronto: Cassell and Company, 1917.

Green, Martin. *The Adventurous Male: Chapters in the History of the White Male Mind*. University Park: Pennsylvania State University Press, 1993.

Greenhous, Brereton, ed. *A Rattle of Pebbles: The First World War Diaries of Two Canadian Airmen*. Ottawa: Department of National Defense, 1987.

_____, and Stephen Harris. *Canada and the Battle of Vimy Ridge, 9–12 April 1917*. Ottawa: Minister of Supply and Services, 1992.

Grey, W.E. *With the French Eastern Army*. Toronto: Hodder and Stoughton, 1915.

Groves, Edith. *The Making of Canada's Flag*. Toronto: William Briggs, 1916.

_____. *Britannia*. Toronto: McClelland and Stewart, 1917.

_____. *Drills and Exercises*. Toronto: McClelland and Stewart, 1917.

Gwyn, Sandra. *Tapestry of War: A Private View of Canadians in the Great War*. Toronto: HarperCollins, 1992.

Hadley, Michael L. and Roger Sarty. *Tin-Pots and Pirate Ships: Canadian Naval Forces and German Sea Raiders, 1880–1918*. Montreal: McGill-Queen's University Press, 1991.

Hahn, Major J.E. *The Intelligence Service Within the Canadian Corps, 1914–1918*. Toronto: The Macmillan Company of Canada, Limited, 1930.

Hall, James Norman. *Kitchener's Mob: The Adventures of an American in the British Army*. Toronto: Thomas Allen, 1916.

Hallin, Daniel. *The `Uncensored War: The Media in Vietnam*. New York: Oxford University Press, 1986.

Harris, Stephen J. *Canadian Brass: The Making of a Professional Army*. Toronto: University of Toronto Press, 1988.

Harrison, Charles Yale. *Generals Die in Bed*. Owen Sound: Richardson, Bond and Wright ed., 1976.

Haste, Cate. *Keep the Home Fires Burning*. London: Lane, 1977.

Hawgood, John Arkas. *The Tragedy of German America*. New York: Arno Press, 1970.

Hay, Ian. *All in it! K(1) Carries On*. Toronto: William Briggs, 1917.

Hibbert, Christopher. *The English: A Social History, 1066–1945*. London: Grafton Books, 1987.

Hilliker, John. *Canada's Department of External Affairs*. Vol. 1. Montreal: McGill-Queen's, 1990.

Hillmer, Norman, Bohdan Kordan, and Lubomyr Luciuk, eds. *On Guard for Thee: War, Ethnicity and the Canadian State, 1939–1945*. Ottawa: Canadian Committee for the History of the Second World War, 1988.

Hodder-Williams, Ralph. *Princess Patricia's Canadian Light Infantry, 1914–1919*. Toronto: Hodder and Stoughton, 1923.

Hopkins, J.C. *Canadian Annual Review (1914–1919)*. Toronto: Canadian Annual Review Publishing Company, 1915–20.

———. *Canada at War: A Record of Heroism and Achievement, 1914–1918*. Toronto: The Canadian Annual Review Limited, 1919.

Howard, Philip. *We Thundered Out: 200 Years of the Times*. London: Times Books, 1985.

Howell, Colin. *Northern Sandlots: A Social History of Baseball in the Maritimes*. Toronto: University of Toronto Press, 1994.

James, Fred. *Canada's Triumph: Amiens-Arras-Cambrai*. London: Charles & Son, 1919.

Joynt, W.D. *Saving the Channel Ports 1918*. North Blackburn: Wren Publishing, 1975.

Kallmann, Helmut, Gilles Potvin, and Kenneth Winters, eds. *Encyclopedia of Music in Canada*. Toronto: University of Toronto Press, 1981.

Kaplan, William. *State and Salvation: The Jehovah's Witnesses and Their Fight for Civil Rights*. Toronto: University of Toronto Press, 1989.

Kaye, V.J. *Ukrainian Canadians in Canada's Wars*. Toronto: Ukrainian Canadian Research Foundation, 1983.

Keegan, John. *The Face of Battle: A Study of Agincourt, Waterloo and the Somme*. Toronto: Penguin, 1976.

Keene, Louis. `Crumps': The Plain Story of a Canadian Who Went*. Boston: Riverside Press, 1917.

Kennedy, David. *Over Here: The First World War and American Society*. New York: Oxford University Press, 1964.

Kennedy, J.M. *The Campaign Around Liege*. Toronto: Hodder and Stoughton, 1914.

Kent, Tom, et al. *Royal Commission on Newspapers*. Ottawa: Ministry of Supplies and Services, 1981.

Kesterton, W.H. *A History of Journalism in Canada*. Ottawa: Carleton University Press, 1984.

Kipling, Rudyard. *Sea Warfare*. Toronto: Macmillan, 1916.

Knightley, Phillip. *The First Casualty From Crimea to Vietnam: The War Correspondent as Hero, Propagandist, and Myth Maker*. New York: Harcourt Brace Jovanovich, 1975.

Krawchuk, Peter. *The Ukrainian Socialist Movement in Canada, 1907–1918*. Toronto: Progress Books, 1979.

Lamb, Dave. *Mutinies, 1917–1920*. Leeds: Solidarity Press, 1977.

Lane, John, ed. *The Love of an Unknown Soldier Found in a Dugout*. Toronto: McClelland, Goodchild & Stewart, 1918.

Laswell, Harold. *Propaganda Technique in the World War*. London: Keagan, Paul, Trench, Trubner & Co., 1938.

Lauder, Harry. *A Minstrel in France*. Toronto: McClelland, Goodchild & Stewart, 1918.

Leacy, F.H., ed. *Historical Statistics of Canada*, 2nd edition. Ottawa: Statistics Canada, 1983.

Leed, Eric J. *No Man's Land: Combat and Identity in World War I*. Cambridge: Cambridge University Press, 1979.

Lippmann, Walter. *Public Opinion*. New York: Macmillan, 1960.

Livesay, John Frederick Bligh. *Canada's Hundred Days*. Toronto: Thomas Allen, 1919.

Luebke, Frederick C. *Bonds of Loyalty: German Americans and World War One*. De Kalb: Northern Illinois University Press, 1974.

Maccas, Leon. *German Barbarism: A Neutral's Indictment*. Toronto: Hodder and Stoughton, 1916.

Macdonald, Lyn. *1914*. London: Penguin Books, 1987.

MacIntyre, D. *Canada at Vimy*. Toronto: Peter Martin Associates. 1967.

Macksey, Kenneth. *The Shadow of Vimy Ridge*. Toronto: Ryerson, 1965.

Macphail, Sir Andrew. *Official History of the Canadian Forces in the Great War 1914–1919: The Medical Services*. Ottawa: King's Printer, 1925.

Mandle, W.F. *Going it Alone: Australia's National Identity in the Twentieth Century*. Victoria: Penguin, 1977.

Manion, R.J. *A Surgeon in Arms*. New York: D. Appleton and Company, 1918.

Mansfield, John. *Gallipoli*. Toronto: S.B. Gundy, 1916.

Masters, D.C. *The Winnipeg General Strike*. Toronto: University of Toronto Press, 1950.

Mathieson, William. *My Grandfather's War: Canadians Remember the First World War, 1914–1918*. Toronto: Macmillan, 1981.

McBride, Herbert. *A Rifleman Went to War*. Onslow: Small-Arms Technical Publishing Company, 1935.

McClung, Nellie. *The Next of Kin*. Toronto: Thomas Allen, 1917.

McCormick, Robert R. *With the Russian Army*. Toronto: Macmillan, 1915.

MacKenzie, John. *Propaganda and Empire: The Manipulation of British Public Opinion, 1880–1960*. Manchester: Manchester University Press, 1984.

McKenzie, F.A. *Canada's Days of Glory*. Toronto: William Briggs, 1919.

McLuhan, Marshall. *The Gutenberg Galaxy: The Making of Typographic Man*. Toronto: University of Toronto Press, 1962.

McNaught, Kenneth. *A Prophet in Politics*. Toronto: University of Toronto Press, 1959.

Metcalfe, Alan. *Canada Learns to Play: The Emergence of Organized Sports, 1807–1914*. Toronto: McClelland and Stewart, 1987.

Middleton, Jesse Edgar, ed. *Sea Dogs and Men at War*. Toronto: McClelland, Goodchild and Stewart, 1918.

Mock, James R. *Censorship 1917*. Princeton: Princeton University Press, 1941.

Mock, James and Cedric Larson. *Words that Won the War*. New York: Russell & Russell, 1968.

Montreal Chamber of Commerce. *Bulletin de la Chambre de Commerce Francaise*. Montreal: 1915.

Morris, Peter. *Embattled Shadows: A History of the Canadian Cinema, 1895–1939*. Montreal: McGill-Queen's University Press, 1978.

Morton, Desmond. *Canada and War*. Toronto: Butterworths, 1981.

_____. *A Peculiar Kind of Politics: Canada's Overseas Ministry in the First World War*. Toronto: University of Toronto Press, 1982.

_____. *A Military History of Canada*. Edmonton: Hurtig Publishers, 1985.

_____. *When Your Number's Up: The Canadian Soldier in the First World War*. Toronto: Random House, 1993.

_____, and Glenn Wright. *Winning the Second Battle: Canadian Veterans and the Return to Civilian Life, 1915–1930*. Toronto: University of Toronto Press, 1987.

_____, and J.L. Granatstein. *Marching to Armageddon: Canadians and the Great War, 1914–1919*. Toronto: Lester & Orpen Dennys, 1989.

Morton, W.L. *The Progressive Party in Canada*. Toronto: University of Toronto Press, 1950.

Mosley, Sidney A. *The Truth About the Dardenelles*. Toronto: Cassell and
    Company, 1916.

Mosse, George. *Fallen Soldiers: Reshaping the Memory of World Wars*. New York:
    Oxford University Press, 1990.

Mould, David H. *American Newsfilm, 1914–1919: The Underground War*. New
    York: Garland Publishing, 1983.

Moyles, R.G. and Douglas Owram. *Imperial Dreams and Colonial Realities:
    British Views of Canada, 1880–1914*. Toronto: University of Toronto Press,
    1988.

Murray, Marr. *The Russian Advance*. Toronto: Hodder and Stoughton, 1914.

Murray, Robert K. *Red Scare: A Study in National Hysteria, 1919–1920*.
    Minneapolis: University of Minnesota Press, 1955.

Nasmith, George G. *On the Fringe of the Great Fight*. Toronto: McClelland,
    Goodchild and Stewart, 1917.

Naylor, James. *The New Democracy: Challenging the Industrial Order in Industrial
    Ontario, 1914–1925*. Toronto: University of Toronto Press, 1991.

New York Times Editorial Staff. *New York Times Film Reviews, 1913–1968*. Vol. 1.
    New York: Arno Press, 1970.

Nicholson, G.W.L. *Canadian Expeditionary Force 1914–1919*. Ottawa: Queen's
    Printer, 1962.

Oliver, Frederick Scott. *Ordeal by Fire*. Toronto: Macmillan, 1915.

Oxford Faculty of Modern History. *Why We Are at War: Great Britain's Case*.
    Toronto: Oxford University Press, 1914.

Palmer, Frederick. *My Year of the Great War*. Toronto: McClelland, Goodchild &
    Stewart, 1917.

Palmer, Howard. *Patterns of Prejudice: A History of Nativism in Alberta*. Toronto:
    McClelland and Stewart, 1982.

Parrot, Sir Edward. *The Children's History of the War*. 31 vols. Toronto: Thomas
    Nelson and Sons, Limited, 1917.

Pearson, George. *The Escape of a Princess Pat*. Toronto: George H. Doran, 1918.

Penner, Norman. *The Canadian Left: A Critical Analysis*. Toronto: Prentice-Hall,
    1977.

Pilli, Arja. *The Finnish Press in Canada, 1900–1939*. Turku, 1982.

Prentice, Allison, Paula Bourne, Gail Cuthbert Brandt, Beth Light, Wendy
    Mitchinson, and Naomi Black. *Canadian Women: A History*. Toronto:
    Harcourt Brace Jovanovich, 1988.

Preston, William Jr. *Aliens and Dissenters: Federal Suppression of Radicals,
    1903–1933*. New York: Harper & Row, 1963.

Rae, John. *Conscience and Politics: The British Government and the Conscientious Objector to Military Service, 1916–1919.* London: Oxford University Press, 1970.

Rawling, Bill. *Surviving Trench Warfare: Technology and the Canadian Corps, 1914–1918.* Toronto: University of Toronto Press, 1992.

Ray, Anna Chapin, ed. *Letters of a Canadian Stretcher Bearer.* Boston: Little, Brown and Company, 1916.

Read, Daphne, ed. *The Great War and Canadian Society.* Toronto: New Hogtown Press, 1978.

Read, J.M. *Atrocity Propaganda.* New Haven: Yale University Press, 1972.

Reeves, Nicholas. *Official British Film Propaganda During the First World War.* London: Croom Helm, 1986.

Roberts, Barbara. *Whence They Came: Deportation from Canada, 1900–1935.* Ottawa: University of Ottawa Press, 1988.

Roberts, Charles G.D. *Canada in Flanders.* Vol. 3. Toronto: Hodder and Stoughton, 1918.

Robertson, Heather, ed. *A Terrible Beauty.* Toronto: James Lorimer & Company, 1977.

Robbins, Keith. *The First World War.* Toronto: Oxford University Press, 1984.

Rodney, William. *Soldiers of the International: A History of the Communist Party of Canada, 1919–1929.* Toronto: University of Toronto Press, 1968.

Roetter, Charles. *Psychological Warfare.* London: B.T. Batsford, 1974.

Rotundo, E. Anthony. *American Manhood: Transformations in Masculinity from the Revolution to the Modern Era.* New York: Basic Books, 1993.

Roy, Reginald, ed. *The Journal of Private Fraser.* Victoria: Sono Nis Press, 1985.

Rutherford, Paul. *The Making of the Canadian Media.* Toronto: McGraw-Hill Ryerson, 1978.

Saunders, M.L. and Philip Taylor. *British Propaganda During the First World War.* London: Macmillan, 1982.

Saywell, John, and George Vegh, eds. *Making the Law: The Courts and the Constitution.* Toronto: Copp Clark Pitman Ltd., 1991.

Scheiber, Harry. *The Wilson Administration and Civil Liberties, 1917–1921.* Ithaca: Cornell University Press, 1960.

Schmeiser, D.A. *Civil Liberties in Canada.* Toronto: Oxford University Press, 1964.

Scott, Cannon Frederick George. *The Great War as I Saw It.* Toronto: F.D. Goodchild, 1922.

Scott, F.R. *Essays on the Constitution: Aspects of Canadian Law and Politics.* Toronto: University of Toronto Press, 1977.

Sheldon-Williams, Ralf. *The Canadian Front in France and Flanders*. London: A & C Black, 1920.

Snell, James G. *In the Shadow of the Law: Divorce in Canada, 1900–1939*. Toronto: University of Toronto Press, 1991.

Socknat, Thomas. *Witness Against War: Canadian Pacifists and the State, 1900–1945*. Toronto: University of Toronto Press, 1987.

Souter, Gavin. *Lion and Kangaroo: The Initiation of Australia, 1901–1919*. Sydney: Collins, 1976.

Squires, James. *British Propaganda at Home and in the United States from 1914 to 1917*. Cambridge: Harvard University Press, 1935.

Stamp, Robert. *The Schools of Ontario*. Toronto: University of Toronto Press, 1976.

Stearns, Peter N. *Be a Man! Males in Modern Society*. New York: Holmes and Meier Publishing Inc., 1979.

Steinhart, Allan L. *Civil Censorship in Canada During World War I*. Toronto: Unitrade Press, 1986.

Sullivan, Mark. *Our Times: The United States 1900–1925*. Vol. 5, *Over Here, 1914–1918*. New York: Charles Scribner's Sons, 1933.

Sutherland, Neil. *Children in English-Canadian Society: Framing the Twentieth-Century Consensus*. Toronto: University of Toronto Press, 1976.

Swettenham, John. *Canada and the First World War*. Ottawa: Canadian War Museum, n.d.

_____. *To Seize the Victory: The Canadian Corps in World War I*. Toronto: Ryerson, 1965.

Taylor, A.J.P. *Beaverbrook*. New York: Simon and Schuster, 1972.

Thompson, John Herd. *The Harvests of War: The Prairie West, 1914–1918*. Toronto: McClelland and Stewart, 1978.

_____, and Allen Seager. *Canada 1922–1939: Decades of Discord*. Toronto: McClelland and Stewart, 1985.

Thompson, Paul. *The Voice of the Past*. New York: Oxford University Press, 1978.

Tippett, Maria. *Art at the Service of War*. Toronto: University of Toronto Press, 1984.

Tompkins, Stuart Ramsay. *A Canadian's Road to Russia: Letter's From the Great War Decade*. Ed. Doris H. Pieroth. Edmonton: University of Alberta Press, 1989.

Turner, E.S. *The Shocking History of Advertising*. London: Penguin, 1952.

Turner, John, ed. *The Canadian Feature Film Index, 1913–1985*. Ottawa: National Archives of Canada, 1987.

Urquhart, M.C., and K.A.H. Buckley, eds. *Historical Statistics on Canada*. Toronto: Macmillan, 1965.

Van Paasen, Pierre. *Days of Our Years.* New York: Hillman-Carl Inc., 1939.

Vaughn, Stephen. *Holding Fast the Inner Lines: Democracy, Nationalism and the Committee on Public Information.* Chapel Hill: University of North Carolina Press, 1980.

Volkogonov, Dmitri. *Lenin: A New Biography.* New York: Free Press, 1995.

Wallace, W. Stewart, ed. *The Macmillan Dictionary of Canadian Biography.* Toronto: Macmillan, 1976.

Ward, Russell. *The Australian Legend.* Melbourne: Oxford University Press, 1958.

Ward, W.P. *White Canada Forever: Attitudes and Public Policy Towards Orientals in British Columbia.* Vancouver: University of British Columbia Press, 1978.

Weinrich, Peter. *Social Protest from the Left, 1870–1970: A Bibliography.* Toronto: University of Toronto Press, 1982.

White, William Allen. *The Martial Adventures of Henry and Me.* Toronto: Macmillan, 1918.

Wilson, Barbara. *Ontario and the First World War.* Toronto: Champlain Society, 1977.

Wilson, Henry Beckles. *From Quebec to Picadilly.* London: Jonathan Cape Ltd., 1929.

Winter, Denis. *Death's Men: Soldiers of the Great War.* Toronto: Penguin, 1979.

Wise, S.F. *Canadian Airmen and the First World War: The Official History of the Royal Canadian Air Force.* Vol. 1. Toronto: University of Toronto Press, 1980.

Wood, James Playsted. *The Story of Advertising.* New York: The Ronald Press, 1958.

Wood, Herbert Fairlie. *Vimy!* Toronto: Macmillan, 1967.

Woodson, Harry M. *Private Warwick: Musings of a Canuck in Khaki,* Toronto: Sovereign Press, 1915.

3 Articles

Allen, Frederick L. "The Revolution in Manners and Morals." In *The 1920's: Problems and Paradoxes,* ed. Milton Plesur, 253–66. Boston: Allyn and Bacon, 1969.

Andrews, Eric. "The Media and the Military: Australian War Correspondents and the Appointment of a Corps Commander, 1918—A Case Study." *War & Society* 8, 2 (1990): 83–103.

Avery, Donald. "European Immigrant Workers in Western Canada, 1900–1930: A Case Study of the Ukrainian Labour Press." In *Labor Migration Project: Labor Newspaper Preservation Project,* ed. Christiane Harzig and Dirk Hoerder. Bromen, 1985.

Badsley, S.D. "'The Battle of the Somme': British War Propaganda." *Historical Journal of Film, Radio and Television* 3, 2 (1983): 99–116.

Bassler, Gerhard P. "The Enemy Alien Experience in Newfoundland, 1914–1918." *Canadian Ethnic Studies* 20, 3 (1988): 42–62.

Bausenhart, Werner A. "The Ontario German Language Press and its Suppression by Order-in-Council in 1918." *Canadian Ethnic Studies* 4 (1972): 35–48.

Bercuson, David Jay. "Labour Radicalism and the Western Industrial Frontier, 1897–1919." *Canadian Historical Review* 58, 2 (1978): 176–200.

Burns, E. Bradford. "Conceptualizing the Use of Film to Study History." *Film and History* 4, 4 (1974): 1–11.

Bliss, J.M. "The Methodist Church and World War One." In *Conscription 1917*, ed. Carl Berger, 53. Toronto: University of Toronto Press, 1970.

Bliss, Michael. "War Business as Usual: Canadian Munitions Production, 1914–1918." In *Mobilization for Total War: The Canadian, American and British Experience, 1914–1918, 1939–1945*, ed. N.F. Dreisziger, 45–55. Waterloo: Wilfrid Laurier University Press, 1981.

Bray, Robert Matthew. "Fighting as an Ally: The English-Canadian Patriotic Response to the Great War." *Canadian Historical Review* 61, 2 (1980): 141–68.

———. "A Conflict of Nationalism: The Win-the-War and National Unity Convention of 1917." *Journal of Canadian Studies* 15, 4 (1980–81): 18–30.

Brown, Robert Craig and Donald Loveridge. "Unrequited Faith: Recruiting the C.E.F., 1914–1918." *Revue internationale d'histoire militaire* 54 (1982): 53–79.

Buchanan, Russell. "American Editors Examine War Aims and Plans in April 1917." *Pacific Historical Review* 9, 3 (1940): 253–65.

Cameron, Brian. "The Bonne Entente Movement, 1916–1917: From Co-operation to Conscription." *Journal of Canadian Studies* 13, 2 (1978): 42–56.

Casty, Alan. "The Films of D.W. Griffiths: A Style for the Times." *Journal of Popular Film* 1, 1 (1972): 67–79.

Cook, Ramsay. "Laurier, Dafoe and the Formation of the Union Government." *Canadian Historical Review* 42, 3 (1961): 185–208.

Crago, Hugo. "The Incorporative Mode in a Propaganda Novel of the Great War." *Journal of Popular Culture* 13, 2 (1979): 274–81.

Crerar, Duff. "The Church in the Furnace: Canadian Anglican Chaplains Respond to the Great War." *Journal of the Canadian Church Historical Society* 35, 2 (1993): 75–104.

Cripps, Thomas. "Film: The Historian's Dangerous Friend." *Film and History* 5, 4 (1975): 6–9.

Cuff, Robert. "Organizing for War: Canada and the United States During World War I." *Canadian Historical Association, Historical Papers*, 1969, 141–56.

_____. "Ernest Poole: Novelist as Propagandist." *Canadian Review of American Studies* 19, 2 (1988): 183–94.

Eggleston, Wilfrid. "Press Censorship." *Canadian Journal of Economics and Political Science* 7, 3 (1941): 313–23.

Entz, W. "The Suppression of the German Language Press in September 1918 (With Special Reference to the Secular German Language Papers in Western Canada)." *Canadian Ethnic Studies* 8, 2 (1976): 56–70.

Evans, Raymond. "Some Furious Outbreaks of Riot: Returned Soldiers and Queensland's `Red Flag' Disturbances, 1918–1919." *War & Society* 3, 2 (1985): 75–95.

Federowich, Kent. "Society Pets and Morning Coated Farmers: Australian Soldier Settlement and the Participation of the British Ex-Serviceman." *War & Society* 8, 2 (1990): 38–56.

Ferro, Marc. "Does a Filmic Writing of History Exist?" *Film and History* 17, 4 (1987): 81–89.

Fewster, Kevin. "The Operation of State Apparatuses in Times of Crisis: Censorship and Conscription, 1916." *War & Society* 3, 1 (1985): 37–54.

Fisher, Robert. "Film Censorship and Progressive Reform: The National Board of Censorship of Motion Pictures, 1909–1922." *Journal of Popular Film* 4, 2 (1975): 143–56.

Fry, Ken. "Soldier Settlement." *Labour History* 48 (1983): 29–43.

Gartner, Lloyd P. "Jewish Gold and Prussian Iron." *Jewish Journal of Sociology* 19, 2 (1977): 197–201.

Grenke, Art. "The German Community of Winnipeg and the English-Canadian Response to World War One." *Canadian Ethnic Studies* 20, 1 (1988): 21–44.

Griffin, Patricia. "Film Document and the Historian." *Film and History* 2, 3 (1972): 1–5.

Hantover, Jeffrey P. "The Boy Scouts and the Validation of Masculinity." In *The American Man*, ed. Elizabeth H. Pleck and Joseph H. Pleck, 285–301. Englewood Cliffs: Prentice-Hall, 1980.

Haycock, Ronald. "Recruiting." In *Canadian Military History: Selected Readings*, ed. Marc Milner. Toronto: Copp Clark Pitman, 1933.

Henige, David. "Where Seldom Is Heard a Discouraging Word: Method in Oral History." *Oral History Review* 14 (1986): 35–42.

Hiley, Nicholas. "Sir Henry Le Bas and the Origins of Domestic Propaganda in Britain." *Journal of Advertising History* 10, 2 (1987): 30–45.

Hopkins, Deian. "Domestic Censorship in the First War." *Journal of Contemporary History* 4, 4 (1970): 151–69.

Horrall, S.W. "The Royal North-West Mounted Police and Labour Unrest in Western Canada." *Canadian Historical Review* 61, 2 (1980): 168–90.

Howlett, Charles F. "Academic Freedom Versus Loyalty at Columbia University During World War I: A Case Study." *War & Society* 2, 1 (1984): 44–53.

Hull, Deborah. "'The Old Lie': Teaching Children about the War, 1914–1939." *Melbourne Historical Journal* 20, 1 (1990): 88–110.

Hyatt, A.M.J. "Arthur Currie: Corps Commander." In *Canadian Military History: Selected Readings*, ed. Marc Milner. Toronto: Copp Clark Pitman Ltd., 1993.

_____. "Canadian Generals of the First World War and the Popular View of Military Leadership." *Histoire Sociale/Social History* 12, 24 (1979): 418–30.

_____. "Corps Commander: Arthur Currie." In *Canadian Military History: Selected Readings*, ed. Marc Milner. Toronto: Copp Clark Pitman Ltd., 1993.

Inglis, K.S. "A Sacred Place: The Making of the Australian War Memorial." *War & Society* 3, 2 (1985): 99–126.

Issenberg, Michael T. "World War I Film Comedies and American Society: The Concern With Authoritarianism." *Film and Society* 5, 3 (1975): 7–15, 21.

_____. "An Ambiguous Pacifism: A Retrospective on World War One Films, 1930–1938." *Journal of Popular Film* 4, 2 (1975): 98–115.

_____. "The Mirror of Democracy: Reflections on the War Films of World War I, 1917–1919." *Journal of Popular Culture* 9, 4 (1976): 878–85.

Johnston, Hugh. "The Surveillance of Indian Nationalists in North America, 1908–1918." *B.C. Studies* 78 (1988): 3–27.

Jowett, Garth S. "The First Motion Picture Audiences." *Journal of Popular Film* 3, 1 (1974): 39–54.

Kealey, Gregory. "1919: The Canadian Labour Revolt." *Labour/Le Travail* 13 (1984): 11–44.

_____. "The State, the Foreign-Language Press and the Canadian Labour Revolt of 1917–1920." In *Labor Migration Project: Labor Newspaper Preservation Project*, ed. Christiane Harzig and Dirk Hoerder. Bromen, 1985.

_____. "The Surveillance State: The Origins of Domestic Intelligence and Counter-Subversion in Canada." *Intelligence and National Security* 7, 3 (1992): 179–210.

_____. "State Repression of Labour and the Left in Canada, 1914–1920: The Impact of the First World War." *Canadian Historical Review* 78, 3 (1992): 281–314.

_____. "The Early Years of State Surveillance of Labour and the Left in Canada: The Institutional Framework of the Royal Canadian Mounted Police Security and Intelligence Apparatus, 1918–26." *Intelligence and National Security* 8, 3 (1993): 129–48.

Kitchen, Martin. "The German Invasion of Canada in the First World War." *International History Review* 7, 2 (1985): 245–60.

Keyserlingk, R. "Allies or Subversives? The Canadian Government's Attitude towards German Canadians in the Second World War." In *North America and Australia during the Two World Wars*, ed. Panikos Panayi. Providence: Berg Publishers, 1993.

Laine, Edward W. "Finnish Canadian Radicalism and Canadian Politics: The First Forty Years, 1900–1940." In *Ethnicity, Power and Politics in Canada*, ed. Jorgen Dahlie and Tissa Fernando, 94–112. Toronto: Methuen, 1981.

Lang, Gladys Engel and Kurt Lang. "Mass Communication and Public Opinion Strategies for Research." In *Social Psychology: Sociological Perspectives*, ed. Morris Rosenberg and Ralph Turner, 653–82. New York: Basic Books, 1981.

Lockhart, John. "Sir William Wiseman Bart—Agent of Influence." *RUSI Journal* 134, 2 (1989): 63–67.

Lovelace, Colin. "Press Censorship During the First World War." In *Newspaper History from the Seventeenth Century to the Present Day*, ed. George Boyce, James Curran, and Pauline Wingate. London: Sage, 1978.

Luciuk, Lubomyr. "Internal Security and an Ethnic Minority: The Ukrainian Internment." *Signum* 4, 2 (1984): 31–64.

Lutz, Robert. "Studies of World War Propaganda." *Journal of Modern History* 5, 4 (1933).

Lyons, Timothy L. "Hollywood and World War One, 1914–1918." *Journal of Popular Film* 1, 1 (1972): 15–30.

MacDonald, J. Frederick. "'The Foreigner' in Juvenile Series Fiction, 1900–1945." *Journal of Popular Culture* 8, 3 (1974): 534–48.

Makuch, Andrij. "Ukrainian Canadians and the Wartime Economy." In *Loyalties in Conflict*, ed. John Herd Thompson and Francis Swyripa, 69–77. Edmonton: Canadian Institute for Ukrainian Studies, 1982.

Makuch, Nestor. "Influence of the Ukrainian Revolution on Ukrainians in Canada, 1917–1922." *Journal of Ukrainian Graduate Studies* 6 (1979): 42–61.

Malvern, Sue. "'War As It Is': The Art of Muirhead Bone, C.R.W. Nevinson and Paul Nash, 1916–1917." *Art History* 9, 4 (1986): 487–515.

Marquis, Alice Goldfarb. "Words as Weapons: Propaganda in Britain and Germany During the First World War." *Journal of Contemporary History* 13, 3 (1978): 467–98.

Martel, Gordon. "'Generals Die in Bed': Modern Warfare and the Origins of Modernist Culture." *Journal of Canadian Studies* 16, 3–4 (1981): 2–13.

Martynowych, Orest. "The Ukrainian Socialist Movement in Canada, 1900–1918." *Journal of Ukrainian Graduate Studies* 1 (1976): 27–44, and 2 (1977): 22–31.

McEwan, John M. "The National Press During the First World War: Ownership and Circulation." *Journal of Contemporary History* 17, 4 (1982): 459–86.

_____. "'Brass Hats' and the British Press During the First World War." *Canadian Journal of History* 18, 1 (1983): 43–67.

McKenna, Marian. "The Melting Pot: Comparative Observations in the United States and Canada." *Sociology and Social Research* 53 (1969): 433–47.

Melnycky, Peter. "The Internment of Ukrainians in Canada." In *Loyalties in Conflict*, ed. John Herd Thompson and Francis Swyripa. Edmonton: Canadian Institute for Ukrainian Studies, 1982.

Mitchinson, Wendy. "The WCTU: 'For God, Home and Native Land': A Study in Nineteenth-Century Feminism." In *Not an Unreasonable Claim: Women and Reform in Canada, 1880s–1920*, ed. Linda Kealey, 151–67. Toronto: The Women's Press, 1979.

Morton, Desmond. "The Supreme Penalty: Canadian Deaths by Firing Squad in the First World War." *Queen's Quarterly* 79, 3 (1972): 345–52.

_____. "Sir William Otter and Internment Operations in Canada During the First World War." *Canadian Historical Review* 55, 1 (1974): 32–57.

_____. "Polling the Soldier Vote: The Overseas Campaign in the Canadian General Election of 1917." *Journal of Canadian Studies* 10, 4 (1975): 39–58.

_____. "'Kicking and Complaining': Demobilization Riots in the Canadian Expeditionary Force, 1918–1919." *Canadian Historical Review* 61, 3 (1980): 334–60.

_____. "'Noblest and Best': Retraining Canada's War Disabled, 1915–1923." *Journal of Canadian Studies* 16, 3 & 4 (1981): 75–85.

Moss, John. "The Great War as an Ideological Conflict—An Australian Perspective." *War & Society* 7, 2 (1989): 55–77.

Mott, Morris. "One Solution to the Urban Crisis: Manly Sports and Winnipeggers, 1900–1914." *Urban History Review* 12, 2 (1983): 57–70.

Naylor, James. "Toronto 1919." *Canadian Historical Association, Historical Papers*, 1986, 33–55.

Neuenschwander, John A. "Remembrance of Things Past: Oral Historians and Long-Term Memory." *Oral History Review* 6 (1978): 45–53.

Palmer, Howard. "Mosaic versus Melting Pot: Immigration and Ethnicity in Canada and the United States." *International Journal* 31, 3 (1976): 488–528.

Prassad, Yuvaran. "William Randolph Hearst and Pro-Germanism During World War I." *Indian Journal of American Studies* 17, 1–2 (1987): 93–100.

Ramkhalawansingh, Ceta. "Women during the Great War." In *Women at Work: Ontario, 1850–1930*, ed. Janice Acton, 261–307. Toronto: Women's Press, 1974.

Ramstead, Ken. "The 'Eye-Witness': Lord Beaverbrook and Canada in Flanders." *The Register* 12 (1984): 295–314.

Rawls, Walton. "Wake Up America." *American History Illustrated* 23, 5 (1988): 32–45.

Reeves, Nicholas. "Film Propaganda and its Audiences: The Example of Britain's Official Films During the First World War." *Journal of Contemporary History* 18, 3 (1983): 463–94.

Robertson, Peter. "More Than Meets the Eye." *Archivaria* 1, 2 (1976): 33–43.

_____. "Canadian Photojournalism During the First World War." *History of Photography* 2 (1978): 40.

Robinson, Daniel. "'Planning for the Most Serious Contingency': Alien Internment, Arbitrary Detention, and the Canadian State, 1938–39." *Journal of Canadian Studies/ Revue d'etudes canadiennes* 28, 2 (1993): 6–20.

Roger, Andrew C. "Amateur Photography by Soldiers of the Canadian Expeditionary Force." *Archivaria* 26, 2 (1988): 10–13.

Ropp, Theodore. "War as a National Experience." In *The Second World War as a National Experience*, ed. Sidney Aster, 1–11. Ottawa: Canadian Committee for the History of the Second World War, 1981.

Ruff, Allen. "Repression of the Press in the World War I Era: The Case of Charles H. Kerr & Company." *Journal of Newspaper and Periodical History* 5, 2 (1989): 2–19.

Sandwell, Bernard. "Financial Measures." In *Canada in the Great War: An Authentic Account of the Military History of Canada From the Earliest Days to the Close of the War of Nations*. Vol. 2. Toronto: United Publishers of Canada Ltd., 1921.

Sarty, Roger and Greenhous, Brereton. "The Great War." In *Readings in Canadian History: Post Confederation*, 3rd ed., ed. R. Douglas Francis and Donald B. Smith, 325–30. Toronto: Holt, Rinehart and Winston of Canada, 1990.

Saunders, M.L. "British Film Propaganda in Russia, 1916–1918." *Historical Journal of Film, Radio and Television* 3, 2 (1983): 117–30.

Sayer, John. "Art and Politics: Dissent and Repression." *American Journal of Legal History* 32, 1 (1988): 42–78.

Sears, Allan. "Immigration Controls as Social Policy: The Case of Canadian Medical Inspection, 1900–1920." *Studies in Political Economy* 33 (1990): 91–112.

Selig, Michael. "The Espionage Case of Producer Robert Goldstein (1917)." *Journal of Popular Film and Television* 10, 4 (1983): 168–74.

Siemiatycki, Myer. "Munitions and Labour Militancy: The 1916 Hamilton Machinists' Strike." In *Canadian Labour History*, ed. David Bercuson, 119–37. Toronto: Copp Clark, 1987.

Simcovitch, Maxim. "The Impact of Griffith's `Birth of a Nation' on the Modern Ku Klux Klan." *Journal of Popular Film* 1, 1 (1972): 45–53.

Small, Melvin. "Motion Pictures and the Study of Attitudes." *Film and History* 2, 1 (1972): 1–5.

Smith, David Edward. "Emergency Government in Canada." *Canadian Historical Review* 50, 4 (1969): 429–48.

Strong, Edward K. "Psychological Methods as Applied to Advertising." *Journal of Educational Psychology* 4 (1913): 393–404.

Susman, Warren. "History and Film: Artifact and Experience." *Film and History* 15, 2 (1985): 26–36.

Taylor, Philip. "The Foreign Office and British Propaganda During the First World War." *The Historical Journal* 23, 4 (1980): 875–98.

Thompson, Eric. "Canadian Fiction of the Great War." *Canadian Literature* 91, 4 (1981): 81–96.

Travers, Tim. "Learning and Decision-Making on the Western Front, 1915–1916: The British Example." *Canadian Journal of History* 18, 1 (1983): 87–97.

Tucker, Leigh. "English Friends and Censorship, World War I." *Quaker History* 71, 2 (1982): 111–24.

Twomey, Paul. "Small Power Security Through Great Arms Control? Australian Perceptions of Disarmament, 1919–1930." *War & Society* 8, 1 (1990): 71–97.

Tylee, Claire M. "`Maleness Run Riot' — The Great War and Women's Resistance to Militarism." *Women's Studies International Forum* 14, 3 (1988): 199–210.

Uisikin, Roz. "`The Alien and Bolshevist in Our Midst': The 1919 Winnipeg General Strike." *Jewish Life and Times* 5 (1983): 28–49.

Valverde, Mariana. "`When the Mother of the Race is Free': Race, Reproduction, and Sexuality in First Wave Feminism." In *Gender Conflicts: New Essays in Women's History*, ed. Franca Iacovetta and Mariana Valverde, 13–20. Toronto: University of Toronto Press, 1992.

Van Dopperen, Ron. "Shooting the Great War." *Film History* 4, 2 (1990): 123–29.

Vipond, Mary. "Canadian Nationalism and the Plight of Canadian Magazines in the 1920's." In *Partners Nevertheless: Canadian-American Relations in the Twentieth Century*, ed. Norman Hillmer, 237–58. Toronto: Copp Clark, 1989.

Vizram, Rozina. "The First World War and the Indian Soldiers." *Indo-British Review* 16 (1989): 17–26.

Weigand, Wayne A. "In Service to the State: Wisconsin Public Libraries During World War I." *Wisconsin Magazine of History* 72, 3 (1989): 199–224.

White, Richard. "The Soldier as Tourist: The Australian Experience of the Great War." *War & Society* 5, 1 (1987): 63–77.

Williams, David. "The Bureau of Investigation and its Critics, 1919–1921: The Origins of Federal Political Surveillance." *Journal of American History* 68 (1981–82): 560–89.

Wilson, J. Donald. "The Finnish Organization of Canada, the 'Language Barrier,' and the Assimilation Process." *Canadian Ethnic Studies* 9, 2 (1977): 105–16.

Young, Allan R. "'We Throw the Torch': Canadian Memorials of the Great War and the Mythology of Heroic Sacrifice." *Journal of Canadian Studies* 26, 4 (1990): 5–27.

Young, William R. "Conscription, Rural Depopulation and the Farmers of Ontario, 1917–1919." *Canadian Historical Review* 53, 3 (1972): 289–320.

4 Pamphlets and Miscellanea

DEPARTMENT OF AGRICULTURE, OTTAWA, ONTARIO

Can, Store and Dry For Victory (1915)
Canadian Food Bulletin (1917–19)
Eat More Fish (1918)
Fancy Meats in Newest Dishes (1918)
Food Service: A Handbook for Speakers (1918)
Fruits and Vegetables: Canning, Drying and Storing (1918)
Glucose for Household Use (1918)
Livestock—Canada's Opportunity (1918)
One Week's Budget (1918)
Potatoes and How to Cook Them (1918)
Poultry Rather Than Beef (1918)
Recipes For Jam Making (1918)
Report of the Milk Committee (1917)
War Meals: Practical Suggestions to Save Bacon, Wheat and Flour to Meet War Needs Overseas (1917)

DIRECTORATE OF HISTORY, DEPARTMENT OF NATIONAL DEFENCE, OTTAWA, ONTARIO

Recruiting in Canada, 1914–1917

CANADIAN WAR MUSEUM, OTTAWA, ONTAIO

The Canadian Army From Ypres to Mons, 1915–1918. Catalogue, C.W.R.O.
Photographic Exhibition. Grafton Galleries, London, England, 1919.
Catalogue, C.W.R.O. Art Exhibition. London, England, 1919.
Catalogue, War Trophy Exhibition. Hamilton, Ontario, October 1919.

ARCHIVES OF ONTARIO, TORONTO, ONTARIO

Canadian Imperial Bank of Commerce, *Letters from the Front*, 1918.
Wrong, George. *The War Spirit of Germany*, 1915.

UNITED CHURCH, TORONTO, ONTARIO

T.B. Kirkpatrick, *The War and the Christian Church*.
Murray T. Lovell, *The Call of the World Task*.
J.M. Shaw, *The War and Divine Providence*.
George Workman, *Armageddon, or the World Movement*.

METROPOLITAN TORONTO LIBRARY

Theatre Programmes
Song Sheets

5 Films

NATIONAL FILM, TELEVISION AND SOUND ARCHIVES, OTTAWA, ONTARIO

Battle of Courcelette
Dawson City Museum Collection
Great War Home Front
James and Sons Collection
Recruiting Rally
Round Przemsyl
Sons of Our Empire
Supremacy in the Air
11th Battalion of Galt
204th Battalion Sham Battle

York University, Toronto, Ontario

D.W. Griffiths: An American Genius, Film Classics Presentation, 1977.
Hearts of the World, D.W. Griffiths' Productions, 1918.

6 Interviews

National Film, Sound and Television Archives, Toronto, Ontario

C.B.C., Flanders' Field Series

Multicultural History Society of Ontario, Toronto, Ontario

J.H. Baetz
W.L. Bitzer
B. Kayfetz
W. Krystia
H.A. Lachner
F. Levine
E. Shantz
E. Weber
A. Yanke

7 Unpublished Theses and Manuscripts

Allain, Robert. "Sir Thomas White and Canadian Wartime Financial Policy."
    Unpublished M.A. Thesis, Queen's University, 1975.
Baxter, T.C. "Selected Aspects of Canadian Public Opinion on the Russian
    Revolution." Unpublished M.A. Thesis, University of Western Ontario, 1973.
Boudreau, Joseph A. "The Enemy Alien Problem in Canada, 1914–1921."
    Unpublished Ph.D. Thesis, University of California, Berkeley, 1965.
Boyko, Michael. "The First World War and the Threat of Invasion." Unpublished
    Ms., York University, n.d.
Brandstaetter, Maureen. "Deutschtum on the Prairies: A Study of Prairie German-
    Canadian Newspapers During the First World War." Unpublished M.A.
    Thesis, University of Calgary, 1986.

Bray, Robert Matthew. "The Canadian Patriotic Response to the Great War." Unpublished Ph.D. Thesis, York University, 1977.

Bruce, Jean. "The Toronto *Globe* and the Manpower Problem, 1914–1917." Unpublished M.A. Thesis, Queen's University, 1967.

Cole, Curtis Johnson. "The War Measures Act 1914: Aspects of the Emergency Limitation of Freedom of Speech and Personal Liberties in Canada, 1914–1919." Unpublished M.A. Thesis, University of Western Ontario, 1980.

Ens, Adolf. "Mennonite Relations With the Governments of Western Canada, 1870–1925." Unpublished Ph.D. Thesis, University of Ottawa, 1978.

Fell, Brian John. "A Question of Conscience: British and Canadian Quakers and Their Socialist and Parliamentary Allies Face the Great War." Unpublished M.A. Thesis, University of Manitoba, 1969.

Fewster, Kevin. "Expression and Suppression: Aspects of Military Censorship in Australia During World War I." Unpublished Ph.D. Thesis, University of New South Wales, 1980.

Fyfe, Robert. "Sir Thomas White, the Victory Loans and the Canadian Financial Community, 1917–1919." Unpublished M.A. Thesis, Carleton University, 1986.

Hanks, Robert. "The Humane Dimension of War: Fraternization and Community on the Western Front, 1914–1918." Unpublished Ms., University of Toronto, 1989.

Haynes, Nancy Jane. "A History of the Royal Alexandra Theatre, Toronto, Ontario, Canada, 1914–1918." Unpublished Ph.D. Thesis, University of Colorado, 1973.

Indra, Doreen. "Ethnicity, Social Stratification and Opinion Formation: An Analysis of Ethnic Portrayal in the Vancouver Newspaper Press, 1905–76." Unpublished Ph.D. Thesis, Simon Fraser University, 1979.

Kalbfleisch, Herbert Karl. "A History of German Newspapers in Ontario, Canada, 1835–1918." Unpublished Ph.D. Thesis, University of Michigan, 1953.

Keller, Phyllis. "German-America and the First World War." Unpublished Ph.D. Thesis, Kent State University, 1969.

Killian, Crawford. "The Great War and the Canadian Novel, 1915–1926." Unpublished M.A. Thesis, Simon Fraser University, 1972.

Kuitunen, Alan Neil. "The Finnish Canadian Socialist Movement, 1900 to 1914." Unpublished M.A. Thesis, University of Calgary, 1982.

Lamb, Bessie. "Origin and Development of Newspapers in Vancouver." Unpublished M.A. Thesis, University of British Columbia, 1942.

Lindsay, Alexander Mollison. "The Effect of Public Opinion on the Borden Administration During World War I, 1914–1918." Unpublished M.A. Thesis, Acadia University, 1953.

Linstrom-Best, Varpu. "A History of Organized Socialism and Communism Among the Finnish-Canadians From 1905 to 1929." Unpublished Ms., York University, 1974.

Lubek, Melvyn. "The Uncaring Blind: Or Freedom of Expression in Canada During World War One." Unpublished LL.M. Thesis, Osgoode Hall Law School, 1980.

Magney, William. "The Methodist Church and the Conscription Crisis of 1917." Unpublished Ms., University of Toronto, 1968.

Mah, Valerie. "An In-Depth Look at Toronto's Early Chinatown, 1913–1933." Unpublished Ms., University of Toronto, 1977.

Matheson, R. Neil. "The Business of War: Publisher John Bayne Maclean and the Great War." Unpublished Ms., York University, 1986.

McKegney, Patricia Roy. "Germanism, Industrialism and Propaganda in Berlin, Ontario, During World War One." Unpublished M.A. Thesis, University of Waterloo, 1979.

Miller, J.A. "The Alberta Press and the Conscription Issue." Unpublished M.A. Thesis, University of Alberta, 1974.

Mitchell, Peter M. "Canada and the Chinese Labour Corps, 1917–1920." Unpublished Ms., York University, 1982.

Mott, Morris K. "The 'Foreign Peril': Nativism in Winnipeg, 1916–23." Unpublished M.A. Thesis, University of Manitoba, 1970.

Novak, Dagmar. "The Canadian Novel and the Two World Wars." Unpublished Ph.D. Thesis, University of Toronto, 1988.

O'Neill, Mora. "A Partial History of the Royal Alexandra Theatre, Toronto, Canada, 1907–1939." Unpublished Ph.D. Thesis, Louisiana State University and Agricultural and Mechanical College, 1976.

Pateman, Andrew. "Keeping the Home Fires Burning: Fuel Regulation in Toronto During the Great War." Unpublished M.A. Thesis, University of Western Ontario, 1988.

Patterson, David. "Loyalty, Ontario, and the First World War." Unpublished M.A. Thesis, McGill University, 1986.

Pinsonneault, Gerard. "La Propagande de Recrutement Militaire au Canada, 1914–1917." Unpublished M.A. Thesis, Université de Sherbrooke, 1981.

Porter, V.R. "The English-Speaking Labour Press and the Great War." Unpublished M.A. Thesis, Memorial University, 1981.

Purcell, Gillis. "Wartime Press Censorship in Canada." Unpublished M.A. Thesis, University of Toronto, 1946.

Raynolds, Tracy. "A Case Study in Attitudes Towards Enemy Aliens in British Columbia, 1914–1919." Unpublished M.A. Thesis, University of British Columbia, 1973.

Rider, Peter. "The Administrative Policy of the Chief Press Censor of Canada." Unpublished B.A. Thesis, Carleton University, 1966.

_____. "The Imperial Munitions Board and its Relationship to Government, Business and Labour, 1914–1920." Unpublished Ph.D. Thesis, University of Toronto, 1974.

Samuels, Elliot. "The Red Scare in Ontario: The Reaction of the Ontario Press to the Internal and External Threats of Bolshevism, 1917–1919." Unpublished M.A. Thesis, Queen's University, 1971.

Steward, Linda Rae. "A Canadian Perspective: The Fictional and Historical Portrayal of World War One." Unpublished M.A. Thesis, University of Waterloo, 1983.

Straus, Melvin Potter. "The Control of Subversive Activities in Canada." Unpublished Ph.D Thesis, University of Illinois, 1959.

Thielman, George C. "The Canadian Mennonites." Unpublished Ph.D. Thesis, Western Reserve University, 1955.

Unger, Molly. "A Subtle Re-Shaping: Effects of World War I on Canadian Soldiers Who Fought in It." Unpublished Ms., McMaster University, 1987.

Zdunich, Darlene. "Tuberculosis and the Canadian Veteran." Unpublished M.A. Thesis, University of Calgary, 1988.

Index

Amiens, 174
Amsterdam, 242n8
Anderson, A.
    diary, 254n114
    letters home, 250n59
Anglican Church, 227n90
Anglo-American Telegraph Co., 100
Anglo-Protestant superiority, belief in,
        4, 8, 16
Antwerp, Belgium, 114
Apostolic Faith, 80
Arabic language, 81
Archangel, Russia, 86
Armageddon, 228n94
Armenia, 5
armistice, 11, 67, 86, 183–84, 210
arms' race seen as a factor in the
        Great War, 192
Armstrong, —, 243n33
Army and Navy Veterans' League, 202
Arras, 174
Ashmead-Bartlett, Ellis, 119–20,
        246n83
Asquith, Herbert Henry, 31, 114, 116
Atkinson, Joseph E., 234n109
Australia, 209, 215
    1917 election, 121
    Aliens Restrictions Order, 121
    Anzac Day, 212
        first anniversary of Gallipoli,
            118
        "Anzac legend," 118, 211
    Anzacs (Australian and New
        Zealand Army Corps), 29,
        119–20, 211
        casualty toll, 49, 118, 210
        number sent into action, 118
        vote against conscription, 49
    censorship, 118–19, 246n83
    Chief Censor, 119, 121
    citizens
        fail to comprehend the real
            battle situation, 120

fear imported coloured
        workers, 120–21
    see war as a glorious enterprise,
        117
civilians
    divisions between Anzacs
        and, 210
    ready to greet strong, heroic
        veterans, 210
colony to nation, 210
Commonwealth Crimes Act
    (1921), 122
conscription referendum, 47, 49,
    118, 120–21
Directorate of War Propaganda, 118
enemy aliens
    religious publications serving,
        121
Gallipoli reports downplayed,
    118–19
government
    allotment for national
        memorial, 211
    opposed to any future arms
        race, 210
    policy of military
        entrenchment, 210
hopes for an equal footing in the
        Empire, 117
Labour Party of Australia, 121
left-wing press
    anti-draft articles, 240n88
letters from soldiers
    censored, 118
levels of enlistment, 40, 48, 118
military postal system, 157–58
newspapers
    censors on premises, 119
    editors, 119
    foreign-language, 121
organized labour, 121, 240n88
    demands conscription of
        wealth before men, 120

percentage of males in uniform,
231n48
poor economic conditions, 118,
121, 210
public opinion
management, 117
social welfare
expanded to veterans, 210
troops. *See* Anzacs
Unlawful Associations Act (1917),
122
veterans
demand increase in post-war
gratuity, 210
on Anzac Day, 212
war correspondents, 29, 34
war debt, 210
war memorials, 211
War Precautions Act (1914), 121–22
penalties under, 119
Australian Returned Soldiers' and
Sailors' Imperial League,
210
Austria, 3, 47
Ambassador to the U.S., 68
Austrian-Canadians
language restrictions after
armistice, 67
Austro-Hungarian Empire, 9

B

Baden-Powell, Robert Stephenson
Smyth, Lord, 128
Baetz, J.H., 8
Bainbridge, Isaac, 240n97
Balfour, Arthur James, 116
Banks, William, 72, 108
Barrie, Ontario, 78
Batten, A.C., 106
The Battle and Fall of Przemsyl, 19
Battle Cry of Peace, 20
battlefield
contradictory portrayals of, 12

notions of heroes and clean deaths
on the, 127–28, 185
slaughter unsurpassed, ix
See also combat
Battle of the Somme, 107–8, 188
Baymaster, 105
B.C. Federationist, 124
Bean, Charles Edwin Woodrow, 29,
118, 210–11
Belgium, 13, 146, 172
alleged German outrages in, 14
as portrayed in church sermons, 23
as portrayed in movies, 20
churches, 14, 43
in political cartoons, 24
invaded by German army, 3
refugees, 14
relief for, 5
Bell, F. McKelvey, 17, 99
Bell, George, 180
Bennett, Richard Bedford, 46–47,
252n75
Benzinger, I., 228n95
Berlin, Ontario, 8
Berliner Journal, 82
Berlin Press Bureau, 80
Berton, Pierre, 214
Bethune, 208
Bexhill-on-Sea tactical school, 172
Big Bear, 71
Big Bertha (bomb), xi
Billings, Warren K., 87
Bird, William, 196
Bishop, William Avery "Billy," 17, 214
Blackston, J. Stuart, 20
Blighty
a wound, serious but not
permanent, 143, 167, 179
Blondin, Pierre Edouard, 45, 237n42,
238n58
Bloxham, Private —, 79
Boag, Ernest, 72
Boer War, 5, 36

deaths in, xii
participation urged by *Canadian Military Gazette*, 71
press criticized Kitchener during, 28
soldiers' letters to papers gave classified information, 153
used fewer shells than 35 minutes at Neuve Chappelle, 178
war correspondent for the *Globe*, 72
war correspondents telegraphed troop movements, 65
Bohn, John, 33, 238n48, 243n28
Boland, M., 224n36
Bold, J., 256n40
Bolsheviks, 86
Bolshevism in Russia, 57
Bolshevist threat, 67
Bolton, F.
    diary, 254n114
Boni and Livewright publishers, 98
Borden, Robert Laird, 10, 14, 33, 41, 72, 222n15, 224n40, 231n55, 239n72, 250n46
    decides for conscription, 48
    demands British consult on use of Canadian troops, 12
    descends to bigotry, 49, 67
    despatches troops to Russia, 86
    eager for Canadian input into Empire strategy, 40
    emotionally moved by wounded Canadians, 48
    equivocates over manpower survey cards, 47
    Hughes a political liability to, 44
    instructs O'Connor on War Measures Act, 65
    lets election tracts deepen the French-English cleavage, 50
    misuses the military to influence the vote, 49
    on books by Mees being suppressed, 97
    on the issue of coalition with Laurier, 48, 50
    pledges a volunteer army of a half million, 40
    quoted as standing with Britain, 5
    quoted regarding Bourassa, 77
    seems reluctant to spend on recruiting, 46
    shows gross disrespect for democracy, 48–49
    submits to G.W.V.A., 83
    told by Gwynne of soldiers' discontent with officers, 229n24
    told by veteran of having to sell war mementos, 204
    vacationing as Britain declared war, 3
    visits Camp Borden — late, 78
    warned of danger from Germans near U.S. border, 6–7
    writes in diary about long casualty lists, 236n15
Bourassa, Henri, 5, 31, 75, 77
Bovey, Tom, 176, 252n81
Boy-Ed, Carl, 7
Boy Scouts of Canada, 42, 128
Brade, Sir Reginald, 37
Bradley, Russell
    diary, 250n14
Brady, William, 20
Brandon, Manitoba, 92
Brantford (Ontario) Board of Trade, 231n55
Bray, Roger, 205
Brest-Litovsk, Treaty of, 86
Britain, 13, 60, 117, 192
    Admiralty Office, 36
    advertising agencies in, 15
    Aitken aims to promote Canada in, 32
    army instructors of Canadian troops, 164

army staff schools, 173
Board of Film Censors, 27, 36
books, 116
    banned in Canada, 97
Camp Whitley, 164
Canadian-born soldiers do not
    care much for, 163
casualty toll, 29, 37, 178
censors, xiv, 33
charges of drunkenness against
    Johnny Canuck, 164
citizens, 76
    as seen by Graves and Sassoon,
        110
    deaths, 110
    dismayed by rioting Tommies,
        191
    hatred of things German, 113
    see their soldiers on leave, 191
climate, 163
Colonial Office, 28–29, 80
conscientious objectors, 113, 115,
    243n57
conscription, 37, 108
Defence of the Realm Act, xiii,
    113, 115
Department of Information, 116
doctrine that Canada always goes
    to war with, 4
Foreign Office, 28, 116
government, ix, xiii, 108
    allows greater access by
        photographers, 35
    calls for more Canadian troops,
        40, 46
    declares war against the
        Central Powers, 3
    ends embargo on Hearst
        papers, 81
Indian Home Office, 101
Intelligence, 102
intercepts revolvers bound for
    Germany, 242n8
Irish Republicans in, 113, 115

journalists
    battles for free expression, 113
military authorities, 33
    confiscate wireless facilities, 27
military newspapers
    printed at print shops and news
        plants, 134
    Wiper's Times, 134
Ministry of Information, ix, 116
movies, 36
    censored in Canada, 66, 106
National Insurance Commission,
    245n72
newspaper
    circulation, xiii, 11, 114
    criticism of military strategy,
        xiv, 114
    descriptions of battle, 33, 114
    editors, 113–14
    fines for misconduct, 114
    ownership, xiii, 31, 76
    publication of troop positions
        in Boer War, 65
    received by Canadian
        combatant, 141
    reports of Allied losses, xiv
    technology, 11
    voluntary blackouts, 113
    war photos by C.W.R.O., 36
newsreels, 19, 36, 116
    abridged in Canada, 107
    Aitken sees potential of, 37
    Allies liberating towns, 38
    Canadians at casualty clearing
        stations, 38
    censored, 37
    first of tanks in action, 38
    German P.O.W.s, 38
    shots of dead bodies excised, 38
    technology inadequate for long
        shots, 38
    ten-minute bi-weekly from the
        War Office, 37
    percentage of males in uniform, 47

government trys to boost
acceptance of, 51, 57
helps radical left, xv
Methodist Church promotes, 23
National Service survey and,
13, 47
pressure is on Borden for, 46
sends 24,000 men to France, 50
constitution
of "peace, order and good
government," 111
Criminal Code, 93, 124
Dominion Publicity Committee, 193
amount spent on advertising
by, 55
enemy aliens, x
Chambers's view of, 110, 122
interned, xv, 8
promised fair treatment by
government, 9
regulations governing, 9–10
veterans beat and destroy shops
of, 83
farmers, 52, 83, 90–91, 97
in the army, 132
film distributors
regulated by Chambers, 107
Finance, Department of
contract with C.P.A., 55
follows Britain into war, 4
food, 117
conservation posters, 39, 53
control, 52–53
shortages, x, 51
French-Catholic and Loyalist
roots, 111
French-English cleavage, 4–5
fuel, 117
control, 51–52
"gasless Sundays and heatless
Mondays," 51
shortages, x, 51
Gentleman Usher of the Black
Rod, 71–72

government, 241n97
afraid to call by-elections, 47
appoints Aitken as *eye-witness*, 30
arrests socialists under War
Measures Act, 91
assistance to veterans, 57–60,
201–4, 206
attempts to combat spies and
saboteurs, 6, 99
authorizes 65e Regiment, 45
broadsides, 46
by Order in Council, 66–68,
91, 235n11
commissions a national war
memorial, 193
creates censor's office, 66
declines to ban *Le Devoir*, 77
deports Finns, 104
deports Slavs complicit in
Winnipeg strike, 93
election posters, 50
fears a repeat of U.S. pension
episode, 203
finds internment helps unemployment dilemma, 10
funds newspaper for Johnny
Canuck, 134
grant to C.W.R.O., 31
infantry battalions authorized
by, 41
labour bureaus, 204
letters of appeal to community
leaders, 46
newsletters to all community
leaders, 57
news management, ix, 236n15
not decisive enough for
Chambers, 89
offers to pay war
correspondents, 34
on censorship, 66–69
promises aliens fair treatment, 9
propaganda arm, 57

casualty lists, 40
censorship, xi, 60, 76–78, 159
circulation, xi, 11–12, 68
comments on C.W.R.O. art
    collection, 195
coverage of strikes, 86
editors, xiii–xiv, 12, 24, 68–69,
    75, 79, 90, 100
foreign-language, 67–68, 74,
    87
has no constitutional guarantee
    of freedom, xiii
imperialism, xii
jingoism, xii–xiii
letters to, 79, 203
limited clout of, xiii
mass distribution, xii, 12
"Memorandum on the Duties
    of the Press in War," 68
partisanship, xii, 12
patriotism, xii, xvii
political cartoons, 12
propaganda, 12
publishers, xii–xiii, 12, 34, 68
received by combatants, 141
reporters, xiii, 69
reports from overseas, 31, 127,
    145, 163, 177
reports of classified
    information, 99–100
socialist, 87, 91
stories of sabotage, 7
support for ban on Hearst
    papers, 80
technology, 11
war photographs by C.W.R.O.,
    35–36
1917 election, 46, 56
election boxes stuffed, 49
enlisted voters watched by
    officers, 49
pamphlets and posters, 50
results, 50
nurses, 161, 167

Old Age Pensions, 206
Parliament buildings
    House of Commons
        demolished by fire, 8
        Ontario and Quebec farmers
            march on, 91
    photographs
        censored, 27, 106
        theme of soldier as tourist, 161
    pilot, 225n62
        contradictions in the life of, 17
    Post Office, 56, 73, 204
        control of obscene or immoral
            mail, 68
        employees assigned to
            censorship, 74
        rates raised, 53
    post-war recession, 207
    profiteering scandals, 54, 85
    prohibition, 197
        bootlegging, 198, 207
    provincial
        boards of health, 199
        movie censors, 106–7
    Public Information, Department
        of, 56, 117
        pamphlet describing Bolshevist
            Russia, 57
        War Lecture Bureau, 57
    public opinion
        management, 51, 187
    Public Safety Branch, 67, 85, 92
    recruiting, 33
        at church services, 22
        bribery charges over, 41
        broadsides, 46
        by civilians on commission, 41
        fear that war death scenes will
            thwart, 19
        in movie theatres, 13
        in Quebec, 43–45
        letters of appeal, 46
        newspaper advertising, 41–42,
            45–46

photographs of dead, 36
resents and despises officers,
    161, 171–72, 229n24, 252n82
resents the C.W.R.O.
    trivializing of war, 141, 153
resolved to bear the brunt like
    men, 133, 153, 157
routine at the front, 177–78, 208
sees irony of the term Great
    War, 28
shot for desertion or cowardice,
    167, 179
suicide, 179
supports Union government,
    49
treatment or consequences of
    trenchfoot, 174–75
who retained his concepts of
    duty and honour, 183
widow's pension, 167
wounded, 38, 57, 79, 143, 157,
    164, 167–68, 179, 184
writes narratives of the war,
    16–17
Soldiers' Civil Re-Establishment,
    Department of (D.S.C.R.),
    204
certificates rejected by unions
    and employees, 203
pamphlets re: War Service
    Gratuity, 59
Repatriation Committee, 59
Soldier Settlement Act (1919), 204
songs of war, x, 21–22
Statute of Westminster (1931), 213
taxation, 51, 53–54, 202, 233n102
telegrams and telephone calls
    monitored, xi, 66, 100, 103–5
    Regulations for Censorship of
    … Telegraph Messages,
    242n9
temperance advocates, 97–98, 144
theatre owners
    regulated by Chambers, 107

trade unions
    city police forces form, 85
    demand collective bargaining,
        85
    demand conscription of wealth
        before manpower, 13, 85
    industrial or craft, 85
    protest jailing of Bainbridge,
        241n97
    strikes, 4, 76, 85
troops, 37, 243n38
    1st Canadian Siege Battery, 164
    2nd Field Artillery Brigade, 161
    4th Infantry Brigade, 170
    5th (Western Cavalry)
        Battalion, 145, 196
    7th (1st British Columbia
        Regiment) Battalion, 142,
        144
    11th Infantry Brigade, 142–43
    13th (Royal Highlanders of
        Canada) Battalion, 163, 171
    14th (Royal Montreal
        Regiment) Battalion, 147
    19th (Central Ontario)
        Battalion, 193
    21st (Eastern Ontario)
        Battalion, 42
    22e Regiment, 43
    27th (City of Winnipeg)
        Battalion, 142
    43rd (Cameron Highlanders of
        Canada) Battalion, 174
    49th Battalion, 141
    58th Howitzer Battery C.F.A.,
        142
    72nd (Seaforth Highlanders of
        Canada) Battalion, 137
    85th (Nova Scotia
        Highlanders) Battalion, 196
    86th Battalion, 42
    98th Battalion, 42
    107th Battalion, 136
    118th Battalion, 8

bans foreign-language
publications, xiv, 79–81,
83–84, 88, 101, 103
begins to allow dual-column
format, 89
bans gramaphone records, 109
bans illustrations of dead soldiers,
194
bans Jehovah's Witness's
publications, 80
bans some Canadian papers for
unacceptable copy, 76
bans some U.S. movies and stage
productions, 107–8
bans U.S. pacifist and anti-British
publications, 80, 243n45
bans U.S. socialist publications,
87, 89
Battle of the Somme abridged by,
107–8
biographical sketch, 70
books banned or abridged by,
97–99
calls upon others for help, 73,
106–7
continues censorship after
armistice, 87, 102, 104
controls Canadian riot reports,
78
distinguishes between fiendish foe
and refined Anglo, 77
exceeds his mandate, 94, 123
fears a Bolshevik revolution in
Canada, xv, 104, 117
finds American newspapers
troublesome, 78
has words with M.P. of German
descent, 82
having banned a tract did not
reconsider, 81
Hearts of the World abridged by,
108
imperialism of, 110–11, 236n25
instructions to booksellers, 98

instructions to cable operators,
100, 102–4
instructions to postal employees,
74
legacy is post-war oppression of
minorities, xv, 95, 124
letters to editors of five
newspapers, 238n52
number of publications
suppressed by, xiv, 79–80
personal diplomacy of, 75, 100, 123
photograph of, 64
post-war fight against socialists, 124
powers granted to, 66, 100, 106,
108–9
protects democracy by cutting free
expression, 123
racism of, xv, 81, 101, 103, 106,
123–24, 242n20
rebukes Montreal, Ottawa, and
Toronto papers, 78–79, 106
regimental historian, 236n25
restrained by government on
Canadian socialist papers,
90–91
retirement as Chief Censor, 190
screens letters from soldiers to
publications, 79
seeks a warrant to ban the *Western
Clarion*, 89–90
supposes most ethnics to be pro-
German, xv
workaholic conduct, 72–73
Chambers, Thomas, 70
Chanak, 192
Chartinoff, Michael, 91
Château Thierry, 131
Chesney Gold Medal, 211
Chicago, 98
Chicago *Tribune*, 78
Child, Philip, 207
Children's History of the War, 24
Chillicothe, Ohio, 112
China, 101, 103

Minister of the Interior
  assassinated in Victoria, 104
Chinese-Canadians, 104
  assumed to be sympathetic to
    Germany, 101
  head tax applied to, 102–3
  target of police surveillance, 103
Chinese language, 81
  translation, 74
Chinese Nationalist League, 103–4,
    235n11, 242n20
Chinese National Reform
    Association, 104, 235n11
Chown, Samuel Dwight, 22
Christie, Loring Cheney, 97
Christopher, R.L., 255n22
Churchill, Winston Spencer, 114
Citizens' Recruiting League
  Hamilton branch, 46
  Montreal branch, 42, 44
Clan-na-gael (anti-British Irish-
    Catholic group), 6
Clark, Hugh, 229n25
Claxton, Brooke, 159
Cleopatra, 19
Cockburn, C.B., 159
Coderre, Louis, 82
Cody, Henry John, 162
Coleman, W.
  diary, 253n97, 254n106
The Colonials and the Flag, 227n87
Colson, —, 237n29
Columbia Record Company, 109
combat, xv, 168, 170
  at Amiens and Arras results in 14
    percent casualties, 174
  British orthodoxy traded for Can-
    adian innovation, 13, 173
  Canadians' idealistic conceptions
    of, x
  depicted as an intense sporting
    contest, 132, 167

during which artillery salvos could
    last for days, 178
  four million shells churn the
    muck waist deep, 34
  illustrated in American books, 98
  in which a men are decapitated,
    208
  in which artillery forced "games of
    hide and seek," 178
  in which artillery smashes bodies
    to pulp, 166
  Mark IV tanks integrated into
    attack formation, 173
  poison gas used in, 14, 18, 22, 32,
    208
  promoted as a manly game, 42
  psychological effects, xvii–xviii
  Ross Rifle in, 171
  supporting artillery aimed at
    Canadian troops, 32
Congregational Church, 22
Connor, Ralph. *See* Gordon, Charles
    William
The Conquerers, 194–95
The Conquering Hero, 195
"Conscription," 232n79
Conservative Party of Canada, 4, 44,
    47
Coolican, —, 242n23
Co-operative Commonwealth
    Federation, 23, 208
Correll, Robert
  letters home, 162
Costain, Thomas, 237n41
Coulter, R.M., 74, 89, 240n88
Courcelette, 38, 195
Der Courier, 83–84
Courlage Fish and Game Club, 71
Craig, Claude G.
  diary, 252n74
Crandall, C.F., 229n25, 243n27
Creelman, J.J., 161

diary, 250n30

letters home, 250n34

Crerar, Thomas Alexander, 92

Croatia, 194

Croation language, 67

La Croix (Quebec City), 76

Crothers, Thomas, 10

Cubitt, B.B., 230n37

cult of the superior soldier, 215

Curll, M.H., 196

Currie, Arthur William, 13, 34, 171,
173–74, 184

D

Dafoe, John Wesley, 13

The Daily Advertizer, 82

Daily Chronicle, 28

Daily Express, 30, 32

Daily Mail, 115

Dalhousie University, 245n75

Dancocks, Daniel, 214

Dardenelles, 118, 246n83

Das, Tarkat, 101

Daughter of the Sun, 108

Davidson, Judson, 222n3

anti-war pamphlet by, 4

Davy, Iona, 164

Dawson, Albert, 19

Dawson, Corningsby, 17

Dawson, S.W., 16

Days of Our Years, 208

Deacon, Ben, 72

Deeds That Won the Empire, 23

Defeat, 97

de Mille, Cecil B., 20

de Panet, B., 230n37

Despised and Rejected, 115

Le Devoir, 77, 94

Devonshire, Victor Christian William
Cavendish, 9th Duke of,
228n1, 238n58, 238n59,
243n35

Dickinson, T. Kelly, 233n104

Doctor Cassell's Dyspepsia Tablets, 15

Doherty, Charles Joseph, 69, 98,
238n68, 241n97

Dollard Des Ormeaux, Adam, 43

Dominion Alliance, 97

Dominion Feature News Service, 55

Dominion Police, 84

budget to coordinate activities
with R.N.W.M.P., 6

Budka under surveillance of,
224n30

combined with R.N.W.M.P. to
become R.C.M.P., 93

Commissioner, 102

created following assassination of
McGee, 6

roster, 7

Doughty, Sir Arthur, 38–39, 193

Douglas, J. Harvey, 18

Dublin, 120

Duggan, Kenneth

letters home, 249n13

Dunlop, Hugh MacDonald, 249n3

Dutch language, 81

E

Eastman, Max, 112

Eaton, Sir John, 234n109

Eayrs, Hugh S., 16

Eddelstein, H., 74

Edmonton, 92, 242n20, 250n59

Edward VIII, King, 213

Ellis, M.

letters home, 250n52

Ellis, S., 159

Empire Day

in Ontario, 23

Empire Parliamentary Association

Ottawa branch, 71

Enderby Press, 78

England, 107, 215

prostitution, 182
Tower of London, 113
London, Ontario, 22
Long, —, 243n35
Longstaff, Will, 211
Loos, 40
"lost generation," 206
Lucas, I., 98, 222n16, 224n36, 241n3
Lusitania, 8, 14, 20
Lutheran Church, 11
L.W. Walter Company, 98
Lyon, Stewart, 34

M

MacBrayne, W., 242n20
McBride, Herbert, 208
Macdonald, J.A., 12
MacDonald, J.M., 225n43
MacDougall, J.C., 169–70
McGee, D'Arcy, 6
McGill University, 74, 173, 209
McIntyre, D.E., 170, 254n119, 254n121
    diary, 179, 252n73
MacKenzie, John, 247n22
McKenzie, Lester
    letters home, 162
Macksey, Kenneth, 214
Maclean, John Bayne, 76, 85, 237n41
Maclean's, 19, 76, 86–87, 195
McLeod, H.C., 250n46
McMaster University, 209, 245n75
McNab, John P., 237n37
McNaughton, Andrew George Latta,
    173
MacNutt, E.A., 234n110
Magrath, Charles Alexander, 51–52
Maheaux, F.
    letters home, 250n54, 250n61
Mail and Empire (Toronto), 229n24
Maison de la Presse (France), x
The Major, 16
Maltese in Australia, 120
The Manchester *Guardian*, 114–15
Mandle, W.F., 211

Manitoba, 8, 52, 78
Manitoba Free Press, 12–13, 226n81,
    238n52
Manley, Morris, 227n85
Manley-Sims, J.F., 29, 229n16
manly stereotype
    appears in war novels, 16
    building on the ethos of muscular
        Christianity, 130
    imperialists connect militia
        service with, 130
    imposed upon young men, 128
    influences many to enlist, 132–33
    Johnny Canuck abides by the, xvi,
        16–17, 118, 146, 153, 159, 165,
        169
    of Dominion's northern warriors, x
    of duty and self-respect in war
        songs, 21
    taps into the theme of adventure,
        3, 131
    utilized by G.H.Q., 179
The Man Who Stayed Home, 226n81
Maple Leaf Club (London), 182
Marne, Battle of the, 115, 143
Maron, G.L., 83–84
Martin, —, 252n67
Masses, 112
Masterman, Charles Frederick
    Gurney, 36, 115–16, 245n72
Mathieson, —, 242n10
Mattagami Pulp and Paper
    Company, 11
Matthews, Frank G.
    letters home, 250n57
Mearling, Colonel —, 183
Mees, Arthur, 97–98
Meighen, Arthur, 10, 48, 192, 224n30,
    238n47
Mendelssohn, Felix, 109
Menim Gate at Midnight, 211
Men in War, 98–99
Menzies, A.P.
    letters home, 250n55

Norwegian language, 81
Novy Mir, 84
Nuarteva, Sateria, 87

O

O'Brien, W.J.
    diary, 163, 183, 250n45, 252n77
O'Connor, W.F., 65
Ode to a Louse, 142
Odlum, Victor, 181
Ontario, 23, 78, 82
    Bruce County, 146
    farmers march on Parliament, 91
    jail registers, 8
    recruiting, 45
    restricts French-language
        instruction, 45, 77, 232n72
    shortage of agricultural labourers,
        52
Ontario Provincial Police, 92, 98,
    224n36
Ontario Teachers' Federation, 24
On the Fringe of the Great Fight, 18
Onward Christian Soldiers, 22
Open Court Publishing Company, 98
opium trade, 242n20
Orange Order, 43, 72, 108
Orpington Military Hospital, 143, 168
Ottawa
    Russell Theatre, 108
Ottawa *Citizen*, 238n52
Ottawa *Evening Journal*, 8, 78–79,
    238n52
Ottawa *Evening Telegram*, 238n56
Ottawa Golf Club, 71
Otter, Sir William Dillon, 237n28
Over There, 226n81
Overton, Johnny, 131
Owram, Douglas R., 163

P

pacifism, 12, 113, 115, 125, 208, 226n81,
    240n97
Papal Zouaves, 43

Papen, Franz von, 7
Papineau, Talbot, 31
    letters home, 250n58
The Parasite, 97
Paris, xi, 108, 134
Parker, Sir Gilbert, 220n4
Parrot, Sir Edward, 24
Passchendaele, 31, 34, 167, 174, 193
Patenaude, Esioff Lèon, 237n42,
    238n55
Paths of Glory, 194
Paull, Francis H.
    diary, 250n43
Peace at any Price, 107
Pearce and McKim, 55
Pearson, George, 18
Pedley, P.P., 22
Pelletier, Georges, 77
Pembroke, Ontario, 223n21
Perley, Sir George, 173
Perth, Ontario, 223n21
Petawawa, Ontario, 9
Philippines, 74
Phillips, F.R., 203
Pickford, Mary, 20, 56
Pierce, —, 243n39
Pinkerton Detective Agency, 6,
    242n20
Der Plauderer, 84
poison gas, 14, 18, 32, 167, 208
Polish language, 81
Pope, Sir Joseph, 222n13, 222n15,
    238n59, 239n72, 242n22,
    243n48
Port Arthur/Fort William, 89, 104
    Austro-Hungarians arrested in, 10
    sympathy walkout for Winnipeg
        strike, 92
postcard
    new and popular form of
        communication, 161–62
Power, C.G., 79
Pozieres, 49
Presbyterian Church, 22

Roberts, Charles George Douglas, 31
Roberts, Theodore Goodridge, 31
Robertson, Gideon, 241n97
Robertson, John Ross, 34, 70
Robidoux, F.J., 231n55
Robitnyche Slovo, 88
Robotchyi Narod, 88, 91
Rogers, Joseph, 92, 224n36
Rolls-Royce Ltd., 30
Roman Catholic Church, 22
Romanian language, 81
Roosevelt, Theodore, 28, 112, 130
Rose, H., 22
Ross, A.E., 253n99
Ross, J.G., 229n9
Ross, Philip Dansken, 79
Ross Rifle, 171
Rowell, Newton Wesley, 92
Roy, A.C.
    diary, 253n94
Royal Academy, 71
Royal Bank of Canada, 196
Royal Canadian Mounted Police, 93,
    124
Royal Canadian Navy, 209
Royal College of Music, 71
Royal Commission on Pensions and
    Soldiers' Civil Re-
    establishment, 206
Royal Navy, 27, 68, 114
Royal North-West Mounted Police, 6,
    84, 90, 93
Russell, Bertrand, 113
Russell, Thomas, 98
Russia, 87, 239n78
    collapse of the Tsar, 47
Russian-Australians, 121
Russian-Canadians, 86
Russian language
    banned from print and public
        gatherings in Australia, 122
    newspapers banned in Canada, 81,
        84
    texts suppressed in Australia, 121

Russian Revolution, xv, 84, 88,
    239n78
Russian Revolutionary Group, 235n11
Russian Social Democratic Party,
    235n11
Russian Social Revolutionists, 235n11
Russian Workers Union, 235n11
Russkoye Slova, 84
Ruthenian language, 67
Rutherford, Charles
    diary, 168

S

sabotage, 6–7, 11, 106
St. Croix River railway bridge
    dynamited, 7
St. Eloi, 173, 183, 193
    air reconnaissance, 32
St. Honore, Quebec, 45
St. Julien, 42
St. Lawrence River, 69
St. Marie, Quebec, 45
St. Omer, 29, 33
Salvation Army, 144, 177
Sanctuary Wood, 146
San Francisco, 87, 101
sapper, 233n91
Saskatchewan, 6, 52
Saskatoon, 92
Sassoon, Siegfried, 110, 206
Saturday Night, 14, 80, 167, 196,
    250n16
Sault Ste. Marie, 92
Saunders, Sir Charles, 70
Schlieffen Plan, 3
The School, 24
Scott, W., 223n30
Searchlight, 124
Seattle, 101
Senate Standing Committee on
    Social Affairs, Science and
    Technology, 258n85
Serbia, 3, 5
Serbian language, 81

Service, Robert William, 79
Shakespeare, William, 227n81
Shell Committee, 44
shell-hole bath tub, 176
   photograph, 175
Sherwood, Percy, 6–7, 102, 123
Sikhs in Canada, 6, 101–2, 110
Sinclair, Ian, 254n112
Singh, Bhag and Balwant, 101
The Sky Pilot in No Man's Land,
   195
Sladen, —, 237n27
Smith, Frederick Edwin "F.E.," 113
Smooth Rock Falls, Ontario, 11
Social Democratic Party of Canada
   (S.D.P.C.), 92, 235n11,
   240n97
Social Gospel, 23, 208
Socialist Party of Canada, 89
Social Labour Party, 235n11
Soldiers of the Soil campaign, 53
Somme, 113–14, 116, 169, 193
   better medical care could have
      saved one third of dead,
      252n63
   brings pessimism and despair
      about winning, 183
   British casualties, 29
   Canadian troops needed to
      resupply the, 46
   fabricated photo of Canadian
      troops at, 36
   fraternization and cooperation at
      the, 180–81
   Haig calls a costly failure, 29
   Haig ignores advice about troop
      advances at the, 173
   trenching improved after the, 175
South Africa, 118
South African War. *See* Boer War
Spanish-American War, 130
Sparticus League, 86
Speakers' Patriotic League, 42, 57
Specialty Film Import Company, 57

Spence, Benjamin, 97–98
Spirit Lake internment camp, 10
sports
   baseball gaining favour in U.S., 128
   contact, to develop manly will, 128
   football requires bravery and
      prowess, 128
   fostered healthy bodies and
      healthy minds, 130
   ice hockey, 128
   likened to military life, 131
   soccer, 128
Springfield, W.E., 41
Spurr, J.B., 22
The Spy, 21
Staatszeitung, 238n60
Stamfordham, Arthur John Bigge,
   Lord, 116
Stanfield, Frank, 231n55
Stanton, E.A., 236n17
Steele, Samuel Benfield, 169–70
Stein, Gertrude, 206
Stephens, R.N., 103, 236n17
Stephenson, —, 234n107
Sterling Bank of Canada, 79
Stewart, R.M, 238n68
Stratford, Ontario, 11
Students' Christian Movement, 208
Sudbury, Ontario, 89
Sung, M., 74
Sun Yat-Sen, 103–4
Superfeatures Inc., 107
Surrender of Kroonstad to Lord
   Roberts, 36
Swedish language, 81
Swettenham, John, 213
Swinton, Ernest Dunlop, 28
Switzerland, 15, 143
Sydney *Morning Herald*, 118
Symmons, John H.
   letters home, 166
Syrett, Victor
   diary, 174
Syrian language, 81

daily life in the, 144, 177, 208
described by Private Bloxham, 79
drying out brings improved
    conditions, 175
front-line inspections want tidy
    uniforms in, 171
German, protected by barbed
    wire, 173
in Flanders flooded by Germans, 174
kit bags unsuitable for use in, 170
latrines in, 175
likened to a common grave, 177
meals in, 176
mud in, 142, 174, 214
photograph of, 166
play baseball (called scrub) in the,
    177
"rat shoots" popular in, 177
rats in, 142
referred to in *Canada in Flanders*, 33
sleeping in, 165
soldiers can not follow war from,
    140
visiting offices not admired by
    men in, 172
Trinity College Council, 113
Trotsky, Leon, 84
Turkey, 192
Turkish language, 67
Turner, Richard E.W., 173
Tyokansa, 89

U

Ukraine, 88
Ukrainian-Canadians, 86
    consistently vote Liberal, 48
    interned, 8–9, 87–88
Ukrainian immigrants
    as seen by Canadians, 8–9
Ukrainian internees, 10
Ukrainian language
    newspapers
        anti-communist, 88
        banned, 81, 88

Catholic, 88
in dual-column format, 67
translated, 88
outlawed in print or public
    meetings, 67
Ukrainian Social Democratic Party
    (U.S.D.P.), 88–89, 235n11
The Unbeliever, 20
Underwood and Underwood, 106
Union Jack, 11, 22–23, 39, 42,
    236n25
Union of Russian Workers, 122
Union of Socialist Soviet Republics
    (U.S.S.R.), 104
    Comintern, 86
United Empire Loyalists, xii, 111
United Kingdom. *See* Britain
United States of America, 100, 215
    Austrian ambassador to, 68
    baseball popularity, 128
    Bill of Rights, 111
    books banned or abridged in
        Canada, 98–99
    Canada bans anti-British or
        pacifist material from, 80
    Canada bans foreign-language
        tracts from, 79, 89, 103
    Canada bans leftist material from,
        79, 87, 89
    Canada monitors German-
        language tracts from, 81
    Canadian militia kills hunters
        from, 7
    Canadian war trophies lent to,
        231n46
    censorship, xiv, 112
    citizens
        jail suspected pro-Germans
            and Bolshevists, 111
        protected from books, 111
    civil liberties record, 111
    Civil War pensions, 203
    Committee on Public
        Information, x, 20

operation costs, 115
war posters, 245n70
Criminal Code
outlaws postage of "indecent
material," 111–12
declares war, 47, 51, 81, 111
detectives monitor Germans in
Northern, 6
espionage, 242n20
Espionage Act (1917), 111–12
Federal Bureau of Investigation,
243n53
first amendment to the
constitution, xiv, 111–12
Generals Die in Bed published
and distributed in, 207
German information service
actions in, 106
Germany distributes newsreels
to, 36
government monitors left-wing
publications, 85
Liberty Bond campaigns, 56,
231n46
library boards
remove books from shelves,
111
Lord Northcliffe envoy to, 237n38
mail censored in Canada, 74
market for Canadian war
products, 51
Michigan-based subversives, 7
Mississippi, 82
movie industry, 19–20, 106
movies, xiv, 18–21, 107, 206
censored in Canada, 66
Liberty Bond promotions, 56
neutrality, xv, 27, 33, 79–80, 110,
220n4
newspapers, 19, 28–29, 31, 112
carry Canadian war photos, 36
circulation, 11
prefer German photographs, 35
technology, 11

Pennsylvania anthracite coal, 51
postmasters
allowed to demand translation,
111–12
post-war surveillance of leftists,
243n53
recruiting, 111
Robert Service reports to papers
in, 79
Russian-language papers
published in, 84
Russian Soviet Bureau in, 84
Secret Service, 78
Sedition Act (1918), 111–12
soldiers, 212
stage production halted in
Canada, 108
Trading with the Enemy Act, 111
troops
102nd infantry battalion, 191
two years in war, 191
veterans
reap vengeance against
"slackers," 191
Vietnam War bred anti-war
attitudes, 214
Wall Street Crash, 207
war correspondents, 33
Universal Studios, 20
University of Alberta, 245n75
University of Manitoba, 245n75
University of Saskatchewan, 245n75
University of Toronto, 23, 245n75
Unsere Zeit, 112
"The Unthinking Chatter of our Rag-
Tag Press," 237n41

V

Vanceboro, Maine, 7
Vancouver, 72
anti-Asian riots, 101
Chambers and the *Western
Clarion* in, 89–90
China's Consul-General in, 103